Nation-building in Malaysia
1946–1974

Nation-building
in Malaysia
1946–1974

James P. Ongkili

Singapore

Oxford University Press

Oxford New York

1985

Oxford University Press
Oxford London New York Toronto
Kuala Lumpur Singapore Hong Kong Tokyo
Delhi Bombay Calcutta Madras Karachi
Nairobi Dar es Salaam Cape Town
Melbourne Auckland
and associates in
Beirut Berlin Ibadan Mexico City Nicosia

© *Oxford University Press 1985*

OXFORD *is a trademark of Oxford University Press*

ISBN 0 19 582574 8

Printed in Singapore by Koon Wah Printing Pte. Ltd.
Published by Oxford University Press
10, New Industrial Road, Singapore 1953.

Preface

THIS book is a thematic study, an examination of the process of political evolution which gave birth first to Malaya and then to Malaysia and the major problem that had to be faced by those directly involved in guiding the destiny of the country, namely, communalism. Malaysia might not have gone through a phase of violent struggle to achieve independence but the way to nationhood was nonetheless thorny because of the plural nature of the society.

Undoubtedly, communalism was the fundamental problem of nation-building in Malaysia during the period under study. Communal groups, such as the various political parties, ranging from the UMNO–MCA–MIC Alliance, the PAP, the PMIP, to the SUPP, BARJASA, UPKO, USNO and others, sought representation during the period of nation-building from the Malayan Union of 1946 to the formation of Malaysia in 1963. Every major effort to establish a nation highlighted communalism in the country; but the same problem of communalism also determined at length the nature of politics and political system which the Malaysians adopted.

It is pertinent to mention here that what is attempted is a broad historical view of the efforts made by the Malayan/Malaysian leadership to weld together disparate parts so that there would emerge a general sense of national consciousness. It is not a study of the psychological and sociological aspect of communalism. Malaysia's peculiar communal problems have been studied by many scholars belonging to various disciplines. Very few indeed have been inclined to look at the problem from the perspective of those who have been entrusted with the serious responsibility of running the government of the country.

Although at the time when I first began this academic study my own experience was limited to that of a former civil servant, I was subsequently placed in a situation where I had first-hand experience of the kind of problems which the Malayan/Malaysian leadership had to grapple with in dealing with a very heterogeneous society. If there is an easy

solution to the very acute problem of communalism, I am certain it
would have been adopted a long time ago.

The sources used here have been as varied as possible. In addition to
published official and unofficial documents, I have been fortunate in
being able to interview and have discussions with Malaysian, Singaporean and British leaders and personalities who played significant roles
in the events of the period under study.

I would like to record my appreciation and deep gratitude to the
numerous individuals and institutions that have helped me in the course
of preparing this work which was originally written as a Ph.D. dissertation. Among these must be mentioned Professor S. Arasaratnam who
initially supervised the research. As the second and greatly involved
supervisor, Royal Professor Ungku A. Aziz, sacrificed a lot of his busy
time as Vice-Chancellor to the benefit of the present writer. Among
many other academics who gave the benefit of their varied and valuable
viewpoints on the issues and problems of nation-building in Malaysia
were Professors K. J. Ratnam, Wang Gungwu, Khoo Kay Kim, J. M.
Chandran, Zainal Abidin bin Abdul Wahid, (the late) Wong Lin Ken,
Nicholas Tarling and Damador Prasad Singhal.

Through the assistance of the University of Malaya, I was able to go to
Britain to consult records on Malaya, Sarawak and Sabah, particularly at
the Public Record Office and the State Papers Room of the British
Museum. Professor C. D. Cowan of the School of Oriental and African
Studies helped greatly with suggestions as to where to locate various
research materials in London.

In Malaysia itself, the Arkib Negara (National Archives) proved helpful and useful. Both the Sarawak Museum and Archives and the Sabah
Central Archives assisted me in obtaining sources which helped to fill in
gaps in the histories of the two Borneo states. The staffs of these
institutions were very obliging indeed.

Had it not been for the fourteen months which I was invited to spend
at the Institute of Southeast Asian Studies, Singapore, the dissertation
would not have been completed so soon. The Director, Professor Kernial
Singh Sandhu, and his staff were immensely helpful, while Peggy Lee
Giok Huay, Celina Heng Sang Noi and Ong Beng Thye patiently typed
the dissertation.

Department of History   JAMES P. ONGKILI
University of Malaya
Kuala Lumpur
1982

Contents

Tables

Abbreviations

AJPH	Australian Journal of Politics and History
AMCJA	All-Malaya Council of Joint Action
API	Angkatan Pemuda Insaf
BARJASA	Barisan Raayat Jati Sarawak
BMA	British Military Administration
CCO	Clandestine Communist Organization
CCP	Chinese Communist Party
CEC	Central Executive Committee
CIAM	Central Indian Association of Malaya
CLC	Communities Liaison Committee
CMC	Central Military Committee
Cominform	Communist Information (Bureau)
Comintern	Communist International
CPA	Commonwealth Parliamentary Association
DAP	Democratic Action Party
DAS	Dayak Association of Sarawak
FAMA	Federal Agricultural Marketing Authority
FAS	The Facts About Sarawak (book, q.v.)
FELCRA	Federal Land Consolidation and Rehabilitation Authority
FELDA	Federal Land Development Authority
FIDA	Federal Industrial Development Authority (now known as Malaysian Industrial Development Authority)
FIMA	Federal Industrial Marketing Authority
FMS	Federated Malay States
FOA	Farmers' Organization Authority
FRU	Federal Reserve Unit
GLU	General Labour Union
HMSO	His/Her Majesty's Stationery Office
IBRD	International Bank for Reconstruction and Development

IGC	Inter-Governmental Committee
IIL	Indian Independence League
IMP	Independence of Malaya Party
INA	Indian National Army
ISEAS	Institute of Southeast Asian Studies
JEBAT	Journal of the Historical Society, Universiti Kebangsaan Malaysia
JHSUM	Journal of the Historical Society, University of Malaya
JMBRAS	Journal of the Malayan Branch, Royal Asiatic Society
JSBRAS	Journal of the Straits Branch, Royal Asiatic Society
JSEAH	Journal of Southeast Asian History
JSEAS	Journal of Southeast Asian Studies
JSSS	Journal of the South Seas Society
KMM	Kesatuan Melayu Muda
KMS	Kesatuan Melayu Singapura
KMT	Kuomintang
KRIS	Kesatuan Raayat Indonesia Semenanjong
LPN	Lembaga Padi dan Beras Negara
MARA	Majlis Amanah Ra'ayat
MARDI	Malaysian Agricultural Research and Development Institute
MCA	Malayan Chinese Association
MCP	Malayan Communist Party
MDU	Malayan Democratic Union
MIC	Malayan Indian Congress
MIDF	Malaysian Industrial Development Finance
MNP	Malay Nationalist Party
MNUS	Malay National Union of Sarawak
MPABA	Malayan People's Anti-British Army
MPAJA	Malayan People's Anti-Japanese Army
MPU	Malayan Planning Unit
MRLA	Malayan Races Liberation Army
MSC	Malaysian Solidarity Convention
MSCC	Malaysia Solidarity Consultative Committee
NAP	National Association of Perak
NCC	National Consultative Council
NEP	New Economic Policy
NOC	National Operations Council
PANAS	Party Negara Sarawak

PAP   People's Action Party
PBDS   Parti Bangsa Dayak Sarawak
PERNAS   Pertubuhan Nasional
PETA   Pembela Tanah Air
PKMM   Partai Kebangsaan Melayu Malaya
PMCJA   Pan-Malayan Council of Joint Action
PMFTU   Pan-Malayan Federation of Trade Unions
PMIP   Pan-Malayan Islamic Party
PPP   People's Progressive Party (before 1956 called
             Perak Progressive Party)
PUTERA   Pusat Tenaga Raayat
RIDA   Rural Industrial Development Authority
RISDA   Rubber Industry Smallholders' Development Authority
SAYA   Sarawak Advanced Youths' Association
SCA   Sabah Chinese Association
SCA   Sarawak Chinese Association
SCBA   Straits Chinese British Association
SEAC   South-East Asia Command
SEDC   State Economic Development Corporation
SFTU   Singapore Federation of Trade Unions
SITC   Sultan Idris Training College
SMR   Standard Malaysian Rubber
SNAP   Sarawak National Party
STS   Special Training School
SUPP   Sarawak United People's Party
TCLP   Tan Cheng Lock Papers
UDA   Urban Development Authority
UDP   United Democratic Party
UMNO   United Malays National Organization
UNKO   United National Kadazan Organization
UPKO   United Pasok Momogun Kadazan Organization
USNO   United Sabah National Organization
YMAS   Young Malay Association of Sarawak

1
Background

In order to be able to examine the course of nation-building and the problem of communalism in Malaysia properly it is important, first and foremost, to understand the background of the people who make up Malaysian society. That society was of multiracial origin and each ethnic group had its distinctive place and predilection before the Second World War. Indeed by 1946 it was this multiracial background which dictated the nature and course of the political development that began the process of nation-building in Malaysia.

Malay Society

The Malays were the first politically-organized indigenous people of the Peninsula in that the earliest political states were founded by them. It has been aptly remarked that:

The Malays owed allegiance territorially to their sultans. Culturally their allegiance was to Islam, and most specifically to the maritime branch of it speaking Malaysian languages and having a common tradition of culture, trade and intermarriage among the royal families, extending along the coasts of Malaya, Sumatra and Borneo and parts of Java and other islands.[1]

Migration from island South-East Asia to the Peninsula was a common phenomenon in the days before Britain and Holland introduced some measure of control in the twentieth century. The rise of the Malacca Sultanate led to migration from Sumatra to the Peninsula. The process of migration continued throughout the succeeding centuries. Most of the Malay migrants from the neighbouring islands were easily absorbed or assimilated into the existing Malay population of the Peninsula. No doubt this was facilitated by their cultural similarities. Their linguistic and religious affinities in particular fostered cultural adaptation and the process was accentuated from the nineteenth century onwards as their common rural pattern of life contrasted more and more with that of the non-Malay immigrants.

The traditional sultanates were often riverine centres which were largely self-sufficient and isolated from their neighbours. Indeed it was often only in times of war or disputes about succession that one sultanate had much to do with another.[2] It was this self-sufficiency and the compact nature of the sultanates which to some extent engendered a spirit of contentedness among many Malays until recently. Most Malays lived a simple kampong life. Despite the lush primeval jungle which always threatened to invade their kampongs, these indigenous people were blessed by Nature with a climate and habitat which readily produced food and other basic necessities of life. It was this ease with which life could be tolerably sustained that gave not only the Malays but also the Dayaks, Melanaus, Kadazans, Bajaus and other indigenous communities time for leisure as well as hard work.[3]

It is to be noted that the use of leisure was often misunderstood or purposefully characterized as laziness by some members of the ruling British group and the non-Malay communities. This accusation became more pronounced in the increasingly competitive world of tin and rubber exploitation in the twentieth century so that the Malays and other indigenous communities were branded as unreliable, erratic workers; they supposedly looked upon wage-earning often as a merely temporary means of occupying themselves, especially if they were farmers who usually preferred to return to their kampongs for their more permanent occupations. In point of fact, there were hundreds of thousands of Malays who proved their diligence by staying steadfastly and faithfully in their jobs and spending longer hours than others as civil servants, teachers, drivers, engine operators and farmers in their kampongs.[4]

It is interesting to note the words of a Malay who claimed to be the first to analyse the psychology of his own race; he wrote in 1928:

of their failings and weaknesses, the worse that has been said against them is that they are lazy and improvident. Even in these, one is tempted to refute the charge, since those that have made this observation had probably formed their opinion from the minority who live in towns and work generally as servants to Europeans and others. But these Malays are as a rule the degenerate examples of the race who are stupefied by the glare of the luxurious life of civilisation and are easily victimised by the temptations that abound in towns. The majority that live in the country escape the notice of the ordinary European observer, and though they made bad coolies as compared to other races, it cannot be doubted that they work sufficiently hard on their small holdings to enable them to get all their wants which, as country people are naturally few and limited.[5]

The use of non-indigenous labour in the years of the expansion of the tin and rubber industries was often prompted by very simple practical considerations. In the case of the tin industry, it has been said that:

Except for the work of clearing the forests and bushes on the land, which was given to the Malays or the Sakais who were more dexterous in the use of the *parang*, all the work in the mines was done by the Chinese. Difference in race, religion, temperament, languages, customs, and mining superstitions, obvious economic self-interest, and the social requirements of living together in a mine precluded Chinese employers from employing non-Chinese labourers.[6]

As a result even Indian labour, cheaper than Chinese labour, was not considered for the mining industry.

In the case of rubber the position of indigenous labour has been explained in the following manner:

The use of local people for regular tasks on the rubber estates was mainly confined to the states of Johore, Kedah and Kelantan; here fewer immigrant workers were available. Elsewhere Malays were employed chiefly for the clearing of land under contract, for their seasonal preoccupation with activities on their own farms usually made them unsuitable as members of a regular labour force. By 1917 the total number of indigenous Malay workers on estates in the Peninsula is likely to have reached around 20,000 including the estimated 8,900 in the FMS.... The drop in numbers thereafter probably coincided both with worsening economic conditions and with the coming to maturity of rubber trees planted on the workers' own holdings.[7]

Certainly the conditions under which, at least in the early years of the industries, the labourers lived, uprooted from normal family life and practically fenced in with limited physical mobility, could hardly attract the indigenous population who, even if they were poor, were not contractually tied to anyone and therefore not forced to work to a rigid timetable. Drastic and intolerable socio-economic conditions in China and India compelled large numbers of people to emigrate from time to time, hoping to improve their lot before returning to their homeland. Similar conditions did not exist in Malaya to induce the Malays to abandon their existing occupations. Landlessness was not a problem for the Malays in the nineteenth century; increasingly, it became so in the twentieth century which has therefore witnessed a gradual drift of Malay population to the urban areas.

The Indigenous Society of Sarawak and Sabah

While Melaka was the focus of the Malay world in the Malay Peninsula, Brunei emerged as a similar focus further to the east of the Straits of Melaka. Both Sarawak and Sabah were parts of the Brunei Sultanate before coming under foreign administration in the course of the nineteenth century.[8]

The Brunei Sultanate shared many similarities with those in the

Peninsula. The Sultan was the apex of political authority and below him there was a hierarchy of chiefs: four *wazir*, eight *cheteria* and sixteen *menteri*.[9] Except that the titles were different, Kedah, Pahang and Perak also subscribed to the multiple-four system of chiefs.

Owing to physical vastness and the absence of an efficient system of transport and communication, there was also a wide dispersal of political power in the Brunei political system and various major chiefs wielded significant power in specific territories. This was accentuated by the decline of the Sultanate after the prosperous and notable reign of Sultan Bulkiah in the early sixteenth century.

The indigenous people of Sarawak and Sabah are more heterogeneous than those of the Peninsula and—an important point—many of them are not Muslims. The indigenous communities of Sarawak include the Ibans or Sea Dayaks, the Bidayuhs or Land Dayaks, the Kayans, the Kenyahs and the Kelabits, all of whom are non-Muslim. The Muslim groups are the Kedayans, the Bisayas and a good proportion of the Melanaus. In the case of Sabah, the largest indigenous groups are the Muruts and the Kadazans (formerly known as Dusuns). These are largely non-Muslim. There are also numerous groups of people who are physically and culturally akin to the Malays of the Peninsula and are Muslim, namely the Bajaus, the Bruneis, the Sulus, the Illanuns, the Kedayans and other smaller groups.[10]

Although Brunei was also an important trading centre, the kingdom was relatively remote from the commonly-used trade route between East and West Asia whereas the Peninsula was the meeting point for traders from these two regions. More frequent contacts with the external world required a higher degree of adaptation of the indigenous people. For example, there was greater intellectual-literary ferment in the Peninsula–Sumatra region than in Brunei. The development of Malay literature in the Peninsula–Sumatra region owed much to the coming of Islam. Evidence of this is the existence of a number of works known to posterity such as the *Hikayat Raja-Raja Pasai*, *Sulalatus-Salatin* (more popularly known as the *Sejarah Melayu*), *Hikayat Muhammad Hanafiah*, and *Hikayat Amir Hamzah*. Intellectual-literary leadership, not surprisingly, was provided by the *ulama* (religious scholars) from outside the region such as Sheikh Nuruddin Al-Raniri or by locals such as Shamsuddin Pasai, Hamzah Fansuri, and Abdul Rauf Singkel.[11] Brunei too came under Islamic influence but, perhaps again because of its geographical position, it did not draw as many Islamic scholars from West Asia. Furthermore, there is no evidence that Brunei ever produced any scholar of the standing of Hamzah Fansuri or Abdul Rauf Singkel.

Similarly, in the nineteenth century, although Sarawak, Sabah and the

Peninsula all came under official or unofficial British administrative control, technological developments in the Malay Peninsula occurred at a far faster rate owing largely to the growth of the tin-mining industry. The transformation which occurred in the Peninsula beginning in the last quarter of the nineteenth century had a deep impact on the Malays, so that increasingly Malay thinking was preoccupied with the necessity to check the spread of non-Malay influence. The indigenous society in Sarawak and Sabah, being less exposed, did not have to cope with the challenge faced by the Peninsular Malays in the early decades of the twentieth century.

The Growth of Immigrant Communities

The Chinese and Indians had been visiting the Malaysian region as early as the beginning of the Christian era but it was only after the establishment of British control in the region that they began to come in large numbers and stayed.

The Chinese who ventured to Malaysia in the early days were mostly traders who frequented Melaka, Pulau Pinang and then Singapore as these entrepôts developed. Not a few decided to settle permanently and became the forefathers of the present 'Baba Chinese', especially in Melaka and Pulau Pinang.[12] The number of Chinese immigrants increased rapidly in the second half of the nineteenth century as they were attracted to the lucrative exploitation of tin-bearing districts in Perak and Selangor.[13] Simultaneously the Chinese moved into Johor from Singapore to open up large gambier and pepper plantations. Temenggong Ibrahim's famous *kangchu* system ensured a modicum of stability which did not prevail in the mining areas of Larut and Kelang.[14]

From the later nineteenth century to 1934 indentured Chinese labourers were brought to Malaya in ever increasing numbers through the *sin-kheh* method of recruitment.[15] Even during the Depression years the number of arrivals often exceeded the number who returned to China. In Sarawak, Rajah Charles Brooke employed a basically similar method of engaging Chinese contractors to obtain Chinese labourers at the turn of the century; while in Sabah the Chartered Company made many attempts to get Chinese peasants and refugees from the 1911 Chinese revolution and 1937 Sino-Japanese War for the rubber plantations and public works of the territory.[16] By the time restrictions were imposed on Chinese immigration to Malaya in 1933, the community comprised a very significant proportion of the total population of the Peninsula, namely well over one-third.[17] Far more Chinese eventually settled in Malaya than in Sarawak and Sabah.[18] Consequently the political impact of the Chinese tended to be more heavily felt in the Peninsula than in northern Borneo.

From their traditional role as traders in sailing junks, the Chinese expanded their economic activities so that by the beginning of the twentieth century they had become the principal owners of commercial tin-mining in Malaya. It was only at the beginning of the 1930s, with the increasing use of mining technology, that the European share of the capital outlay overtook theirs.[19] Chinese ownership of the other major export earner of Malaya, rubber, also became increasingly important, amounting to 12.5 per cent of all the estates (excluding those less than 100 acres which were classified as small-holdings) in the Straits Settlements and the Federated Malay States. The importance of the Chinese in the Malayan economy by the time of the Second World War (1941) is perhaps best summed up by Purcell:

Chinese ownership of tin-mines and rubber estates is no real indication of their share of the wealth of the country. Chinese had, for instance, large holdings in European rubber companies. Malaya's important and growing secondary industries were very largely in Chinese hands. The pineapple industry, the creation of the last two decades, is entirely a Chinese enterprise. Canned pineapples in 1938 accounted for 1.2 per cent of Malaya's entire export trade. In Singapore, Penang, Kuala Lumpur, Klang, Ipoh and elsewhere the Chinese owned oil mills, biscuit factories, rubber works for the manufacture of shoes, tyres &c., iron foundries, sawmills, and sauce factories; there were Chinese shipping companies; they ran motor agencies and repair shops; the bulk of the retail trade everywhere was in their hands. One indication of the wealth of the community is the fact that in 1941 the Malayan Chinese remitted to China over $110,000,000 (£12,833,000).[20]

It is instructive to note that the Chinese were not only divided into different clans with their distinctive dialects but that their business activities were conducted largely along exclusive clan–dialect lines. The discipline within each clan group was often so effective that it could undercut and ruin the economic position of a rival group when it chose to do so. The majority of pre-war Chinese in Malaysia retained some links with the homeland, although such ties loosened in the course of time. By the 1930s many of those born in China had begotten children in Malaya, but many regarded this as the unfortunate consequences of revolution, civil war and the Sino-Japanese conflict in their homeland.

Although Indians[21] came to Malaya in noticeable numbers as early as the British acquisition of Pulau Pinang in 1786, it was only around the beginning of the twentieth century that they began to arrive at a steadily increasing rate. The growth of the rubber industry after 1910 and the development of railways and roads in Malaya necessitated a greatly increased labour force which the Indian immigrants helped to supply. By 1907 the governments of the Straits Settlements and the Federated Malay States had set up an Indian Immigration Committee to take charge of and promote the immigration of Indian labour. The Committee ran an Indian Immigration Fund which defrayed the passage, accommodation and other expenses of Indian labourers attracted to Malaya, especially under the *kangany* method of recruitment.[22]

The *kangany* system drew mainly persons from South India so that although Punjabis, Bengalis and other North Indians also came to Malaya, the Tamils, Malayalees and Telegus predominated among the immigrants. Eventually, four-fifths of the Indians who came to Malaya were Tamils. The largest number of Indians who came before the Japanese Occupation found their way into the rubber plantations, the railways and public works of Malaya.[23] An Agent of the Indian Government was appointed in 1923, with the consent of the Labour Department of Malaya, to supervise the employment conditions of Indian labourers. He was given the legal right to visit any estate during working hours and make enquiries among labourers. He sent annual reports to India:

These reports were as much directed at officialdom in India, as at Indian public opinion. They served to transform the nature of the Indian emigrant problem. It changed from one of exclusive concern with the mechanics and procedures of emigration and recruitment to a concern for the living and working conditions, and the welfare and prospects of the large numbers of Indians who had come to live in Malaya. The Indian Government now began to look closely into the wages, cost of living, and housing and health facilities experienced by their nationals in Malaya.[24]

It has also been pointed out that 'the presence of the agent of the Government of another country as a protector of labourers' interests naturally aroused some political feelings and helped to keep the Indian labourer conscious of the influence of Indian nationalism, even though the Agent was not a political officer'.[25] The average Indian worker stayed only for a few years in Malaya and following the Depression years of the early 1930s nationalist public opinion made the Indian Government impose a total ban on all forms of assisted emigration of labour to Malaya in 1938.[26]

It might have been thought that this curtailment of labour supply would have encouraged those who were already in Malaya to remain in their new home. But it has been said that 'demographically the suspension of the flow of migrants was one of the causes of the comparative failure of Indians to settle, and of the decline in importance, both absolutely and relatively, of the Indian component in Malaya's population.[27] The Indians comprised 15.1 per cent in 1931 and 10.8 per cent in 1947 of the total population of Malaya, not including Singapore.[28]

Few Indians migrated to northern Borneo. Even by 1960, when immigration to Sarawak and Sabah had become severely restricted, Indians comprised less than 1 per cent of the population of Sarawak and less than 4 per cent of that of Sabah. Efforts by the Brooke and Chartered Company Governments to attract Indian immigrants had a singular history of failure, one which was repeated during the colonial period from 1946 to 1963.[29]

The Development of Foreign Administration

(a) Malaya

British rule in Malaya was launched when the English East India Company, in its effort to foster and protect its lucrative trade route between India and China, obtained Pulau Pinang from Sultan Abdullah of Kedah in 1786; in 1819 Stamford Raffles hoisted the Union Jack over Singapore. The Anglo-Dutch Treaty of 1824 gave the British complete control over the Straits of Melaka.[30] The three outposts of Pulau Pinang, Singapore and Melaka became the Straits Settlements in 1826 and formed the stepping-stones to subsequent British intervention in the Malay Peninsula. Still the process of British penetration of the Peninsula took a long time. Even when the Straits Settlements began to prove a drain on the coffers of the East India Company after the company lost its monopoly of the China trade in the 1830s, the British Government made no move to take over responsibility for these outposts despite persistent expressions of dissatisfaction with Indian administration by the merchants of the Straits Settlements. It was only in 1867 that the Settlements were transferred to the Colonial Office and collectively became a Crown Colony.[31] The Settlements remained a Colony until the Japanese invasion in 1941.

The Transfer of 1867 in a sense laid the foundation for the subsequent forward movement. It has been shown that the British movement into the Peninsula cannot be easily attributed to any single factor.[32] Still Emerson's observation is not without validity:

The British forward movement in the Malay Peninsula coincided very closely in time with that of the Dutch across the Straits of Malacca after the treaty of 1871 had removed the earlier treaty restrictions on Dutch action in Achin, but there seems no reason to suspect that the slightly later date of the British advance can be attributed to any fear of an expansion of Dutch ambitions to include the Peninsula as well as Sumatra. Both were symptomatic of the new imperialist spirit which was beginning to be felt at the time, as was the continued French advance in Indo-

China. There can be no doubt that imitation is a real factor in the stimulation of the imperialist sentiment, and it may well be that the Dutch declaration of war on the Achinese strengthened the determination of the merchants and officials to put an end to the continual disturbances in the Malay States, but this determination was of far earlier birth. The British action was clearly determined by local considerations rather than by any foreign pressures, although it might have been delayed even longer if neighbouring regions had continued their half-century of calm.[33]

Although at the time he wrote Emerson had no access to confidential documents, his reference to local considerations as the prime factor determining the British action rested on a firmer foundation than he realized. By the early 1870s the Straits merchants had successfully established their influence in London itself. Their persistent lobbying at the Colonial Office could hardly have been an insignificant factor in Lord Kimberley's decision to consider the possibility of interfering actively in the Malay States.[34] It is now well known that Sir Andrew Clarke acted beyond the instructions given to him but the Pangkor Engagement of 1874 was nonetheless ratified. Setting the pattern of British intervention, the sixth article of the Engagement stated, 'That the Sultan receive and provide a suitable residence for a British Officer to be called Resident, who shall be accredited to his Court, and whose advice must be asked and acted upon on all questions other than those touching Malay Religion and Customs.'[35] It has been well said that during the twenty years following the intervention in Perak 'a colonial government, ruling its own population through colonial departments and recognizing no native authority as an executive instrument, had brought into being a system of rule in which the native authority was sovereign, native hierarchies preserved, and native institutions used as agencies of government'.[36] To carry out the paraphernalia of indirect rule, Britain's colonial officials, headed by the Governor of the Straits Settlements, proceeded to make arrangements which witnessed Selangor coming under British protection in 1874, Pahang accepting a British Resident in 1888, and Negeri Sembilan requesting in 1889 and receiving in 1895 a British Resident.[37] These three states, together with Perak, were grouped to form the Federated Malay States (FMS) in 1896. The FMS arrangement remained until the Japanese Occupation.

The expansion of British intervention led to further extension of indirect rule when in 1909 the Anglo-Siamese Treaty stated that 'The Siamese Goverment transfers to the British Government all rights and suzerainty, protection, administration, and control whatsoever which they possess over the States of Kelantan, Trigganu, Kedah, Perlis and adjacent islands.'[38] Thus Britain acquired the four northern Malay states.

Each of the four states accepted the appointment of a British Adviser with powers similar to those of the British Resident in each of the FMS. Meanwhile Johor in the south, having lost its nominal suzerainty over Pahang and Terengganu, also gradually gravitated into British influence and control. A British promise of protection came in 1885, and in 1914 a treaty provided for the appointment of a British General Adviser whose powers were again broadly similar to those of the Residents and the other four Advisers.[39] However Kelantan, Terengganu, Kedah, Perlis and Johor remained outside the FMS and were collectively known as the Unfederated Malay States (UFMS). The administrative arrangements of the FMS and the UFMS continued to be the forms by which Britain sought to implement its policies in the Peninsula until the Second World War. As one British student of Malayan affairs put it, 'From the borders of Siam down to Singapore all the Malay States had accepted British advice and Britain had secured a zone of influence against trespass by any other European power'.[40]

As a Crown Colony from 1867 onwards the Straits Settlements had an Executive Council and a Legislative Council composed of official and unofficial members. The FMS had a Federal Council which was established in 1909 and was empowered to legislate on matters of federal importance. A British officer styled Resident-General (later renamed Chief Secretary and then Federal Secretary) coordinated the administrative affairs of the FMS. Each of the nine Malay states had a State Council presided over by the Ruler and responsible for legislating on matters pertaining to the individual states. As in Sarawak and Sabah in the pre-war period, no universal suffrage was ever employed to elect members of these legislative and state councils in Malaya. The unofficial members were nominated, not elected, to their seats by the British authorities.

The Governor of the Straits Settlements was also High Commissioner to the Malay States and, from 1888, the Borneo territories of Sarawak, Brunei and North Borneo (Sabah). He presided over both the Settlement Executive and Legislative Councils and the Federal Council, thus ensuring the coordination of British direct and indirect rule in the Colony and the nine Malay states. As the highest-ranking British official in Malaya, the Governor cum High Commissioner, with the aid of his usually energetic Residents and Advisers, was able not only to represent the views of Whitehall but also to promote the growth of a British Malaya in which, from the days of intervention in the late nineteenth century until the Japanese invasion in 1941, his advice had to be 'asked and acted upon on all questions other than those touching Malay Religion and Customs'. The Malay Rulers, though nominally still sovereign, had come under the effective dominance of the British officials.

Nevertheless, although it is clear that Britain imposed an effective administrative control over Malaya between 1874 and the Second World War, it is important to bear in mind that not the whole of the Peninsula was directly colonized. While the Straits Settlements were a Crown Colony from 1867, the nine Malay states remained legally autonomous. Each state had its own civil service, albeit heavily influenced by the British Resident or Adviser, and the *Kerajaan* (Government) functioned in the name of the Ruler. Wide-ranging though the British control over Malaya was in the pre-war period, the indirect rule over the Malay states allowed the survival of a lingering impression and belief among the Malay Rulers that they still held the patrimony of their states and that the British were in their midst as friends and protectors who therefore should be treated with Malay traditional courtesy and afforded the dignity due to any well-meaning ally.

Britain in fact grew increasingly conscious of her lack of direct control, especially over the UFMS. It was largely for this reason that in the 1920s and 1930s High Commissioners Sir Lawrence Guillemard (1920–7) and Sir Cecil Clementi (1930–3) advocated Decentralization (of powers) in the FMS in order to foster administrative uniformity with the UFMS.[41] But the Malays, in particular, suspected that if the idea was to loosen the FMS in order to tie up the UFMS with it in one all-embracing British administrative loop the Decentralization proposal would be detrimental to Malay interests. The Malay Rulers of the UFMS therefore generally opposed the idea. On the whole, however, the British encountered few problems in the maintenance of their dominance over pre-war Malaya. The Settlement, FMS and UFMS legislatures functioned in the manner of typical colonial legislatures, with their members having to take an oath of allegiance to the British Crown. Without the introduction of the electoral process, no popular representation was possible and the different communities of Malaya lived in a plural society with little political consciousness or nationalist awareness towards Malaya.

(b) Sarawak

In the late 1830s rebellion broke out in Siniawan, Sarawak, against a local chief, the Pangiran Mahkota. The Sultan of Brunei was unable to suppress the uprising and eventually James Brooke, an Englishman, entered the scene and helped to quell the rebellion. The result was that the Sultan of Brunei formally recognized James Brooke as the Rajah of Sarawak in 1841.[42]

The ensuing century saw the development of a highly personalized and paternalistic rule which left little room for political initiative among the communities of Sarawak.[43] The Brookes treated the indigenous people of their kingdom with a Victorian humanitarianism which, among other things, sought to insulate them from harsh treatment of the sort meted out to colonized peoples elsewhere. James Brooke propounded:

I have, both by precept and example, shown what can be done; but it is for the [British] Government to judge what means, if any, they will place at my disposal. My intention, my wish, is to extirpate piracy by attacking and breaking up the pirate towns; not only pirates direct, but pirates indirect. Here again the Government must judge. I wish to correct the native character, to gain and hold an influence in Borneo proper, to introduce gradually a better system of government, to open the interior, to encourage the poor natives, to remove the clogs on trade, to develop new sources.[44]

As did the British in the Peninsula, the Brookes in Sarawak paid considerable attention to the Malays. Their leaders were awarded honorific titles akin to those of aristocratic Brunei, such as Datu Patinggi, Datu Bandar and Datu Imam,[45] and so accustomed had the Malays become to Brooke paternal treatment that in 1946, when the Rajah decided to deliver his once romantic kingdom to the British Crown, there were anti-cession protests from sections of the Malay community (as well as others).

The Brookes devoted their attention also to protecting the Dayaks and kindred non-Malay indigenous peoples of Sarawak. In particular, the second Rajah, Charles Brooke, spent long years as an administrator among the Ibans and firmly believed that nothing could be more unjust than to expose his peace-loving native wards to the predatory activities of joint-stock companies, privateers and imperialists. He drew examples from the Dutch policy of native subjugation in which the Javanese were reduced to 'a very abused and oppressed people, being forced both to provide labour for the Government, as well as to comply with the demands of their own native chiefs'.[46] The Brookes made use of traditional native chiefs as much as the Dutch did in the Netherlands East Indies but being more simply paternalistic and less economically motivated than the Dutch, the Rajahs, in principle if not in practice, continually emphasized the welfare of the Sarawak indigenous leaders and their people.

When he succeeded James Brooke in 1868, Charles Brooke continued the protective policy of his uncle. While he was still the chief administrator under his uncle, Charles Brooke initiated a forum in which the local leaders of Sarawak could know one another and exchange views by establishing a General Council in 1867.[47] Despite the expansion of the

administration and the associative role of this Council, Sarawak remained
politically backward. Towards the end of his long reign, Charles Brooke
indirectly attempted to vindicate the nature of his own rule in Sarawak
when he brooded philosophically over the future of Asia and wrote in
1907, 'My own opinion is that before we reach the middle of this century
all nations now holding large Colonial possessions will have met with
very severe reverses, and that the tens of millions of Europeans will not be
able to hold their own against the hundreds of millions of Easterns who
are daily gaining substantial power.'[48] In an age when almost all the states
of Asia were helplessly under Western dominance[49] and the dawn of
Asian nationalism was a mere glimmer,[50] Charles Brooke certainly
deserves some credit for his prophetic overview of Western imperialism
in Asia.

But despite this perceptiveness about the course of Asian political
changes, it is to be noted that in his own Sarawak Charles Brooke, and
also his successor, fell far short of fulfilling their declared intention to
prepare their subjects for eventual self-government. The third and last
Rajah, Charles Vyner Brooke, who succeeded his father in 1917, ruled
very much in the tradition of his predecessors; and during the centenary
of Brooke rule he publicly admitted in the preamble to the 1941 Sarawak
Constitution that the time had only then come for 'terminating for ever
the Era of Autocratic Rule which has so far characterised our Government'.[51] The 1941 Sarawak Constitution itself appeared prima facie to be
a liberal document which provided for a new state council, the Council
Negri, and an executive council, the Supreme Council. Yet fourteen of
the twenty-five Council Negri members were official members while all
the eleven unofficial members were appointed by the Rajah-in-Council.
The majority of the members of the Supreme Council, likewise, were
'members of the Sarawak Civil Service ... a majority of whom shall be
members of the Council Negri'.[52]

In practice, the 1941 Sarawak Constitution merely transferred the
personal rule of the Rajah into the hands of his own bureaucrats. It merely
glossed the 'Autocratic Rule' the Rajah was so conscious of; there was no
substantive political change, inasmuch as the members of the two
Councils were clearly the faithful servants of the Rajah himself. No less
significant, especially in terms of the political evolution of a modern state,
the 1941 Sarawak Constitution was silent on any system of adult suffrage
which would have introduced the people to democratic processes of
government. In the event, the new Council Negri had only a short
existence before the Japanese overran Sarawak in December 1941.

The Sarawak administration grew and expanded with the faithful
service of British civil servants who were recruited almost entirely from

Britain. In commemorating the centenary of Brooke rule, the nine 'Cardinal Principles of the Rule of the English Rajahs' were reaffirmed. The eighth Principle is of particular interest: 'That the goal of self-government shall always be kept in mind, that the people of Sarawak shall be entrusted in due course with the governance of themselves, and that continuous efforts shall be made to hasten the reaching of this goal by educating them in the obligations, the responsibilities and the privileges of citizenship.'[53] In some ways, therefore, the second and third Rajahs anticipated the time when their personal rule would become untenable and their successors would have to give way to demands for self-rule from the people. But partly because education was neglected by the Brookes, who entrusted this important matter to rival Christian missions, Chinese school boards and a few Malay pedagogic centres,[54] civic and political understanding likewise saw only a very inconsequential advance in the pre-war years. This was especially true among the largest ethnic grouping, namely the non-Malay indigenous peoples.

That Brooke rule insulated the indigenous peoples of Sarawak from abuse and colonial exploitation can hardly be denied. The Malay and non-Malay peoples of Sarawak were certainly more humanely treated under their English Rajahs than were the Javanese under the Dutch 'culture system' or the Vietnamese under the so-called 'assimilation' and 'association' programmes of the French.[55] But it can be said that the benevolent Rajahs over-protected the indigenous peoples of Sarawak: in a manner of speaking, the indigenous peoples were like birds in a golden cage, pampered and unruffled by winds of change; but when the cage door was opened, first by the Japanese in 1941 and then by the British Government in 1946, it was found that the birds had lost the art of flying. The different communities of Sarawak were largely unharmed but they were also politically innocent under Brooke rule. Clearly, the time of nationalist awareness was yet to come.

(c) Sabah

The beginning of the end of Brunei rule in Sabah occurred in December 1877 when some sections of Sabah were ceded to Baron von Overbeck who was acting on behalf of the British firm of Dent Brothers. In subsequent years more territory was ceded piecemeal. A limited Provisional Association was formed to exploit Sabah and several stations were established by employees of the Association. By 1881 the Association was able to persuade the British Government to grant a charter of corporation and Sabah came under the administration of the British North Borneo (Chartered) Company.[56]

At a time when joint-stock companies were clearly considered anachronistic instruments of government, the granting of the Royal Charter to the North Borneo Company by the British Government was a demonstration of the backwardness of the territory.[57] Nevertheless, the Charter laid down the political and administrative bases upon which the Company Court of Directors in London and their Governor and officers in Sabah should manage an area of over 29,000 square miles. The Charter, which was closely adhered to by the Company until the Japanese invasion in 1941, required *inter alia* that the Company should by degrees abolish slavery, refrain from interfering with the religion of any clan or people of the territory, develop the area, make and maintain public works, promote immigration, grant lands to investors, afford free access to British shipping, and impose no monopoly of trade in the territory.[58]

The Chartered Company, like the Brooke Rajahs, was preoccupied with the establishment of a bureaucracy in Sabah. In this respect the most significant provision of the Charter, in so far as the peoples of the territory were involved, was Article 9 which required that:

In the administration of justice by the Company to the people of Borneo, or to any of the inhabitants thereof, careful regard shall always be had to the customs and laws of the class or tribe or nation to which the parties respectively belong, especially with respect to the holding possession transfer and disposition of lands and goods, and testate or intestate succession thereto, and marriage, divorce, and legitimacy, and other rights of property and personal rights.[59]

Here at least is evidence that the territory was constituted into a political entity, separate from the Brunei Sultanate, at a period in British history when some regard for the well-being of the subject peoples, albeit paternalistic, was manifest. As the Rajahs of Sarawak were imbued with Victorian humanitarianism, so the promoters of the Chartered Company were enjoined to protect the welfare of the indigenous and other communities of Sabah from 1881 onwards. Notwithstanding that, it must be pointed out that a stable government was of paramount importance to the Company itself in its overriding effort to open up the territory and thereby attract investors, planters and speculators to Sabah.[60] The chief aim was to establish good government in order to ensure the success of a business concern which had been launched with the blessing of the British Government.[61]

An Advisory Council was set up in 1883 with the aim of providing to the Governor and his officers a channel of communication with the various communities in the territory. But in practice this Council hardly promoted political understanding among the people. Its members were composed of the higher officers of the Company, representatives of the European planters and Chinese merchant groups.[62] Not only were all the members nominated by the Governor, but it is also significant to note that the indigenous peoples of the territory were not represented on this Council. Despite the Charter provision *vis-à-vis* the welfare of the indigenous communities, their non-representation on the Advisory Council clearly demonstrates the fact that the Company was far more interested in the economic than in the political advancement of the territory.

Late in the nineteenth century the Company's rule in Sabah faced a major challenge. Beginning in 1894, intermittent disturbances erupted on the east and west coasts as well as in the interior of Sabah. The problem for the Company centred on a man of mixed Bajau and Sulu parentage called Mat (Muhammad) Salleh. He was married to a relative of the Sultan of Sulu and lived as the chief of a small village up the Sugut River on the east coast.[63] Under the *ancien régime* he would have remained an influential headman but the presence of the Company changed that. It has been remarked that a discerning government would have incorporated him into the administration; instead it began to harass him.[64]

There is no evidence that Mat Salleh was implicated in the initial trouble in late 1894 which involved the killing of two Dayak traders who had penetrated to the headwaters of the Sugut. Mat Salleh was prepared to come to terms with the Company but none of the British administrators looked upon him as the legitimate indigenous leader which he was. They insisted on submission and further required that he should allow himself to be banished. Later a promise made to him that he and his followers would be forgiven and that the Company would delegate its authority over the people in the Tambunan Valley to him was not fulfilled. And so Mat Salleh resisted the Company until he was killed in January 1900. This was not the end of the resistance; other recalcitrant groups rose from time to time though without ever really threatening to break the hold the Company had over Sabah.[65]

On its part, the Company fought determinedly to ensure the stability which it perennially sought in order to make Sabah an attractive area for investment. In 1912 a Legislative Council was established to replace the Advisory Council. All nominated, the members of the new Council comprised official members, representatives of the European economic interests and a representative of the Chinese community. While the Chinese representation was later increased to two members, the Council again included no representative of the indigenous peoples of the territory.[66] In any event, despite the change in its name, the new Legislative Council remained largely advisory in practice. It functioned as a source of information on the economic temperament and development of the territory for the Governor and the Court of Directors rather than as a training ground for local leaders in an eventually self-governing Sabah. The Legislative Council existed uneventfully and apolitically until the Japanese invasion in late 1941.

An interesting experiment in local government was attempted in 1936. A local authority was formed by combining villages in the Bingkor area of the Interior Residency for administrative purposes. The Committee formed to run the day-to-day affairs of the Authority was led by O. K. K. Sedomon bin Gunsanad. At first the Authority functioned promisingly; but lack of financial support and experience beset its native leaders, who were expected to rely almost entirely upon the meagre revenue of the poor Bingkor area for the implementation of their projects and local authority services. The local authority received some financial assistance from the Education and Medical Departments, but this made no difference to the increasing budgetary needs of the authority.[67] Ultimately the experiment failed, thereby demonstrating the impossibility of initiating even grassroots political education successfully without the long-term assistance of a governing Company disposed towards the granting of eventual self-government to Sabah.[68]

Whereas the Brooke Rajahs at least repeatedly stated that it was their intention to lead the people of Sarawak to self-rule and attempted to substantiate their pledge by granting the 1941 Constitution to their subjects on a silver platter,[69] the Chartered Company never in its sixty-year rule indicated such a wish for the people of Sabah. Undisturbed by other imperial powers, thanks to the British protectorate of 1888, the Company portrayed itself by 1941 as a management concern which to all intents and purposes was happy to continue to husband Sabah as its economic domain well into an indeterminate future.

Political Activity in Malaya prior to 1941

Until recently there has been little research into the subject of political activity in Malaya before the Second World War. Yet there has been a widespread impression that, compared to other countries in South-East Asia, there was a conspicuous absence of political activity in Malaya until after 1945. While it is undeniable that political activity here never reached the degree of turbulence observable, for example, in Burma or Indonesia, Malaya and Singapore were by no means politically dormant. Singapore, in fact, was the headquarters of Kuomintang (KMT) activity[70] as well as the nerve centre of the Chinese communist movement in the *Nanyang* (the Chinese term for South-East Asia).[71] During the Second World War, it was the base of the Indian Independence Movement led by Subhas Chandra Bose.[72]

But Malaya's politics before 1945 were highly cosmopolitan in nature, reflecting the multiracial character of the population. Any political development in China and India found an immediate response here, though not always on a large scale—the extent of each response was determined by the size of the particular ethnic or sub-ethnic group involved. Hence political activities involving the Chinese always tended to be more difficult for the British Government to control.[73]

The Malays were comparatively less turbulent and in fact, between 1900 and 1941, there was less internal turmoil and unrest in Malay society than in Chinese society (in China) or in Indian society (in India). Admittedly, Malay society was exposed to developments in the Middle East as well as to those in Indonesia.[74] The Kaum Muda Islamic reformist movement, which emerged in the early twentieth century and neither progressed nor retrogressed within a period of about forty years, is one example.[75] The Kesatuan Melayu Muda (KMM), an anti-establishment political party founded in 1938, was indirectly influenced to some extent by the radicalism then prevailing in Indonesia.[76] There were also some Malays from time to time involved in the Malayan Communist Party (MCP), which was founded around 1930–1.[77] But, by and large, the Malays did not respond to external political stimuli. Numerically, the activists and the radicals were a small minority. They made little significant impact on Malay society. Although, since the 1920s, there had emerged a literate and vocal group which consistently aired Malay grievances and anxieties about the future of the Malays in their own country, the pattern of leadership in Malay society remained relatively unchanged.[78] Political associations which were not led by the traditional ruling class found it difficult to make any impression on the common people.

However, on the eve of the Second World War the political situation in Malaya and Singapore could, by no stretch of the imagination, be considered calm. Owing to the Sino-Japanese War, the Chinese—both the Kuomintang and the communists—were actively involved in anti-Japanese campaigns. The communists, for once, found massive support among Chinese workers. They fomented strikes throughout Malaya and Singapore.[79] The Indians, egged on by developments in India and Nehru's visit in 1937, formed the Central Indian Association of Malaya (CIAM) whose leaders were to be among the most important supporters of Subhas Chandra Bose.[80]

The Malays were obviously alarmed by the activities of the non-Malays and began to organize themselves more elaborately. Malay state associations emerged in Perak, Selangor, Kelantan, Pahang and Negeri Sembilan.[81] That pan-Malayan Malay consciousness grew at this time is shown by the organization of the first 'national' Malay congress in Kuala Lumpur in 1937. This was followed by a second congress in Singapore in 1938; a third was held in Kuala Lumpur in 1939 and a fourth in Singapore in 1940. A fifth congress scheduled to be held in Ipoh in 1941 did not materialize because of the war.[82]

But in all these political activities, there was clearly no cohesion among the various ethnic groups. The idea of a future Malayan nation was perhaps already in the minds of some of the more radical Malay leaders but its shape and dimensions were not very clear. In the ensuing years, many of the radical leaders aimed for political union with Indonesia.[83] The traditional leaders, at this stage, did not think of independence. The non-Malays were too preoccupied with China and India, except for a handful of the local-born. The principal representative of this small group was Tan Cheng Lock who, when he was in the Straits Legislative Council until his retirement in 1934–5, campaigned strenuously for the admission of Malayans into the Civil Service, for the abandonment of the official majority in the Legislative Council, for the introduction of elections and for the inclusion of non-Europeans in the Executive Council;[84] he can be said to have at least foreseen the dawn of self-government in the not too distant future. What further developments would have taken place subsequent to 1941 had the war not broken out is open to speculation. Suffice it to say that when the Japanese ousted the British from Malaya, the door was opened to developments which few could have anticipated before 1941.

The Impact of the Japanese Occupation

Because there had been little political awakening among the indigenous communities of Sarawak and Sabah when the Japanese invaded the territories in December 1941, the occupying power encountered little or no opposition and found it relatively easy to induce many of these who worked in the Brooke and Chartered Company administrations, with the exception of the Europeans, to serve the new regime.[85] In Malaya[86] leaders of the KMM who had been arrested by the British on the eve of the war were released by the Japanese following the fall of Singapore on 15 February 1942.

Owing to the earlier contact between KMM leaders and the *Fujiwara Kikan* (a fifth column organization based in Bangkok), KMM members gave every assistance to the conquering Japanese army. While their leader, Ibrahim Yaacob, was still detained in Singapore, some members of the KMM in Ipoh under the leadership of Mustapha Haji Hussein (Vice-

President of KMM) and Onan bin Haji Siraj (brother-in-law of Ibrahim Yaacob) formed the *Barisan Pemuda Kesatuan Melayu Muda* whose immediate objective was to ensure the safety of KMM members detained in Singapore upon the Japanese conquest of the island. It seems likely that the *Barisan Pemuda* was needed because KMM itself was in disarray owing to the imprisonment of the majority of its leaders.[87]

After the release of Ibrahim Yaacob and his close associates, there was still little that KMM could do in the ensuing months to achieve its political objective of working towards eventual independence for Malaya. KMM had no clear idea as to Japanese future policy for Malaya; above all, its initial concern was to render protection to the Malays in the wake of atrocities committed by the conquering Japanese soldiers.[88]

The Japanese, on their part, were quite clear what Malaya meant to them. The available war documents now reveal that:

In the draft plan for military government under the command of the Southern Expeditionary Forces (...Nampo Sogun), Sogun military administrators conceived Malaya to be 'Japan's economic and military base' in order to 'establish an economic self-sufficiency in the South'. For this end, in another document, they brushed aside any consideration for granting independence to Malaya and planned to incorporate the territory into 'permanent' Japanese possessions. Tokyo had consistently maintained through the war years until July 1945 this policy of granting no independence to the Malays.[89]

After the Japanese had completed their conquest of Malaya in February 1942 and that of Java and Sumatra a month later, KMM could sense that it had outlived its usefulness. In an endeavour to keep the spirit of its struggle alive, leaders of the KMM such as Ishak Haji Muhammad, Hassan Manan, Abdul Karim Rashid, Onan bin Haji Siraj, Ahmad Boestamam, Taharuddin Ahmad, Jaafar Sidek, Pachik Ahmad and Ibrahim Yaacob himself, visited various states on the west coast and Pahang on the east to consolidate KMM bases. This was, possibly, the immediate cause which prompted the Japanese administration, in June 1942, to direct Ibrahim Yaacob to disband the KMM.[90] The ban was imposed on KMM because the Japanese feared that if KMM was allowed to expand its activities, other groups might ask for similar privileges.[91]

KMM leaders, however, were absorbed into the Japanese establishment. Ibrahim Yaacob became the adviser on Malay affairs to Watanabe, the Director-General of the Japanese Military Administration, while Ishak Haji Muhammad, Abdullah Kamel, Taharuddin Ahmad and Mohamed Zallehuddin were employed on the *Berita Malai* and other publications brought out by the Propaganda Department.[92]

The Japanese dealt another serious blow to KMM's ambition of achieving independence for Malaya by formally transferring, on 18

October 1943, the four northern Malay states of Perlis, Kedah, Kelantan and Terengganu to Thailand. To comfort Ibrahim Yaacob further, the Japanese chose him to establish the *Giyu Gun* (Volunteer Army) and *Giyu Tai* (Volunteer Corps) in Malaya. *Giyu Gun* was a fighting force whereas *Giyu Tai* was more specifically concerned with the preservation of public peace and order. In Indonesia, the *Giyu Gun* was more popularly known as the *Pembela Tanah Air* (PETA). Both units were to comprise Malay youths and they contributed substantially to the growth of political consciousness and nationalism. By the middle of 1944, some 2,000 Malay youths were said to have been recruited into the *Giyu Gun* with a central training camp and barracks in Johor Bahru. In July 1944 the *Giyu Gun* was used in anti-guerrilla operations and clashes with the MPAJA occurred in the jungle of Kota Tinggi, Johor. But the Japanese kept a tight control over the *Giyu Gun* allowing little room for the unit to develop into a truly independent army.[93]

Even while the Japanese administration was keeping a vigilant watch over the activities of the ex-KMM leaders and their followers, the political situation was changing rapidly. Japan's defeat in the war appeared increasingly imminent. Hence Indonesia had been promised independence in September 1944 and the decision was soon made to grant it to Malaya also. In mid-1945 Ibrahim Yaacob and his associates were called upon to form *Kesatuan Raayat Indonesia Semenanjong* or KRIS (All-out Effort of the People) to prepare for independence. In the words of Yoichi Itagaki, the specialist in Malay affairs sympathetic to Ibrahim Yaacob's cause:

The plan of the KRIS movement directly resulted from the Second Singapore Conference of Secretary-Generals [*sic*] of the Military Administrations of Java, Sumatra, Celebes and Malaya on July 2y, 1945. The aim of the Conference was to discuss the problem of 'Quick Independence of Indonesia' and related issues. Military Administration of Malaya had to take a necessary step for the unavoidable political repercussions of Indonesian independence upon the Malays in Malaya, in view of the fact that they highly rejoiced when Malaya and Sumatra were treated as a unit area of Military Administration immediately after the Japanese occupation. Furthermore, on the occasion of the declaration of future independence for Indonesia made by Prime Minister Koiso on September 7, 1944, the Malays of Singapore attempted to hold celebration meetings and to form Indonesian Association, which, however, was not permitted by the Japanese Authority.

What was more important might have been the fact that the desperate decrease in Malay population after the cession of four northern Malay States (Perlis, Kedah, Kelantan and Trengganu) to Thailand . . . the increasing difficulties in living conditions due to the rising prices, and the accumulation of discontent and disappointment in the Japanese Military Administration, were causing it to lose the support of Malays. In such conditions, therefore, it was very natural that the idea was taken up to encourage their political awakening by recognizing their long-cherished 'Indonesia Raya' and also by inspiring them who have the language, culture, religion, customs, and race in common with Indonesians.[94]

Ibrahim Yaacob lost no time in attempting to revive the former branches of KMM all over the country as the branches of KRIS. His plan was for Malaya to be granted independence as an integral part of Indonesia.[95] While he was still in Taiping engaged in negotiations with his Japanese advisers on 13 August 1945, he met a returning delegation of Indonesian nationalists at the Taiping airstrip. The Indonesian group, led by Soekarno and Mohammad Hatta, was continuing its return journey to Indonesia after independence negotiations with the Japanese at Saigon.[96] It was at this meeting in Taiping that Soekarno reportedly shook hands with Ibrahim Yaacob and said, 'Let us form one single Motherland for all the sons of Indonesia.' Ibrahim Yaacob answered, 'We, the Malays in Malaya, are with loyalty in full support of the idea of a single Motherland, with Malaya as a part of Free Indonesia.'[97] Two days later, Japan announced her surrender; Soekarno and Hatta proclaimed the Republic of Indonesia on 17 August 1945, without Malaya and British Borneo; and the KRIS had no option but to resolve to continue an obviously down-hearted struggle for the independence of the Peninsula.

The Malays in general were not as anti-Japanese as the Chinese, but this was not so much because 'loyalty to their Sultans was in their blood' or because the Chinese boycott of cheap Japanese goods prompted Malays to 'align themselves with the Japanese rather than with the Chinese'.[98] (The proportion of Malays who were adversely affected by such boycotts was small, in view of the fact that the great majority of them, despite a general shortage of consumer goods, remained tolerably self-sufficient in their kampongs.) In the first place, the Japanese needed the cooperation of the Malays against the British. Secondly, the Japanese shelved their initial plan to abolish the status of the Sultans and reverted to a policy in many ways similar to that of British paternalism in pre-war days by reinstating all the trappings of Malay royalty by January 1943.[99] Thirdly, as the Japanese professed to assist nationalist movements in the lands which they occupied, they obviously regarded the Malays as the logical inheritors of the British political legacy in Malaya. Thus the Japanese adopted a comparatively lenient attitude towards the Malays, which contrasted markedly with the harsh treatment meted out to the Chinese and which engendered among the Malays themselves a feeling—albeit far from universal—of tolerance towards the occupying regime.

The bitterness of the Chinese towards the Japanese had been increasing since the latter's invasion of Manchuria in 1931. In the hearts of most Chinese in Malaya and northern Borneo, the Japanese Occupation was simply an extension of the war in the homeland where even the rival KMT and Communists had managed to form a united front, although an uneasy one, to fight the Japanese in 1937. The more conservative and westernized Chinese here organized a small volunteer force—DALFORCE—and, together with a few hundred known communists, fought the Japanese in the northern outskirts of Singapore. Following the fall of that Island, the Japanese rounded up and executed many of the Chinese, especially those whom they suspected to be communists, 'the total number perishing in this way exceeding five thousand'.[100] This further incensed the Chinese and deepened their grudge against the Japanese.

A significant development was the understanding reached between the retreating British Military officers and MCP leaders to organize a resistance movement in the Peninsula. Guerrillas were trained in Singapore and sent out in separate Independent Forces which became the components of the Malayan People's Anti-Japanese Army (MPAJA). The MPAJA guerrillas were mostly Chinese and they proclaimed as their objectives the liberation of Malaya from the Japanese and the setting up of an independent Malayan People's Republic.[101] For all practical and ideological purposes, the MPAJA was a communist organization. Although only a small number of Malays joined the MPAJA, it had an understanding with the Malay radicals. In point of fact they all wished to end Japanese rule and establish power bases for themselves in Malaya. To this end, the MPAJA, in particular, agreed with the returning British to plan a joint operation against the Japanese but the dropping of atomic bombs on Hiroshima and Nagasaki and the resulting abrupt proclamation of Japanese surrender made the execution of the planned operation unnecessary.[102]

It is significant that while collaborating with the MPAJA, the British made little attempt to mobilize the Malays as allies against the Japanese. There were thousands of Malays who were in various departments and sections of the civil service and police force who could have been far better organized than actually happened in the months before the fall of British Malaya. Indeed, in Johor alone Malay volunteer forces numbered over a thousand but they were hardly encouraged by the British authorities to fight with them against the invading Japanese. Similarly, the Pahang Wataniah (Pahang Volunteers) functioned almost entirely on their own nationalistic initiative. As one Malay, who was trained as a radio operator before the Japanese Occupation, posed the matter, 'Why were not the Malays told to form resistance groups, as the MPAJA were, by the British? Thousands of technically-trained Malays were not put to the jungle. Could it be that if the British had done so a Malay 3-Star guerrilla movement would have emerged in Malaya?'[103] (The 3-Star was the MPAJA emblem.) At any rate, the overall impression is that there were ample signs of Malay political and nationalist fervour as demonstrated by the activities of the Malay Unions and the KMM in the 1930s and that Britain's anxiety not to promote such nationalist Malay aspirations so long as Whitehall wished to maintain its dominance in Malaya was to a considerable degree responsible for the lack of mobilization of the Malays during the Japanese Occupation.[104]

In northern Borneo, the Allies parachuted advanced reconnaissance patrols into the interior of Sarawak and these eventually made contact with local anti-Japanese resistance groups. Heavy fighting between these guerrillas and the Japanese took place, especially along the lower and middle reaches of the Batang Rajang in the Third Division of the territory.[105] By and large however, the indigenous communities—with the exception of small numbers in Kuching, Sibu and Miri—lived much as the majority of Malays did in the Peninsula. Comparatively few were singled out for oppression by the Japanese, notwithstanding the fact that most laboured under the fear that the occupying regime might actually ravage their kampongs and longhouses.[106] As in Malaya, too, the Chinese in Sarawak and Sabah bore the brunt of Japanese machinations and high-handedness, and for basically the same reasons as in Malaya. Apart from the Japanese being their traditional enemy, the Chinese forming the highest income group of all the non-European communities attracted the attention of the Japanese. This became increasingly so as the occupation wore on and as, among other debilitating things, the value of the Japanese paper currency—supposed to be at par with the Straits dollar—depreciated to almost nothing.[107] Chinese and European property became irresistible sources of revenue for the insolvent occupation government. The Japanese evoked the wrath of the Chinese further by inhumanly rounding up Chinese women and girls and forcing them into prostitution or plain rape orgies.[108]

While the Chinese in Malaya and Singapore organized their anti-Japanese activities almost independently of the other communities, in Sarawak and Sabah they often worked closely with the indigenous communities to sabotage their common enemy. In Sabah, a multiracial resistance movement known as the Kinabalu Guerrillas, was organized in 1942. Led by Albert Kwok Fen Nam, Musa, Korom and others, these guerrillas established liaison with the American-backed resistance movement in the southern Philippines.[109] A plan was drawn up whereby a general uprising against the Japanese in Sabah with assistance from Sulu would be organized. However, a serious breakdown in communications occurred between the guerrilla headquarters in Sabah and their much needed allies in Sulu and when the armed struggle, known as the Double Tenth Uprising, was launched on 10 October 1943, the guerrillas gained an initial advantage but were soon subdued by the Japanese who poured reinforcements into the affected areas in Jesselton, Inanam, Menggatal, Tuaran and Tamparuli.[110] The anti-Japanese guerrillas in Sarawak were not as well organized as those in Sabah, but multiracial groups of local people fought the Japanese with determination in the coastal urban centres. The Muruts of Pensiangan and Tenom in the interior of Sabah and many of the Ibans and kindred indigenous groups of Sarawak re-enacted their half-forgotten cultural habit of head-hunting; scores of heads of retreating Japanese were taken by these independent-minded peoples as they helped the Allies in the manner they thought best to beat out Japanese still hiding in the Borneo jungle in 1945.[111]

As Sarawak and Sabah did not have large numbers of Indians, it was not there but in Malaya, where they accounted for over 10 per cent of the population, that this community played a rather conspicuous role in the war. In many ways, the Japanese attitude towards the Indians was similar to that which they adopted towards the Malays. Indians were en-couraged to free themselves and their motherland (India) from the clutches of the British and to work for national independence as part of Japan's 'Greater East Asia Co-Prosperity Sphere' with the 'Great Spirit of Cosmocracy' as its guiding principle.[112] The Indian revolutionary nationalist, Rash Behari Bose, was chosen by the Japanese to lead the Indian Independence League (IIL) which had been formed in Thailand, before the outbreak of the war in Malaya, as the political arm of a movement by Indian leaders in South-East Asia to liberate India. The military arm of the movement, the Indian National Army (INA), was formed in December 1941 and was led by Capt. Mohan Singh of the British Indian Army stationed in Malaya (which had surrendered to the Japanese). Broad agreement had been reached and conferences were held in Tokyo and Bangkok but the Indian leaders were suspicious of Japanese intentions and were inclined to heed more the nationalist voice of the Indian National Congress. 'There were tensions between the Japanese and the Independence League, and between the League and the Indian National Army. Because of these disputes no concrete progress was achieved.'[113] Rash Behari Bose, who had long lived in Japan 'proved unpopular and unsuccessful. He was too obviously a Japanese puppet, and it is said in Malaya that his Japanese cap did more than any other one thing to alienate Indian support.'[114] Six months after its formation, the INA had attracted about 16,000 volunteers but Mohan Singh, who had been made a Major, subsequently resigned because *inter alia* he reasoned that there were insufficient soldiers for the INA to take action independently of the Japanese who were hovering around watching closely the activities of the Indian nationalist movement.

The Indian independence movement received widespread Indian support only after the arrival of Subhas Chandra Bose in Singapore in July 1943. A former president of the Indian National Congress, he had been in Germany where he attempted to secure assistance for the Indian nationalist cause from Hitler. Transported to Singapore in a German submarine, Bose took steps to rejuvenate the INA which 'became under his leadership a united, disciplined body trained in the use of arms; and he attracted a large personal following that was fanatically devoted to him'.[115] He toured Malaya and attracted not only new volunteers for the INA but also members for the IIL, branches of which were opened in every main town and even in the estates.[116] The seriousness and determination of the Indian nationalists at this time were demonstrated by the establishment of their provisional government in exile, the Azad Hind Government, proclaimed in Singapore in October 1943 with Chandra Bose as its Prime Minister and Malayan Indian leaders occupying some of its other offices.[117] The provisional Government received much moral and financial support from wealthy and educated Indians in Malaya but its fortunes declined with those of the Japanese regime as the Second World War wore on.

Chandra Bose, as one opinion put it, 'was distinctly authoritarian, not only because he had studied German political and social philosophy, but also because the mental constitution of a middle-class Bengali is likely to harbour a perceptible bias in favour of dictatorial regimes'.[118] His powerful personality instilled life into the movement but the INA and the Azad Hind Government failed to achieve the goal of liberating India because these organizations had inadequate means to work independently of the Japanese. The support of the Indians in Malaya and Singapore failed to rectify this shortcoming. The INA had its only real campaign in Burma at the beginning of 1945 and in this, despite Japanese aid, it suffered reverses and a number of its men deserted to the British.[119]

•   •   •

It is evident that the Japanese Occupation produced varying effects upon the different ethnic communities of Malaysia. Because of the comparatively lenient attitude of the Japanese towards the Malays and the indigenous communities of northern Borneo, relatively fewer of them suffered death or extreme deprivation. This accounted partly for the lesser participation of these communities in the war effort. (There was also, of course, the British decision not to train many Malay guerrillas, as mentioned earlier.) It seems likely that if the Japanese had treated them more brutally, the Malays, Ibans, Melanaus, Kadazans, Bajaus and kindred indigenous groups might have mustered far stronger resistance to the occupying regime. However, Japanese treatment of the Chinese and occasionally the rest of the population was so brutal that it led to sabotage and various forms of chicanery, extortion and double-dealing. Such laxities were embarked upon sometimes as forms of reprisal against the Japanese or those who collaborated with them but often they were simply ways of sustaining life in conditions of economic and social chaos. Inevitably large fortunes were made, especially by those who had little or no scruples about legality or conventional behaviour.

It would be untrue to suggest that only the Chinese fell into the social malaise engendered by the chaotic conditions of the occupation years. In varying degrees all the communities found it expedient and necessary, for the sake of sustaining life, to succumb from time to time to the pattern of behaviour cogently described in a discussion of the effects of the Japanese Occupation on the Chinese: 'Bribery of individual Japanese, black market deals, smuggling and racketeering in various degrees, became the keys to success and prosperity.... But the habits of law and order were largely lost in the business sector.'[120]

To some extent, the Indians were on the horns of a dilemma. The Japanese courted them ostensibly to struggle for the independence of their motherland. But it soon became obvious to the Indian nationalists in Malaya that it was not the intention of the occupying regime to hand over real power to their protégés in the foreseeable future. Consequently, an atmosphere of dismaying political stalemate prevailed in Indian–Japanese relations. Partnership with the Japanese also had its divisive effects upon the Indian community. While the INA sometimes used coercion, backed by the Japanese *kempeitai*, to gain financial help from wealthy Indians, there were those among the wealthy who chose to use their material contribution as insurance against the brutal arm of the Japanese police state but, especially as the INA demands grew, 'the wealthy Indians felt harassed, and avoided payment by various means'.[121]

Yet, like other political upheavals elsewhere, the Japanese invasion and subsequent rule of three years and eight months proved catalytic in several important respects to the various communities of Malaysia. The Japanese Occupation produced changes, especially in Malaya and Singapore, which were hardly anticipated by the British. While Britain remained 'Great' in Sarawak and Sabah where she took over from the semi-private Brookes and Chartered Company and turned the two territories into Crown Colonies in 1946, the developments during the occupation years led the population of Malaya to question the right of Britain to re-impose her pre-war hegemony. The more conservative and usually well-to-do Chinese continued to support the KMT. Their nationalist feeling continued to be chiefly directed towards helping in Generalissimo Chiang Kai-shek's struggle against the Communists in the homeland. Many Chinese in Malaya remained politically apathetic, while other Chinese (and other Asians) who were treated as equals in Japanese internment camps were disappointed to find their former British POW mates treating them as subject people again in 1946. Of more pregnant consequence, the Chinese communists who had formed their MCP in pre-war days had now well-nigh perfected their guerrilla tactics; not long after the end of the Japanese Occupation, they were to employ the same tactics against the British.

While Jawaharlal Nehru had characterized the Indians in Malaya as living in a 'political backwater' in 1937,[122] he himself must have been amazed at the turn of events which not only awakened many Indians politically but also turned that 'political backwater' into the seedbed of a movement which sought to liberate his own motherland by forming the IIL, the INA and the provisional Azad Hind Government. The Malayan Indians involved in the independence movement were to found the Malayan Indian Congress (MIC) in 1946.

Two strands of political mobilization were evident among the Malays. The formation of the Kesatuan Melayu Singapura (KMS) in 1926 in many ways marked the real beginning of a modern Malay political movement. It inspired the formation of similar politically-orientated bodies during the following decade and especially from 1937 onwards, when the various Malay Unions in the Peninsula fostered political mobilization by holding the four congresses and enlivening the columns of the literary societies and pamphlets. At the same time, it cannot be denied that Indonesian nationalism had influenced another group of Peninsular Malays who formed the KMM and pursued a more radical approach to political progress for their people. While many of the more pliant and conservative Malays were induced to enter the Japanese administration, the KMM stole the political limelight by outwardly co-operating with the Japanese but actively plotting to discredit Japanese rule and win independence for the Peninsula. Ironically, both the conservative and the radical Malay intelligentsia were much influenced by Japanese anti-colonialism and leadership of Asian nationalism. Someone wrote in anticipation of the return of the pre-war colonial power, 'The British will find that the people of this new Malaya are vitalised by a new political outlook, so that they should not be surprised if they do not find the former docility and limp submissiveness to authority'.[123] It was thus hardly surprising that the politically awakened Malays challenged the British when the latter attempted to impose a highly-centralized form of government under the guise of the Malayan Union in 1946. This brings us to a very crucial point within the context of this study of race relations in Malaysia.

As has been shown above, a conglomeration of developments, outside and within Malaya, resulted in a sharp division between the Malays and the Chinese during the Japanese Occupation. The same situation did not arise in Sarawak and Sabah mainly because there was no indigenous political movement with an anti-British stance and prepared to co-operate with the Japanese in pursuing independence and because, accordingly, the Japanese did not find the situation suitable for whipping up the spirit of indigenous nationalist feeling. Moreover, and by no means less important, owing to the comparative lack of economic development, Sabah and Sarawak never became important centres of overseas Chinese nationalism. Therefore, while in Sarawak and Sabah the indigenous population and the Chinese were able to make common cause against the Japanese, in Malaya the intensity of anti-Japanese feeling among the Chinese and the official pro-Malay policy of the Japanese together tended to stir up hostility between the two major racial groups which had already had a mild confrontation, confined to the press and debates in legislative councils, in the 1920s and 1930s regarding questions of citizenship and privileges.[124]

The growing strength of the Chinese-dominated MPAJA, as the war drew to an end, served only to accentuate Malay fears and the situation was aggravated during the brief interregnum after the Japanese surrendered and before the British returned to assume control of Malaya. One writer comments, 'For the first few weeks [after the Japanese surrender] as the only power in Malaya, the MPAJA virtually held complete control of the peninsula, especially the more remote inland regions'.[125] They indiscriminately carried out a campaign of vendetta against those they considered Japanese collaborators, including a large number of Malays. All at once, it appeared to the Malays that the possibility of Chinese political control in Malaya had become a probability. With some instigation from the Japanese, the Malays retaliated. From late 1945 to early 1946 several parts of the country were torn by racial clashes, the most serious of which probably occurred in the Batu Pahat–Muar area and Sungai Manik near Teluk Anson.[126] A great deal of Malaya's politics, in the early post-war years, can be understood only against this background. The clashes of 1945–6 have influenced the growth of communalism in Malaysia's politics[127] more than most people realize.

The total effects of the Japanese Occupation period, not only in Malaya but also in South-East Asia as a whole, have been succinctly summed up by a scholar of Harvard University:

The war...did accentuate nationalist sentiments and the determination to achieve independence. First, Japan granted at least the illusion of independence to [some South-East Asian countries]; and at the time of capitulation sanctioned the formation of the Republic of Indonesia and Vietnam in Indochina. During the war a second source of encouragement to independence was the Atlantic Charter and the formation of a United Nations Organization in San Francisco. To South-east Asians news of these two pledges were heard over short-wave radio sets at the risk of reprisal. Promises concerning the autonomy of dependent peoples were accepted with deep trust and literalness.

In addition to nationalism the immediate aftermaths of V-J day accentuated another tendency present before the war in Southeast Asia. It was a tendency which the rapid capitulation of Western powers in the winter of 1941–42 had re-inforced, namely, loss of prestige for Europeans. Before the war the European colonials may not have been held in high esteem, but at least their assumption of power went unquestioned by the man in the street and field. During and immediately after the war, neither power nor prestige were available to bolster European colonial claims in Southeast Asia.[128]

It will be apparent that if, in any one of the comparatively more homogeneous societies of South-East Asia, the war effected a major trans-formation in almost every aspect of life, in Malaya the consequences were far greater. The two largest communities in the country—the Malays and the Chinese—emerged from the war with high expectations, believing that the colonial powers would, sooner rather than later, embark on a policy of decolonization. The need to prepare for imminent independ-ence was strongly felt especially among the younger generation whose traumatic experience during the war enabled them to reach political maturity more rapidly than the older generation. Unfortunately, the two major communities did not share the same vision of Malaya's political future. The Chinese either continued to look to China as the principal object of their political loyalty or spoke in terms of a single Malayan citizenship which should confer equal rights on all inhabitants who chose to make Malaya their home. The Malays, on the other hand, either jealously asserted their claim of 'Malaya for the Malays' or cherished the hope of early independence within 'Greater Indonesia'. The stage was therefore set for a period of political bargaining or attempts by one group to outmanoeuvre the other. But it was the British administration which made the first move on the political chess board.

1. T. H. Silcock and Ungku A. Aziz, 'Nationalism in Malaya', in W. L. Holland (ed.), *Asian Nationalism and the West*, New York, 1953, p. 279. It should also be observed that the traditional allegiance of the Malay was to the state or sultanate, for example Terengganu or Pahang, rather than to his race. There was 'state' or 'nationalist' rather than racial consciousness in the Malay world.

2. J. M. Gullick, *Indigenous Political Systems of Western Malaya*, London, 1958; C. C. Brown (trans.), *Sejarah Melayu or Malay Annals*, Kuala Lumpur, 1970.

3. F. Swettenham, *British Malaya*, London 1907, especially ch. 7; R. O. Winstedt, 'The Circumstances of Malay Life' in R. J. Wilkinson (ed.), *Papers on Malay Subjects*, Kuala Lumpur, 1925; B. Sandin, *The Sea Dayaks of Borneo*, London, 1967; A. Richards (ed.), *The Sea Dayaks and other Races of Sarawak*, Kuching, 1963 (reprint of 1912 edition); I. H. N. Evans, *Among Primitive Peoples in Borneo*, London, 1922; and T. R. Williams, *The Dusun: A North Borneo Society*, New York, 1965.

4. See M. G. Swift, *Malay Peasant Society in Jelebu*, London, 1965; and Wan A. Hamid, 'Religion and Culture of the Modern Malay' in Wang Gungwu (ed.), *Malaysia: A Survey*, New York, 1964, pp. 179–89.

5. One of them [Abdul Majid bin Haji Zainuddin], *The Malays in Malaya*, Singapore, 1928, p. 78. For a more analytical discussion of the subject, see S. H. Alatas, *The Myth of the Lazy Native*, London, 1977.

6. Wong Lin Ken, *The Malayan Tin Industry to 1914*, Tucson, 1965, p. 65.

7. Colin Barlow, *The Natural Rubber Industry: Its Development, Technology, and Economy in Malaysia*, Kuala Lumpur, 1978, pp. 48–9.

8. H. Low 'Selesilah (Book of Descent) of the Rajahs of Brunei', *JSBRAS*, No. 5, June 1880, pp. 1–35; H. R. Hughes-Hallet, 'A Sketch of the History of Brunei', *JMBRAS*, 18, Pt. 2, 1940, pp. 23–42; J. P. Ongkili, 'Pre-Western Brunei, Sarawak and Sabah', *Nusantara*, Bil. 3, January 1973, pp. 49–68.

9. Peter Leys, 'Observations on the Brunei Political System 1883–1885' (with notes by Robert M. Pringle), *JMBRAS*, 41, Pt. 2, December 1968, p. 118.

10. See L. W. Jones, *The Population of Borneo*, London, 1966, pp. 12, 15; Lee Yong Leng, *North Borneo (Sabah)*, Singapore, 1965, pp. 58–62.

11. See, for example, A. Johns, 'Muslim Mystics and Historical Writing' in D. G. E. Hall (ed.), *Historians of South East Asia*, London, 1961; Syed Naguib Al-Attas, *The Mysticism of Hamzah Fansuri*, Kuala Lumpur, 1970; and Mohd. Taib Osman, *Kesusasteraan Melayu Lama*, Kuala Lumpur, 1965, pp. 73–86.

12. See J. D. Vaughan, *The Manners and Customs of the Chinese of the Straits Settlements*, Kuala Lumpur, 1971 (reprint of 1879 edition); I. L. Bird, *The Golden Chersonese and the Way Thither*, Kuala Lumpur, 1967 (reprint of 1883 edition), pp. 132–4, 188–92, and 288–91; and Song Ong Siang, *One Hundred Years' History of the Chinese in Singapore*, Singapore, 1967 (reprint of 1923 edition).

13. Khoo Kay Kim, *The Western Malay States, 1850–1873*, Kuala Lumpur, 1972, Pts. II and III; N. Ginsburg and C. F. Robert, Jr., *Malaya*, Seattle, 1958, ch. 8.

14. C. M. Turnbull, 'Gambier and Pepper Trade in Johore in the Nineteenth Century', *JSSS*, 15, Pt. 1, 1959; J. C. Jackson, *Planters and Speculators: Chinese and European Agricultural Enterprise in Malaya, 1786–1921*, University of Malaya Press, Kuala Lumpur, 1968, pp. 15–22, 24–30; Carl A. Trocki, 'The Origin of the Kangchu System, 1740–1860', *JMBRAS*, 44, Pt. 2, 1976.

15. This resembled the *kangany* method for Indian labour mentioned below and entailed the employment of Chinese recruiters or brokers who went to China to obtain prospective labourers. The recruiter, known as *kheh thau*, arranged the passage in return for which the labourers, or *sin-kheh*, very often peasants from rural Chinese provinces, signed contracts or

made explicit undertakings to work for employers associated with the recruiter. The employers in Malaya usually paid off the recruiters while the labourers remained tied to the employers until all debts had been paid. Not uncommonly, the employers imposed high rates of interest which kept the labourers indentured for years. See J. N. Parmer, *Colonial Labor Policy and Administration: A History of Labor in the Rubber Plantation Industry in Malaya, c.1910–1941*, New York, 1960, pp. 27–37; and R. N. Jackson, *Immigrant Labour and the Development of Malaya, 1786–1920*, Kuala Lumpur, 1961, chs. 4, 6 and 14.

16. See A. M. Cooper, *Men of Sarawak*, Kuala Lumpur, 1968, chs. 4 and 11; W. J. Chater, *Sarawak Long Ago*, Kuching, 1969, pp. 66–70; and K. G. Tregonning, *A History of Modern Sabah, 1881–1963*, Singapore, 1965, ch. 7.

17. Excluding Singapore, the Chinese comprised 33.9 per cent in 1931 and 38.4 per cent in 1947 of the population of Malaya. Federation of Malaya, *Official Year Book, 1961*, p. 36. See also C. A. Vlieland, 'The 1947 Census of Malaya', *Pacific Affairs*, 22, No. 1, March 1949, pp. 59–63.

18. In Sarawak, there were 123,626 (24 per cent) Chinese in 1939, and 145,158 (26 per cent) in 1947; while in Sabah, there were 50,056 (18 per cent) Chinese in 1931, and 74,374 (22 per cent) in 1951. The figures are from Jones, op. cit., p. 63; and the percentages—approximate—are of the total population of the territory in each case. By comparison there were 1,285,000 Chinese in 1931 and 1,885,000 in 1947 in Malaya (excluding Singapore). Federation of Malaya, *Official Year Book, 1961*, p. 36.

19. V. Purcell, *The Chinese in Malaya*, Kuala Lumpur, 1967 (reprint of 1948 edition), p. 237.

20. Ibid., pp. 241–2. See G. W. Skinner, *Leadership and Power in the Chinese Community of Thailand*, Ithaca, N.Y., 1958, chs. 4 and 5 and R. J. Coughlin, *Double Identity: The Chinese in Modern Thailand*, Hong Kong, 1960, chs. 3 and 6 for the economic roles and clan life of the Chinese which were in many ways similar to those in Malaya.

21. Unless otherwise stated, the term 'Indian' is used in this study to include all persons of related origin, for instance Pakistanis and Ceylonese.

22. Under this arrangement, Malayan employers sent Indian agents (*kangany*) to India to persuade prospective labourers, especially in the *kanganys'* own home districts, to apply for free passage to Malaya. The *kangany* method of labour recruitment is discussed in S. Arasaratnam, *Indians in Malaysia and Singapore*, Kuala Lumpur, 1970, pp. 16–20.

23. There were Indian middle class people in Malaya, such as doctors, lawyers, teachers and clerks, but most of these came originally from similar classes in India or Ceylon rather than from the ranks of the immigrant labourers in Malaya. See Usha Mahajani, *The Role of Indian Minorities in Burma and Malaya*, Bombay, 1960, pp. 98–103.

24. Arasaratnam, op. cit., p. 24.

25. Silcock and Aziz, op. cit., p. 287.

26. Usha Mahajani erroneously states that the ban was on 'unassisted emigration of Indian labour' to Malaya, op. cit., p. 109.

27. Silcock and Aziz, op. cit., p. 276.

28. Federation of Malaya, *Official Year Book, 1961*, p. 36.

29. Jones, op. cit., p. 203.

30. N. Tarling, *Anglo-Dutch Rivalry in the Malay World, 1780–1824*, London, 1962, ch. 5; and R. Bonney, *Kedah 1771–1821: The Search for Security and Independence*, Kuala Lumpur, 1971.

31. C. M. Turnbull, *The Straits Settlements, 1826–67*, London, 1972, chs. 9 and 10; and N. Tarling, *British Policy in the Malay Peninsula and Archipelago, 1824–1871*, Kuala Lumpur, 1969.

32. See C. D. Cowan, *Nineteenth-Century Malaya: The Origins of British Political Control*,

London, 1961; and D. McIntyre, 'Britain's Intervention in Malaya: the Origin of Lord Kimberley's Instructions to Sir Andrew Clarke in 1873', *JSEAH*, 2, No. 3, 1961.

33. R. Emerson, *Malaysia: A Study in Direct and Indirect Rule*, Kuala Lumpur, 1964 (reprint of 1937 edition), p. 112.

34. For a detailed discussion of the subject, see Khoo Kay Kim, 'The Origin of British Administration in Malaya', *JMBRAS*, 39, Pt. 1, 1966.

35. C. N. Parkinson, *British Intervention in Malaya 1867–1877*, Singapore, 1960, App. A.

36. E. Sadka, *The Protected Malay States 1874–1895*, Singapore, 1968, p. 379.

37. W. G. Maxwell and W. S. Gibson (eds.), *Treaties and Engagements Affecting the Malay States and Borneo*, London, 1924, pp. 35–6; 63–4; and 68–9.

38. Ibid., p. 88.

39. E. Thio, *British Policy in the Malay Peninsula 1880–1910*, Singapore, 1969, *passim*.

40. R. O. Winstedt, *A History of Malaya*, Kuala Lumpur, 1968, p. 240.

41. J. S. Sidhu, 'Decentralization of the Federated Malay States 1930–34', *Peninjau Sejarah*, 1, No. 1, June 1966, pp. 17–28.

42. For a history of the establishment of the Brooke regime in Sarawak see S. Runciman, *The White Rajahs*, London, 1960; and N. Tarling, *Britain, The Brookes and Brunei*, Kuala Lumpur, 1971.

43. In 1960, the population of Sarawak comprised: indigenous 68 per cent, Chinese 31 per cent, and Europeans and others 1 per cent. See L. W. Jones, op. cit., p. 203.

44. R. Payne, *The White Rajahs of Sarawak*, London, 1960, pp. 59–60.

45. S. Baring-Gould and C. A. Bampfylde, *A History of Sarawak Under its Two White Rajahs, 1839–1908*, London, 1909, chs. 3 and 7.

46. C. Brooke, *Ten Years in Sarawak*, London, 1866, Vol. 2, p. 317.

47. Of the twenty-one 'members' of the first Council meeting at Bintulu in September 1867, 'no one represented the great interior hinterland; and direct representation of the *ulu* to any extent was not to come for more than thirty years. The early Councils were drawn mainly from the accessible coastal plain of the south-west.' Government of Sarawak, *Council Negri Centenary, 1867–1967*, Kuching, 1967, p. 1.

48. Payne, op. cit., p. 137. Charles Brooke penned the opinion quoted in a tract titled 'Queries, Past, Present and the Future' which he published in London.

49. See K. M. Panikkar, *Asia and Western Dominance*, London, 1959; R. Emerson, *From Empire to Nation*, Cambridge, Mass., 1962; and D. P. Singhal, 'Nationalism and Communism in South-East Asia', *JSEAH*, 3, No. 1, March 1962.

50. W. L. Holland (ed.), *Asian Nationalism and the West*, New York, 1953; G. A. Almond and J. S. Coleman (eds.), *The Politics of the Developing Areas*, New Jersey, 1960; and Emerson, *From Empire to Nation*, especially chs. 1–3.

51. Government of Sarawak, *The Sarawak Government Gazette*, Kuching, 24 September 1941, p. 616.

52. Ibid., p. 617.

53. Runciman, op. cit., p. 249.

54. Prior to 1939, there were 25 government schools which were entirely Malay (Islamic) and in which the use and teaching of English was debarred before 1930, 37 mission schools, and over 100 Chinese schools. (Interview with A. G. Smith former Director of Education, Sarawak, Hull, March 1972.) See also Jones, op. cit., pp. 57–60; No survey of literacy was ever undertaken during the Brooke period.

55. J. D. Legge, *Indonesia*, New Jersey, 1964, pp. 68–78; D. G. E. Hall, *A History of Southeast Asia*, London, 1964, chs. 28, 35 and 42; and D. J. Steinberg (ed.), *In Search of Southeast Asia: A Modern History*, Kuala Lumpur, 1971, chs. 18, 20 and 24.

56. See O. Rutter, *British North Borneo*, London, 1922; L. R. Wright, *The Origins of*

British Borneo, Hong Kong, 1970.

57. K. G. Tregonning, 'Steps in the Acquisition of North Borneo', *Historical Studies: Australia and New Zealand*, 5, No. 19, 1952.

58. For the text of the Royal Charter, see the Company's *Handbook of British North Borneo, 1886*, pp. 113–28.

59. Ibid., p. 123.

60. Rutter, op. cit., chs. 5 and 10. For an illustrative study of one of the main products, see D. W. John and J. C. Jackson, 'The Tobacco Industry of North Borneo: A Distinctive Form of Plantation Agriculture', *JSEAS*, 4, No. 1, March 1973, pp. 88–106; see also J. P. Ongkili, 'Kelekaan Ekonomi Kompeni Berpiagam Sabah, 1881–1941', *Malaysia in History*, 16, No. 1, June 1973, pp. 9–15.

61. K. G. Tregonning in his *Under Chartered Company Rule*, Singapore, 1958 (2nd edn., 1965, as *A History of Modern Sabah, 1881–1963*) gives the impression that the Chartered Company was a very humane institution which husbanded Sabah faithfully and brought it to stability and progress. There is a lot of truth in such an assertion and admittedly the Company brought relative peace to a once-wild country. Yet, such an impression is one-sided unless it is also pointed out that the Company had an overriding economic wish to do well for the sake of its shareholders. Indeed, the Company made little effort to hide this paramount objective. One has only to scan the pages of the reports of the Company to find major spaces perennially devoted to trade, timber and other forest products, geology and minerals, commercial agriculture, careful reproductions of documents on trade returns, 'openings for capitalists and settlers' and the prospects for European life in the territory. See *Handbook of British North Borneo* for 1886, 1890 and 1934.

62. The Advisory Council was so much a creature of the Company Government, and so little a body representing the people of the territory, that Rutter saw no distinction between it and the Company administration. See Rutter, op. cit., ch. 6.

63. K. G. Tregonning, 'The Mat Salleh Revolt (1894–1905)', *JMBRAS*, 29, Pt. 1, 1956, pp. 20–36.

64. K. G. Tregonning, *A History of Modern Sabah*, pp. 200–1.

65. Ibid., see chapter on 'Rebels', pp. 197–222.

66. The locus of power and extent of political participation by the people were summed up by the Company *Handbook* in 1934: 'The Government is assisted by a Legislative Council consisting of nine official and five unofficial members, the unofficial members being nominated by the different communities and appointed by the Governor subject to the approval of the Court of Directors. Ordinances are enacted by the Governor, with the advice of the Council, but the Court of Directors reserve the right to disallow any such Ordinances in the same way as the Crown retains a power of veto in the case of Crown Colonies.' (p. 44) The position remained so until the Japanese Occupation.

67. Tregonning, *A History of Modern Sabah*, pp. 127–8.

68. Interviews with Datuk G. S. Sundang, O. K. K. Tambakau, O. K. K. Zainal bin Kerahu about their experiences in the pre-war period. All agreed that the Chartered Company rule was oppressive and debilitating.

69. The communities of Sarawak made no demand for a constitution at the time, thereby manifesting that they were not politically prepared or nationalistically aware. Neither was there any significant reaction to that Constitution.

70. See Wang Gungwu, 'Sun Yat-sen and Singapore', *JSSS*, 15, Pt. 2, December 1959, pp. 55–68; Lee Ah-chai, 'Policies and Politics in Chinese Schools in the Straits Settlements and Federated Malay States, 1786–1941' (M.A. Thesis, University of Malaya, Singapore, 1957); Png Poh Seng, 'The Kuomintang in Malaya, 1912–1941', *JSEAH*, 2, No. 1, March 1961, pp. 1–41; V. Purcell, *The Chinese in Malaya*, pp. 209–18.

71. See Khoo Kay Kim, 'The Beginnings of Political Extremism in Malaya 1915–1935' (Ph.D. Thesis, University of Malaya, Kuala Lumpur, 1973), pp. 197–303; G. Z. Hanrahan, *The Communist Struggle in Malaya*, Kuala Lumpur, 1971, pp. 19–60.

72. See G. P. Ramachandra, 'The Indian Independence Movement in Malaya 1942–45' (M.A. Thesis, University of Malaya, Kuala Lumpur, 1970).

73. See Khoo Kay Kim, 'The Beginnings of Political Extremism in Malaya'.

74. See W. R. Roff, *The Origins of Malay Nationalism*, Singapore, 1967; Radin Soenarno, 'Malay Nationalism, 1900–1945', *JSEAH*, 1, No. 1, March 1960, pp. 1–28; Silcock and Aziz, op. cit., pp. 284–6.

75. See W. R. Roff, 'Kaum Muda–Kaum Tua: Innovation and Reaction Amongst the Malays, 1900–1941' in K. G. Tregonning (ed.), *Papers on Malayan History*, Singapore, 1962, pp. 162–92.

76. See W. R. Roff, *The Origins of Malay Nationalism*, pp. 221–34.

77. See Khoo Kay Kim, 'The Beginnings of Political Extremism in Malaya', pp. 128–9, 254–346.

78. See Khoo Kay Kim, 'Malay Society, 1874–1920's', *JSEAS*, 5, No. 2, September 1974, pp. 179–98.

79. See Stephen Leong, 'Sources, Agencies and Manifestations of Overseas Chinese Nationalism in Malaya 1941–1945' (Ph.D. Thesis, University of California, Los Angeles, 1976); Norman Parmer, 'Chinese Estate Workers' Strikes in Malaya in March 1937' in C. D. Cowan (ed.), *The Economic Development of Southeast Asia*, London, 1964; M. R. Stenson, *Industrial Conflict in Malaya*, London, 1970, pp. 19–24.

80. Arasaratnam, op. cit., pp. 96–111; Stenson, op. cit., pp. 25–33.

81. See W. R. Roff, *The Origins of Malay Nationalism*, pp. 211–47.

82. Muhammad Yunus Hamidi, *Sejarah Pergerakan Politik Melayu Semenanjong*, Kuala Lumpur (1961?), pp. 5–6.

83. See Radin Soenarno, op. cit., pp. 16–22; Ahmad Boestamam, *Dr. Burhanuddin: Putera Setia Melayu*, Kuala Lumpur, 1972, pp. 4, 77.

84. Soh Eng Lim, 'Tan Cheng Lock', *JSEAH*, 1, No. 1, March 1960, p. 33.

85. See M. Hall, *Kinabalu Guerrillas*, Sarawak Press Ltd., Kuching, [1949?], ch. 1; and S. Runciman, op. cit., p. 255.

86. For a contemporary account of the Japanese invasion of the Peninsula and Singapore, see I. Morrison, *Malayan Postscript*, London, 1942.

87. Abd. Malek Haji Md. Hanafiah, 'Sejarah Perjuangan Kesatuan Melayu Muda 1937–1945' (B.A. Hons. Academic Exercise, Department of History, Universiti Kebang-saan Malaysia, 1974), pp. 233–6.

88. Ibid., pp. 261–2. On the subject of KMM's cooperation with the Japanese, see Lt.-Gen. Fujiwara Iwaichi, *F. Kikan Japanese Army Intelligence Operations in Southeast Asia during World War II*, Hong Kong, 1983. Translated by Yoji Akashi.

89. Yoji Akashi, 'Education and Indoctrination Policy in Malaya and Singapore under the Japanese Rule, 1942–1945', *Malaysian Journal of Education*, 13, No. 1/2, December 1976, p. 1.

90. Abd. Malek Haji Md. Hanafiah, op. cit., p. 274.

91. Halinah Bamadhaj, 'The Impact of the Japanese Occupation of Malaya on Malay Society and Politics' (M.A. Thesis, Auckland University, 1975), pp. 93–4.

92. I. K. Agastja (Ibrahim Yaacob), *Sedjarah dan Perdjuangan di Malaya*, Jogjarkata, 1951, p. 101.

93. Ibid., p. 106; Abd. Malek Haji Md. Hanafiah, op. cit., pp. 287–97; Interview with Ishak Haji Muhammad, Ulu Langat, March 1978. For the war-time activities of KMM, see also F. S. Chapman, *The Jungle is Neutral*, London, 1949, *passim*.

94. Yoichi Itagaki, 'Some Aspects of the Japanese Policy for Malaya Under the Occupation, with Special Reference to Nationalism' in K. G. Tregonning (ed.), *Papers on Malayan History*, Singapore, 1962, pp. 262–3.

95. Ibrahim Yaacob, *Sekitar Malaya Merdeka*, Djakarta, 1957, p. 28.

96. Abd. Malek Haji Md. Hanafiah, op. cit., pp. 302–7; Khoo Kay Kim, 'Ibrahim Yaakob dan KMM', *Widya*, No. 21, May 1979, p. 39.

97. Soenarno, op. cit., p. 25; Ibrahim Yaacob, *Sekitar Melaya Merdeka*, p. 29.

98. B. Simandjuntak, *Malayan Federalism, 1945–1963*, Kuala Lumpur, 1969, p. 10.

99. For an extended discussion, see Yoji Akashi, 'Japanese Military Administration in Malaya—Its Formation and Evolution in Reference to Sultans, the Islamic Religion, and the Moslem-Malays, 1941–1945', *Asian Studies*, 7, No. 1, April 1969, pp. 81–110.

100. V. Purcell in his Introduction in 1954 to G. Z. Hanrahan, op. cit., pp. 10 and 62. Writing earlier in 1948, however, Purcell stated that between 40,000 and 100,000 perished in the purge. See V. Purcell, *The Chinese in Malaya*, p. 251.

101. Hanrahan, op. cit., ch. 3. The KMT in Malaya, although officially banned as a political party since 1925, also actively participated in the anti-Japanese effort by collecting funds for the parent organization in the homeland and organizing resistance groups, such as DALFORCE.

102. Another guerrilla resistance group was built by the British in their plan to re-occupy Malaya. Known as Force 136, its Malayan Section gained enlistments from members of the various communities from July 1942 onwards. It worked out a *modus operandi* with the MPAJA while anticipating its major military supply and direction from the Allies. However, it disbanded without seeing much action when the War ended abruptly. Hanrahan, op. cit., pp. 77–88; and R. Clutterbuck, *The Long Long War*, London, 1967, p. 16.

103. Discussion with Ungku A. Aziz.

104. See G. Maxwell, *The Civil Defence of Malaya*, London, 1944; V. Purcell, *Malaya: Outline of a Colony*, London, 1946; and R. Winstedt, *Britain and Malaya, 1786–1948*, London, 1949, for apologetic versions of the British position in Malaya.

105. M. Hall, *Labuan Story*, Jesselton, 1958, pp. 254–70; and T. Harrisson, *World Within: A Borneo Story*, London, 1959.

106. As the occupation years wore on, Japanese atrocities became commonplace in Borneo, as they did in the Peninsula and Singapore. See Chin Kee Onn, *Malaya Upside Down*, Singapore, 1946; and Morrison, op. cit.

107. See M. R. Stenson, *Industrial Conflict in Malaya*, London, 1970, pp. 67–8.

108. Tregonning narrates, 'There was widespread conscription of women for prostitution and a regimentation of men and women for labour.... As in Malaya, the first signs of dissatisfaction came from the Chinese. Their shops had been looted, their trade had been eliminated, their women had been raped or appropriated.' (*A History of Modern Sabah*, pp. 216–17.) See also Chin Kee Onn, op. cit., ch. 2.

109. Interviews with Assistant Superintendents of Police, Mohammed Yassin Anik and Ansibin, both of Sabah, who were active in the resistance movement from 1943 to 1945. Kuala Lumpur, June 1971. See also F. G. Whelan, *Stories from Sabah History*, Singapore, 1968, ch. 5.

110. For a vivid narrative of the Double Tenth Uprising, see M. Hall, *Kinabalu Guerillas*, chs. 2 and 3.

111. K. G. Tregonning, *North Borneo*, London, 1960, p. 164; and Harrisson, op. cit.

112. W. H. Elsbree, *Japan's Role in Southeast Asian Nationalist Movements, 1940 to 1945*, Cambridge, Mass., 1953, pp. 15–41.

113. Arasaratnam, op. cit., p. 105; see also Ramachandra, op. cit.

114. Silcock and Aziz, op. cit., p. 296.

115. C. Chaudhuri, 'Subhas Chandra Bose—His Legacy and Legend', *Pacific Affairs*, 26, No. 4, December 1953, p. 356.

116. Usha Mahajani, op. cit., pp. 145–8.

117. Arasaratnam, op. cit., p. 105; and J. Lebra, 'Japanese Policy and the Indian National Army', *Asian Studies*, 7, No. 1, April 1969, pp. 44–9.

118. Chaudhuri, op. cit., p. 356. See also S. P. Cohen, 'Subhas Chandra Bose and the Indian National Army', *Pacific Affairs*, 36, No. 4, winter 1963–64, pp. 411–29.

119. K. K. Ghosh, 'The Indian National Army—Motives, Problems and Significance', *Asian Studies*, 7, No. 1, pp. 4–5; and Arasaratnam, op. cit., p. 107.

120. Silcock and Aziz, op. cit., p. 295.

121. Arasaratnam, op. cit., p. 106.

122. Silcock and Aziz, op. cit., p. 287.

123. Chin Kee Onn, op. cit., p. 208. See also C. Du Bois, *Social Forces in Southeast Asia*, Cambridge, Mass., 1959, ch. 3, for (*inter alia*) the outlook of nationalism in the area after 1946.

124. For some idea of this confrontation, see Roff, *Origins of Malay Nationalism*, pp. 207–10.

125. Hanrahan, op. cit., p. 87.

126. There are few published works on the subject of Sino-Malay clashes during this period. The best known source is K. O. L. Burridge, 'Racial Relations in Johore', *Australian Journal of Politics and History*, 2, 2, 1957, pp. 151–68; see also Hairi Abdullah, 'Kebangitan dan Gerakan Tentera Selendang Merah dalam Sejarah Daerah Muar dan Batu Pahat', *JEBAT*, 3/4, 1973/75; unpublished sources include Mohd. Noordin Sopiee, 'The Communities Liaison Committee and Post-War Communal Relations in Malaya: A Historical Source Book' (University of Malaya, Microfilm 861); Ghazali Basri, 'Hilir Perak: Sejarah Hubungan Ras Zaman Pendudukan Jepun sehingga Pemerintahan Tentera Inggeris (BMA), 1942–1946' (B.A. Hons. Thesis, Department of History, University of Malaya, 1974/75); Musak Mantrak, 'Sejarah Masyarakat Majemuk di Mukim VII, Batu Pahat, Johor, 1900–1945' (B.A. Hons. Thesis, Department of History, University of Malaya, 1974/75).

127. For a study of the nature of communal politics in Malaya, see K. J. Ratnam, *Communalism and the Political Process in Malaya*, Kuala Lumpur, 1965.

128. See Du Bois, op. cit., pp. 52–3.

2
The Unification of
the Malay Peninsula, 1946–1948

DESPITE her complete defeat by the Japanese with the fall of Singapore on 15 February 1942, Britain, for economic, imperial and strategic reasons, worked conscientiously for her return to Malaya. As early as July 1943 the Colonial Office set up a Malayan Planning Unit (MPU) composed mainly of British officials with Malayan experience and charged with the responsibility of working out future British policy for Malaya and Singapore.

The MacMichael Mission

The outcome of the planning and preparation by the MPU was summarized by the Secretary of State for the Colonies in answering a question in the House of Commons on 10 October 1945:

His Majesty's Government have given careful consideration to the future of Malaya and the need to promote the sense of unity and common citizenship which will develop the country's strength and capacity in due course for self-government within the British Commonwealth.

Our policy will call for a constitutional Union of Malaya and for the institution of a Malayan citizenship which will give equal citizenship rights to those who can claim Malaya to be their homeland. For these purposes fresh agreement will need to be arranged with the Malay State Rulers and fresh constitutional measures for the Straits Settlements. . . .

The Malayan Union will consist of the nine States in the Malay Peninsula and of the two British Settlements of Penang and Malacca. The Settlement of Singapore at this stage requires separate constitutional treatment and in view of its special economic and other interests provision will be made for it to be constituted as a separate Colony.[1]

It was recognized that in order to implement the new proposals, it would be necessary to obtain the consent of the nine Malay states with which Britain had signed treaties enabling her to exercise indirect rule in Malaya before the Japanese Occupation. For this purpose, Sir Harold Mac-Michael was despatched to Malaya concurrently with the statement made in the House of Commons.

Since it was the British policy for post-war Malaya which highlighted Malay loyalist and patriotic sentiments at the time, it is instructive to see how MacMichael proceeded to secure the signatures of the Malay Rulers to the new Agreements. MacMichael's terms of reference directed him to 'invite each Malay Ruler's co-operation in the establishing of a fresh constitutional organisation of Malaya which has been approved by His Majesty's Government and communicated to' him. More revealingly, MacMichael was 'authorised as Special Representative of His Majesty's Government to conclude with each Ruler on behalf of His Majesty's Government *a formal Agreement by which he will cede full jurisdiction to His Majesty in his State*'.[2] Clearly, the British intention was to gain much wider control over the Malay Rulers than they had had in pre-war days.

MacMichael toured all the nine states of the Peninsula. He claimed that he had observed propriety and due respect in his meetings with the Rulers. His Majesty's Special Representative vouched that before every Ruler:

I opened the proceedings in all cases by explaining the object of my mission and my terms of reference and thereafter, in general terms, but always with complete frankness, the salient features and justification of the policy which had been adopted by His Majesty's Government and which it was proposed to carry out *after the grant of jurisdiction*, namely, the creation of a Malayan Union and the grant of common citizenship to all who had made Malaya their real home.[3]

During his stay of eighty-two days in Malaya, from 11 October 1945 to 1 January 1946, MacMichael succeeded in obtaining the signatures of the nine Malay Rulers to the new Agreements. Britain's wish to possess and exercise full jurisdiction over the internal and external affairs of Malaya was realized in so far as the Rulers signed the British-drafted Agreements before the Special Representative. It is difficult to deny, however, that the Special Representative went about his mission not only with a strong element of haste but also with undisguised arrogance; the Malay Rulers and their subjects soon represented the proceedings as a dictatorial and opportunistic attempt on the part of Britain to colonize directly the Malay states which were no more than British protectorates in pre-war days. This attempt was a clear breach of promise: the pre-war British promise to uphold the sovereignty of each of the nine Malay states. But, beside the impression of a British conspiracy, it was the astounding provisions of the Malayan Union proposals of 1946 which really aroused Malay sentiments.

The Malayan Union Proposals

Pursuing her post-war policy for Malaya in a planned manner, Britain published two White Papers—on 22 January and 4 March 1946—which clearly showed a drastic change in attitude and approach towards the Malay states. Undoubtedly, the second White Paper contained the clearest and most precise definition of the Malayan Union proposals and it demonstrated the fact that Britain was set in her policy of dividing her Malayan dependencies into two distinct entities, namely, the Malayan Union and Singapore.

Briefly, the Malayan Union, comprising the nine Malay states and Pulau Pinang and Melaka as earlier announced, would have a central Legislative Council with up to twenty-two official and twenty-one nominated unofficial members presided over by the Governor of the Malayan Union. The Governor would have a veto power over bills passed by the Council. There would be a central Executive Council with six official and five unofficial members, the latter to be appointed by the Governor. Clearly, these central government bodies were almost identical with those usually found in British crown colonies. There was no intention of introducing the electoral process in the Malayan Union; the people's voice was obviously regarded as a thing of the distant future.

In so far as consideration had to be given to the position of the Malay Rulers whose sovereignty in their respective states Britain had recognized and maintained throughout the pre-war period, provision was made for the setting up of a Council of Sultans which was to consist of the Governor as President and the Rulers, the Chief Secretary, the Attorney-General and the Financial Secretary of the Malayan Union as members. More systematic than the periodic *durbar* of the pre-war era, this Council would meet twice a year.[4] The Council's functions were 'to consider legislation, relating solely to matters of Muhammadan religion, which the Malay Advisory Council in any State has approved for enactment; and to advise the Governor on any matter which he may refer to the Council for discussion, or on any matter which, with his prior consent, any Sultan may propose for discussion'.[5] In short, even Muslim religious affairs were to be controlled by the British authorities.

There was to be a State Council in each of the Malay states and Settlement Councils in Pulau Pinang and Melaka. 'Each such Council will consist of the Resident Commissioner of the State or Settlement as Chairman, and of such ex-officio Members, Nominated Official Members, Nominated Unofficial Members and Elected Members as may be prescribed by law or regulation'.[6] The State and Settlement Councils were empowered to make laws on any subject which was declared by the

Governor-in-Council to be of a purely local nature or in respect of which powers of legislation had been 'delegated to them by the Legislative Council, but any such law may be altered or repealed by the Union Legislature and will be void if repugnant to Union legislation'.[7] The arrangement demonstrated unequivocally the Malayan Union Government's responsibility for initiating a strong central government in Kuala Lumpur, one which would rectify the failure of the pre-war decentralization.

Also at state level, the Malay Advisory Council in each state would, as mentioned earlier, consist of the Ruler and other Malays he might appoint. This Advisory Council was given the function, as the title implies, of advising the Ruler on all matters affecting Islam in the state or which might 'be referred to the Council at the request of the Resident Commissioner with the Governor's approval, and on the making of laws which relate solely to Muhammadan religion and do not involve taxation or tithes'.[8] Thus, at state level, too, Islamic affairs which were expressly the domain of the Rulers in pre-war days were to come under the enormous, all-embracing powers of the Malayan Union Governor and his lieutenants, the Resident Commissioners.

The provisions on citizenship in the Malayan Union proposals must be clearly understood, not only because they accounted to a considerable extent for the heightening of Malay sentiments but also because they bore significance in relation to subsequent developments on the matter. The second White Paper laid down that the Order-in-Council on the matter would provide that the following persons would be Malayan Union citizens:

(a) Any person born in the Malayan Union or Singapore before the date when the Order comes into force, who is ordinarily resident in the Malayan Union or Singapore on that date.

(b) Any person of eighteen years of age or over ordinarily resident in the Malayan Union or Singapore on the date when the Order comes into force, who has resided in the Malayan Union or Singapore for a period of ten years during the fifteen years preceding the 15th of February, 1942, and who swears or affirms or takes the oath of allegiance (i.e. to be faithful and loyal to the Government of the Malayan Union).

(c) Any person born in the Malayan Union or Singapore on or after the date when the Order comes into force.

(d) Any person born outside the Malayan Union and Singapore on or after the date when the Order comes into force, whose father is a Malayan Union citizen at the time of that person's birth and either was born in the Malayan Union or Singapore or was a Malayan Union citizen under (b) above or had obtained a certificate of naturalization. The minor children (viz: children under eighteen) of persons in categories (a) and (b) will also be Malayan Union citizens.[9]

At the discretion of the Governor, and subject to certain residential and character qualifications, certificates of naturalization as Malayan Union citizens could be granted; but 'a Malayan Union citizen who becomes naturalized in a foreign state will cease to be a Malayan Union citizen'.[10]

At least three significant points can be seen in the provisions on citizenship above. First, despite the decision to separate Singapore from the rest of Malaya in 1946, the British kept the door open for those in Singapore to become Malayan Union citizens if they qualified and chose to do so. Secondly, for the first time in its history the Peninsula was to be unified under one form of citizenship. Thirdly, category (c) meant that *jus soli* citizenship was advocated for all 'Malayans' irrespective of race, colour or creed. It was this third point on citizenship which the Malays found threatening and considered damaging to their community. But, this particular aspect apart, the Malayan Union proposals as a whole bore testimony to the British wish to return to Malaya in a position of administrative strength and political prestige. Britain brought with her a neat bundle of colonial proposals which the Malays found astonishing and deeply disappointing when compared to the benevolent British indirect rule of the pre-war period. The Malays thereupon reacted against the Malayan Union scheme.

Malay Reactions

Because of the prevailing unsettled conditions in the Peninsula resulting from the Japanese Occupation, it was not surprising that the majority of the Rulers tended to welcome the returning British who had been far more benevolent in pre-war days than the high-handed and harsh Japanese during the occupation years. It was in this relatively pro-British atmosphere that MacMichael pressed on with his efforts to acquire the Rulers' signatures. Yet it is significant that the earliest adverse reactions of Malays to the Malayan Union proposals were those of the Rulers themselves. Before signing the new Agreement on 14 November 1945, the Yang di-Pertuan Besar of Negeri Sembilan, Tuanku Abdul Rahman, is reported to have been given very little time to consider the proposals. Speaking also on behalf of the four *Undang* (territorial chieftains) whose concurrence was necessary before his signing the British document, the Ruler maintained that 'During the two days which was all the time Sir Harold MacMichael and his party could give us there was the veiled implication that what we had been compelled to do might be held against us and furthermore we were told that as Johore, Selangor and Pahang had already signed it was pointless our not doing so'.[11] There was a much stronger reaction in Kedah where the question of sovereignty was deeply involved. Article 3 of the Anglo-Kedah Agreement of 1923 stated that 'His Britannic Majesty will not transfer or otherwise dispose of his rights of suzerainty over the State of Kedah to another power and will not merge or combine the State of Kedah or her territories with any other State or with the Colony of the Straits Settlements without the written consent of his Highness the Sultan in Council.'[12] Indeed, it was in the case of Kedah that haste and the use of threat on the part of the British Representative were clear. Sultan Badlishah later wrote to Sir Frank Swettenham:

I was presented with a verbal ultimatum with a time limit, and in the event of my refusing to sign the new agreement, which I call the Instrument of Surrender, a successor, who would sign it, would be appointed Sultan. Members of the State Council were compelled to sign an undertaking that they would advise me to sign it. I was told that this matter was personal and confidential, and was not allowed to tell my people what had taken place.[13]

It is also recorded that while maintaining his politeness until his guest had left, Sultan Badlishah later 'called for his yellow Rolls-Royce and rode down to Alor Setar post office to send, that very evening, a telegram *en clair* to the Secretary of State declaring that as he had signed under duress the treaty was null and void'.[14]

As in the cases of Negeri Sembilan and Kedah, MacMichael gave little more than twenty-four hours' notice to the Sultan of Perak to consider and sign the Agreement. While the Yang di-Pertuan Besar of Negeri Sembilan and the Sultan of Kedah were refused any opportunity to consult other Malay leaders in their states about the proposals in the Agreements, Sultan Abdul Aziz of Perak was allowed to do so and found that all the major Perak chiefs had serious reservations and doubts about the proposals. Sultan Abdul Aziz deplored the severely short notice given and subsequently emphasized:

The transaction savours of haste. One cannot but regret the necessity for extreme speed in deciding the destiny of a nation when a little delay would have been conducive to wider counsel. In signifying my assent to the Agreement against my better judgement, I did so because I was caught in the atmosphere of haste and because I was engrossing my unshaken loyalty to the British Crown with full confidence that my rights and the rights of my people would not be disturbed.[15]

In Selangor, the signature-collecting mission displayed the same abrupt and high-handed manner. The British Special Representative imperiously told Sultan Hisamuddin Alamshah, 'The object of the Union is to ensure peace and progress for Malaya. It would be best for you to *surrender your powers to the King. The Sultan of Johore has signed and surrendered his powers.* I ask Your Highness and the other Rulers to give your consent and not to be recalcitrant.'[16] The amazing aspect of the whole episode was that while Britain realized she was one of the victorious 'big powers' at the end of the Second World War, Whitehall feared that any delay in the implementation of a British post-war policy for Malaya would lead to fissiparous tendencies, uncertainties and objections from the Malay Rulers and their people. The haste and arrogance with which that policy was carried out must have recalled the adage 'might is right' to the generally well-informed Malay Rulers.

From the above excerpts of statements by the Rulers, it is undeniable that the traditional Malay leaders had forebodings about the new Agreements from the beginning. Even the Sultan of Johor, who had long taken a liking to many aspects of British institutions and society in his lengthy life, soon felt that there was something definitely untoward in the Agreement which Britain, his long-time ally, had edged him into signing. In fact Sultan Ibrahim of Johor displayed more than anyone else the unfolding disappointment of the Malays towards the British in 1946. He was Anglophile and even incurred the anger of some of his subjects over the British proposals. But once he had fully comprehended the import of the new Agreement, Sultan Ibrahim, who was regarded as the doyen of the Malay Rulers at the time, was prompt in stating his views in what can only be described as diplomatic language of a high order:

I was not in any way coerced or stampeded by Sir Harold MacMichael into signing the agreement he placed before me. I signed it quite willingly, firstly, because I was so happy and relieved at the liberation of Malaya from the Japanese occupation, and secondly, because I felt confident that I would not be asked to sign anything that was not in the interests of the Malays.... But after thinking the matter over carefully and lengthily, I came to the conclusion that I had signed the agreement without scrutinizing it as closely as I should have done and that I had, unfortunately, not realised its far-reaching implications. I accordingly wrote to the Secretary of State for the Colonies on February 15 [1946], telling him this and informing him that in the circumstances I could no longer maintain the unqualified approval I had originally given.[17]

In his letter of 15 February 1946, Sultan Ibrahim explained that as a result of the publication of the first White Paper there had been very serious reactions to the Malayan Union proposals from the Malays. The Malay Rulers were obviously becoming aware not only of the importance of maintaining their dignity as traditional leaders and foci of loyalty and patriotism in Malay society but also of the political dangers confronting the Malays as a whole. The 73-year-old Johor Ruler mirrored this awareness in his letter to the Colonial Office:

This grave situation has convinced me, after long and careful consideration, that it would be wrong of me if I were to adhere to the unqualified approval I gave originally to the scheme. . . . I am sure you will agree that it is my first duty to do everything in my power to safeguard the legitimate interests of the Malays not only in my own State but in Malaya generally.[18]

Sultan Ibrahim's decision to withdraw his signature to the new Agreement was significantly influenced by the opposition to the Malayan Union proposals from prominent Johor leaders at the time. On 3 January 1946, a group headed by Onn bin Jaafar,[19] who was then the district officer of Batu Pahat, formed the Pergerakan Melayu Semenanjung (or Peninsular Malay Movement) with the principal aim of uniting all Malays in an effort to undermine the Malayan Union proposals. In Johor Bahru, opposition was so intense that it was subsequently referred to as the Johor 'conspiracy'. After Sultan Ibrahim had signed the MacMichael Agreement and left for London, some of the Johor leaders who had had altercations with the Ruler before or during the Japanese Occupation, held a protest meeting at the Abu Bakar mosque, Johor Bahru, on 2 February 1946. At the head of this opposition group was Dato Abdul Rahman bin Mohd. Yasin, the pre-war State Treasurer and a member of the Johor Councils of Ministers and State. The meeting was sponsored by the Persatuan Melayu Johor (based in Johor Bahru) whose President was Dato Abdul Rahman bin Mohd. Yasin.[20]

Clause 15 of the Johore Constitution (1891) prohibited the Ruler from dividing or handing over the state and territories of Johor to any foreign power without the consent of the State Council. Though Britain never formally recognized the Constitution, it was significant for the internal affairs of Johor. It was Sultan Ibrahim's failure to consult the Council which roused the leaders of the Persatuan to unprecedented action. In wild speeches, they called for Ibrahim's replacement by a ruler worthier of the throne. The meeting was punctuated by cries of 'Down with the Sultan' and 'Get the old man down'. Dato Onn, who unexpectedly arrived from Batu Pahat during the course of the meeting, opposed the call for the ruler's abdication and managed to stem the extremism.[21]

The British Government acted swiftly. On 19 February 1946, with the concurrence of the Regent, the ringleaders (seven of them) were suspended from their government appointments. However, it did not alter their antagonism towards the Ruler. Sultan Ibrahim's subsequent volte-face only provoked fresh outbursts and a telegram was sent to him on 9 March 1946 which read, 'Your own confusion now proves your disloyalty and breach of trust to the Johore Malays stop We can fight our battle stop No need for you any more God's help and protection sufficient for us.'[22] Dato Onn himself was bitterly criticized for his allegedly 'equivocal role' during the 'conspiracy'. Members of the Persatuan Melayu Johor maintained that Onn at first wholeheartedly supported the abdication movement but later sought to dampen the vehemence of the demonstration at the Abu Bakar mosque.

Sultan Ibrahim's action undermined his own popularity somewhat. More important still, it created fertile soil for the subsequent growth of radical politics resulting in conflict within the Malay nationalist movement. (The Kesatuan Melayu Johor (based in Muar), led by Dr Hamzah bin Haji Taib (whose anti-British remarks in 1939 had almost led to his imprisonment) and Ungku Abdullah (a disaffected Johor prince), worked in unison with the Malay Nationalist Party (MNP)[23] against Dato Onn and the United Malays National Organization (UMNO) when this was formed. *Hizbul Muslimin* (greatly feared by Dato Onn), the first Islamic political party to be established in Malaya, was founded in Gunong Semanggol on 14 March 1948 and set up its first branch in Johor Bahru on 14 April 1948. One of the leaders of the branch was Dr Ismail bin Dato Abdul Rahman; many years later Dr Ismail became the Deputy Prime Minister of Malaysia.[24])

Despite the instability of his own position in Johor, Sultan Ibrahim played a prominent part in the coordination of Malay reactions to the Malayan Union proposals. While he and his advisers were in London during the first half of 1946–the period when the proposals were being widely and seriously debated, questioned and evaluated in both Britain and Malaya–Sultan Ibrahim was the liaison man between Britons who opposed the proposals[25] and the Malays who increasingly organized themselves in a united opposition to the British scheme. One by one, the Rulers declared that their signatures on the new Agreements had been affixed under duress and were therefore null and void. But there was a more profound reason for this about-turn.

The Malay states had long been in existence, most of them for centuries, and they had developed their own socio-cultural, economic and political norms. Loyalty and patriotism within these states had become ingrained characteristics of the public life of their people.[26] Many of the Rulers by 1946 were descended from long lines of ancestry which imposed upon them a duty to be true to the traditions set by their forebears: above all they had always to uphold the safety, integrity and sovereignty of their states. Granted that they were largely feudal aristocrats; but there is not a shadow of doubt that the Malay Rulers of 1946 understood deeply that in their persons rested the ultimate responsibility for the survival and well-being of their states. Their statements after being asked in haste to sign the new British-drafted Agreements in 1946 proved this beyond doubt. But in addition, the existence of well-established nationalist concepts of loyalty and patriotism within the nine states was thrown into bold relief when the Malays in general and from different strata of their society rallied and united to oppose the British proposals and defend the sovereignty of their Rulers and states.

In point of fact, even during his visit, MacMichael had encountered a peaceful demonstration by about 10,000 Malays in Kelantan on 15 December 1945. These people declared that they were not so much anti-British as anti-Malayan Union. The demonstrations, organized by the Persatuan Melayu Kelantan, marched to the Sultan's palace in Kota Bharu to meet the British Special Representative with placards which read: 'Malaya Belongs to the Malays. We do not want the other races to be given the rights and privileges of the Malays'.[27] These slogans epitomize the vehement reaction towards the Malayan Union. The events occurring shortly afterwards in Johor, at the other corner of the country have already been described, among them being the formation of Dato Onn's Pergerakan Melayu Semenanjung or Peninsular Malay Movement. Membership of the Movement rose rapidly to 120,000 while in the other states the pre-war Malay unions and other new associations came to life.[28] In May 1946 two British MPs, Captain L. D. Gammans and D. R. Rees-Williams, 'toured Malaya in order to sound out national sentiment. In every hamlet, village and town that we visited we were met by what appeared to be the whole of the population. For the first time in their history, the Malays had become politically conscious'.[29]

The vernacular press took a prominent role in the movement to rally Malay opinion. The leading Malay daily, *Utusan Melayu*, warned, 'At this moment our future is in danger. The new [British] plan is a big question that will affect us and our grandchildren. If we are inactive and lazy our grandchildren will curse us.'[30] A month later the *Warta Negara* urged that a central organization should be established by the various Malay associations that had sprung up.[31] Malay Peninsula-wide unity was in effect being urged for political and cultural reasons. Another daily, *Majlis*, urged at the beginning of 1946, 'join and take part in associations as soon as possible if you love your grandchildren. Look at your people— what will befall them—they will be left far behind. There is no other remedy than to organise yourselves into associations through which we unite to face the danger.'[32] For the first time in their history the Malays throughout the Peninsula were avidly thinking and mobilizing as a community in which the state boundaries mattered far less than the overriding need to act in concert against a common threat.

The call to join various associations and unite reached a dramatic point when no less than thirty-nine Malay bodies held a congress in Kuala Lumpur from 1 to 4 March 1946.[33] Dato Onn was elected chairman, and among those who attended the congress were Zainal Abidin bin Ahmad

(Za'ba), Sardon bin Jubir, Senu bin Abdul Rahman, Dato Panglima Bukit Gantang and Dr Burhanuddin Alhilmy. One by one, the associations rejected the Malayan Union scheme. There was profuse evidence of disappointment at the very discourteous manner in which MacMichael obtained the signatures of the Rulers. The delegates stressed that the new Agreements were signed by the Rulers not only under duress but also without the knowledge of Their Highnesses' subjects. The Agreements thus violated the tradition, customs and usage of the Malays.

The Selangor Malay Association had prepared a letter of protest which it hoped would be adopted by the congress. The letter demonstrated the political awareness of the Association: among other things, it declared that any new agreement between Britain and the Malay states must be only with full consultation with the Malay people; citizenship must be given only to those who truly merited it; Malay must progressively replace English as the official language; the armed forces were to be made up entirely of Malays; Malay Land Reservations must be maintained and increased; and the Malays must be given opportunities and financial help to enable them to carry out trade, industry and agriculture.[34] The congress felt, however, that it was unable to make the letter the final document of protest as it had not been circulated beforehand for study by the other associations.

The Perak Malay Alliance declared that the doings of MacMichael were illegal; and the Kedah Malay Association reiterated the charge that the MacMichael treaties were *ultra vires* because they allowed Britain to capture sovereignty from the Malay Rulers without the consent of the Malay people as a whole.[35] Debating important aspects of the Malayan Union proposals, the Singapore Malay Union argued:

Dalam Malayan Union itu majlis penasihat ugama terletak di-bawah Governor Malayan Union. Sa-bagai kaum Muslimin orang2 Melayu tidak akan sabar bahawa hal ehwal Ugama mereka di-ganggu2 dimikian ini, dan akan menjadi bahaya membangkitkan perang Ugama yang akan bergema ka-seluroh dunia Muslimin. Pada masa ini sa-bahagian daripada kaum China sedang mengachau keamanan dan ketenteraman negeri ini dan dukachita-lah jika kera'ayatan di-beri kepada mereka. Dan oleh sebab itu seluroh umat Melayu dalam negeri yang di-chintai ini sa-bagaimana yang di-wakili oleh Pertubohan Kebangsaan Melayu Bersatu dengan kuat-nya membangkang semua sa-kali chadangan Malayan Union yang di-dalam Kertas Puteh itu. Dan perjanjian yang di-buat oleh Great Britain dengan Raja2 Melayu memberi kuasa membuat undang2 kepada baginda King itu batal dan tidak sah.[36]

The Saberkas party, made up mostly of peasants and the ordinary Malays of Kedah, asserted that if the MacMichael treaties were recognized the Malay race would become a colonized race forever;

Britain would be free to sell or pawn the Malay states to other governments: 'Kerana Malayan Union ini menghanchorkan nasib Melayu maka hendak-lah Malayan Union itu kita leborkan, biar-lah kita rugi dalam suatu keturunan asalkan sa-ribu keturunan akan datang selamat'.[37]

The Malay Nationalist Party (MNP–also known as Partai Kebangsaan Melayu or PKMM) had been formed in Ipoh in October 1945. A radical, leftist party, it was undoubtedly one of the most important groups which attended the March congress. The MNP charged that the British had attempted to bring about a similar form of Malayan Union in the 1920s, but the Malay Rulers were secure enough to have been able to reject the pre-war British proposals outright. The MNP explained that in the unsettled political climate of the immediate post-war period, when the people had just freed themselves from the clutches of the Japanese 'fascists', the British took advantage of the situation by despatching a dictatorial representative, MacMichael, to take over the powers of the Malay Rulers of the Peninsula. It is notable that, although the MNP later characterized the Rulers and Malay aristocracies as reactionary and feudal, at this stage it evinced the impression of a patriotic party that was as loyal to the traditional Rulers as the other Malay groups. The MNP, with vehemence and flourish, declared:

P.K.M.M. bersedia menerangkan jikalau sa-benar-nya akuan kita sekarang ini bahawa surat akuan Sultan2 Melayu itu tidak sah, maka tidak-lah akan undur daripada melawan terus, dan terus membangkang Kertas Puteh itu dengan chara diplomacy yang halus. Dia sudah tipu kita. Kita sudah di-ajar chara menipu dalam politik dan jika demikian tidak-kah terlebeh baik kita tidak mahu sama sa-kali dengan Kertas Puteh itu melainkan kita mempadukan pemerintahan Malaya jadi satu dengan tuntutan Malaya Merdeka? Malaya di-perentah oleh Melayu sendiri untuk umat Melayu. Lagi sa-kali P.K.M.M. menjelaskan kita menuntut terus merdeheka–habis perkara. Ini-lah balasan menipu kita, dan kita mesti berjaya–Insha Allah.[38]

It reminded the delegates that Britain, as a signatory to the San Francisco United Nations Charter, had the obligation to help promote the political advancement of Malaya towards self-government and independence. Instead, she was colonizing Malaya.

Almost to a man the participants from the other states of Malaya deplored the high-handed manner in which the Rulers' signatures to the MacMichael treaties had been obtained and rejected the Malayan Union scheme. They declared that it was a tight, colonial administrative set-up designed not only to strip the Malay Rulers of their traditional powers but also to deprive the Malays of their birthright in the Peninsula. That the Malayan Union proposals acted as a stimulus which enabled Malay nationalism to develop and find its proper place in 1946 is seen in the following highly patriotic and nationalist passage from a memorandum submitted at the end of the March congress:

It is submitted that with all the failings of the Malay race in the past the Malays of the Atomic Age do not consider themselves at present to be so generous as to share their birthright with others and to accept dictation from others as to what form of government they should adopt. They believe that they are also entitled to self-determination as other peoples in the rest of the world, and it would be wise to leave it to them to decide as to when and in what form they wanted a change of their government. If they were at one time Independent and Sovereign in their own State, there is no reason why they should not be so at some future time, which should and would be decided by themselves. It is submitted that Great Britain has no right, morally and otherwise, in this matter. And, therefore, the whole Malay population in this beloved country of theirs, as represented by the United Malays National Organisation, exercising the Malay national will, do declare that the Agreements made by Great Britain with the Malay Rulers giving full jurisdiction to H.M. the King, is null and void, and at the same time do strongly oppose and entirely reject the Malayan Union proposal as set out in the White Paper.[39]

This is reminiscent of the United States Declaration of Independence of 1776. The pro-Malay bias was undeniably there. But what was far more striking, especially when contrasted with the largely uncoordinated patriotic Malay efforts in pre-war days, was the firm grasp the Malay leaders had of the political situation of 1946. They comprehended very well one cardinal aspect of the problem: sovereignty and the possible loss of it through the threat of outright British colonization by the implementation of the Malayan Union proposals. Thus in their carefully discussed telegram to the British Government at the conclusion of the four-day congress, the delegates declared 'Bahawa chadangan Kerajaan Baginda King hendak menjalankan kuasa penoh di-dalam negeri2 Melayu yang tersebut dan menidakkan kuasa Duli Yang Maha Mulia Sultan2 berma'ana di-rampas sama sekali negeri2 Melayu dan ia-itu berlawanan dengan semangat dan kehendak Atlantik Charter.'[40]

The congress devoted much time and serious attention to the citizenship provisions of the Malayan Union proposals. The delegates found, above all, the British proposal 'to promote a broad-based citizenship which will include, without discrimination of race or creed, all who can establish a claim, by reason of birth or a suitable period of residence, to belong to the country'[41] a portentous threat to the political future of the nine Malay states and one which would lead to 'the wiping from existence of the Malay race along with their land and Rulers'.[42]

The strength of Malay patriotism at the time was graphically shown when the Malay leaders succeeded in dissuading their Rulers from attending the installation ceremony of the first and last Governor of the Malayan Union, Sir Edward Gent, on 1 April 1946. The Malays, largely through the efforts of Dato Onn bin Jaafar, continued to demonstrate their loyalty to their Rulers; but they also warned them that by attending the installation, which the Malay leaders averred amounted to 'the funeral rites of their birthright and liberty',[43] the Rulers would have forfeited their mandate to rule over their states and their subjects would have had no further obligation to remain loyal to them.[44] The blending of loyalty to the Rulers with patriotism towards their Semenanjung Tanah Melayu (the Peninsular Malay Land, meaning Malaya) was evident in the campaign of the Malays to prevent the implementation of the Malayan Union scheme.

On the whole, the Rulers tended to come to terms with the wishes of the Malay population and its leaders. Indeed, by April 1946 the Rulers contemplated going to London together to plead their case against the Malayan Union before His Majesty King George VI. Although the position of the Rulers was duly stressed in the opposition to the Malayan Union, it was the question of the loss of Malay sovereignty as well as the implementation of the *jus soli* citizenship provision of the proposals which the Malays were most concerned with. Among other things, *jus soli* citizenship would have enabled the flood of new non-Malay citizens not only to acquire equal political rights with the Malays but also to gain other concessions such as positions in the public services which had been traditionally restricted to the Malays, wider opportunities in the commercial sector and possibly even easier means of acquiring landed property.[45] These have become the perennial problems of Malaysian politics.

The United Malays National Organization was mooted during the 1–4 March 1946 Pan-Malayan Malay Congress at Kuala Lumpur when a select committee comprising the following Malay leaders was elected by the representatives of some thirty-nine organizations to prepare the constitutional and administrative bases of the new central organization: Dato Panglima Bukit Gantang of Perak, Dato Setia Raya Kelantan, Dato Orang Kaya Menteri Selangor, Tuan Zainal Abidin bin Ahmad (Za'ba), and Dato Onn bin Jaafar.[46] At a subsequent congress in Johor Bahru, UMNO was proclaimed a full-fledged political party on 11 May 1946 with a constitution which provided for the opening of branches throughout Malaya.[47] Dato Onn was its first President. From its inception until the inauguration of the Federation of Malaya on 1 February 1948, it can be said that UMNO undertook a 'struggle for the restoration of Malay sovereignty'.[48] The inauguration of UMNO was followed by another demonstration of Malay solidarity when the community and its Rulers boycotted the installation of the Governor-General of the Malayan Union and Singapore (Malcolm MacDonald) on 22 May 1946. The combined front effected by the Malay leaders and their Rulers since the installation of Gent on 1 April had turned out to be such a formidable closing of ranks that it prompted British officials to seek some peaceful way of avoiding a direct confrontation with the Rulers (if they did arrive in London to plead their case) and with the increasingly organized Malays throughout the Peninsula. The Malay leaders, principally those in UMNO who, in truth, commanded the largest following from the community as soon as the party was established, declared that they would agree to negotiations with the British representatives only on condition that the new Agreement were first revoked. The Malay leaders were quite obdurate on this point and there were increasing indications that some sections of the community were beginning to lose patience. A spirit of non-cooperation with the British was becoming evident while a number of Malay resignations from the police force boded ill for Anglo-Malay relations.

Faced with a solidly united Malay opposition, Gent had virtually no alternative but to seek a compromise as best he could. After an informal meeting between them at Kuala Kangsar from 2 to 4 May 1946, Gent and the Rulers came out in support of the establishment of a federation in place of the Malayan Union. It was an arrangement which the five Unfederated Malay States (UFMS) had refused to entertain in the pre-war period. In the meantime, UMNO had also demanded that any fresh negotiations must be only between the British on the one hand and the Rulers and UMNO representatives on the other. This exclusive approach was to have its repercussions in the subsequent course of Malaya's political history. Nonetheless, exhaustive and friendly negotiations again took place at Kuala Kangsar from 28 to 30 May, this time attended by MacDonald, Gent, the Rulers and UMNO representatives led by Dato Onn. Major problems on the political future of Malaya were obviously discussed. D. R. Rees-Williams was in Malaya at this time, as mentioned above. He had been asked by the British Government to stop by after a visit to Sarawak and to observe and report privately to London what was happening in the Peninsula. He attended the second Kuala Kangsar meeting and said of it years later, 'At the Kuala Kangsar meeting, the Malays did not present proposals for the political future of Malaya; we got it out of them. These were important matters and they became the basis for the arrangement that led to the formation of the Federation of Malaya in 1948.'[49] From the second Kuala Kangsar meeting onwards the demise of the Malayan Union proposals[50] and the acceptance of the federal arrangement in its place proceeded almost as a matter of course.

The Federation of 1948

Although the Malayan Union scheme had been attempted and found unacceptable to the community that mattered most, namely the Malays, Britain had no intention of relinquishing Malaya forthwith. The only feasible alternative was to placate the nationalistic Malays by agreeing to modify the original British proposals as much as necessary to suit the circumstances of the time. Without fully or obviously capitulating, Britain put forward her modified proposals in the form of a federation. It was a calculated move and for a good reason.

Historically the pre-war FMS, notwithstanding the indirect rule of the British, did preserve substantially some local autonomy and the façade of sovereignty of each of the Malay states. Another post-war federation could not be as inimical to Malay political and cultural survival as the unfortunate Malayan Union which would have been a crown colony. Moreover, the Malayan Union proposals had been incubated in the confidential rooms of Whitehall solely by British officials only a minority of whom had an adequate knowledge of Malayan problems and needs whereas Britain positively encouraged the Malays to participate in the negotiations to replace the Malayan Union with a federation. The point is that with politeness and courtesy the Malays, as a rule, were seldom difficult to persuade; and with such an affable approach from Gent and MacDonald, the Rulers and UMNO leaders relaxed their opposition and began cooperating with their British 'protectors' to formulate the new Federation proposals during the second half of 1946.

The first clear suggestion in favour of a federation to replace the Malayan Union may have come from a former British diplomat, John G. Foster, M.P., Q.C. (later Sir John Foster), whom the Rulers had engaged jointly as their legal adviser. From London, on 26 March 1946 'Foster cabled all the Rulers advising them to withdraw their signatures from the MacMichael Treaties and to offer to re-open negotiations, after time for consultation with their people, on the basis of a federation.'[51] Sir John later attested:

I was not very involved in the affairs of Malaya, except that I advised the Rulers at a critical point in 1946.... The Union was virtually imposed on the Rulers. Alleged collaboration with the Japanese was used as a powerful lever. As I remember it you are correct in saying the idea of Federation came from Whitehall. I went with H.H. the Sultan of Johore to the Colonial Office. The Rulers were protesting at the deprivation of their sovereignty. This was altered as the result of their very strong objections.[52]

If the Malayan Union proposals were the bitter beginnings, the federation proposals which followed formed the bases of constitutional

developments which were to lead to the birth of first the Malayan and
then the Malaysian states. A close look at the main and relevant provisions
of the federation proposals is therefore pertinent. After a series of
meetings between MacDonald and Gent on the one hand and the Rulers
and UMNO leaders on the other, during which both sides submitted new
draft proposals, a Working Committee consisting of six British officials,
four Rulers and two UMNO leaders was appointed on 25 July 1946 to
bring up matters for both sides to examine and criticize. The trend of
future constitutional developments was clearly set by the following
principles or terms of reference which the Working Committee adopted
as the basis for its discussion:

(a) that there should be a strong central government to ensure economical and
effective administration of all matters of importance to the welfare and progress
of the country as a whole;

(b) that the individuality of each of the Malay States and of the Settlements
should be clearly expressed and maintained;

(c) that the new arrangements should, on a long view, offer the means and
prospects of development in the direction of ultimate self-government;

(d) that, with a view to the establishment of broad-based institutions necessary
for principle (c) to become effective, a common form of citizenship should be
introduced which would enable political rights to be extended to all those who
regard Malaya as their real home and as the object of their loyalty;

(e) that, as these States are Malay States ruled by Your Highnesses, the subjects
of Your Highnesses have no alternative allegiance, or other country which they
can regard as their homeland, and they occupy a special position and possess rights
which must be safeguarded.[53]

It is evident from the above terms of reference that the Working
Committee had achieved a good position of compromise in relation to
Malayan Union proposals and Malay nationalist aspirations. Matters of
state and issues of nationalism were involved and decided upon: while
Britain managed to maintain what she regarded as her 'own fundamental
objectives of essential cohesion and a basis for common loyalty'[54] in (a)
and (d), the Rulers, UMNO and the Malays in general were accorded
very substantial concessions in the restoration of the sovereignty of their
individual states, the ultimate goal of self-government for their Peninsula
and the concomitant upholding of their birthright in (b), (c) and (e).
Indeed, it can be seen with hindsight that the spirit of compromise so
prominent in future stages of Malaysian political development, in efforts
to work out solutions to problems of state, was set as a precedent by the
Working Committee of 1946.

The Report of the Working Committee, containing the draft
proposals for a federation, was published on 24 December 1946. But

because the new proposals had been formulated between British and Malay representatives alone, it was 'declared that there can be no question of their reaching any final decision on any matters involved until all the interested communities in Malaya have had full and free opportunity of expressing their views.'[55] Accordingly in December 1946 a Consultative Committee composed mainly of influential representatives of the non-Malay communities was appointed to study– '. . . opinion from interested individuals, communities, bodies and groups'.[56] The Consultative Committee, whose Report was published on 31 March 1947, endorsed the retention of the main structure of the federation proposals; and after reconvening on 17 April, the Working Committee produced the final drafts of the federation and state agreements.

The final drafts for a federation discarded the Malayan Union and in its place aimed to 'establish under the protection of Great Britain a Federation, to be called the Federation of Malaya, and in Malay, Persekutuan Tanah Melayu, which will consist of the nine Malay States and of the Settlements of Penang and Malacca'.[57] Some of the major changes from the Malayan Union may now be pointed out. Instead of a Governor there was a British High Commissioner as requested by some of the Malay leaders. The legislative arrangements, however, still smacked of the usual British colonial ethos: the British High Commissioner would preside over both the new Federal Executive Council and Federal Legislative Council; the unofficial members in both Councils were appointed by the High Commissioner; and, initially, all the official members were Europeans.[58]

There was, however, one particular undertaking which augured well–at any rate on paper–for the future political development of Malaya:

The Federal Agreement will record that it is the desire of His Majesty and of Their Highnesses the Rulers that progress should be made towards eventual self-government, and as a first step to that end, that His Majesty and Their Highnesses the Rulers have agreed that as soon as circumstances and local conditions will permit, legislation will be introduced for the election of members to the several legislatures which will be established under the agreement.[59]

The electoral process was promised for the first time by these words.

Instead of the Council of Sultans under the strict control of the Governor of the Malayan Union, the Federation would have a Conference of Rulers consisting of the nine Malay Rulers who would meet whenever necessary, not under the chairmanship of the High Commissioner but under that of one of the Rulers whom the Conference would select. It is of interest to note that the system of a Conference of

Rulers was subsequently retained as a unique aspect of constitutional government in Malaysia, being included in both the 1957 Federation of Malaya Constitution and the 1963 Malaysia Federal Constitution. As against the veto power of the Malayan Union Governor, bills passed by the Federal Legislative Council required the assent of the High Commissioner and that of the Rulers expressed by a Standing Committee consisting of two Rulers. Significantly, in terms of the restoration of the Rulers' sovereignty, the prerogative of pardon over cases occurring in any of the Malay states was to be exercised by the Ruler of the State concerned in Council. Again, this provision was to remain as an aspect of constitutional government in Malaysia until the present.

There was to be a State Council in each of the nine Malay states and a Settlement Council in each of the two Settlements. In each Malay state there would also be a state Executive Council which would aid and advise the Ruler in the exercise of his functions. The chief executive officer in each state, nevertheless, was the Menteri Besar (Chief Minister). This new development too was to become the basis of constitutional practice at state level in the remaining period under study. Each state was to have written constitution. Even though there was to be a British Adviser in each state (Resident Commissioner in the case of a Settlement), there was a change in that bills passed by the State Council would require the assent of the Ruler and not of the British authorities. The State Council was empowered to legislate on matters relating to Islam and Malay customs: a significant change from the Malayan Union, under which even the Council of Sultans and the state Malay Advisory Councils could not legislate on those matters without the sanction of the Governor or his representatives, the Resident Commissioners.[60] In these several important aspects the federation proposals formed the bases of future constitutional developments in Malaya.

As citizenship is one of the recurring problems in nation-building in Malaysia, it is pertinent to look into the provisions regarding this matter in the federation proposals. The most important development was that the acquisition of citizenship was rendered more difficult. This was obviously undertaken in order to meet the demands of the patriotic and nationalist Malays who feared the loss of their birthright should *jus soli* or liberal citizenship provisions be upheld as the Malayan Union had intended. Citizenship would be *automatic* (that is, by operation of law) or acquired by *application*. Again, the citizenship provisions of the federation proposals formed the bases of determining who were to be made the nationals of Malaysia in future years; for this reason also it is appropriate to deal more closely with those provisions. Under the federation proposals, the following persons would be automatically federal citizens:

(a) Any subject, whenever born, of His Highness the Ruler of any State;

(b) Any British subject born at any time in either of the Settlements, who was permanently resident (that is to say had completed a continuous period of fifteen years residence) anywhere in the territories to be comprised in the Federation.

(c) Any British subject born at any time in any of the territories to be comprised in the federation whose father, either

    (i) was himself born in any of the territories;

    or

    (ii) had resided therein for a continuous period of not less than fifteen years.

(d) Any person born at any time in any of the territories to be comprised in the Federation, who habitually spoke the Malay language and conformed to Malay customs.

(e) Any other person born in any of the territories at any time, both of whose parents were born in any of such territories and had been resident in them for a continuous period of not less than fifteen years.

(f) Any person whose father was, at the date of that person's birth, a Federal citizen.[61]

The provisions regarding acquisition of citizenship by *application* required the person who applied to satisfy the High Commissioner:

(a) That either

    (i) he was born in any of the territories to be comprised in the Federation and has been resident in any one or more of such territories for not less than eight out of the twelve years preceding his application; or

    (ii) he had been resident in any one or more of those territories for not less than fifteen out of the twenty years immediately preceding his application.

It was further required that:

(b) The applicant must satisfy the High Commissioner that he was of good character, possessed an adequate knowledge of the Malay or English language, had made a declaration of permanent settlement in the prescribed form and, if his application was approved, that he was willing to take the citizenship oath. An applicant for citizenship must be of the age of eighteen years or over.

It is to be noted that, unlike the Malayan Union proposals, the federation proposals excluded birth and residence in Singapore as qualifications for citizenship in the Federation. This exclusion tended to emphasize the separate political development of Malaya and Singapore from 1948 onwards.

A number of other cogent developments can be seen in those provisions. Provisions (a) and (d) regarding automatic citizenship clearly amounted to the granting of a prior right to Malays to become citizens of the Federation. This development assuaged the fear of the patriotic Malays of the Peninsula that *jus soli* citizenship would have swamped their community. Furthermore, this concession—or in fact restoration of previously-protected Malay rights—was reinforced by the strict provisions for acquisition of citizenship by non-Malays, as can be seen in (b), (c), (e) and in the entire provisions for acquisition of citizenship through application. The provision for citizenship by birth alone, or *jus soli*, which became one of the very controversial points about the Malayan Union proposals, was effectively negated by the citizenship provisions of the federation proposals. Furthermore, an applicant for citizenship had to fulfil a language requirement: 'an adequate knowledge of the Malay or English language'. This requirement, modified as time went on, was to become a central aspect of subsequent citizenship arrangements in Malaysia.

When it is recognized that the main point of consideration during the early years after the Second World War was the birthright of the Malays as well as their claim to be the indigenous people of the Peninsula, it becomes understandable that the federation proposals of 1948 sought to meet the demands of the Rulers and UMNO for tight controls over the acquisition of citizenship in Malaya by the non-Malays. In addition to this, the Malays were in fact given the power to control future immigration to Malaya. The High Commissioner was required 'to consult the Conference of Rulers from time to time upon the immigration policy of the Government'.[62] This was a significant change when viewed against the background of the Malayan Union in which the Governor had, in effect, absolute power over citizenship and immigration (especially under the general escape clause, 'Nothing in the order will affect the power of His Majesty in Council to make laws from time to time for the peace, order and good government of the Union').[63] Furthermore, if the High Commissioner and the Rulers disagreed on any major change in immigration policy, the matter would be referred to the Federal Legislative Council which would, by resolution, confirm or reject it. On such a resolution only the unofficial members could vote. Because there was a preponderance of Malays over non-Malays in the Council (thirty-one out of fifty), in the last resort it was possible for the Malay members, if they voted together, to defeat any major change in immigration policy when they and the majority of the Rulers considered it necessary to do so.[64]

By and large, it can be said that the Federation proposals succeeded in meeting the demands of the leaders of UMNO, who challenged the imposition of the colonial Malayan Union scheme, but not those of the MNP leaders who were opposed to any scheme which did not provide for the least immediate self-government. The United Malays National Organization, as the largest Malay organization, accepted the federation proposals and on 21 January 1948 the Rulers and Sir Edward Gent, on behalf of Britain, signed the federation and state agreements in Kuala Lumpur. On 1 February 1948, the Federation of Malaya began its separate existence as a combined entity—a nation in the making, guided and protected yet by Britain. The basic political and constitutional framework of Malaya had been established and it was left to the people, in the years to come, to provide the sinews which would transform that framework into the reality of nationhood.

Opposition to the Federation Proposals

The first half of 1946 was conspicuous for both the strength of Malay opposition and the lack of non-Malay reaction to the Malayan Union scheme. A number of reasons accounted for this relative quiet on the part of the other big communities of Malaya, that is to say, the Chinese and the Indians. In so far as the Chinese were concerned, the traumatic destruction caused by the Japanese Occupation, of which they bore the brunt, kept the community preoccupied with the basic needs of survival and the speedy resumption of their business activities. The Indians were similarly in a quandary, lacking not only basic human necessities but also organization and leadership.[65] The post-war skirmishing between the Kuomintang (KMT) and the increasingly stronger Mao-led communist armies in China, as well as the Indian Congress demands for independence for the sub-continent from the British also tended to continue to draw the political and nationalist aspirations of the Chinese and Indians in Malaya away towards their motherland rather than inwards within Malaya as their new permanent home.[66]

A political group led by English-educated and Westernized Chinese, Eurasians and Indians namely, the Malayan Democratic Union (MDU), was formed in December 1945 *inter alia* to work for the self-government of Malaya, including Singapore, on the basis of universal suffrage, a freely-elected legislature, complete freedom of speech and social justice. News editor, Gerald de Cruz, and lawyer, John Eber—both Eurasians—later became active in the MDU, but it was Philip Hoalim Senior, Lim Hong Bee, Lim Kean Chye and Wu Tian Wang who initiated the formation of the party.[67] The MDU criticized the Malayan Union scheme on the grounds that it excluded Singapore, restricted civil liberties and provided no universal suffrage. One of the founders of the MDU later said in reminiscence:

I have always believed in Singapore regaining its unity with the mainland; but I have also been convinced that it is a difficult and complex operation which cannot be bulldozed into existence. I therefore, together with my party the MDU, was strongly opposed to the constitution emanating from the British Government after the war, if only because it separated Singapore from the mainland.[68]

But the MDU was an isolated political group and at first tended to devote its energy to the island setting of Singapore. In general, it was only at the end of 1946, many months after the Malay Rulers and UMNO had mobilized themselves politically, that groups of non-Malays rallied to present a coordinated standpoint regarding the future of Malaya. This coordination took the form of the All-Malaya Council of Joint Action (AMCJA) which was inaugurated on 22 December 1946. Its formation is believed to have been inspired by the MCP and prompted largely by the setting up of the Working Committee and the formulation of the federation proposals. Leaders of the MDU played a prominent role in its creation.

The body was first called the Council of Joint Action, then it was renamed the Pan-Malayan Council of Joint Action (PMCJA): and later the All-Malaya Council of Joint Action (AMCJA): 'The Pan-Malayan Council of Joint Action was formed on December 22, 1946, two days before the proposals of the Working Committee of Government, Sultans and U.M.N.O. were published.'[69] The initial membership of the AMCJA comprised the Malayan Democratic Union (MDU), the Singapore Federation of Trade Unions (SFTU), the Clerical Union, the Straits Chinese British Association (SCBA), the Malayan Indian Congress (MIC), the Indian Chamber of Commerce, and the Ceylon Tamil Association. Later, in September 1947, the following were listed as AMCJA affiliates: the Pan-Malayan Federation of Trade Unions (PMFTU) the Malayan People's Anti-Japanese Army (MPAJA), Ex-Service Comrades' Association, the Malayan New Democratic Youth League, and twelve Women's Federations from Malaya. The AMCJA claimed a membership of 400,000 in August 1947.

With Tan Cheng Lock[70]—a fourth-generation Malayan Chinese—as its Chairman, the AMCJA argued that negotiations pertaining to the revision of the Malayan Union scheme should not be undertaken solely by the British, the Malay Rulers and the UMNO leaders. The AMCJA maintained that it was the only body representing all sectors of the population of Malaya and it therefore should be consulted by the British on the proposal to form a federation. As a body representating the growing political awareness of the non-Malays in the post-war period, the AMCJA demonstrated the Westernized, liberal outlook generally found among similar South-East Asian movements towards self-rule. This outlook was eloquently summed up by Tan Cheng Lock himself in a memorandum he wrote on the federation proposals:

The entire plan should be reconstructed on a new basis by a competent body, such as a Royal Commission, which will re-examine the whole Constitutional issue affecting Malaya, and which after examining and discussing any proposals for constitutional reform and consulting with various interests and all sections of Malayan opinion concerned with the subject of constitutional reform, will proceed to evolve a Constitution for this country which, while offering ample scope for the development of responsible self-government in a United Malaya, inclusive of Singapore, in which equality of status and rights will be ensured to all who make Malaya their real home and the object of their loyalty, will bring about the best feelings of friendship and spirit of co-operation and brotherhood among the different racial elements making up its composite population, so that such a Constitution may prove to be a foundation upon which may ultimately be built a future Malaya in the enjoyment of full dominion status as an integral part of the British Commonwealth of free nations, the ultimate ideal of British statesmanship being the fusion of Empire and Commonwealth.[71]

The passage clearly shows the awareness of the need for a Malayan nation; but it more starkly demonstrated the influence of Western concepts of liberal rule. The eulogistic part about the British Commonwealth was probably more perfunctory than sincere, inasmuch as any nationalist political group in Malaya at the time had to maintain some working relationship with the British authorities if it hoped to achieve self-rule in a peaceful, democratic manner.

At about the same time that the AMCJA was agitating for a liberal constitutional arrangement, a section of the Malays who had disagreed with those in UMNO concentrated their political efforts in the MNP which, as already mentioned, had been formed in Ipoh in October 1945. Led by radical and often leftist Malays who included former leaders of the erstwhile KMM, PETA and KRIS such as Ahmad Boestamam, Ishak Haji Muhammad and Dr Burhanuddin Alhilmy, the MNP had attended the 1–4 March 1946 Malay Congress in Kuala Lumpur. However, it thereafter withdrew from the UMNO-led groups on the grounds that UMNO was too conservative and that the MNP was not getting an adequate voice in it:

Kalau kita bermaksud hendak mengubah pandangan politik UMNO ini dari dalam saya tidak perchaya kita akan berjaya melakukannya sebab pemberian undi didalamnya sangat tidak adil—tidak demokratik. Badan yang kechil diberi dua suara dan badan yang besar saperti kita ini pun di-beri dua suara juga. Mustahil dengan undi dua suara itu kita akan dapat mengubah pandangan politik kira2 50 buah badan lain yang bererti hampir2 100 suara semuanya, sedang badan2 itu badan2 kanan belaka. Hanya kita satu saja yang merupakan badan kiri didalam golongan mereka.[72]

Although the MNP had members and supporters from different parts of the Peninsula, its following was clearly much smaller than that enjoyed by UMNO. In February 1946, the MNP had issued a manifesto on the Malayan Union proposals in which the party agreed that the cumbersome pre-war administrative arrangements in Malaya should be reformed. But the MNP manifesto bared its pro-Indonesian tendency when it stated that 'National Birthrights are reserved only for the native *Malays in Malaya having blood relationship with those living in the other parts of the Malay Archipelago*'.[73] The MNP joined the 1–4 March Pan-Malayan Malay Congress to denounce the MacMichael treaties and the Malayan Union proposals which it argued must 'be amended subject to the approval of the Malay people'.[74] In April, the MNP reiterated its opposition to the British proposals and again demonstrated its pro-Indonesia bias when it declared, 'Malaya *is a part of Indonesia*'.[75]

Because of its disagreement with and consequent dissociation from UMNO, the MNP began to look around for new allies. When the British refused it participation in the Working Committee negotiations, the MNP teamed up with non-Malay bodies and almost joined the PMCJA. Nevertheless, disagreement over the choice of chairman for the coalition led the MNP to hold back and to conclude rightly that it would be in a better bargaining position if it could rally the support of the Malays who had not followed UMNO. Thus in February 1947 the Pusat Tenaga Raayat (PUTERA) was established, composed of leftist and radical Malay groups which, by and large, shared the anti-colonial platform of the MNP. The groups were the MNP itself, the Angkatan Pemuda Insaf (API), the Peasants' Union, the Angkatan Wanita Sedar, and eighty other smaller bodies. PUTERA claimed a total membership of more than 150,000. By March 1947, PUTERA was again working with the PMCJA to try to form a coalition for airing their views and demands for the self-government and constitutional future of Malaya.

It is not often realized that the PUTERA-PMCJA combination was the first inter-communal alliance of any consequence in the post-war period. The PMCJA, as a largely non-Malay body, clearly showed its Westernized democratic orientation as well as some grasp of Malay needs in the following six principles which it adopted:[76]

1. A United Malay, inclusive of Singapore.

2. A fully-elected central legislature for the whole of Malaya.

3. Equal political rights for all who regarded Malaya as their real home and as the object of their royalty.

4. The Malay Rulers to assume the position of fully sovereign and constitutional rulers, accepting the advice, not of British 'advisers' but of the people through democratic institutions.

5. Matters of the Muslim religion and Malay custom to be under the sole control of the Malays.

6. Special attention to be paid to the advancement of the Malays.

The above principles were drawn up in close consultation with the leaders of the MNP. When the MNP spearheaded the formation of the PUTERA, the latter in turn had ten principles, the first six being identical with those of the PMCJA. The remaining four PUTERA principles were:[77]

1. that Malay should be the official language of the country;

2. that foreign affairs and defence of the country should be the joint responsibility of the government of Malaya and His Majesty's Government;

3. that the term 'Melayu' should be the title of any citizenship or national status in Malaya; and

4. that the national flag of the country should incorporate the red and white colours of the Indonesian national flag.

It was on the basis of the above ten principles that the PUTERA-AMCJA[78] manifested the nationalist content of their response to the Anglo-Malay Working Committee and federation proposals. Clearly, the PUTERA-AMCJA wanted a nation based on Western democratic lines; but they also bore in mind the need to incorporate the Malay ethos into the national community they wished to realize. The seriousness of the grand coalition in its effort to translate into reality its nationalist aspirations and political framework for the future of Malaya is best seen in the historical document which it jointly discussed for months, drafted and presented in November 1947 under the title *The People's Constitutional Proposals for Malaya*.

In addition to presenting the ten principles, the PUTERA-AMCJA constitutional proposals carried a lengthy analysis of the Working Committee's federation proposals. The PUTERA-AMCJA declared that it 'could not accept the Proposals drawn up by the Working Committee, in view of the undemocratic manner in which these Proposals had been drawn up in secret consultation with members of the Malay aristocracy; and in view of the failure of the Working Committee Proposals to embody those provisions which are essential to any stable constitution for Malaya'.[79] In a rather poignant vein, the PUTERA-AMCJA said of the Working Committee's federation proposals:

It is sufficient to say here that they will perpetuate Malaya as a real colony with all legislative and executive power in the hands of His Majesty's Government through the Secretary of State for the Colonies and the High Commissioner; and that they propose an empty and dangerous type of citizenship, which would prevent the stable development of national unity and democracy in Malaya.[80]

It can be seen that the leaders of the PUTERA-AMCJA were as aware of the need to create a nation-state in Malaya as the nationalist Malays in UMNO. Their visions of nationhood were equally clear; they differed mainly on what was adjudged fundamental to the viability of that future Malayan national community.

The PUTERA-AMCJA questioned the repeated pledge of the British authorities that 'there was no question of a final decision being taken until all the interested communities in Malaya had been given a full and free opportunity of expressing their views'.[81] The PUTERA-AMCJA had expected only those who regarded Malaya as their real home and as the object of their loyalty to be given the opportunity to express their views; and that such expressions of views or consultations would be received directly by the Malayan Union Government. When that Government itself delegated the task of receiving the views of 'the interested communities in Malaya' to the Consultative Committee, the PUTERA-AMCJA deplored the action because the Committee was 'headed by a Government official [the Director of Education, H. R. Cheeseman] whose members had not the shadow of a claim to represent those who regarded Malaya as their real home and as the object of their loyalty'.[82] There was no opportunity for direct contact, let alone discussion, with the Government. The Consultative Committee was characterized as a mere collecting agency for the views of interested individuals, communities and groups who in many cases were not 'representatives of those and only those who regard Malaya as their real home and as the object of their loyalty'.[83] The PUTERA-AMCJA therefore decided to boycott the Consultative Committee. Because the Consultative Committee recommended the retention of the main structure of the Working Committee's federation proposals, the PUTERA-AMCJA continued to project and publicize its own political beliefs and nationalist demands for a future self-governing Malaya.

The response of the PUTERA-AMCJA to the political developments of the period can be seen more explicitly through many of the clauses of its constitutional proposals. In addition to or in amplification of the ten principles, the PUTERA-AMCJA stated that eligibility for citizenship should make no distinction between Malays and non-Malays; and all citizens were to 'enjoy equal fundamental rights and opportunities in the political, economic, educational and cultural spheres, regardless of race, creed, colour or sex'.[84] Safeguards for the Malay community were reflected in the provision whereby, during the first three assemblies, 55 per cent of the seats in the proposed Legislative Assembly were to be reserved for Malays, and in the provision that every citizen was to be referred to as 'Melayu', while Malay was to be the official language.[85] It may be argued that while the Anglo-Malay Working Committee produced a set of federation proposals which took cognizance of and supported the primacy of the Malays in the political evolution and development of Malaya, the PUTERA-AMCJA showed itself to be not averse to meeting the demands of the Malays to some extent but at the same time it insisted on a liberal–democratic, egalitarian constitutional arrangement for the proposed united Malaya.

Attempts to eradicate communalism by the PUTERA-AMCJA can be further observed in other clauses of its constitutional proposals. There was to be a Council of Races consisting of two members from each of the following communities: Malay, Chinese, Indian, Eurasian, Ceylonese, Aborigine, Arab, European, Jew and 'Others'. Every bill passed by the proposed Legislative Assembly was to be sent to the Council which would consider whether or not it was discriminatory. A discriminatory bill was 'any Bill which, either as a whole, or in any particular provision, is discriminatory on racial or religious grounds'.[86] The socialist orientation of many of the bodies affiliated to the PUTERA-AMCJA was expressed in the provisions for a minimum wage; at least two weeks' vacation leave with full pay annually for every worker; guarantee for the 'right to strike'; 'the right to maintenance in old age and also in the case of sickness or loss of capacity to work'; two months' maternity leave with full pay for women workers; and the right to leisure.[87]

The socialist provisions of the People's Constitution brings to mind the popular belief that the PUTERA-AMCJA was a formal organization of the Malayan Communist Party (MCP).[88] A recent writer summed up thus: 'the PUTERA-AMCJA was the principal vehicle of the MCP policy of constitutional struggle. To this was subordinated the labour struggle from 1947 to early 1948, much to the disadvantage of the MCP-controlled labour movement in particular and of the MCP policy in general'.[89] There is ample evidence to show that the MCP sought to infiltrate as much as possible the various bodies which became affiliated to the PUTERA-AMCJA; and both the MDU and the MNP which spearheaded the combination of the two coalitions definitely had liaisons with the MCP.[90] But that is not necessarily to say that the MCP dominated PUTERA-AMCJA. What is clear is that the radical leaders of the PUTERA-AMCJA, in their endeavour to gain as wide a hearing as possible, sought to rally the support of the trade and labour unions which, on the other hand, were mainly dominated by the MCP:

This suggests that the A.M.C.J.A. and PUTERA conferences and negotiations suited Communist plans very well. It certainly does not prove that they were mainly the result of Communist planning. There are clauses here and there in the People's Constitution that appear to have been inserted by Communists, but it is impossible to read it closely and believe it a mainly Communist document. Probably the efforts of the Malayan Communist Party were mainly devoted to preventing any effective negotiation on the basis of this Constitution; and in this task they fully succeeded.[91]

At all events, the PUTERA-AMCJA also received substantial support from the various chambers of commerce, especially the Associated Chinese Chambers of Commerce through the efforts of Tan Cheng Lock, who was active in both the AMCJA and the Chambers.

While John Eber actively promoted the establishment of the grand coalition, de Cruz, the Secretary-General, 'virtually controlled the daily administration of the PMCJA-PUTERA, supervised the anti-Federation activities of the member bodies, and had the authority to convene extraordinary meetings of the coalition. In this way the MDU projected itself in the forefront of the movement'.[92] To publicize the political beliefs of the PUTERA-AMCJA and to rally support, its leaders travelled to the main towns of the Peninsula. They demanded immediate self-government for Malaya. When it appeared increasingly clear that the British were not only intent upon staying on to rule Malaya but were also showing a marked preference for the relatively conservative Malay Rulers and UMNO, the PUTERA-AMCJA strove to intensify its opposition to the Anglo-Malay federation proposals. Apparently mooted by Tan Cheng Lock as a result of his war-time sojourn in India, hartal, a form of passive resistance, whereby the PUTERA-AMCJA urged its supporters to stop work for a specific period with the intention of disrupting public and commercial life, was employed. The first hartal was a one-day affair in Malaya on 9 September 1947. Encouraged by a good response, Tan Cheng Lock, as the main organizer, obtained the cooperation of the Associated Chinese Chambers of Commerce to mount an all-Malaya hartal with the specific aim of highlighting what the PUTERA-AMCJA had argued were major defects of the federation proposals. The all-Malaya hartal, staged on 20 October 1947, received the support of the MCP and had its effects in Kuala Lumpur and other main towns on the west coast of Malaya. The costs incurred by closure of business and organizing the hartal 'caused an estimated loss of £4 million'.[93] Despite the protests of the PUTERA-AMCJA, however, the British authorities continued to give their support to the greater number of Malay leaders in UMNO rather than to the leftist ones in PUTERA and their coalition partners in the AMCJA. When Britain announced in January 1948 that the Federation of Malaya was to be brought into being soon, and the Malay Rulers and UMNO supported the British in the matter, the PUTERA-AMCJA saw the impossibility of implementing its People's Constitution. By April 1948 the grand coalition had split up.

Overview

The first step towards providing a constitution and thereby laying the foundation for the development of a Malayan nation was taken by the colonial government. The initial effort—the promulgation of the Malayan Union—ended in failure; the subsequent attempt—the federation proposals—led to the birth of the Federation of Malaya in 1948 and it was the 1948 constitution which provided the bases for the development of a Malayan, and later, a Malaysian nation.

But in the process of implementing both the Malayan Union and the federation schemes, problems of a clearly communal nature arose. There was only one major reason why Malay opposition to the Malayan Union was so vehement—it would enable a large number of non-Malays to secure equal political status with the Malays and this, the Malays believed, would lead eventually to their complete subjugation in Malaya. Since before the war the Malays had been conscious of the economic superiority of the non-Malays, especially the Chinese. The brief period of intimidatory 'rule' by the Chinese-dominated MPAJA immediately after the Japanese Occupation convinced the Malays that they could not possibly share political power with the immigrant communities if they wished to survive. Out of the movement against the Malayan Union, UMNO was born and adopted as its slogan 'Hidup Melayu' (Long Live the Malays). The Malay attitude at that juncture was that Malaya was for the Malays.

The demise of the Malayan Union and the implementation of the Federation proposals, which had been arrived at as a result of consultation with Malay leaders, to a large extent placated Malay fears. But this change, in turn, produced resentment among sections of the non-Malay population comprising mainly the English-educated, radicals and leftists (including the communists) who had a better grasp of British constitutional procedures. They formed themselves into the AMCJA which also included the MNP. But the MNP's participation in the AMCJA was more by accident than by design. The Malay Nationalist Party had opposed the Malayan Union for the same reason as those who founded UMNO. But because its members were inclined to oppose rather than support the traditional structure of Malay society, it was viewed with suspicion, if not hostility, by the more conservative Malays. Feeling left out, it hastily looked for new allies and found the AMCJA a convenient bandwagon to jump on. But it soon withdrew and only re-allied with AMCJA on a more autonomous basis after it had formed a grand coalition of Malay radical parties—the PUTERA.

Although there was seemingly close understanding between AMCJA and PUTERA on a number of issues regarding the future constitution of a Malayan nation, PUTERA's pro-Indonesian tendencies could not have been acceptable to the AMCJA.[94] Moreover, it has to be borne in mind that non-Malay support for AMCJA came largely from those who had leftist leanings and were therefore more willingly to accommodate Malay demands for the sake of achieving independence from colonial rule. The large majority of Chinese and Indians, at this juncture, had not yet begun to think seriously about their political future in Malaya. For the Chinese, the turning point was 1949 when China came under the control of the Communist Party. It was in that same year that the Malayan Chinese Association (MCA) was founded. For the Indians, the emphasis on communal politics began after the Malayan Indian Congress (MIC) was no longer dominated by leaders who were more concerned with the politics of anti-colonialism.[95]

It was therefore largely through indifference on the part of the majority of the non-Malay population that there was no serious political confrontation in either 1946 or 1948. But it was nonetheless clear that Malay thinking about the future political constitution of Malaya differed sharply from that of the non-Malays. This was the primary reason why the colonial government found it difficult to design a constitution which was acceptable to all. Finding that the Malays were able to harness greater political force, the British Government was quick to change its policy thereby avoiding a more violent demonstration of Malay opposition. The legitimization of Malay political demands in the process of forming the 1948 Federation established precedents in such a way that certain nationalist Malay political and socio-economic privileges were incorporated into the constitutional machinery of the country. These included the adoption of Malay as the national language; a special position for Malays in recruitment to the public services, in the granting of state scholarships and in the granting of commercial licences; and the reservation of land for Malays.[96] It would not be far-fetched to say that the problems which emerged during the period 1946 to 1948 within the context of relations between Malays and non-Malays were to recur repeatedly in the course of the development of the Malaysian nation.

1. V. Purcell, 'A Malayan Union: The Proposed New Constitution', *Pacific Affairs*, 19, No. 1, March 1946, pp. 27–8; and Great Britain, *Hansard (House of Commons)*, 414, 1945–6, 9–26 October, col. 254.

2. Malayan Union Government, *Report on a Mission to Malaya by Sir Harold MacMichael, G.C.M.G., D.S.O.* (hereinafter referred to as *MacMichael Report*), Kuala Lumpur, 1946, para. 10. Emphasis added.

3. *MacMichael Report*, para. 13. Emphasis added.

4. See R. O. Winstedt, *A History of Malaya*, Kuala Lumpur, 1968, pp. 242–5; and B. Simandjuntak, *Malayan Federalism, 1945–1963*, Kuala Lumpur, 1969, pp. 24–32.

5. Great Britain, *Malayan Union and Singapore: Summary of Proposed Constitutional Arrangements* (hereinafter referred to as *Malayan Union and Singapore: Summary*), London, 1946, para. 7.

6. Ibid., para. 9.

7. Ibid.

8. Ibid., para. 8.

9. Ibid., para. 23. The proposals also stipulated, 'Japanese nationals will be debarred from obtaining Malayan Union citizenship under the above provisions'.

10. Ibid., paras. 24 and 27.

11. J. V. Allen, *Malayan Union*, New Haven, 1967, p. 172. For a background to the Undang system of Negeri Sembilan, see J. M. Gullick, *Indigenous Political Systems of Western Malaya*, London, 1958, pp. 16 and 39.

12. W. G. Maxwell and W. S. Gibson (eds.), *Treaties and Engagements Affecting the Malay States and Borneo*, London, 1924, p. 104. The texts of the Agreements which the nine Rulers signed in 1945 were identical, except for the names of the states and their respective Rulers. See *MacMichael Report*, Appendix II.

13. Allen, op. cit., Appendix D.

14. Ibid., p. 32.

15. Great Britain, *Hansard (House of Commons)*, 420, 1946–7, cols. 659–62.

16. Ibid. Emphasis added. The Sultan of Johor was the most senior among the Malay Rulers.

17. Great Britain, *Hansard (House of Commons)*, 420, 1946–7, cols. 659–62. See also M. Ardizzone, *A Nation is Born: Being a Defence of Malayan Union*, London, 1946, p. 86 and A. J. Stockwell, 'The Development of Malay Politics During the Course of the Malayan Union Experiment 1942–1948' (Ph.D. Thesis, University of London, 1973), p. 99.

18. From the papers of Sir George Maxwell, *et al.*, British Association of Malaysia and Singapore, Northumberland Avenue, London. The letter was dated 15 February 1946.

19. Dato Onn bin Jaafar was born in 1895 of a Johor noble family. Educated in Britain from an early age and at the Kuala Kangsar Malay College, he joined the Johore Civil Service; he left for Singapore for some years in the 1920s and 1930s as a result of disagreements with Sultan Ibrahim who nevertheless secretly admired Dato Onn and wished him to be at his side as much as possible. Dato Onn's father and two elder brothers had been Menteri Besar (Chief Minister) of Johor, a post which Dato Onn himself held from 1946 to 1949. After successfully leading the Malays and the formation of UMNO of which he was president until 1951, Dato Onn formed the Independence of Malaya Party (IMP) and the Party Negara, both of which he led until his retirement from active politics in the early 1960s. He died on 20 January 1962.

20. See Allen, op. cit., p. 34.

21. Ibid., also discussion with Ungku A. Aziz who was present at the meeting.

22. A. J. Stockwell, op. cit., p. 107.

23. Ibid., pp. 108–9.

24. Nabir bin Haji Abdullah, *Maahad Il Ihya Assyariff Gunung Semanggol 1934–1959*, Kuala Lumpur, 1976, p. 185.

25. A number of retired British civil servants who had formerly served in Malaya, including Sir Frank Swettenham, Sir George Maxwell, Sir Lawrence Guillemard, Sir Cecil Clementi and Sir Richard Winstedt, as well as MPs such as Tom Driberg, L. D. Gammans and Lord Marchwood, criticized the British Government for embarking on the Malayan Union proposals. In doing so, these Britons significantly assisted the Malays in their

concerted opposition to the Malayan Union. Winstedt later condemned the Malayan Union which 'was to be under a British Governor, who would usurp the rights the Sultans had enjoyed (subject to the guiding advice of British Resident or Adviser) of ratifying laws, making grants of land and pardoning offenders or commuting sentences', op. cit., p. 258.

26. See W. G. Shellabear, *Sejarah Melayu*, Kuala Lumpur, 1967; and C. C. Brown (trans.), *Sejarah Melayu or Malay Annals*, Kuala Lumpur, 1970.

27. *Utusan Melayu*, 22 December 1945.

28. The revived Malay unions were the Persatuan Melayu Selangor, Persatuan Melayu Kelantan, Persatuan Melayu Pahang and Persatuan Melayu Perak.

29. D. R. Rees-Williams, 'The Constitutional Position in Malaya', *Pacific Affairs*, 20, No. 2, June 1947, p. 174.

30. *Utusan Melayu*, 10 October 1945. (Author's translation.)

31. *Warta Negara*, 10 November 1945; and S. W. Jones, *Public Administration in Malaya*, London, 1953, p. 139.

32. *Majlis*, 5 January 1946. (Author's translation.) See also Ishak bin Tadin, 'Dato Onn and Malay Nationalism 1946–1951', *JSEAH*, 1, No. 1, March 1960, p. 59.

33. See Muhammad Yunus Hamidi, *Sejarah Pergerakan Politik Melayu Semenanjong*, Kuala Lumpur [1961?], pp. 17–24, for a list of the associations represented at the congress.

34. Ibid., p. 60.

35. Ibid., pp. 61–3.

36. Ibid., pp. 64–5: 'In the Malayan Union the religious advisory council is placed under the Governor of the Malayan Union. As a Muslim community the Malays will not tolerate that their religious affairs are meddled with in this manner, and [this issue] will become a danger which will bring about religious war that will reverberate throughout the Muslim world. At present a section of the Chinese community is endangering the peace and stability of this country and it is regrettable if citizenship is given to them. And because of that the whole Malay community in this beloved country as represented by the United Malays National Organization strongly and completely opposes the Malayan Union proposal contained in the White Paper. And the agreement made by Great Britain and the Malay Rulers giving power to make laws to His Majesty the King [George VI] is null and void.' All translations from Malay to English are by the present writer.

37. Ibid., p. 65. 'Because the Malayan Union destroys Malay destiny therefore we must destroy Malayan Union, never mind that we lose within a generation so long as a thousand future generations will be safe.'

38. Ibid., p. 66. 'P.K.M.M. is ready to explain that if our consensus now is that the agreement signed by the Malay Rulers is void, then we should not be deterred from continuing to fight, and continuing to oppose the White Paper by peaceful diplomatic means. She [Britain] has cheated us. We have been taught the way to cheat in politics and in that case is it not better that we completely reject the White Paper and instead we unite the government of Malaya into one by suing for an Independent Malaya? Malaya ruled by Malays themselves for the Malay community. Once again P.K.M.M. wishes to emphasize that we demand immediate independence—and that is it. This is the price for cheating us, and we shall succeed—God Willing.'

39. Ibid., p. 114.

40. Ibid., p. 83. 'That the proposal of His Majesty's Government to exercise full jurisdiction in the said Malay States and to abolish the powers of Their Highnesses the Sultans means the outright annexation of the Malay States in the Malay Peninsula and that proposal is contrary to the spirit and aim of the Atlantic Charter.'

41. Great Britain, *Malayan Union and Singapore: Statement of Policy on Future Constitution* (hereinafter referred to as *Malayan Union and Singapore: Statement*), London, 1946, para. 10.

42. United Malay National Organization, *Ten Years of UMNO, 1946–1956*, Penang, 1957, p. 25.

43. *Malay Mail*, 2 April 1946.

44. As early as 8 February 1946, the Kesatuan Melayu Johor, in expressing disappointment with Sultan Ibrahim's signature of the new Agreement brought by MacMichael and 'for the information of our fellow-citizens of the State of Johore in particular and for the Malays of the Peninsula in general', declared 'that the act of the Sultan in ceding the State and Government of Johore to the British Government amounts to a breach of trust laid upon him by God, and consequently it is no longer necessary for citizens to extend their loyalty to him'. Allen, op. cit., Appendix F, paras. 1 and 3.

45. See E. MacFayden, 'A Political Future for British Malaya', *Pacific Affairs*, 17, No. 1, March 1944, pp. 49–55, where the author summed up in full relief:

In the Straits Settlements the Chinese had been firmly established for generations. They already outnumbered the Malays there before the Peninsula came into the picture. Once British protection was extended, the same disproportion was established in the Peninsula. The small number of Malays in Malaya (discounting recent migrants from the Netherlands Indies) is the chief anomaly in the composition of the population. The administration held a watching brief for the few there were, and, in particular, for the interests of the Sultans: Malays were privileged in government employment. Land policy aimed at preserving their hold on their native soil although more could perhaps have been done to protect them from the usurers, generally of Indian origins.

There were, of course, usurious persons of other ethnic origins, as will be seen subsequently in this study.

46. Muhammad Yunus Hamidi, op. cit., p. 56.

47. Properly speaking, therefore, UMNO was formed in March rather than May 1946. See also D. E. Moore, 'The United Malays National Organization and the 1959 Elections' (Ph.D. Dissertation, University of California, Berkeley, 1960); and UMNO, *UMNO Dua Puluh Tahun*, Kuala Lumpur, 1966.

48. Salleh Daud, UMNO, *Image and Reality*, Kuala Lumpur [1966?], p. 7. See also Stockwell, op. cit.

49. Interview with the present writer, London, April 1972. Rees-Williams was in Malaya in the inter-war period, practising as a lawyer in Penang from 1930 to 1934 when he got to know many Malayan leaders. He died in 1976, as Lord Ogmore.

50. The Malayan Union Government took over from the British Military Administration (BMA) on 1 April 1946 and administered Malaya until 1 February 1948. The Governor of the Malayan Union, however, ruled Malaya with the aid of an Advisory Council rather than with the projected Legislative and Executive Councils. See Malayan Union Government, *Advisory Council Proceedings, 1st April, 1946*, Kuala Lumpur, 1946, pp. 1–14, for the records of the inaugural meeting of the Advisory Council.

51. See Allen, op. cit., p. 39.

52. Sir John Foster, K.B.E., Q.C. to the present writer, 11 December 1973.

53. Great Britain, *Federation of Malaya: Summary of Revised Constitutional Proposals* (hereinafter referred to as *Federation of Malaya: Revised Proposals*), London, 1947, para. 4.

54. Ibid., para. 6.

55. Confidential source: telegram. Governor of Malayan Union to Colonial Office, 6 July 1946.

56. Ibid., telegram. Governor of Malayan Union to Secretary of State for the Colonies, 23 December 1946. See also Malayan Union Government, *Constitutional Proposals for Malaya: Report of the Consultative Committee Together with Proceedings of Six Public Meetings, a Summary of Representations Made and Letters and Memoranda Considered by the Committee*, Kuala Lumpur, 1947, especially chs. 2–4.

57. *Federation of Malaya: Revised Proposals*, para. 12.

58. Ibid., para. 16.

59. Ibid., para. 12.

60. See *Malayan Union and Singapore: Summary*, paras. 7 and 8.

61. *Federation of Malaya: Revised Proposals*, para. 24.

62. Ibid., para. 18.

63. See *Malayan Union and Singapore: Summary*, para. 13 (d).

64. Out of the fifty unofficial members, there were twenty-two Malays; in addition, the nine Menteri Besar who could vote as unofficial members were also Malays.

65. G. Hawkins, 'Reactions to the Malayan Union', *Pacific Affairs*, 19, No. 3, September 1946, p. 281.

66. See V. Purcell, *The Chinese in Southeast Asia*, Oxford University Press, 2nd edn., London, 1965, pp. 322–3; and Hawkins, op. cit., p. 282: 'The Indian Press [in Malaya], preoccupied with Indian politics, accepted the basic features of the [Malayan Union] scheme with satisfaction rather than enthusiasm'. See also M. R. Stenson, 'The Malayan Union and the Historians', *JSEAH*, 10, No. 2, September 1969, pp. 344–54, for a view which argues that non-Malay reactions to the Malayan Union scheme were more substantial than they were often made out to be.

67. See Cheah Boon Kheng, 'The MDU: A Brief History', *JHSUM*, 7, 1968–9, pp. 8–20; and C. Gamba, *The Origins of Trade Unionism in Malaya*, Singapore, 1962, pp. 433–7. John Eber, born of a leading Singapore Eurasian (R. L. Eber) lawyer and an English mother, was educated at Harrow and Cambridge. Before the Second World War, he lived very much like an Englishman although, as a Eurasian, he was not admitted into the Civil Service. He suffered further discrimination during internment in the Sime Road Camp between 1942–5 which was largely instrumental in changing his outlook. He emerged from the war a severe critic of colonialism and, not unexpectedly, campaigned zealously for the Malayanization of the Civil Service as well as the end of racial discrimination. By 1947 he had become actively involved in politics being the Vice-President of the Malayan Democratic Union. He spoke at a number of rallies and meetings held by the communists. He was also the defence counsel for several communists and left-wing trade unionists who were arrested by the police at picket sites and demonstrations. He was on holiday in Australia and New Zealand when the Emergency was declared in the middle of 1948 one year after his return but in early 1950 he was detained and charged with being a communist sympathizer. Although released in 1953, he decided to leave Singapore for London. He never returned. In London he became a political activist again pursuing clearly the communist line. He was consequently banned from re-entry into Malaya and Singapore. (For more information, see Cheah Boon Kheng, *The Masked Comrades: A Study of the Communist United Front in Malaya, 1945–1948*, Singapore, 1979, pp. 106–8 and 112.)

68. P. Hoalim, Sr., *The Malayan Democratic Union: Singapore's First Democratic Political Party*, Singapore, 1973, p. 17.

69. T. H. Silcock and Ungku A. Aziz, 'Nationalism in Malaya', in W. L. Holland (ed.), *Asian Nationalism and the West*, New York, 1953, p. 315.

70. Tan Cheng Lock was born on 5 April 1883 into a long-established Malacca family. Educated at the Malacca High School and Raffles Institution Singapore, he began his career as a schoolmaster at Raffles Institution but soon chose the commercial sector which saw him rise to numerous managerial positions, directorships and trusteeships in the rubber, banking, export–import and other industries. Apart from holding the presidency and patronship of various professional and voluntary bodies, he served as a Justice of the Peace and was an unofficial member of the Straits Settlements Legislative Council from 1923 to 1934 and likewise of the Straits Settlements Executive Council from 1933 to 1935 when he officially

THE UNIFICATION OF THE MALAY PENINSULA

retired. A polished speaker and writer of English, he had travelled with his family in 1935 to Europe where they remained until 1939; he was in India from 1942 to 1946. He became the first chairman of the AMCJA in late 1946, worked for a united multiracial Malaya, was elected first president of the Malayan Chinese Association (MCA) in 1949, was a member of the Communities Liaison Committee (CLC) of 1949–51, and initially supported the Independence of Malaya Party (IMP) in 1951. Partnered Tunku Abdul Rahman to the unsuccessful talks with Chin Peng at Baling in 1955; and was in semi-retirement thereafter. Received a knighthood (K.B.E.) from Britain and the ranks of Dato (D.P.M.J.) from Johor and Tun (S.M.N.) from the Federation of Malaya Government. Died on 8 December 1960.

71. Tan Cheng Lock, *Miscellaneous Speeches*, Malacca (n.d.), p. 18. The 'Memorandum on the 1946 Constitutional Proposals for Malaya' was dated 10 March 1947.

72. Ahmad Boestamam, *Merintis Jalan Ke Punchak*, Kuala Lumpur, 1972, p. 87. 'If we mean to change the political outlook of UMNO from within I do not believe that we would succeed in doing so because the allocation of votes in it is very unfair—undemocratic. Small bodies are allocated two voices [votes] and large bodies like ours are likewise given two voices. It is unlikely that with the two votes we would be able to change the political outlook of about 50 other bodies which means nearly 100 voices in all, when they are all rightist bodies. We alone constitute a leftist body among them'.

73. Malay Nationalist Party, 'The Manifesto of the Malay Nationalist Party, Malaya, with Regard to the British "White Paper on Malayan Union"', Kuala Lumpur, 1946. Mimeographed, p. 2. Emphasis added.

74. Ibid.

75. Confidential source: PB/PKMM/26/46/25, MNP to Governor of the Malayan Union, 16 April 1946. Emphasis added.

76. PUTERA-AMCJA, *The People's Constitutional Proposals for Malaya* (hereinafter referred to as *PUTERA-AMCJA Constitutional Proposals*), Kuala Lumpur, 1947, pp. 2–3.

77. Ibid., pp. 3–4.

78. The name All-Malaya Council of Joint Action was adopted in August 1947 (i.e., PMCJA changed to AMCJA) because PUTERA objected to the term 'Malayan', considered by the Malays at that time to refer only to non-Malays.

79. *PUTERA-AMCJA Constitutional Proposals*, p. 4.

80. Ibid. See also Penang Chinese Constitutional Consultative Committee, *The Humble Petition of the Chinese Town Hall—Penang, the Chinese Chamber of Commerce—Penang, the Straits Chinese British Association—Penang to the Right Honourable Arthur Creech Jones, P.C., M.P., H.M. Secretary of State for the Colonies*, 9 March 1947. (A copy of the Petition is extant in the Library of the Institute of Southeast Asian Studies, Singapore.)

81. *Federation of Malaya: Revised Proposals*, para. 6.

82. *PUTERA-AMCJA Constitutional Proposals*, p. 5.

83. Ibid.

84. K. J. Ratnam, *Communalism and the Political Process in Malaya*, Kuala Lumpur, 1965, p. 150.

85. See *PUTERA-AMCJA Constitutional Proposals*, Sections 2, 24 and 34. The life of each assembly was to be three years.

86. Ibid., Section 26.

87. Ibid., Sections 12–17.

88. V. Purcell, *Malaysia*, London, 1965, p. 110; and M. R. Stenson, *Industrial Conflict in Malaya*, London, 1970, pp. 129–30.

89. Yeo Kim Wah, 'The Anti-Federation Movement in Malaya, 1946–48', *JSEAS*, 4, No. 1, March 1973, p. 50.

90. See Stenson, *Industrial Conflict in Malaya*, ch. 8. The MCP is discussed more extensively in ch. 3.

91. Silcock and Aziz, op. cit., p. 322.

92. Yeo Kim Wah, op. cit., p. 40.

93. V. Purcell, *Malaya: Communist or Free?* London, 1954, p. 118.

94. Abdul Samad Ismail, who was an active leader in the Malay leftist movement from the KRIS to the MNP period (1945–8) stated that 'the MNP was not a direct result of the nationalist movement against the Japanese but rather a result of Indonesian political activities.... As late as 1944 the Indonesians wished to leave Malaya out of their future nation.' Interviews with the present writer, Kuala Lumpur, October 1972 and May 1973.

95. The early leadership of MIC comprised men who were involved in the Indian independence movement. It is important to note that MIC was formed soon after Nehru's visit to Malaya just as the CIAM was formed before the war soon after Nehru came here.

96. See Federation of Malaya, *The Federation of Malaya Agreement 1948*, Kuala Lumpur, 1948.

3
In Quest of Racial Unity

THE racial clashes of 1945–6, the impassioned Malay opposition to the Malayan Union which attempted to grant citizenship to large numbers of non-Malays, and the rather vocal expression of discontent by sections of the non-Malay population because of the pro-Malay tendencies of the federation proposals, altogether resulted in very severe damage to the relationship between Malays and non-Malays. Time might yet have allowed the mutual suspicion and animosity to abate. But Malayans were not given that time. Hardly six months after the inauguration of the Federation of Malaya, a state of emergency was declared by the government in an attempt to crush the activities of the Malayan Communist Party.

The Emergency and Race Relations

As already mentioned the MCP was founded some time between 1930 and 1931.[1] By the mid-1930s it had made significant headway notwithstanding setbacks due to vigilant police action. It was later able to benefit considerably from the anti-Japanese feelings of the Chinese population in Malaya. When the Japanese invaded the country, it managed to come to terms with even the British Government. In order to build up a resistance force against the Japanese the British agreed to provide for the military training of younger members of the MCP. Soon four 'regiments' of varying strength and size passed through a Special Training School (designated 101 STS); these were the founding troops of what came to be known as the MPAJA.[2]

The MCP emerged from the war a hardened and well-organized force. However, despite being allowed legal room to move about, it found itself gradually inhibited and forced to comply with the regulations of the British Military Administration (BMA). Still it was able to promote industrial and urban unrest as well as economic dislocation. The Malayan Union Government responded to the increasing militancy of the labour unions by raiding their offices and detaining union leaders. It became clear at this juncture that with the consolidation of British rule after the war, the MCP would not be allowed to function openly for long.

A series of increasingly violent incidents occurred, including the killing of opponents of the MCP by Chinese gunmen and, on one occasion, of seven rioters by the police. In mid-June 1948, the murder of three European planters in Sungai Siput was followed by the Government's declaration of a state of Emergency. The details of these events do not concern the present study and are recounted elsewhere.[3] However, it may be useful to trace briefly the course of the Emergency until about 1955, since it had a significant bearing on the Sino-Malay relationship in the country.

The MCP was strong and effectively on the offensive during the first three years of the Emergency. Planters, miners and many other Europeans (including Americans) in the private sector of the Malayan economy were earmarked for killing by the MCP and its military arm, the Malayan People's Anti-British Army (MPABA). Some Malayan Chinese and Indians incurred the same treatment. Initially the majority of the Malays were left alone because the MCP, in June 1948, found them to be as insusceptible to Marxist, Leninist or Maoist indoctrination as they had been since the communist movement began in the 1920s.

In 1925, writing from Singapore after having made some attempts to spread communism in Malaya, Tan Melaka, the leading Indonesian communist, said:

So far not the slightest advantage is to be seen from the work of our dealers (propagandists?) at (Singapore) or at (Penang). You may say that they are quite incapable, but in criticising it must not be forgotten that the proper (indigenous?) inhabitants there, who form only a minority, are all conservative in their manner of living and thinking, and are petty bourgeois. On the departure of Hadji Moek from (Singapore) his kindness was involved to make a visit to the F.M.S. The impression which he obtained everywhere did not differ from those gained from (Singapore) and (Penang). The section of the people which understands (economy) and (politics) are the (Chinese). In the harbours, in buildings, in the trains, and above all in commerce, the (Chinese) are the most prominent. None the less their Federation is very weak.

You will understand that in these circumstances it is impossible for us to effect a union. The railway personnel and those in establishments connected with the railway are all Klings. In their circles no beginning has been made to set up any association. There is not a single daily paper in the Straits or F.M.S. that is read by Malays. In brief, if one looks for a movement in the F.M.S., it is not to be sought from the side of the Malays. It will certainly come from the Chinese and Klings, whatever sort of movement it may be.[4]

Although Tan Melaka made no direct reference to the problem of race relations, his awareness of the differences among the various racial groups in Malaya may be construed to mean that he knew Malaya's multiracial character constituted a major barrier to any attempt to effect political unity.

It is interesting to note that in the mid-1930s, when analysing the trend of Malay politics, the Special Branch singled out the Malay attitude towards non-Malays as the most dominant aspect of Malay political consciousness. For example, in 1936 the Special Branch remarked, 'Malay "nationalism" continued to be fostered by certain of the Malay Vernacular newspapers. An anti-foreign undercurrent chiefly anti-Chinese and Indian, was noticeable in the Malay press during the year, particularly in "Warta Malaya" of Singapore and "Saudara" of Penang.'[5] The communist movement in Malaya, as is now well known, was dominated from the beginning by the Chinese. The Japanese Occupation, as mentioned earlier, aggravated Sino-Malay friction. First, many Malays, especially those involved in the KMM movement, cooperated with the Japanese while the communists formed the MPAJA to resist Japanese hegemony. Then in late 1945 and early 1946, as a result of the 'reign of terror' mounted by the MPAJA during the interregnum (between the surrender of the Japanese and the return of the British), Sino-Malay fighting occurred in several parts of the country, as mentioned in the previous chapter.

However, despite adverse conditions, the MCP was optimistic that it could win a constitutional battle against the British in the immediate post-war period. It made concerted efforts to assist the formation of Malay as well as non-communal political organizations which it hoped to dominate. Hence the formation of the Malay Nationalist Party was initiated by Mokhtaruddin Lasso, of Sumatran origin and a member of the MCP.[6] The communists were also conspicuously present in the committees of the MDU[7] and played an important role in the formation of the Pan-Malayan Council of Joint Action.[8] Communist representatives, in the persons of Rashid Mydin, Musa Ahmad and Gerald de Cruz, were present during the founding of *Hizbul Muslimin* in Gunong Semanggol.[9] If in June 1948 the MCP came to the same conclusion as Tan Melaka in 1925, about the futility of converting the Malays, it was not for want of trying. The cleavage between the Malays and the Chinese was simply too wide to bridge.

When later the MPABA found that there were some 35,000 Malay special constables working to guard estates, mines, factories and other industrial sites, not to mention the Malay components of the Federation army and police, numerous Malays inevitably also became targets of the

MCP armed forces. The MCP continued to rely, for recruits, food, medicine and other necessities to prosecute its war, upon the Chinese civilian population. Its forces formed veritable lifelines with—especially—the Chinese squatters who had mostly remained on the jungle fringe after the Japanese Occupation. Even the Malayan Aborigines, timid as many of them were and numbering some 70,000, had little option but to accommodate the wishes of the MCP by performing the tasks of guides, porters and spies, and supplying provisions demanded by the MPABA.[10]

The same Aborigines had, of course, been told to cooperate with the MCP elements during the Japanese Occupation and they were no doubt somewhat confused by the sudden reversal of positions after the war, when they were being urged to assist in suppressing the MCP. Indeed, the Aborigines were to become the object of a struggle for influence between the MCP and government forces in which, for some time, the MCP had the upper hand, causing much concern to the government. It is only in very recent times that the Aborigines have been won over through skilfully conducted psychological warfare operations and social development schemes.[11]

The MCP attempted to conduct its campaign with care and close attention to tactics and manoeuvres against the greater military strength of the British, especially as reinforcements began arriving in the Peninsula following a nation-wide declaration of Emergency on 18 June 1948; but six months after the outbreak of the war the MCP was tenaciously preparing itself for an extended revolutionary venture:

Our Army's objective, then, is self-preservation, attrition of the enemy and, also continued striving for expansion. We must, therefore, refrain from hasty action and adventurism. We will attack only when we are confident and will not attack when we do not feel so. We want to strike hard to gain a victory in every action and to ensure the annihilation of the enemy and the capture of his arms. In this war we will train our forces, expand them and so improve their quality that the superior position and strength of the enemy and our position of weakness and inferiority are reversed. It follows that our Army is adopting a policy of a protracted war. Armed strength in a colonial revolution must develop gradually in a drawn-out struggle. We counsel no fears for such a long-term struggle; on the contrary, we subjectively welcome the strategy of a protracted war.[12]

Mindful of its professed aim of fighting a people's war and in an attempt to attract support from all sections of the Malayan population, the MCP renamed the MPABA the Malayan Races Liberation Army (MRLA) in February 1949. There was no lack of armed encounters between the MCP forces and the British security forces (as these mainly United Kingdom and Commonwealth military contingents came to be called). By the end of 1950 the number of civilians killed as a result of the

Emergency was substantial.[13] But by then the initial strength of the MCP forces had clearly been surpassed by the burgeoning British military paraphernalia in Malaya.

Intent upon safeguarding its strategic and economic interests in the area, Britain steadily poured reinforcements into Malaya, expanded the Federation police force and developed the Special Branch of the Criminal Investigation Department. There were twenty-three battalions of troops by 1954; the police had expanded from 9,000 to 67,000 including some 35,000 special constables, by 1952; to defend their kampongs and new villages, the Malays and Chinese had raised 350,000 part-time Home Guards by 1951; and to undercut MCP tactics and sever the Party's underground communication links, the Special Branch was reorganized, trained with the latest methods, Asianized, and rendered extremely effective:

... the Special Branch of Malaya became one of the finest establishments of its kind in the world. Even countries with more sophisticated intelligence systems sent observers to a training school which had been set up in Kuala Lumpur specially to build up a cadre whose single aim was the complete breaking up of the military and Min Yuen organizations of the MCP.[14]

What particularly brought about an increased determination on the part of the British authorities to defeat the MCP was the killing of Sir Henry Gurney, High Commissioner of Malaya, on 6 October 1951 as his Rolls-Royce was climbing the winding, jungle-clad road to Fraser's Hills. The fatal attack on Gurney, which was led by Siu Mah, commander of the MRLA regiment in Pahang, was received with shock and dismay in the very country which the MCP was striving to turn into a Soviet-type socialist republic by the 'liberation' of its 'races'. It was felt by thousands that if even the High Commissioner was no longer safe, there was little hope of protection and safety for the man-in-the-street in Malaya. There were in fact numerous acts of violence, killing, torture, vengeance and unnecessary persecution by the MCP forces—too numerous to catalogue here—among the civilians of the country.[15] The people of Malaya were like the rest of mankind and naturally found a reign of terror and unmitigated atrocities against their generally decent and law-abiding way of life intolerable. Within a few years from the outbreak of the Emergency, the MCP had succeeded in painting itself as a diabolical intruder intent upon ravaging the decency, peace and future prospects of Malaya and its people. British psychological warfare had little to do with the emergence of such a terrorist image of the MCP; the activities of the Party and its MRLA were largely responsible for it.

Apart from the phenomenal increase in the strength of the British security forces in Malaya, the adverse and disgusted reactions to its harsh terrorism among the Malayan population left the MCP with little choice but to issue its well-known October 1951 Directive; in this the Politburo ordered its state and branch committees to stop all killing among 'the masses' and instead to adopt a conciliatory approach in order to try again to get their support. The reluctant Malays, the small middle class in the towns and the 'running dogs' had all to be won over rather than terrorized. The primary duty was no longer determined by the purely military objective of destroying the enemy but rather by the need to expand and consolidate the organization of the masses:

To win the masses the party must (i) stop seizing identity.and ration cards; (ii) stop burning new villages and coolie lines; (iii) stop attacking post offices, reservoirs, power stations, and other public services; (iv) refrain from derailing civilian trains with high explosives; (v) stop throwing grenades and take great care, when shooting running dogs found mixing with the masses, to prevent stray shots from hurting the masses; and (vi) stop burning religious buildings, sanitary trucks, Red Cross vehicles, and ambulances.[16]

These abstentions ordered by the Politburo implied what the MCP had been wont to do before October 1951. The Directive also enjoined that the consolidation of support among the masses was 'to be attained by creating a united front of all communities and classes by acquiring the support of the bourgeoisie and capitalists and avoiding violent tactics which have antagonized peasants and workers'.[17] The repentant vein of the October 1951 Directive was an admission of failure in the armed revolutionary approach of the MCP; on the other hand, it showed that the Party was prepared to vary its tactics and manoeuvres in the long-term interest of achieving its chief goal of a Malayan People's Republic.

It is to be noted, however, that the MCP switch to conciliatory tactics failed to arrest the Party's decline in military and political strength in Malaya in the ensuring years. After the appointment of General Sir Gerald Templer as Gurney's successor in February 1952, the fortunes of the MCP sank.further with its leaders and forces finding themselves increasingly hemmed in in the compact but mountainous centre of the Peninsula. As early as April 1952, the usually indomitable Chin Peng, the Secretary and leader of the MCP, with the agreement of his colleagues in the Central Executive Committee (CEC), made his decision to withdraw to the comparative safety of South Thailand. By the time Templer left Malaya in June 1954, the defeat of the MCP in its armed revolutionary venture was manifest.[18] Because of the poor prospect of winning the armed struggle against the British and of the need to be a party to the movement towards the political independence of Malaya, the MCP actually took the initiative to hold negotiations with the incumbent Malayan Government. (It has been said that 'The communists' anxiety to discontinue the war in some way which would bring advantage to them could well be understood; terrorism had brought them nothing, and the impending federal elections and the approach of self-government, combined with the British promise of independence, had nullified their claim that they were fighting for freedom on behalf of the Malayan peoples.')[19]

In an attempt to solve the political problems of the Emergency, talks were held between leaders of Malaya and Singapore on the one hand and members of the Central Executive Committee of the MCP on the other. Tunku Abdul Rahman, Dato Sir Tan Cheng Lock and Too Joon Hing represented Malaya and David Marshall Singapore. The MCP delegation consisted of Chin Peng, Chen Tien and Rashid Mydin. At the talks, held at Baling in Kedah on 28 and 29 December 1955, Tunku Abdul Rahman as Chief Minister of Malaya required that the MCP disband its MRLA; Chin Peng agreed provided the MCP was recognized as a legal political party in the future independent Malaya; the Tunku rejected Chin Peng's rider and the talks failed to achieve any meaningful result.

The effects of the Emergency on Malaya's progress were not entirely negative. Initially the British Government had stipulated that independence could only be given to Malaya when the communists had been completely defeated and the country had returned to normal, peaceful conditions. But even as Templer was departing in 1954, local council elections had been held and active preparations were under way for holding the first 'nation-wide' Malayan federal elections in 1955. Templer later affirmed, 'It was clear that independence was to be given to Malaya; but this could not be done unless the enemy was defeated. I had to start with the grass-roots level, and encourage local councils as the beginnings of future political parties'.[20] The change of attitude developed, especially from 1955 onwards, when it was felt that possibly the most effective way to uncover the real objectives of the MCP was to grant independence to Malaya speedily and judge the subsequent attitude and activities of the communists. It was reasoned that the speedy granting of political independence to Malaya would demonstrate whether the MCP was indeed struggling for the emancipation of Malaya from colonial rule or whether the Party was really primarily interested in disseminating communism as widely as possible as the ideological basis of government in Malaya.

It is important to note that a very few days after the declaration of the Emergency, Dato Onn, then President of UMNO, said:

Malays in kampongs are in no mood to tolerate any intimidation or violence. I feel if they are involved physically they will hit back. The Malays are prepared and ready to assist and back up the administration in restoring law and order. The present activities of the Communist Party and other lawless elements have more than confirmed, if confirmation is necessary, that the real background of what is happening today is the avowed objective to create a Malayan Communist republic in Malaya in which the Malays themselves will be completely subservient. No Malay who loves his country will ever be prepared to allow this to happen.[21]

Indeed, the Malays readily joined the armed forces to fight the communist guerrillas and this was a major factor in perpetuating Sino-Malay animosity. As Anthony Short remarks:

From the beginning of the insurrection the situation within Malaya alone was sufficient to create a good deal of tension between the Malay and Chinese communities. Most apparent was the racial composition of the combatant forces: armed Chinese guerillas and numerous Chinese supporters on the one side, Malay police, soldiers and special constabulary on the other. Superficially, this could be and often was taken as the general alignment of the two communities: the Chinese were supporting the insurrection, the Malays were resisting it. The fact that so many leaders of the two communities should call so often for others to trust them was perhaps itself a sufficient indication of the dangerous lack of trust that existed....

Short continues:

It is perhaps worth making the point that in September 1948 the Federation of Malaya was only six months old. The Constitution had already been changed once since the war and the new one seemed open to specific emphasis and even amendments. The extreme statement of Malay opinion, often expressed by *Utusan Melayu*, was that Malaya belonged to the Malays: an argument which principally though not entirely was directed against the Chinese. Thus it was objected that there were too many Chinese consulates in Malaya—representatives, that is, of the Chinese Nationalist Government—and it was feared that the Chinese Government might take advantage of the existing state of emergency to assert the rights of Chinese. Where Malays were counting their numbers in the forces fighting the terrorists, the Chinese consuls, said *Majlis*, were busy calculating the amount of Chinese losses and the total of Chinese casualties.[22]

The British Government itself was well aware of the seriousness of the problem. As early as 1949, one of the most influential and persuasive diplomats that Britain had ever sent to Malaya perceived the wisdom of aiding the multiracial population of the Peninsula to achieve closer unity for its own political benefit. This was Malcolm MacDonald who became Governor-General of the Malayan Union and Singapore in 1946 and later served as British Commissioner-General for South-East Asia.[23] Having established friendly relations with Malayan leaders, especially Dato Onn bin Jaafar, Tan Cheng Lock and E. E. C. Thuraisingham, MacDonald intimated to them that the political future of Malaya would be better assured if they put their heads together and worked for the common good of the country.[24] A direct consequence of this encouragement from MacDonald was the setting up of the Communities Liaison Committee (CLC) in January 1949. The members were E. E. C. Thuraisingham (chairman), Dato Onn bin Jaafar, Tan Cheng Lock, Dato Panglima Bukit Gantang, Yong Shook Lin, Sir Roland Braddell, Dr Mustapha bin Osman, Lee Tiang Keng, Saleh Hakim, C. C. Tan, Zainal Abidin bin Haji Abbas, and Malcolm MacDonald (first as 'liaison officer' and later as an observer).

Although it is true that Dato Onn had convened a meeting of leaders of the main communities in his home in December 1948 for informal exchanges of views on the communal problems of Malaya, particularly 'to discuss and study the sources of inter-racial frictions with a view to finding ways and means of eliminating them', it was after the CLC came into being that concrete efforts were made in the matter.[25] The CLC met several times during the next two years and discussed such fundamental constitutional issues as citizenship, education, the introduction of elect-ions to local councils and the Federal Legislative Council, and ways and means of resolving social and economic disparities between the Malays and non-Malays. On the last point, in particular, there was a general consensus that if the Malays were expected to share their political rights with the non-Malays, the latter must assist the Malays to attain social and economic parity with the non-Malays.[26] The CLC thus promoted a political and economic 'bargain' between the Malays and the non-Malays in the course of deciding the political future of Malaya: 'The Communi-ties Liaison Committee had come to the conclusion that the Malays would sacrifice their privileged political position only if they could be aided in securing a greater share of their country's wealth.'[27]

It can be said that the work of the CLC was the first attempt by a communally representative group of Malayan leaders to pin-point and suggest solutions to the basic problems of their country. Tan Cheng Lock declared emphatically:

One of the principal objects of the Communities Liaison Committee is to bridge the yawning gulf that now exists between the communities. If there was no such gulf there might perhaps be no need for the Communities Liaison Committee. Obviously then we shall have to face squarely the causes for [sic] this gulf, one of which, I take it, is the present Constitution of the Federation of Malaya.[28]

Indirectly, the CLC discussions on citizenship led to the passage of the 1952 Ordinance amending the 1948 Constitution; developments in education policy, such as the appointment of the Barnes and Fenn-Wu Committees, to be discussed below, also owed much to the attention given by the CLC to curriculum and language problems. Last but not least, the CLC initiated moves to demand from the British authorities the speedy introduction of party politics in the Peninsula. Of the political and economic 'bargain' between the Malays and the non-Malays, Dato E. E. C. Thuraisingham said, years later, 'It is true. I and others believed that the backward Malays should be given a better deal. Malays should be assisted to attain parity with non-Malays to forge a united Malayan Nation of equals'.[29]

Notwithstanding the endeavours of Malcolm MacDonald and the CLC, racial animosity continued to exist owing to a number of developments. There was, for example, the problem of National Service. On 15 December 1950 the High Commissioner, Sir Henry Gurney, announced conscription measures which gave authority to the Government to direct all males between 17 and 45 to perform military or police service. The first step was registration for the 18–24 age group. A total of some 290,000 persons were involved. The manpower regulations deeply disturbed the Chinese and by the end of 1951 only 1,800 Chinese had been conscripted. The majority of these were English-educated. Thousands of Chinese youths fled from Malaya first to Singapore and then to Hong Kong or China. The leading Chinese papers did not lend their support to the Government's conscription measures. The *Sin Chew Jit Pao* felt that students, skilled workers in agriculture, commerce and industry and teachers should be exempted as well as the eldest son or only son in a particular family. The *Nanyang Siang Pao* stressed that the Chinese should be granted citizenship first, before they could be called upon to fight the communists. The *China Press* preferred that national service should be on a voluntary basis. Even Tan Cheng Lock, who had no strong political ties with China, came out to defend the Chinese attitude on the ground that it had traditionally been the case that the Chinese would accord loyalty first to the family and locality rather than to the nation. Moreover, the Western idea of social obligation was alien to them.[30] When in 1954 the Singapore Government implemented the National Registration system and the National Service Act, which required everyone to register for an identity card and subjected able-bodied men between 18 and 20 to possible compulsory military service, students of Chinese schools staged protests and as disorder mounted the Government temporarily closed down eight of the schools.[31]

The unwillingness of Chinese youths to serve in the armed forces to fight the communist guerrillas inevitably gave the Malays the impression that the Chinese did not identify themselves politically with Malaya. The Sino-Malay situation had so deteriorated that even the popular leader of UMNO, Dato Onn, could not persuade it to accept non-Malays into the party and Dato Onn's now celebrated resignation from the party in protest did nothing to alter the resolute stand of UMNO members. It is pertinent to note that when, subsequently, Dato Onn proceeded to form a non-communal political party—the Independence of Malaya Party (IMP)—Tunku Abdul Rahman, the new President of UMNO, remarked that by leaving UMNO and forming the IMP, Dato Onn had sold away the Malays' rights and heritage to other races.[32]

The seriousness of the racial situation may be further illustrated by a reference to the subject of the resettlement of the Chinese rural population (otherwise known as the Briggs Plan). One of the significant results of the armed confrontation between the British and the MCP was that the geographical location of a substantial number of the Peninsula's inhabitants was deliberately altered. In a concerted effort to stop the thousands of mainly Chinese squatters on the jungle fringes from continuing to render various forms of aid to the Malayan Races Liberation Army, the Federation Government began mapping out plans as early as 1949, when Gurney was High Commissioner, to resettle these squatters in so-called New Villages located in suitable and accessible parts of the Peninsula. It was not an easy undertaking, inasmuch as the sites of the New Villages had to have basic necessities such as habitable and arable land, roads, water, protection from MRLA incursions and, where funds permitted, an electricity supply.[33]

The first organized settlement was at Mawai, near Kota Tinggi in Johor. Out of a score of such schemes half were abandoned for lack of funds and coordination by the Federal and State Governments in their implementation. 'The situation required not only a comprehensive scheme for the whole of the country and funds to finance this, but also a man able to galvanize the Administration into extraordinary action'.[34] The resettlement effort had in effect become a strategic as well as a major social problem.

More taxing for the planners, the majority of the sites had to be acquired from land gazetted as Malay Reservation which, as the title implies, could be settled and used only by Malays. In accordance with the 1948 Federation Agreement land, which had abruptly become a British responsibility under the Malayan Union proposals, had been 'restored' as a matter of jurisdiction to the Malay Rulers. It took Gurney nearly two years to convince the Rulers that the resettlement scheme 'was not only a question of military survival, but a vital step in promoting racial harmony and equality, without which the date of independence might well be delayed'.[35] The Rulers agreed to release land for siting the New Villages, and the 'villagers were eligible for permanent title to this land'.[36] It has been correctly said that such agreement on land use 'would have been inconceivable in the days before the Emergency when the Malays would have demanded adherence to old promises, which acknowledged the complete rights of the Malays'.[37]

In actual fact, by 1952 security forces, special constables, government officials and social welfare workers had helped to resettle over 423,000 squatters into some 410 New Villages.[38] It should be noted that, though Gurney initiated resettlement, it was Lieutenant-General Sir Harold Briggs who concentrated on the plans for it during his appointment as civilian Director of Operations from April 1950 to November 1951. No less significant, it was Templer, with his soldierly professionalism, who improved upon and made a notable success of the Briggs Plan as a strategic and social programme. Many years later Templer explained, 'Oh yes, the plan was Briggs' all right. But he had no power to implement it effectively, until Sir Winston Churchill appointed me High Commissioner and Director of Operations and I swallowed the Briggs Plan, hook, line and sinker'.[39]

The social and political significance of the resettlement effort has been summarized thus:

At first essentially a security measure, the resettlement programme developed into a battle for the hearts and minds of the people. Victory in this battle, it was hoped, would help to raise a new generation of Chinese with a stake in the country. Completion of this process would change the New Villages from reservoirs of resentment into bastions of loyal Malayan citizenry. It was a dream, but there was a chance of its coming true.[40]

The process involved the removal of about half a million people from isolated areas of the jungle fringes to a community life in the New Villages; these were linked by road and often also by railway to the other population centres of Malaya, which thus enabled the Federal and State Governments to extend social amenities and welfare to the Villages. Ultimately, local government councils were initiated and leaders from among the villagers themselves were entrusted with the responsibility of running their village affairs.[41]

The unfortunate aspect of the Briggs Plan, however, was that most of the New Villages were populated by Chinese. This, and the failure of a few multiracial ones, led to the development of what amounted to Chinese ghettos in many areas. The Villages eventually helped to prolong, if not accentuate, the polarization of voting and political preferences along communal lines, inasmuch as communal bloc votes often came from the Villages. No less important, within the context of this study, is the fact that the resettlement schemes caused not a little resentment among the Chinese affected. Means comments:

Counter-insurgency measures undertaken by the Government also tended to intensify communal antagonisms. Rural Chinese who cultivated vegetable plots or rubber small-holdings were uprooted from their often illegal land holdings and sent to detention camps for 'screening' or, after 1950, to 'new villages' where they could be brought within effective government control so as to prevent their giving willing (or unwilling) support to the guerrillas. The use of collective punishment, preventive detention and summary deportation' were all measures employed almost exclusively to punish Chinese for proven or suspected support of the Communist cause. Food denial measures, which under severe circumstances involved communal cooking of food, added to the grievances of these resettled Chinese 'squatters'. Although the government provided physical amenities and social services to the new villages, the total impact of government policy frequently caused hardship and grievances among the very people whose cooperation was essential for defeating the Communist guerrillas.[42]

Ironically enough the very same measure which the Chinese so resented also caused dissatisfaction among the Malays—what the Chinese regarded as 'punishment', the Malays regarded as 'favour'. In the period 1951–3, Malay leaders and the Malay press repeatedly complained that the Government was neglecting Malay kampongs. One Malay paper pointed out that 'Malays in the kampongs are left with their old lamps, wells in a wretched state and muddy roads. They should ask if that is what they ought to receive in return for the loyalty they show the government, whereas persons whose loyalty the government cannot depend upon are given all amenities and comforts.'[43] In the Municipal Council of Kuala Lumpur, Abdullah Yassin complained that in the adjoining areas of Sentul and Setapak 'Only one pipe is available for the people of three kampongs and that pipe is situated right in the town of Sentul, that is half a mile from each kampong. At the same time, the kampongs are dirty because pigs and cows are allowed to be reared near the kampongs.'[44] The subject was also brought up in the Federal Council in 1951 and again in 1952, on both occasions by Dato Haji Mohammed Eusoff who complained that the Government was apathetic towards the development of Malay society. He warned that if the situation was not remedied then 'in solving one emergency, we start another which might be more serious . . . let us not give too much when it is too late'.[45] The tone of press reports and speeches by Malay councillors and politicians throughout the country was basically the same—the Government was discriminating against Malay kampongs and therefore the Malays were losing confidence in the Government.

It was a symptom of the time: every action, every development was unavoidably seen and interpreted communally. Racial polarization, in fact, was by no means a less serious problem than communism. What made the situation even more acute was the reality that communalism and communism were not two separate problems. Communism and all its ramifications intensified communalism. Yet surprisingly, the country was able to make constitutional progress towards independence.

Constitutional Developments during the Emergency

The imposition of rigid and wide-ranging Emergency Regulations in June 1948 prompted most of the earlier political groupings either to dissolve voluntarily or to suspend activities; some, such as the Malayan Communist Party (MCP) and the Angkatan Pemuda Insaf (API), were banned.[46] Hence, constitutional discussions on the country's future were apparently placed in abeyance until the stringency and threat to stability of the Emergency abated. But, upon closer scrutiny, it can be seen that the stringent years of the Emergency were actually the seed-time of political developments which accelerated Malaya's progress towards independence.

One of these developments concerned the question of Malayan citizenship. The Malayan Union scheme had intended to confer *jus soli* citizenship (i.e., to confer citizenship on all persons born in the Union or Singapore on or after Malayan Union Day) but Malay opposition to this led to the tightening up of citizenship provisions in the 1948 Federation Agreement. In terms of promoting nationhood, too, the federal citizenship provisions of 1948 had one major limitation. Citizenship, it was explained,

... was not a nationality, neither could it develop into a nationality. It would not affect or impair, in any respect whatever, the status of British subjects in the Settlements or the status of subjects of Rulers in the Malay States. It is an addition to, and not a subtraction from, nationality and could be a qualification for electoral rights, for membership of Councils and for employment in Government services, and it could confer other privileges and impose obligations.[47]

Because the 1948 federal citizenship was not a nationality, it failed to instil among many non-Malays who were eligible for it that feeling of Malayan consciousness and allegiance which was a prerequisite for national integration. It tended to delay the realization among Chinese and Indians who were qualified for federal citizenship that they had much more in common with the Malays than with their ethnic brethren in China or India after the Second World War.

Nevertheless, the 1948 citizenship provisions did have some beneficial effects. They brought about a widening interest among the people of Malaya in the importance of citizenship *per se* as their country moved towards independence. It was estimated that the total number of federal citizens by operation of law and by application was 3,275,000 at the end of 1950. Of this figure, 2,500,000 were Malays, 500,000 Chinese and 230,000 Indians.[48] With the population of Malaya at about 5,226,500 in 1950, this meant that in less than three years after the administrative unification of the Peninsula, Malaya had citizens who numbered about 63 per cent of the total population. Thus a citizenry, an essential component of nationhood, had been created by the 1948 Federation.

The widening interest in citizenship led to the passage of the Federation of Malaya (Amendment) Ordinance 1952 which provided two new methods of acquiring federal citizenship. One of these was by being a citizen of the United Kingdom and Colonies and born in the Settlements (Penang and Malacca) or Federation together with certain residential qualifications.[49] Secondly, a person could become a federal citizen by first becoming a subject of one of the nine Malay Rulers.[50] These provisions were meant mainly for non-Malays, as Malays automatically were citizens of the Federation as well as subjects of the Rulers in their respective states. This automatic provision for the Malays had been established and left unaltered since the days of the Malayan Union and its replacement by the 1948 Federation. The definition of a 'Malay' was, and has been until this writing, constitutionally a person who (a) habitually speaks the Malay language; (b) professes the Islamic religion; and (c) conforms to Malay custom.[51]

The 1952 Ordinance maintained the provisions on language qualifications as they existed in the 1948 Federation Agreement. Among other things, reasonable proficiency in 'Malay or English' was required of the applicants for registration or naturalization as federal citizens. Like the Malayan Union proposals, but unlike the 1948 Federation Agreement, the 1952 Ordinance disallowed dual citizenship, that is to say it required the renunciation of any other nationality or citizenship before a person could become a federal citizen of Malaya.[52] This prohibition of dual citizenship acted as a strong incentive for the non-Malays to consider seriously the practicality of taking up federal citizenship for the alternative would have been sooner or later to return to their countries of origin or face life as aliens or stateless persons in the Federation.

The various questions which arose pertaining to citizenship from 1946 to 1952 were important signposts in Malaya's development towards nationhood; that is, they were indicative of the growing preoccupation with evolving a nation-state in the Peninsula. No less significant was the direct result of the passage of the 1952 Ordinance: 'And so from midnight on September 14, 1952, 1,200,000 Chinese—sixty per cent of the Chinese in Malaya—and 180,000 Indians became Malayan citizens. Many others were able to apply for citizenship under the new law which had substantially relaxed the conditions.'[53] Ratnam writes:

> ... it may be established that, at the end of 1953, approximately 4,424,650 persons had either already become citizens or possessed the birth qualification necessary to become registered as such. Since the total population of the country at this time was estimated at 5,705,952, this means that only about 1,281,300 persons were not included in any of the above categories and, significantly, 911,300 of them were in fact born outside the country.[54]

Thus, even though the 1952 Ordinance fell short of declaring a single nationality for Malaya, inasmuch as the Nationality Enactments postulated no less than nine 'different nationalities in a small country'[55] the liberalization of the citizenship provisions of the 1948 Federation Agreement acted as a clear stimulus to the evolution of a Malayan people of different ethnic origins, bound by a common citizenship and moving together towards the goal of full self-government. Ratnam's calculations demonstrate that Malaya was already a state and potentially a nation with nearly 80 per cent of its total population already citizens or clearly eligible to become citizens.

By 1953 too the security situation of the Peninsula had greatly improved so that military orders issuing from King's House, General Templer's headquarters in Kuala Lumpur since he took over as High Commissioner and Director of Operations in February 1952, tended more and more to sound less stringent.[56] The lessening of the threat from the MCP forces from 1953 onwards enabled the Federation Government to place more emphasis on political considerations for the future of the Peninsula. The Emergency itself was to a considerable degree a war between two conflicting ideologies, the communism of the MCP and the liberal parliamentary tradition of the British.[57] In the long run, the British were the more successful for the Malayans at large tended to prefer the ideals of Her majesty's Government to the dialectics of the MCP.

A point to bear in mind is that while constitutional and political developments occurred in the 1950s Malayans experienced the use of some parliamentary processes of government with the encouragement and guidance of the British. Thus, even before party politics developed later in the 1950s, the British authorities made one significant constitutional concession. This was the introduction in April 1951 of the so-called 'Member System' 'whereby in accordance with a resolution of the Federal Legislative Council, nine of the official members were made responsible for various departments and functions of Government'.[58] The nine 'portfolios' introduced were: Member for Home Affairs; Member for Economic Affairs; Member for Agriculture and Forestry; Member for Health; Member for Education; Member for Industrial and

Social Relations; Member for Lands, Mines and Communications; Member for Works and Housing; and Member for Railways and Posts. In February 1954, after some reshuffling of ministerial responsibilities and the addition of the portfolios of Member for Local Government, Housing and Town Planning; Member for Posts and Telecommunications; Member for Transport; and Member for Natural Resources, seven of the portfolios were held by Malayan 'non-official members of the legislature'. These were Dato Sir Onn bin Jaafar (Home Affairs), Tunku Yaacob ibni Al-Marhum Sultan Abdul Hamid Halim Shah (Natural Resources), Dr Lee Tiang Keng (Health), Dato E. E. C. Thuraisingham (Education), H. S. Lee (Transport), Dato Nik Ahmad Kamil bin Haji Mahmood (Local Government, Housing and Town Planning) and Dato Mahmud bin Mat (Posts and Telecommunications).[59]

The Member System turned out to be the precursor of the cabinet system of government in Malaya; but its introduction and use also represented an important stage in the growth of inter-communal cooperation in the country, albeit only at the leadership level. The Member System evidently afforded leaders of the different races opportunities to exercise extensive ministerial responsibilities while working in common for the achievement of independence. It also tended to create a precedent whereby in the future Malayan nation the central cabinet would be multiracial.

The Growth of Party Politics

Party politics had begun with the formation of the Malay Nationalist Party (MNP) in September 1945 as the post-war successor of the KMM, PETA and KRIS; the formation of the Malayan Democratic Union (MDU) in December 1945; the formal establishment of UMNO in May 1946; the quiet formation of the Malayan Indian Congress (MIC) in August 1946 and the establishment of the PUTERA-AMCJA grand coalition. There was, however, little scope for the development of pan-Malayan popular appeal among the political parties until the electoral process was introduced. This was done during the later years of the Emergency, partly in an endeavour to convince the people of Malaya that, unlike the authoritarian MCP, the British believed in giving them the right to choose the type of government and political system they preferred and partly as a corollary of the British pledge contained in the Directive to Templer 'that Malaya should in due course become a fully self-governing nation'. Thus, party politics developed in the 1950s as an agency by which the struggle for political emancipation and the ultimate goal of Malayan nationhood could be widely debated and decided upon in an inter-communal manner by the people of Malaya themselves.

The political parties which functioned during the reactions to and discussions on the Malayan Union and the 1948 Federation proposals took up issues largely from the standpoints of pressure groups agitating for the redress of immediate grievances, such as UMNO's fight for the restoration of traditional Malay political rights and the PUTERA-AMCJA's advocacy of liberal social democracy for Malaya but the party politics which developed in the 1950s evinced more clearly the pattern of a consistent and increasingly steadfast struggle to gain self-rule for Malaya.[60] The introduction of municipal and town council elections between 1951 and 1955 promoted this pattern;[61] and the formation of the Alliance, between UMNO and the MCA, to contest the 1952 Kuala Lumpur municipal elections underlined the awareness of the leaders of the two parties that, in politics as in every other major aspect of public life, there must be inter-communal amity and cooperation if the long-term goal of attaining independence was to be seriously pursued and realized.

The CLC had earlier established the pattern of inter-communal bargaining for the future well-being of Malaya. Dato Onn indeed attempted to convince other UMNO leaders that the Malays 'must get into action and wholeheartedly co-operate with the other communities in order that the aims of UMNO—one nationality speaking one language—can be achieved'.[62] He succeeded in getting UMNO to accept non-Malays as associate members who had no voting right; but, as mentioned earlier, when he pressed for the admission of non-Malay federal citizens as full members of UMNO, he not only faced strong opposition but ended up having to resign and form his own Independence of Malaya Party (IMP) in September 1951.[63]

The IMP was a non-communal party which strove to unite the various communities to work for self-government within ten years; democratic elections to local government by 1953 and to the central legislature based on adult suffrage by 1955; free and compulsory elementary education for all between the ages of 6 and 12 years by 1955; Malayanization of the public service and creation of a Malayan service as opposed to the colonial service; improved social services in the rural areas in particular; subsidies and guaranteed prices to cultivators; the granting of the full fruits of their industry to workers; and reform of the feudal system in the Malay states.[64] In many ways it is fair to say that the IMP 'represented a political crystallization of the co-operative aspirations of the Communities Liaison Committee'.[65] But the IMP failed to gain the support of both Malays and non-Malays which was vital to its programme. The Malays almost entirely opposed the IMP and the Chinese and Indians felt reluctant to support a party which could not even get the confidence of the community its leader hailed from. Essentially, the failure of the IMP demonstrated that, notwithstanding the energetic efforts to foster intercommunal understanding and cooperation, Malayan politics were still heavily charged with communalism at the time. The Malays continued to unite solidly behind UMNO under its new leader, Tunku Abdul Rahman,[66] while the Chinese were to concentrate their political efforts in the MCA for years to come.

The MCA was founded in February 1949, originally as a welfare association to assist in the implementation of the Briggs Plan of resettling squatters into New Villages.[67] While the British managed to exercise better control of the Chinese through it, the MCA also enabled wealthy Chinese to develop a counter-organization to the MCP and moreover helped in orientating the Chinese community towards a Malayan outlook.[68] At the inaugural meeting of the MCA in February 1949 Tan Cheng Lock highlighted what may be described as the pre-occupation of the period, namely the desire for inter-communal understanding in order to attain independence. He said:

The people of Malaya can only constitute a Nationality if the different Communities making up its mixed population are united among themselves by common sympathies and fellow-feeling and reconcile themselves to living together in peace and harmony under equal rights and laws.

Hence it is a matter of supreme significance and an indispensable necessity that a basic purpose of this organization must be the attaining of inter-communal understanding and friendship, particularly, between the Malays and the Chinese, the two major races which form between them about 88% of the population of Malaya....

The Chinese in Malaya have come to stay and *Must Wake up and Unite* not only among themselves but also with the Malays and other Communities to make this land, which feeds, nourishes and sustains us, one country and one nation and the object of their loyalty, love and devotion.[69]

It may be said that the MCA was the first political party to attempt to unify the Chinese in Malaya as a community and in a communal manner for inter-communal purposes. It was the first wide-ranging attempt to make the Chinese in Malaya realize that their social, economic and political welfare were far more deeply involved in the future of Malaya than in that of their traditional homeland. There was a growing awareness, particularly because that homeland appeared to be succumbing to Mao Tse-tung and the Chinese Communist Party, that the number of political options for the mainly capitalist-oriented Malayan Chinese was diminishing; and that one of these was the choice of Malaya as their real home and the object of their loyalty in common with the other communities of the Peninsula.

The wish to cooperate with other communities bore its first fruit when UMNO and the MCA entered an alliance to contest the Kuala Lumpur municipal elections in 1952.[70] Apart from the UMNO–MCA alliance, the IMP was the main contender in the elections. Out of the 12 seats contested the Alliance won 9 and the IMP 2, while the last seat went to an Independent. In the course of 1952 and 1953, the Alliance won 94 out of 124 seats in municipal and town council elections.[71] Mindful of future developments and with much political acumen, the successes were acknowledged in these terms:

The Alliance is grateful to the peoples of the Federation for giving practically 100 percent of the elected seats in the Town, Municipal, State and Settlement Councils to Alliance candidates in elections held so far, and hopes that the people will continue to give its candidates the same measure of support in the Federal elections, to enable it to carry out its policies and programmes for the development of the peoples themselves to a self-governing and then an independent nation.[72]

Their electoral successes encouraged the UMNO and MCA to consider the possibility of making their alliance more permanent, both for future political purposes and to foster a combined leadership in the struggle for Malayan independence. This solidarity between the two largest communities, the Malays and Chinese, who formed 'between them about 88% of the population of Malaya', increasingly became the *sine qua non* of the nationalist move towards independence. The inter-communal leadership of the Alliance was unmistakably becoming the most successful in the popular quest for self-rule. Indeed, this leadership achieved a further triumph in the 1955 federal elections.

The 1955 Elections: the Dawn of Nationhood

While the electoral process was being introduced in the various local councils, serious thinking was taking place about extending it to 'national', Peninsula-wide level. A committee was appointed in July 1953 'to examine the question of elections to the Federal Legislative Council and constitutional changes in the Federal Government arising therefrom'.[73] The Elections Committee advocated the establishment of a partly-elected and partly-nominated unicameral legislature, and gave the explanation vitally connected with nationalism that:

While clearly recognising that the ultimate objective must be a fully elected legislature which would be truly representative of all major elements in the

Federation, it is thought that development and experience in the country have not yet reached the stage when all aspects of the political and economic life of the community would be adequately represented through the electoral process.[74]

Special representation for racial minorities in the legislature was considered, but it 'was felt that separate nomination would be undesirable insofar as it might delay the realization of a united Malayan nation where the separate racial groups would be integrated and would find their political voice through bodies organised on non-racial lines'.[75] Similarly, but clearly of more crucial importance to the political future of Malaya, the Elections Committee rejected any suggestion of a communal voting system:

The Committee is of the opinion that to adopt such a system would not be in keeping with the agreed object of promoting national unity amongst the peoples of Malaya and might arrest the process of assimilation and co-operation which is so essential if the country is to have a single united people. We, therefore, agreed that elections should not take place on a communal basis, but that all communities should participate together in voting on a common basis and that candidates should be elected by individual territorial constituencies and not by individual communities.[76]

The voting age was to be 21 years and over. Out of the total population of Malaya of 5.7 million, 'the number of persons who are or could become citizens would be of the order of 4.4 million of whom approximately one-half are over 21 years of age'.[77] Voting was not made compulsory.

It was eventually agreed that 52 out of 98 members of the Federal Legislative Council would be elected. A Constituency Delineation Commission divided the Federation into 52 single-member constituencies. A system of 'weightage' for sparsely-populated states, such as Kelantan and Trengganu, was employed, 'having regard to the greater difficulty of contacting voters in the country districts and other disadvantages facing rural constituents'.[78] The administrative arrangements necessary for holding the elections were meticulously carried out. These included the registration of voters, the recruitment and training of returning officers and polling station staff, the work of the information services in publicizing the elections and explaining the purposes and value of the electoral process to the public, and the security provisions needed to ensure the safety of the campaign and voting.

It seems clear that the people of Malaya went to their first national poll on 27 July 1955 with an awareness that their country was not only undergoing constitutional development and the institutionalization of party politics but also moving on the road to independence. The 1955 elections were after all a partial fulfilment of the promise, in the Colonial Office Directive quoted earlier, that the people of Malaya could 'count on the powerful and continuing assistance of H.M. Government not only in the immediate task of defeating the terrorists but in the longer-term objective of forging a united Malayan nation'. At all events, the 1955 poll was keenly contested as will be seen below.

Of the 46 nominated seats in the Federal Legislative Council, 3 were for representatives of the Ceylonese, Eurasian and Aboriginal minorities; 22 went to 'scheduled interests' (6 for Commerce, 6 for Planting, 4 for Mining, 2 for Agriculture and Husbandry, and 4 for Trade Unions); 7 were 'nominated reserved seats'; 11 were taken up by the State and Settlement members; and 3 were for representatives of the Ceylonese, Eurasian and Aboriginal minorities (despite the rejection of communal representation by the Elections Commission) because the British Government felt that the interests of these groups should not be submerged. The remaining 3 seats were retained for ex-officio members. In addition, there was to be a Speaker of the legislature.[79] In short, the composition of the new legislature reflected a compromise between direct democracy, in the sense of a fully-elected house, and the demands of immediate Malayan consensus, in that the local social, economic and political realities had to be provided for. But the fundamental spirit and intent of the exercise remained, namely that with the implementation of the electoral process at national level the scope for the people of Malaya to think further and decide upon the national future of their country would be considerably broadened.

Briefly, the parties which contested the 1955 elections were the Alliance, Party Negara, the Labour Party of Malaya, the National Association of Perak (NAP), the Perak Malay League, the Perak Progressive Party (PPP), the Pan-Malayan Islamic Party (PMIP), and 18 Independents.[80] (The Alliance now included the MIC which joined it just before the elections.) The *First Election Report* summed up the results of the poll in clear language:

The UMNO/MCA/MIC Alliance won fifty-one of the fifty-two seats for elected Members in the new Legislative Council. The only seat lost by the Alliance was the Krian Constituency of Perak, which was the scene of a three-cornered fight with the Pan-Malayan Islamic Party candidate just ahead of the Alliance candidate [8,685 to 8,235 votes] and with the National Association of Perak candidate a rather poor third. The Alliance candidates obtained approximately 80 per cent. of the total votes cast, and in each of the 51 constituencies.in which the Alliance was successful, their candidate obtained more than twice as many votes as any of his rivals.[81]

The electoral and therefore political ascendancy of the Alliance was evident from the 1955 poll onwards.[82] Its electoral success also enabled the Alliance to claim that it had the mandate to lead Malaya to independence; this accounts for the fact that the negotiations towards *Merdeka* (Freedom) during the following two years were largely undertaken by the Alliance *vis-à-vis* the British.

The 1955 elections demonstrated some special features in the democratic process in Malaya. Apart from the adoption of different platforms, the various parties also evinced in varying degrees communal preferences in their campaigns. The NAP, which was formed in 1953 and led by the Dato Panglima Bukit Gantang, the Menteri Besar of Perak from 1948 to 1957, had support from mainly conservative and aristocratic Malays even though it professed to be non-communal. In the elections it reached an understanding with Party Negara not to contest the same constituencies. The Perak Malay League, which had existed since 1946, was by 1955 composed of splinter groups from UMNO and the NAP, and supported Independents in addition to fielding its own candidates. The League adopted a communal as well as religious line in its campaign. The Labour Party of Malaya was the re-grouping of several 'labour parties' formed in the early 1950s; it supported trade union demands and advocated socialist policies which included public ownership of basic industries.[83] The PPP likewise was the renamed faction of a 'labour party' in Ipoh and propounded aims similar to those of the Labour Party. The Labour Party and the PPP were the early instances of political groups formed along class as distinct from communal divisions, although both tended to draw their support mainly from the non-Malays.

Party Negara was the successor to the IMP and came into being in February 1954 under the leadership of Dato Onn, who was then Member for Home Affairs in the Federation Government. Unlike the largely non-communal IMP, Party Negara was openly pro-Malay. It was partly due to Dato Onn's identification with the British Malayan administration at the time that Party Negara, in spite of its communal pro-Malay platform, did poorly in the 1955 elections. (Of the total number of registered voters in the elections 84.2 per cent were Malays.)[84] In a valedictory vein, one commentator summed up:

As for the Party Negara, its overwhelming defeat may be regretted in that many considered it the only party capable of offering any effective opposition in the new Council to the Alliance steam-roller. And the defeat of its leaders, Dato Onn, in his home town of Johore Bahru was a sad ending to the career of one who has played such a prominent part in Malayan public life. His downfall must be attributed to serious errors of judgement and to a profound inability to understand the psychology of colonial nationalism.[85]

The PMIP (later known as *Parti Islam Se Tanah Melayu* or PAS) was an off-shoot of UMNO and was another communally-based party.[86] The PMIP sought to re-establish Malaya as a Malay country with an Islamic social system in which there would be no separation between religion and government. Evidently, the 1955 elections were keenly contested and demonstrated the ability of the various parties to pursue specific political, economic and social issues as befits the party-political system.

The very process of introducing the electoral machinery at pan-Malayan level was a recognition on the part of the British that Malaya had to be granted self-government in the foreseeable future. The politics of the 1955 elections were largely the politics of independence. Each of the main parties viewed the political future in terms of Malayan independence and nationhood. The PMIP, while insisting upon the elevation of the Malay community into a nation in which Islam would be established as the state religion and the Malays effectively given primacy over the other communities, nonetheless recognized the imperative need to end British rule and achieve independence before erecting a theocratic state 'and proposing that Malay nationalism should unite the Malays wherever they might be'.[87] Party Negara viewed the 1955 elections as an invaluable step towards self-rule. Its election manifesto pledged *inter alia* 'to secure independence by 1960 under a constitution to be drafted by a Constituent Assembly'.[88]

The British authorities had noted that 'the moderation and good sense of the proposals of the Federal Elections Committee are in themselves an indication of political understanding and maturity which justify making the first step towards a fully elected Legislature substantially greater than has been customary elsewhere'.[89] The orderly electoral victory of the Alliance in the first general elections vindicated the confidence of the British in the political maturity of the Malayan leaders.

For the Alliance leaders, the electorate's solid support for their platform of Merdeka within four years after the poll greatly encouraged them to work for that freedom by moderate constitutional and democratic means. The overwhelming Alliance victory also indicated that the voters preferred an inter-communal approach to politics to the exclusivist and communal policies of Party Negara and the PMIP. As for the Labour Party of Malaya, its failure to gain even one seat in the 1955 elections is largely attributable to its emphasis upon the ideas of socialism without being able to put its message of social justice across, especially to the rural dwellers who should have formed its main source of support along with the urban workers and labourers.

1. For the origins of the Communist Party in Malaya, see Khoo Kay Kim, 'Komunisma di Tanah Melayu: Peringkat Awal', *Jernal Sejarah*, 10, Kuala Lumpur, 1971/72; Hanrahan, *The Communist Struggle in Malaya*, Kuala Lumpur, 1971; E. O'Balance, *Malaya: The Communist Insurgent War, 1948–60*, London, 1966; J. H. Brimmell, *Communism in Southeast Asia*, London, 1959; and R. Onraet, *Singapore—A Police Background*, London, 1947.

2. The Anglo-MPAJA collaboration is well told in F. S. Chapman, *The Jungle is Neutral*, London, 1949.

3. For more detailed accounts of the Emergency, see O'Balance, op. cit.; L. W. Pye, *Guerrilla Communism in Malaya*, Princeton, N.J., 1956; H. Miller, *Menace in Malaya*, London, 1954; D. K. Palit, *The Campaign in Malaya*, New Delhi, 1960; Gwee Hock Aun, *The Emergency in Malaya*, Penang, 1966; R. Clutterbuck, *The Long Long War: The Emergency in Malaya 1948–1960*, London, 1967; N. Barber, *The War of the Running Dogs*, London, 1972; and Anthony Short, *The Communist Insurrection in Malaya, 1948–1960*, London, 1975.

4. Colonial Office Records 273/535, *Malayan Bulletin of Political Intelligence*, October 1926. The letter was dated 6 November 1925. The words in brackets were decoded by the Political Intelligence Bureau in Singapore from the cypher of the original letter.

5. See Khoo Kay Kim, 'The Beginnings of Political Extremism in Malaya 1915–1935' (Ph.D. Thesis, University of Malaya, 1974), p. 326.

6. A. J. Stockwell, 'The Development of Malay Politics During the Course of the Malayan Union Experiment 1942–1948' (Ph.D. Dissertation, University of London, 1973), p. 87.

7. Cheah Boon Kheng, *The Masked Comrades*, pp. 74–5.

8. Yeo Kim Wah, 'The Anti-Federation Movement in Malaya, 1946–48', *JSEAS*, 4, No. 1, March 1973, p. 36.

9. Nabir bin Haji Abdullah, *Maahad Il Ihya Assyariff Gunung Semanggol 1934–1959*, Kuala Lumpur, 1976, pp. 164, 166.

10. See J. B. P. Robinson, *Transformation in Malaya*, London, 1956, ch. 4.

11. S. S. Bedlington, *Malaysia and Singapore: The Building of New States*, Ithaca, N.Y., 1978, pp. 20–1.

12. MCP, 'Strategic Problems of the Malayan Revolutionary War' in Hanrahan, op. cit., App. I.

13. Clutterbuck, *The Long Long War*, p. 70.

14. Miller, op. cit., p. 25. Miller lived in Malaya and covered the Emergency for eleven of its twelve years for *Straits Times*.

15. See Miller, op. cit., p. 181. Barber, op. cit., p. 247, states that there were 2,473 deaths, 1,385 injured, and 810 missing among the Malayan civilian population by 1960.

16. Malayan Communist Party, 'Past Errors' (Party Directive of October 1951, Pt. 1), *The Times*, London, 1 December 1952.

17. Ibid.

18. General Sir Gerald Templer assumed duties as High Commissioner and Director of Operations in February 1952, four months after the death of Gurney. He held these combined appointments until his departure from Malaya in June 1954. Born in 1898, educated at Wellington and Sandhurst, Olympic hurdler in 1924, bayonet-fighting champion in the Army, Templer had a distinguished Second World War record, commanding several divisions, becoming the youngest lieutenant-general in the British Army at 44, and being appointed Director of Military Government in West Germany following Hitler's defeat. Subsequently he was appointed Director of Military Intelligence in the War Office, London. Templer was a professional soldier who had an unusually acute understanding of political matters.

19. H. Miller, *A Short History of Malaysia*, New York, 1966, p. 196.

20. Interview with the present writer, London, June 1972.

21. *Straits Times*, 23 June 1948.

22. Short, op. cit., pp. 156–7.

23. Malcolm MacDonald was born in 1901 and had been a British M.P. since as early as 1929. He was Secretary of State for the Colonies, 1935 and 1938–40; Minister of Health, 1940–1; United Kingdom High Commissioner in Canada, 1941–6; Governor-General of the Malayan Union and Singapore, May–July 1946; Governor-General of Malaya, Singapore and British Borneo, 1946–8; Commissioner-General for the United Kingdom in Southeast Asia, 1948–55; High Commissioner for the United Kingdom in India, 1955–60; Chancellor of the University of Malaya, 1949–61. He passed away recently.

24. See Chapter 2, notes 19 and 70 for the backgrounds of Dato Onn bin Jaafar and Tan Cheng Lock respectively. E. E. C. Thuraisingham was born in Taiping, Perak, in 1898. He was educated at St. Thomas College, Colombo; Selwyn College, Cambridge; and Middle Temple, London. He was a lawyer in Singapore, 1925–34; and also practised law in Malaya; strove to promote the interests of Ceylonese as distinct from the rest of the 'Indian' community, and had been president of the Ceylon Federation of Malaysia since its inception; was chairman of the Communities Liaison Committee, 1949–51; active in the Malayan Estate Owners' Association, 1952–61; was a Senator (member of Dewan Negara) from 1959. Awarded the title of Dato by the Sultan of Johor. Died in 1979.

25. See Ishak bin Tadin, 'Dato Onn and Malay Nationalism 1946–51', *JSEAH*, I, No. 1, March 1960, p. 71; and Anwar Abdullah, *Dato Onn: Riwayat Hidup*, Petaling Jaya, 1971, pp. 165–8 and 237–40.

26. See especially *Straits Times*, 11 January, 10 August and 18 September 1949; and 19 April 1950.

27. G. P. Means, *Malaysian Politics*, London, 1970, p. 130n.

28. Tan Cheng Lock Papers (TCLP): Tan Cheng Lock to chairman of the CLC, 6 May 1949 (privately published, n.p., n.d.). See also I. Morrison, 'Aspects of the Racial Problem in Malaya', *Pacific Affairs*, 22, No. 3, September 1949, p. 250.

29. Dato E. E. C. Thuraisingham to the present writer, 20 November 1973.

30. Short, op. cit., pp. 300–1.

31. Means, op. cit., p. 276.

32. *Straits Times*, 1 July 1952.

33. Earlier, in 1948, a Squatter Committee had been set up to examine squatter problems. Among its recommendations were that wherever possible squatters should be settled in areas already occupied by them, and if that was impossible they should be resettled in a suitable alternative area.

34. K. S. Sandhu, 'Emergency Resettlement in Malaya', *The Journal of Tropical Geography*, 18, August 1964, p. 162.

35. Barber, op. cit., p. 92.

36. Sandhu, op. cit., p. 166. Sandhu confirmed in an interview with the present writer (Singapore, April 1974) that 'the villagers were given to understand that they would get permanent titles to their land three years after settling in the New Villages'.

37. H. Miller, *Menace in Malaya*, p. 233.

38. By 1960, 'a million rural dwellers in more than 600 "new" settlements' were the result of the resettlement efforts. Sandhu, op. cit., p. 157.

39. Interview with the present writer, London, June 1972.

40. Sandhu, op. cit., p. 180.

41. See especially R. Nyce, *Chinese New Villages in Malaya: A Community Study*, Singapore, 1973, ch. 10.

42. Means, op. cit., p. 118.

43. *Warta Negara*, 22 November 1952. (Author's translation.)

44. *Utusan Melayu*, 1 October 1952. (Author's translation.)

45. *Proceedings of the Federal Legislative Council of the Federation of Malaya*, 4th Session, February 1951–February 1952, p. 412.

46. See Federation of Malaya, *The Emergency Regulations Ordinance 1948 (amended up to 31 March 1953)*, Kuala Lumpur, 1953; R. Renick, 'The Emergency Regulations of Malaya', (M.A. Thesis, Tulane University, 1967); and Ahmad Boestamam, *Merintis Jalan Ke Punchak*, Kuala Lumpur, 1972, ch. 7, 14 and 25.

47. Malayan Union Government, *Constitutional Proposals for Malaya: Report of the Working Committee Appointed by a Conference of His Excellency the Governor of the Malayan Union, Their Highnesses the Rulers of the Malay States and the Representatives of the United Malays National Organization*, Kuala Lumpur, 1946, p. 66.

48. K. J. Ratnam, *Communalism and the Political Process in Malaya*, Kuala Lumpur, 1965, p. 84.

49. Federation of Malaya, *Federation of Malaya (Amendment) Ordinance, 1952*, Kuala Lumpur, 1952, Article 124(f).

50. Ibid.

51. It is interesting to note that the Menteri Besar (Chief Minister) of Kedah, Dato Syed Ahmad Shahabuddin, once asserted in the State Legislative Assembly that 'Melayu [or Malay] is any person who professes the Islamic Religion, customarily speaks the Malay language and has, at least, one of his parents a Malay or an Arab. ... An Indian or a Chinese Muslim is not a Malay. ... Likewise, an Indonesian, although normally known as a Malay, is officially also not a Malay'. *Straits Times*, Kuala Lumpur, 24 April 1974.

52. Federation of Malaya, *State Nationality Enactments, 1952*, Kuala Lumpur, 1952, Article 5.

53. N. Barber, op. cit., pp. 162–3. For the numbers of those who gained federal citizenship through registration and nationalization from 1949 to 15 September 1952, see Federation of Malaya, *Annual Report, 1952*, Kuala Lumpur, 1953, p. 33. As of 15 September 1952, the total of such citizens was only 351,826.

54. Ratnam, op. cit., p. 93.

55. J. M. Gullick, *Malaya*, London, 1964, p. 240.

56. Nevertheless V. Purcell castigated many of Templer's Emergency measures, and at one stage burst out that by 1952 'Malaya had become a vast armed camp in which no one could call his soul his own, and the clock of progress, it seemed, had been stopped for the duration of the Emergency. The basic policy was a crude "Divide and Rule"'. See V. Purcell, *Malaya: Communist or Free?*, London, 1954, pp. 5–6.

57. For an appraisal on this aspect, see J. P. Ongkili, 'Darurat dan British, 1948–1960: Suatu Penghargaan', *Jernal Sejarah*, Universiti Malaya, Kuala Lumpur, 1973/74, 12, pp. 58–73.

58. Federation of Malaya, *Annual Report, 1951*, Kuala Lumpur, 1952, p. 289.

59. Federation of Malaya, *Annual Report, 1953*, Government Press, Kuala Lumpur, 1954, pp. 375–9. Dato Sir Onn bin Jaafar's background was given in Chapter 2; Tunku Yaacob ibni Al-Marhum Sultan Abdul Hamid Halim Shah, a brother of Tunku Abdul Rahman became a Malayan High Commissioner and Ambassador subsequently; Dato E. E. C. Thuraisingham (note 24 above) subsequently continued to take an interest in public affairs and the promotion of 'a united Malayan Nation of equals' but found it difficult to work with Indians in the Malayan Indian Congress because of his preoccupation with the welfare and interests of the Ceylonese as a separate community; H. S. Lee later became Minister of Finance in the Federal Cabinet, 1957–9; Dato Nik Ahmad Kamil bin Haji Mahmood

became a High Commissioner and Ambassador, and later grew to be a hard-headed Malay businessman.

60. See Ratnam, op. cit., ch. 5.

61. See Federation of Malaya, *Report on the Introduction of Elections in the Municipality of George Town, Penang, 1951*, Kuala Lumpur, 1953.

62. *Straits Times*, 16 October 1949.

63. Ishak bin Tadin, op. cit., pp. 77–83. Twenty-two years later, Dato Onn's son, Datuk Hussein Onn, who had risen to become Deputy Prime Minister and Minister of Trade and Industry of Malaysia, said of his father's wish to open UMNO to non-Malay membership: 'Apakah ayah saya salah atau betul tidak boleh hendak diukur oleh sesiapa pada waktu itu. Cadangan ayah saya dibuat kerana pandangannya yang jauh. Cadangan itu bukan tidak baik, tetapi boleh jadi terlalu awal untuk dikemukakan. Orang Melayu belum dapat menerimanya lagi. Perkara saperti ini hanya dapat ditentukan oleh masa dan sejarah'. ['Whether my father was right or wrong could not be measured by anyone at that time. My father's proposal was made because of his far-sightedness. The proposal was not bad, but maybe it was premature to suggest it. A matter of this nature can only be decided by time and history.'] Subky Latif, 'Pasang Surut Politik Hussein Onn', *Mastika*, No. 10, October 1973, pp. 4–5.

64. T. H. Silcock and Ungku A. Aziz, 'Nationalism in Malaya', in W. L. Holland (ed.), *Asian Nationalism and the West*, New York, 1953, p. 334.

65. Ratnam, op. cit., p. 155.

66. Tunku Abdul Rahman was born in 1903, a son of Sultan Abdul Hamid Halim Shah of Kedah. Educated first in Malaya, he obtained his B.A. from Cambridge, and became Barrister-at-Law from Inner Temple, London, in 1949. Joined the Kedah and later Federal Legal Department. Became President of UMNO in 1951, and Chief Minister following the Alliance victory in the first Malayan federal elections in 1955. Led Malaya to independence in 1957, and became the nation's first Prime Minister. Led the formation of Malaysia until its inauguration in 1963. Prime Minister of Malaysia until he voluntarily resigned the post in September 1970. He thereafter became Secretary-General of the Islamic Secretariat in Jeddah until 1973. See also H. Miller, *Prince and Premier: A Biography of Tunku Abdul Rahman Putra Al-Haj, First Prime Minister of the Federation of Malaya*, London, 1959.

67. Social Welfare lotteries were run to raise funds for charitable work among the Chinese squatters of the New Villages. It has been observed that 'for several years the MCA exploited the Chinese love of gambling to pay for welfare programs which incidentally helped to consolidate its power among the Chinese of Malaya'. Means, op. cit., p. 121. See Malaysian Chinese Association, *MCA 20th Anniversary Souvenir*, Kuala Lumpur, 1969, pp. 55–6.

68. See M. Roff, 'The Malayan Chinese Association, 1948–1965', *JSEAH*, 4, No. 2, September 1965, pp. 40–53; Chan Heng Chee, 'The Malayan Chinese Association' (M.A. Thesis, University of Singapore, 1965); and Lim San Kok, 'Some Aspects of the Malayan Chinese Association, 1949–1969', *JSSS*, 26, No. 2, 1971, pp. 31–48.

69. Malayan Chinese Association: *Speech by Tan Cheng Lock on the 27th February 1949, at the Inaugural Meeting Of The Proposed Malayan Chinese Association at Kuala Lumpur* (privately published, n.p., n.d), pp. 1–2. Emphasis in the original.

70. The municipalities of George Town (Penang) and Malacca Town and Fort had existed since the beginning of 1948, while the Kuala Lumpur municipality was established later in the same year. 'Local matters in other towns and village areas were controlled by Town Boards in the States and in the Settlements by Rural Boards under the chairmanship of the local administrative officer.' Federation of Malaya, *Annual Report on the Federation of Malaya, 1948*, Kuala Lumpur, 1949, p. 171. See also G. Hawkins, 'First Steps in Malayan

Local Government', *Pacific Affairs*, 26, No. 2, June 1953, pp. 155–8.

71. In 1952, the grassroots democracy of 'elected Local Councils was gradually implemented. Some 135 Local Councils came into being during that year in addition to 12 Town Councils'. Federation of Malaya, *Annual Report, 1953*, Kuala Lumpur, 1954, p. xiv.

72. *TCLP*: 'Alliance Manifesto for Federal Elections'.

73. Federation of Malaya, *Report of the Committee Appointed to Examine the Question of Elections to the Federal Legislative Council* (hereinafter referred to as the *Elections Committee Report*), Kuala Lumpur, 1954, para. 1.

74. Ibid., para. 14.

75. Ibid., para. 19.

76. Ibid., para. 63. It is worthy of note that the Elections Committee set up a Working Party from among its members to study the issues involved; the Working Party included Dato Sir Onn bin Jaafar, Tunku Abdul Rahman, Dato Abdul Razak bin Hussein, Dr Ismail bin Dato Abdul Rahman, E. E. C. Thuraisingham, Dato Nik Ahmad Kamil, Colonel H. S. Lee, Dato Yong Shook Lin, P. P. Narayanan and Dato Zainal Abidin bin Haji Abbas all of whom, in varying degrees, were to continue to play prominent roles in the progress of Malaya towards nationhood. Most of them were at one with the Alliance demand that the elections should be held, 'if practicable, not later than November 1954'. Ibid., paras. 2 and 108. See also V. J. Morais (compiler and publisher), *Who's Who In Malaysia and Singapore*, from 1959 onwards for biographical accounts of these leaders. In general, it may be said that those who supported the Alliance walked the corridors of power and often enjoyed economic success; those who disagreed with the ruling party either ended up in the political wilderness or continued to support opposition parties and concentrated the greater part of their time and energy on personal affairs.

77. *Elections Committee Report*, paras. 51–2, 83, 88 and 96.

78. Federation of Malaya, *Report of the Constituency Delineation Commission*, Kuala Lumpur, 1954, para. 57 and Appendix I. The final allocation of constituencies was as follows: Penang 4; Malacca 2; Perak 10; Selangor 7; Negri Sembilan 3; Pahang 3; Johore 8; Kedah 6; Kelantan 5; Trengganu 3; and Perlis 1. Also interview with W. C. S. Corry, who was a member of the three-man Constituency Delineation Commission, London, April 1972.

79. Federation of Malaya, No. 695/54 and No. 967A: Despatch. High Commissioner to Colonial Office, 10 April 1954, para. 4.

80. T. E. Smith, *Report of the First Election of Members to the Legislative Council of the Federation of Malaya* (hereinafter referred to as *First Election Report*), Kuala Lumpur, 1955, para. 68. See Ratnam, op. cit., ch. 5; and Means, op. cit., chs. 10 and 11 for more detailed backgrounds of the various parties.

81. First Election Report, para. 67. Out of the 1,280,000 who were registered as voters, 84.86 per cent cast their votes in these first federal elections.

82. Of the seven political parties which contested the 1955 elections, the Alliance polled 79.6 per cent of the total votes while the Party Negara captured 7.6 per cent without, however, winning any seat. The PMIP, which won the only remaining seat after the Alliance won handsomely in 51 constituencies, managed to get only 3.9 per cent of the votes.

83. See C. Gamba, 'Labour and Labour Parties in Malaya', *Pacific Affairs*, 31, No. 2, June 1958, pp. 117–30.

84. *First Election Report*, para. 23.

85. F. G. Carnell, 'The Malayan Elections', *Pacific Affairs*, 28, No. 4, December 1955, p. 319.

86. See J. Funston, 'The Origins of Parti Islam Se Malaysia', *JSEAS*, 7, No. 1, March 1976, pp. 58–73 for an account of its early history.

87. Means, op. cit., p. 229. Interview with Datuk Haji Asri bin Haji Muda, Kuala Lumpur, March 1979.

88. Means, op. cit., p. 168n.

89. Federation of Malaya, No. 967A. Despatch. Colonial Office to High Commissioner, 20 April 1954, para. 4.

4
A Nation is Born

THE political developments in Malaya between 1948 and 1955 had plainly prepared the way to self-rule. Since the 1955 elections were largely concerned with the politics of attaining independence, it is not surprising that after its undisputed electoral victory, the Alliance set out to fulfil its pledge of achieving Merdeka for the Peninsula. But there were still some major problems to be surmounted before independence could be achieved, notably those of education, language and citizenship.

Education and Language

Under British rule and 'protection' before 1946, the Straits Settlements, the Federated Malay States (FMS) and the Unfederated Malay States (UFMS) had a systematically thought-out programme of education which was subtly geared to the maintenance of a plural society in Malaya and which kept the Malays backward and rural.

Malay pupils were given free elementary education in Jawi (Malay in Arabic script) and in Romanized Malay from the beginning of the twentieth century. The development of Malay education in the pre-war period has been well summed up as follows:

> The introduction of Malay Schools into the life of the Malays which began in the Nineteenth Century, did not meet with success initially, due to the resistance from the old religious tradition of learning. Gradually however, Malay schools began to be accepted, and after the first quarter of the present century, they were in great demand from the people.
>
> During its approximately sixty years' history, up to 1941, the Malay school system was never raised, nor was it intended to be, beyond its primary level. Its aim was never beyond that of elimination of illiteracy. While the status and the aim never changed, the administration aspect of it did change from time to time.[1]

The Sultan Idris Training College (SITC) at Tanjung Malim began a three-year curriculum to train Malay teachers in 1922. The successful trainees from this College were intended for schools in the Straits Settlements, the FMS and the UFMS. Considerable development took place at the SITC until the Japanese Occupation, its accommodation being extended and its curriculum widened. But, despite all this, the Malay vernacular schools taught only up to Standard Four. The underlying reason has been clearly stated:

> ... it had been accepted as a policy that the Malay education should not go beyond Standard IV. If the idea was to curb Malay education, why then Sultan Idris Training College? The answer is simple. Sultan Idris Training College was not a secondary school. Rather, it was a training college—a College that was meant to be a melting pot for shaping people who would go back to their *kampong* to make the people in the *kampong* more contented with their way of life.[2]

It was only in 1949 that a revised syllabus provided for a six-year course of instruction.[3] Consequently, very few Malays acquired more than knowledge of the 3Rs in pre-war days.

The teaching of non-Malays was carried on in English, Chinese and Tamil. The mosaic of unintegrated sources of education in the pre-war era has been summed up in the following:

> Up to the outbreak of the second world war there was a complexity of schools. There were schools for the Malay children, schools for the Chinese children, schools for the Indian children and schools providing education in English to the children of parents who could afford [it]. There was again an absence of uniformity of policy, though the ultimate aim of all these schools was a practical one. For the Malay child and the Indian child a minimum amount of literacy was considered sufficient. For the Chinese child education was intended to strengthen his bond with China. In the English schools 'the aim was to pass the Cambridge Overseas School Certificate Examination, the certificate having a great economic value.
>
> Again schools were either fully assisted, partially assisted by the Government or totally dependent on charity. All these factors gave rise to different curricula, different methods and different standards. It would therefore be reasonable to surmise that education in Malaya before the war tended more to separate than to unite the various races together.[4]

The post-war period began with a statement of education policy in 1946 which proposed *inter alia* that primary education would be free and would be for a period of six years. The media of instruction would be Malay, Chinese, Tamil and English. Secondary education would be conducted by schools in which English would be the medium of instruction. It was particularly noted that 'In every possible way the essential unity of the various sections of the Primary School will be stressed so that the school may provide a preparation for united service for the country and for the creation of a sense of common citizenship'.[5]

The 1948 Federation Agreement provided for the centralization of control of education in the hands of the Federal Government. The Agreement in fact already envisaged the systematic development of Malayan education by establishing 'Primary, secondary and trade school education to the extent of ensuring a common policy and a common system of administration; higher education; technical education; training of teachers; registration of schools; Federal education institutions; Malay translation bureau'.[6]

These developments are worthy of note, showing as they do that the post-war Malayan policy-makers had come to recognize education as an important factor in the enormous task of building a Malayan nation out of the culturally and ethnically diverse people of the Peninsula. This recognition contrasted with the divisive policy of the pre-war authorities and provided opportunities for the various communities to take seriously their respective roles in the social and political future of Malaya.

In 1949 the Federation Government appointed a Central Advisory Committee on Education consisting of representatives of the Legislative Council, and of official and educational interests, 'to advise Government on the general common policy and wide principles to be followed in education'.[7] Again, the prime intention was to do away with communal barriers and work for the integration of the various racial groups. As it happened, communal views rendered the Committee's efforts ineffective; but it was at least agreed that Malay education required urgent improvement.

A Committee on Malay Education under the chairmanship of L. J. Barnes, Director of Social Training, Oxford University, was appointed in 1951 'to enquire into the adequacy or otherwise of the educational facilities available for Malays'.[8] The Committee comprised, in addition to the British chairman, nine Malays and five Europeans. There were no Chinese or Indian members. The Barnes Report presented the position of the Malays in a highly nationalistic manner. Arguing that the Malay had gradually become enslaved in his own country while the British and the immigrant communities steadily prospered and gained the upper hand in almost everything except administration, the Report lamented, 'Now even if he wanted education he could no longer afford it'.[9] The role of education in nation-building and, above all, in the emergence of an intercommunal approach to the problem of bringing up the younger generation in a future independent country, was underlined when the Barnes Report declared:

We believe that primary schooling should be purposely used to build up a common Malay nationality, and we urge that it should be reorganised on a new inter-racial basis. . . . Our proposed inter-racial primary school we call the National School. . . . In principle we recommend the end of separate vernacular schools and their replacement by a single type of primary school common to all. We recognise, of course, that since this end can come only gradually, vernacular schools will continue for some years concurrently with the development of the National School.[10]

The Barnes Report argued to a considerable extent from a partisan Malay viewpoint. Yet it cannot be denied that the Malay members who were a majority in the Committee were not only conscious of the presence of other communities in their Peninsula but also aware of the complex problems which appeared certain to arise in the implementation of their proposed National School. Thus the Committee stated that its National School scheme 'would be seriously weakened if any large proportion of the Chinese, Indian and other non-Malay communities were to choose to provide their own primary classes independently of the National School'.[11] To reassure the same non-Malay communities that the long-term objective was a common Malayan nationality, the Committee pledged that the National School 'will teach English to all from Standard I onwards, and it will form the broad highway of admission to all Standard post-primary reaches of education'.[12]

However reactions to the Barnes Report which some non-Malays and particularly the Chinese felt was 'saturated with Malay nationalism'[13] prompted the appointment of a Mission of enquiry composed of two prominent Chinese, Dr William P. Fenn and Dr Wu Teh-yau.[14] Among other things, Fenn and Wu looked into 'bridging the gap between the present communal system of school and the time when education will be on a non-communal basis, with English and Malay as the media of instruction and other languages an optional subject' and 'the preparation of textbooks for present use with a Malayan as distinct from a Chinese background and content'.[15] Just as the Barnes Report thought of the educational problems of the Malays against the background of a national pedagogical system, the Fenn-Wu Report sought to elucidate the predicament of the Chinese and their culture in the context of the emergence of Malaya as a nation with its own system and medium of education. It stated:

No element of the population can be 'Malayanized' for the simple reason that there is no 'Malayan' pattern to which to mould it and because such moulding is not produced by fiat. A new culture can come only from the natural mingling of diverse cultural elements for generations. In the process, elements which do not command appreciation disappear, while those which do need no political or external support.[16]

While it argued for 'a proper place' for Chinese Schools in the education system, the Fenn-Wu Mission nevertheless supported the central aim of fostering the development of a Malayan nation. It suggested that there was 'no real advantage for Chinese culture in maintaining the form or, indeed, the methods and content of schools in China. Foreign politics in any form should be eliminated from Chinese schools, and textbooks suitable for Malayan use should be produced'.[17]

The Legislative Council eventually set up a Committee headed by E. E. C. Thuraisingham (who was now Dato Sir Clough Thuraisingham), to study the education problem as a whole: the findings of the Committee were largely incorporated into the 1952 Education Ordinance. This provided for the establishment of a system of national schools with Malay and English as the media of instruction but it also contained the provision that the teaching of other vernacular languages would be allowed in cases where fifteen or more pupils requested the teaching of a particular language. The Committee's report met with hostility from the Chinese. Some of whom considered that the Government had reduced the status of Chinese education to that of 'a prisoner to be condemned'.[18] The MCA leadership, with representatives in the Thuraisingham Committee, expressed satisfaction with the report and came under severe attack not only from those outside the party but also from its rank and file. Education as an issue unavoidably affected relations between UMNO and the MCA. As Means comments:[19]

The political relations between UMNO and the MCA were subject to severe strain in August and September, 1952, when Victor Purcell arrived from London to prepare a report on the Chinese at the invitation of the MCA. The Malays took strong exception to Dr. Purcell's visit because he was a well-known spokesman for the Chinese viewpoint on political and constitutional issues. Tunku Abdul Rahman forbade any UMNO officials to cooperate with Dr. Purcell, and, in apparent retaliation, the MCA withdrew its offer of M$500,000 to set up a Malay Welfare Fund to be administered in cooperation with UMNO.

However, the political partners managed to avoid a serious confrontation. MCA leaders under Tan Cheng Lock appealed for a more tolerant attitude and hence acceptance of the 1952 Education Ordinance.

It can be seen that, at this juncture, the movement among the Alliance leaders to establish a national system of education was pursued with zest, attention to inter-communal considerations and the hope that the system would serve the needs of an independent Malaya. Indeed, in preparation for the 1955 elections, the Alliance promised 'To re-orientate Education to a Malayan outlook.... To establish a type of national schools that will be acceptable to the people of Malaya and will meet their needs in promoting their cultural, economic, social and political development as a nation so as to facilitate the fulfilment of the Alliance aim to adopt Malay as the national language of the country.'[20]

A significant milestone was reached in 1956 when the Federation Government appointed a committee headed by the then Minister of Education, Dato Abdul Razak bin Dato Hussein. The terms of reference of the committee were almost identical with the Alliance election promise just quoted and paid particular regard 'to the intention of making Malay the national language of the country whilst preserving and sustaining the growth of the language and culture of other communities living in the country'.[21]

The Razak Education Report did not abandon the Barnes Reports advocacy of 'national schools'.[22] The Barnes and Fenn-Wu Reports as well as the Report of the Thuraisingham Committee were all concerned, in varying degrees, with the same two aims: to evolve a national education system; and to work out an agreement in which, within that system, Malay would eventually become the sole national language and the principal medium of instruction while accommodating, as far as possible, the other main languages: English, Chinese and Tamil. Separate vernacular schools had to be allowed to exist until the arduous process of compromise could achieve a consensus on the 'national schools'. But there was never a doubt about or objection to the overriding aim of 'establishing a national system of education acceptable to the people of the Federation as a whole', from the time of the Barnes Committee onwards.

Hence, while recommending Malay, the national language, as a compulsory subject in all schools, the Report was strictly realistic:

We cannot over-emphasize our conviction that the introduction of syllabuses common to all schools in the Federation is the crucial requirement of educational policy in Malaya. It is an essential element in the development of a united Malayan nation. It is the key which will unlock the gates hitherto standing locked and barred against the establishment of an educational system accpetable to the people of Malaya as a whole. Once all schools are working to a common content syllabus, irrespective of the language medium of instruction, we consider the country will have taken the most important step towards establishing a national system of education which will satisfy the needs of the people and promote their cultural, social, and political development as a nation.[23]

Clearly, education was meant to be not only an aspect of social development but also a crucial determinant in the rise of a nation in the Peninsula. The Razak Education Report led to the passage of the Education Ordinance 1957 under which Standard Primary Malay Schools with Malay as the medium of instruction, and Standard-Type Primary Schools in which the main medium was English, Chinese or Tamil were established. In secondary education, 'one type of National secondary school open to all races by competitive selection and with a common syllabus, a flexible curriculum permitting the study of all Malayan languages and cultures and room for diversity in the media of instruction' was adopted.[24]

But the Razak Education Report also met with opposition from the Chinese community and because the MCA had been a party to the Report, anti-MCA pamphlets appeared which accused the MCA of having 'swept overboard' the interests and culture of the Chinese in Malaya.[25] Two organizations were particularly vocal in their attacks on the Razak Education Report–the United Chinese School Teachers Association and the All-Malaya Chinese Schools Management Association. Within the MCA itself, there was widespread discontent. The MCA leadership was compelled to form a Central Education Committee to study the implications of the Razak Education Report. At a conference held in February 1957, attended by some 200 delegates, the Alliance Government's education policy, as applied to Chinese schools, was rejected. The MCA leaders, however, were more concerned to preserve their bond with UMNO in pursuit of independence. Hence, when the Razak Education Report was tabled in the Legislative Council in March 1957, it was accepted without a note of dissent from the MCA members.[26] However, within the Chinese community, even after the 1957 Education Ordinance had been passed, disaffection towards the Alliance party continued to be marked and this was manifest during the Ipoh–Menglembu by-election which was held after the sitting MCA member, Leong Yew Koh, was appointed Governor of Malacca in 1957. D. R. Seenivasagam of the People's Progressive Party defeated the Alliance candidate,[27] and Ipoh from then onwards consistently voted for Opposition candidates. The issue of education also continued to plague the Sino-Malay relationship.

The Alliance also continued to regard education and the question of National Language as extremely important aspects of nation-building so that in 1959, after just two years of independence, another committee was appointed to review the implementation of the Razak Education Report.[28] The resulting Rahman Talib Education Report considered that 'the 1956 Committee succeeded in recommending an educational policy which was national in its scope and purpose, while at the same time preserving and sustaining the various cultures of the country'.[29] The importance of language was obvious from the fact that primary education in Malay was 'to be developed by the introduction of national language streams in former Government primary schools'.[30] Furthermore, secondary education would be conducted in only Malay or English; and 'all public examinations in secondary schools [were] to be conducted only in one of the [two] official languages'.[31] Effectively, this meant that, in addition to those in the English streams, the first batch of students in the Malay medium secondary classes begun in 1958 could sit for their Lower Certificate of Education examination (after completing Form III) in 1960, and for their Federation of Malaya Certificate of Education examination (upon completion of Form V) in 1962. Form VI enrolments which could lead to the (Cambridge) Higher School Certificate examination and also matriculation in the University of Malaya, which adjusted its academic year in 1958 to fit in with the school terms were, however, still low and increasing only very slowly.[32]

Citizenship

While all the Malays were subjects of their respective Rulers and automatically became citizens of the Federation from 1948 onwards, the problem of nation-building in this regard was the question who among the non-Malays should be admitted into the privileged fold of Malayan citizenship.

It was very clear by 1955 that the MCA would have a difficult time accommodating Chinese demands and at the same time preserving its bond with UMNO. When the Reid Commission (q.v. *infra*) was set up and prepared, in 1956, to hold hearings on constitutional proposals, the question of citizenship and related issues burst into the open. Several Chinese organizations threatened to call on the Chinese to boycott the MCA and to set up a rival body unless the MCA agreed to ask the Alliance to accept firstly, the principle of equal rights for all races; secondly, the granting of citizenship on the principle of *jus soli*; and finally, the concept of multi-lingualism. In Pulau Pinang and Melaka, certain groups of Chinese also demanded the right to retain their status as British subjects after independence. As has been remarked, 'the Executives of the MCA were, understandably, panicked by the storm that had broken about their heads'.[33] The Chinese, in fact, called for a separate memorandum to be sent to the Reid Commission. When the Alliance refused to allow this, the Chinese guilds began to act independently of the Alliance. In one assembly attended by a thousand delegates representing six hundred associations, resolutions were passed which called for 'nationality by right of birth; citizenship rights after five years' residence; no language test for citizenship; and the adoption of Chinese as an official language in Malaya'.[34]

When the Reid Commission Report was made public in February 1957, it was found that the bulk of the Alliance's recommendations had been accepted. The guilds and associations decided to send their own delegation to London to persuade the British Government to consider more sympathetically the Chinese case in the final negotiations on the Constitution. The delegation which eventually met the Colonial Secretary was headed by Lau Pak Khuan of the Perak MCA, a stalwart in the Federation of Chinese Guilds and Associations. The delegation accomplished nothing but the MCA was greatly embarrassed and therefore decided to suspend five of its members connected with the delegation to London, among them Lau Pak Khuan.[35] But from this point onwards, many Chinese organizations no longer looked to the MCA to espouse the Chinese cause. They felt that the MCA leadership was too concerned with placating the demands of UMNO. This attitude was categorically expressed by an editorial in the *China Press* which stated: 'We feel we can no longer rely on the M.C.A. to accomplish the task of fighting for Chinese rights because it is a political party and not an organization to represent public opinions'.[36]

Happily for the emerging Malayan nation, the Alliance leaders were able to work together. As already indicated, the Reid Commission, after receiving many different citizenship proposals, decided 'that the best proposals for dealing fairly with the present situation are those put forward by the Alliance'.[37] The three parties making up the Alliance had fully considered the matter and had reached broad agreement on it: 'We are satisfied that this agreement is a reasonable and proper compromise between the views of the parties, each of which has the most widespread support from the race which it represents, and we are further satisfied that this agreement is a better way of doing justice between the races than any other that had been suggested or has occurred to us.'[38]

Citizenship was not merely a recurrent problem but also a decisive determinant of nationhood in Malaya. The citizens of a fully self-governing Malaya, like those of other independent nations, had to be made distinct from the rest of mankind. Thus in an independent Malaya, it was agreed 'that all who are citizens before Merdeka Day should continue to be citizens, and that all those born in the Federation on or after Merdeka Day should be citizens by operation of law'.[39] (Merdeka Day was 31 August 1957.) This decision helped to maintain continuity in the criteria and development of Malayan citizenship and nationality.

Very significantly, when the recommendation 'that all those born in the Federation on or after Merdeka Day should be citizens by operation of law' was approved, it clearly meant that *jus soli* citizenship was adopted in independent Malaya, albeit without retrospective effect.[40] From Merdeka Day onwards, the demand of the non-Malays that the acquisition of Federation citizenship should be based solely on a person's birth in Malaya was acceded to.[41] This agreement again demonstrated the spirit of compromise among the Alliance leaders: it is clear that the adoption of *jus soli* citizenship with effect from Merdeka Day amounted to an important concession by the Malays, an essential part of the political and economic 'bargain' between them and the non-Malays.

It was also agreed that those who had become entitled under the 1948 Federation Agreement and the 1952 Ordinance and Nationality Enactments 'to be registered as citizens of the Federation as of right should not be deprived of their privilege to claim to be registered after Merdeka Day . . . provided that these persons claim to be registered within a period of one year from Merdeka Day'.[42] Persons who were born in the Federation before Merdeka Day and had been ordinarily resident therein for five of the preceding seven years, and persons who had been ordinarily resident in the Federation for eight out of the preceding twelve years, could apply for citizenship if they were over 18 years of age subject to certain conditions, including a Malay language test which, however, would be waived if they applied within one year after Merdeka Day.[43] All these provisions were liberal compared to the stringent citizenship paragraphs of the 1948 Federation Agreement.

Aside from the procedures concerning citizenship by operation of law and by registration, the other method of acquiring citizenship in independent Malaya was by naturalization. It was a further measure of the importance which citizenship played in the development of the Malayan nation that the acquisition of citizenship by naturalization was accompanied by the strictest safeguards:

It is proposed that no person of or over the age of 18 years shall be registered as a citizen until he has declared an oath that he absolutely and entirely renounces and abjures all loyalty to any country or state outside the Federation, and swears that he will be a true loyal and faithful citizen of the Federation, and will give due obedience to all lawfully constituted authorities in the Federation. Similarly, it is proposed that a certificate of naturalization shall not be granted to any person until he has taken an oath in this form.[44]

Thus in independent Malaya dual citizenship was made impossible, although, largely as a hangover from Malaya's colonial past, it was decided 'that in accordance with the position of the Federation within the Commonwealth every person who is a citizen of the Federation will enjoy by virtue of that citizenship the status of a Commonwealth citizen in common with the citizens of other Commonwealth countries'.[45]

The Alliance and the Achievement
of Independence

It has been shown that ever since the UMNO-MCA Alliance was formed in 1952, there had been problems in accommodating distinctive party and communal demands. These, of course, included Chinese demands such as those discussed above. On the other hand, Tunku Abdul Rahman was often criticized by more conservative UMNO members for appearing to be less than forthright on the preservation and promotion of Malay rights.[46] When the MIC joined the Alliance prior to the polls of 1955, communal problems within the Alliance were indeed accentuated.[47]

Yet, because of the overriding wish to achieve independence and to continue to represent the three major communities of Malaya, the fragile unity of the Alliance survived the communal dictates of its component parts. A clear example of political cooperation between UMNO and the MCA was the Alliance delegation to London in 1954 to demand not only federal elections in 1954 but also a workable elected majority in the Federal Legislative Council at the forthcoming federal elections. The delegation consisted of Tunku Abdul Rahman, Dato Abdul Razak (deputy president of UMNO) and T. H. Tan (executive secretary of the MCA). When the Colonial Office refused its request for a three-fifths majority in the proposed new Council, the Alliance ordered a boycott lasting three weeks of all Government councils and committees through-out the country: 'At least, 1,000 Malays and Chinese men and women obeyed and handed in their resignations from the bodies on which they were serving'.[48] In the Alliance's own words, 'The boycott was only called off after the High Commissioner [Sir Donald MacGillivray] had agreed to consult the majority party before filling five out of the Special Reserve of Seven Nominated Seats in the Federal Legislative Council'.[49]

The unity of the Alliance was enhanced by the need to maintain a solid front not only against overt political opponents including the IMP, the PMIP and Party Negara but also against the MCP which was still pursuing the objective of setting up a communist Malayan People's Republic. By 1955 the Alliance was demanding self-rule from the British because it believed that independence would undercut the prime objec-tive of the MCP: 'The people of Malaya will not allow the presence of militant Communism to impede the country's progress towards indepen-dence. Independence must and will come in spite of the Communists, and it is obviously to the interests of Britain to see that militant communism is effectively checked'.[50]

It has been argued that the British decided to support UMNO in working towards nationhood in Malaya as early as the period of setting up the 1948 Federation. Furthermore, although the MCP was 'composed almost entirely of Chinese',[51] even during the Emergency the majority of the Chinese population either remained neutral or tended gradually to support the British-encouraged MCA.[52] This meant that while the British decided to support the Alliance, the Malays and Chinese, together with the Indians in the MIC, were able to project a united political front which by and large was representative of the multiracial population of the Peninsula.

Yet it is debatable whether the Alliance would have maintained its unity for long had three further important factors not existed. One was that the armed militancy of the MCP was being effectively checked by 1955, enabling the British to state that the Emergency was no longer an impediment to Malaya's progress towards full self-government and independence. Secondly, while the main opponents of the Alliance, such as the IMP, Party Negara, the PMIP and the PPP, were either too closely identified with the conservatism of the British or were very communal and sectionalist,[53] the Alliance, besides having a broad inter-communal base, also increasingly portrayed itself as a nationalist party, as when it staged the 1954 boycott and in skilful negotiations with the British thereafter.

But undoubtedly the third factor in cementing the Alliance was its overwhelming success in the 1955 elections. What accounted for this success? In addition to the factors already discussed, 'The Road to Independence', the elaborate and well-considered 1955 election manifesto of the Alliance, undoubtedly played a great part in winning the support of the Malayan electorate. The manifesto gave clear expression to the meaning and value of national sovereignty:

We live in an age of political, social and economic revolution. During the last ten years after the Second World War, we have seen several of our neighbouring countries once subject to colonial rule emerging as free and independent nations and taking their rightful place among the free nations of the world.

This naturally is not without its impact on Malaya. And yet Malaya, which is of no less importance than those countries, is still under colonial rule. The Alliance, therefore, resolves to achieve early independence for Malaya by constitutional means . . . in order to ensure that there will not be any falling down in the standards of living and of government administration, and also to prepare the way so that, when the nation becomes free and fully self-governing, it will be able to develop rapidly to take its place with the other nations of the world as well as to flourish and bring greater benefit to the peoples of Malaya.[54]

As a whole, the Alliance manifesto offered to the people of Malaya a pragmatic programme covering all the major aspects of life in a nation of the modern world: forms of national and local government; administration; citizenship; national language; national security; financial and banking systems; land, agriculture and fishery policies; education; health and social welfare services; and a number of other minor matters.[55] As we have seen, the electorate gave the Alliance a mandate to pursue independence by delivering to it 51 out of the 52 elected federal seats in July 1955.

In fulfilment of its independence pledge, the leaders of the Alliance pressed the British for a more definite undertaking to grant full self-government to Malaya. This led to a Constitutional Conference in London between representatives of the Malay Rulers and the Alliance on the one hand and those of the British Government on the other from 18 January to 6 February 1956.[56] Tun V. T. Sambanthan, one of the Alliance leaders who became a federal Minister following the 1955 elections, years later recollected that a number of British officials urged the non-Malays to ensure that their communities were adequately represented at the London constitutional talks. He opposed such a highly communal suggestion, believing that the inter-communal mandate of the Alliance was the best under the circumstances for the people of Malaya.[57]

At all events, the Constitutional Conference achieved significant results. It is clear from its Report that Britain skilfully sought to avoid any drastic adverse effect upon her economic and strategic interests in Malaya even at this relatively late stage, but the main emphasis of the Conference, by far, was on the imminent achievement of Malayan independence.[58] Thus the Conference made arrangements for defence and internal security, financial and economic matters, and the public service of Malaya during a proposed interim period of internal self-government which was to be followed by the granting of complete independence. Regarding the national future of Malaya the Conference stated:

We have further agreed that, in view of the Malayan Delegation's desire that full self-government and independence within the Commonwealth should be proclaimed by August 1957, if possible, a constitution so providing shall be introduced at the earliest possible date consistent with the importance of the task before the Constitutional Commission and that every effort will be made Her Majesty's Government and the Federation Government to achieve this by the time proposed.[59]

Colonial rule, which was partly rescinded by the establishment of the 1948 Federation, was coming to an end at the formal constitutional level. The British Advisers appointed under the 1948 Federation Agreement were to be withdrawn; and in each state the Malayan Menteri Besar (Chief Minister) was to be the principal executive officer.[60] Pending the granting of full independence, the Federal Executive Council was to be further Malayanized with only three British members (the High Commissioner, the Chief Secretary and the Attorney-General) out of its 'not ... less than ten or more than twenty-four' members.[61] A cabinet system of government, initiated by the Member System of 1951, was now being further developed with a Federal Chief Minister increasingly playing the role of a future Prime Minister.

The Alliance manifesto had promised to work for the appointment of a Special Independent Commission to review the 1948 Agreement and 'to make a proper assessment of the fitness of the Federation for progressive constitutional reforms which will prepare the country for self-government and eventual indpendence'.[62] Furthermore, it should be noted that the multiracial leaders of the Alliance had themselves strongly advocated, through their 'Round Table' meetings in 1954[63] and in the 1955 election manifesto, a non-Malayan constitutional commission comprising members from British Commonwealth countries:

Only such a Commission will be able to exercise complete impartiality in the inquiry and in their recommendations. On the other hand, a Commission consisting of local people cannot be completely independent because they are bound to be influenced by local political and other interests. Another great advantage in appointing members of such a commission from Commonwealth countries is that these members will be able to give the Federation the benefit of the experience of their respective countries in their progress towards self-rule and independence.[64]

It was one of the rare instances of a country in the modern world entrusting the constitutional foundations of its future national life to the faculties of foreign legal and constitutional men rather than to the beliefs and aspirations of its own founding fathers.[65] Yet the Malayan leaders, in particular the Alliance leaders who held the mandate to bring the Peninsula to independence, perhaps not unwisely chose this course in order to avoid eroding the inter-communal goodwill and understanding which had been built up since the days of the CLC in 1949. Bickerings over constitutional matters could easily have marred the inter-communal unity which was crucial in demonstrating to the British 'the ability and integrity of the peoples of the Federation to govern themselves'.[66]

The process of attaining independence and thereby building a new nation necessitated a change from a system of sultanates to a constitutional, but by no means republican, modern government. Accordingly, the Malayan leaders faced the necessity of convincing the Malay Rulers that their position and prestige would be safeguarded. The non-Malays gradually came to recognize the necessity for accepting such a safeguard, inasmuch as it was impossible to visualize the total abolition of the nine traditional Malay governments and aristocracies in favour of a non-monarchical government for the whole Peninsula. However, it took much diplomacy and persuasion from the Malay political leaders and in particular from a member of the Malay aristocracy, Tunku Abdul Rahman himself, to convince the Rulers that there really would be such a safeguard in the future Malayan constitution. Even then, the language used to persuade the Rulers that traditional absolutist government had become anachronistic and must be replaced by one with 'the sovereignty of the general will' (to quote Rousseau), was suitably deferential:

In a Petition to Their Highnesses, the Alliance prayed for the appointment of a Special Independent Commission to inquire into constitutional reforms in the Federation. Their Highnesses were gracious enough to consider this Petition, and to express themselves as desirous of ensuring that the Constitution 'should meet with the needs and aspiration of the people and make the fullest provision for their well-being and happiness'.

...in considering the nature of constitutional reforms in the Federation, the Special Independent Commission should aim to create greater autonomy in the Malay States and in the Settlements, giving the Rulers the constitutional power in their States and over their subjects. To do this, the whole present Constitution should be reviewed without touching the special position of the Rulers as constitutional heads of their States.[67]

Subsequently, the Constitutional Commission Report provided that 'The position of a Ruler as Constitutional Monarch in his State would be much the same as that of the Yang di-Pertuan Besar in the Federation'.[68] This last office was an innovation.

As discussed earlier, the 1948 Federation Agreement in many important respects established the basic political and constitutional framework of Malaya. The 1957 Constitutional Commission recommended not only the retention of the Conference of Rulers but also the creation of a unique system of rotating constitutional monarchy. According to this, one of the nine Rulers would be elected by the Conference as the Supreme Head of the Federation with the title of Yang di-Pertuan Agong every five years according to a system of precedence among Their Highnesses. The Governors of Pulau Pinang and Melaka were excluded from election to the post of Yang di-Pertuan Agong, although they were obliged to attend all meetings of the Conference other than those convened for the purpose of such an election.[69]

The institution of the office of Yang di-Pertuan Agong was the culmination of the effort by the Malayan political leaders to persuade the Rulers that their position as constitutional rulers would be safeguarded.[70] The functions of the Yang di-Pertuan Agong were elaborate and in some respects similar to those of the constitutional monarch in Britain.

The Yang di-Pertuan Agong was the symbol of the unity of the country. High Commissioners from Commonwealth countries and Ambassadors or other diplomatic representatives from foreign countries were to be accredited to him. He was to be kept informed with regard to important public affairs and to make his views known to the Prime Minister. He was entitled to confer honours, and commissions and appointments were to be granted or made by him or in his name. Among his formal functions were to choose the Prime Minister, to open and dissolve Parliament as well as to give assent to bills passed by it, to receive visiting foreign Heads of State, and 'to grant pardons, reprieves and respites in respect of all offences which have been tried by court martial'.[71]

These functions of the Yang di-Pertuan Agong as finally approved and incorporated in the 1957 Constitution of the Federation of Malaya gave an institutional basis to the Constitution and at the same time helped to ensure that Malaya would develop as a nation with a parliamentary system of government.

As independence approached there was general agreement 'that the democratic form of Government based on Parliamentary Institutions is the form of Government best suited to Malaya'.[72] Following the Constitutional Commission's recommendation it was decided that there should be a bicameral Parliament consisting of a House of Representatives (Dewan Ra'ayat) as the Lower House and a Senate (Dewan Negara) as the Upper House.[73] The Federal Legislative Council to which elections were held in 1955 and the Federal Executive Council in which Malayan members with portfolios had sat since 1951 were to continue 'in existence until the 31 December 1959',[74] in anticipation of the next federal elections which were to take place in that year, but the adoption in principle of a bicameral legislature together with a Federal Cabinet as the executive branch (and also of an independent judiciary) contributed further to ensuring that independent Malaya would develop along basically parliamentary and non-violent constitutional lines.

Nationhood was on Malaya's doorstep. The Constitutional Commission Report, which included a draft of the Constitution of the Federation, was published in February 1957. It was thereafter examined by Her Majesty's Government and the Conference of Rulers together with the Federation Government; with a number of amendments, the Report and Constitutional Proposals were agreed upon. On 31 August 1957, as envisaged by the 1956 Constitutional Conference, Malaya became a fully self-governing and independent nation within the British Commonwealth. A nation was born.

Of course, the achievement of political independence did not mean the solution of all Malaya's problems of nation-building: Merdeka, the successful dismantling of a colonial system and the establishment in its place of a new nation were merely the beginning of a responsible and challenging national life for the people of Malaya. This was understood outside Malaya, too: joining to welcome the coming Merdeka Day, no less than eighty organizations in different parts of Indonesia cooperated to prepare special programmes but, having experienced the problems as well as the blessings of being independent for twelve years, most of the Indonesians felt constrained to advise their Malayan brethren in the following vein:

Kemerdekaan Malaya sebagaimana kemerdekaan negara-negara lain pasti menimbulkan pekerdjaan-pekerdjaan dan beban-beban baru keatas pundak rakyat.
Kemerdekaan Malaya menimbulkan konsekwensi baru jang tiada sedikit meng-
handaki tjutjuran keringat dan sinsingan lengan badju dimasa depan. Perkataan
kemerdekaan bukan lah perkataan keramat jang langsung dapat melahirkan
sjurga dunia keatas bumi Malaya Merdeka; malah di meminta pengorbanan jang
libih banjak lagi. Perkataan kemerdekaan tidak bisa bekerdja sebagai lampu
wasiat Aladdin.[75]

Indonesia had encountered formidable and sometimes bitter challenges
since declaring independence from the Dutch in 1945.[76]

At the same time, Malayans in Britain also held an elaborate
Convention in London to celebrate and ponder about Merdeka and the
future of their country. The Malayan feeling and inter-communal sense
of goodwill were depicted by the chairman of the planning committee in
his closing address to the five-day Convention: 'We Malayans are very
reasonable people and there is a great amount of goodwill amongst us,
and I sincerely believe that with proper guidance with honest unselfish
and trusted leadership a great Malayan nation would emerge, a nation
which, whatever our culture or creed or racial origin, we shall all be
proud to belong to.'[77] The Convention was well-attended by Malayans
of different ethnic origins and when the chairman concluded by saying,
'many of us must have felt the sense of unity and purpose and mutual
understanding amongst us that we have become more Malayan than we
have been before',[78] he was expressing what millions of his fellow-
countrymen were experiencing in their newly-independent Federation
of Malaya. The Malayans in Britain were thousands of miles away from
home, but they nonetheless welcomed Merdeka with fervour, political
and intellectual hopes, and inter-communal feelings of goodwill and
harmony.

The problems encountered by Malaya on the road to independence
were well known. Not unnaturally, as the new Malayan nation began its
sovereign existence, doubts and caution were expressed regarding its
future. While neighbours in Indonesia concluded that 'Malaya berdjuang
untuk kemerdekaan, menurut landasan evolusi, melalui beberapa fase,
selaku hamparan pengurbanan keberanian, kedjudjuran, kelitjinan ber-
diplomasi dan kesabaran jang luar biasa'[79] and 'menghadapi penduduk
warga negara baru berasal kebangsaan Tionghoa jang menganut aliran
kiri, jang djumlahnja hampir mendekati separoh djumlah penduduk',[80]
Rupert Emerson, who knew both Indonesia and Malaya in the pre-war
colonial days, could say:

It is a hazardous venture on which Malaya is embarking. At a time when the
nation-state remains the basic model for political organization, statehood comes

to a place who can by no stretch of the imagination be regarded as now constituting a nation. That they may in due course become a nation, feeling themselves one as against the rest of the world, is surely a possibility not to be rejected in advance, but for present purposes they figure rather in the contrary role of being a perfect example of the plural society.[81]

Emerson, of course, was adopting a perfectionist attitude towards the concept of the nation.[82] As this study has thus far sought to demonstrate, the complex process of attaining independence had led to the establishment of a nation, at any rate at the formal level, in Malaya. Emerson himself went on to concede that the sinews of nationhood were in effect being established in Malaya and he emphasized that the success of the new nation would depend largely on a political equation whereby 'The Malays must modify their sense that they are the sole rightful inhabitants of the country as the Chinese must be prepared to share their economic predominance.'[83]

So far, in this discussion, attention has been focused on political issues but as Emerson's statement clearly implies, economic questions were no less important as they were also part of the larger problem of the relationship between Malays and non-Malays. The immediate post-independence period therefore saw the Alliance Government attempting to resolve problems of rural poverty and, at the same time, maintain communal harmony.

Economic Planning and Rural Poverty

It is not difficult to establish that an economic problem contributed to the rise of Malay nationalism in 1946. When the Malays feared the loss of their birthright because of the Malayan Union proposals, it needs to be remembered that land, which was the one stable economic anchorage of the Malays and which had been traditionally vested in their Rulers to administer and adjudicate, was being taken over by the British. It was uncompromisingly provided that 'all assets of the Governments of the Federated Malay States and of any Malay State will, after the appointed day, be transferred to the Government of the Malayan Union'.[84] It was not only because 'semua hartabanda tiap-tiap negeri Melayu, melainkan milek peribadi Raja-Raja, terserah kepada kerajaan pusat'[85] but also because 'hak-hak istemewa Melayu telah terhapus'[86] that the Malays then rose with such patriotic fervour that the Malayan Union had ultimately to be abandoned. To the Malays, the abrogation of their special rights which had been recognized by the metropolitan power since the days of British intervention was not only a political but, even more, an economic threat.

The fear of the Malays that the loss of their traditional rights, including special rights over land ownership, would mean the submergence of their community *vis-a-vis* the others in their country can best be understood by reference to the nature of the Malayan economy as a whole. As this economy expanded during the first four decades of the twentieth century, the Malays remained largely in the rural sector, engaged in subsistence farming. At the same time, the other major communities, the Chinese and the Indians, became associated with the expansion of the mercantile, plantation and mining sectors.[87] These trends continued after 1946, bringing in their train not only economic but also social and political consequences. The first major survey of the Malayan economy in the post-war years, made by a Mission from the International Bank for Reconstruction and Development (IBRD), stated in 1954:

Malaya is now the world's largest producer of tin and is second only to Indonesia in the output of natural rubber. The extent to which the economy is specialized on these two commodities may be indicated by the fact that in 1953 their export value accounted directly for a fifth of the national income. Of the two, rubber is of much the greater importance to the economy; it occupies about 65 per cent of the entire cultivated area of Malaya and contributes about 60 per cent of domestic earnings.[88]

The *IBRD Mission Report* went on to point out that 'Next in importance to rubber in terms of area is rice cultivation. Rice is grown on almost 850,000 acres or about 15 per cent of the total cultivated area'.[89] The significant point to remember, however, is that whereas rubber and tin exports accounted for $898 million and $351 million respectively in 1953, rice was a product wholly for domestic consumption which brought meagre economic returns and had no export potentiality.[90] Furthermore, whilst the Chinese and Indians were prominent in more lucrative activities such as rubber cultivation, mining, manufacturing, and commercial and financial undertakings, the Malays had a preponderant role in rice cultivation in which sector many farmers 'live on incomes that are equal to one half or even less than the incomes of rubber farmers and vegetable farmers'.[91]

Following the immediate tasks of rehabilitation and reconstruction after the Second World War, the Federation Government embarked on social and economic planning for Malaya from 1950 onwards. In Malaya's First Development Plan, it was stated that 'the demands of the people for social services and social justice must somehow be met' and the text went on to explain that the second underlying feature of the Plan lay in its emphasis on rural development because it was 'necessary that the producers in the rural areas should enjoy a greater share of the proceeds of their labour than they obtain at present'.[92] This first Plan covered the

period 1950–5 and, indicative of the political temperament of the Emergency years, it was argued 'that the battle against illiteracy, poverty and
all those conditions of social discontent on which communism feeds can
be won ultimately only by a policy aimed at their removal and planned
and carried out in co-operation with the aspirations of the people'.[93]

   The First Development Plan led to two successive Malayan Five-Year
Plans which together covered the decade 1956 to 1965.[94] The results of
planning showed clearly in increases in national output and in economic
growth. Of the First Malayan Five-Year Plan (1956–60), for instance, it
was proudly reported:

Malaya achieved much during those five years. Actual public investment was
nearly double that of the years 1951–1955. Private investment also far exceeded
earlier levels. Along with higher investment, the real output of the economy
increased by about 20 per cent, or at an average annual rate of nearly 3¾ per cent,
compared with an estimated population increase rate of a little over 3 per cent a
year.[95]

Under the Second Five-Year Plan (1961–5), agencies for implementing
various schemes were strengthened or newly established: the National
Development Planning Committee with its secretariat the Economic
Planning Unit in the Prime Minister's Department; the National Operations Room to coordinate development undertakings in military style;
and Rural Development Committees at State, district and kampung
levels.[96] The two Malayan Five-Year Plans were largely the outcome of
the Alliance's own pledge in the 1955 elections to develop the Malayan
economy and to improve the standards of living of the people, in particular those in the rural areas.[97]

   However, despite the efforts at economic planning and development
dating from 1950, and despite the achievement of political independence,
the social and economic discrepancies between the rural and the urban
sectors of the economy had remained substantially unsolved. On the eve
of Malayan independence it was pointed out:

More than half of the rubber and padi farmers do not own the land they work
on. They have to pay rent. This rent takes away between one third and a half of
what they produce. Therefore allowing for costs involved in farm production we
see that these farmers are living on less than half the value of what they produce.
   Frequently, Malay workers on rubber estates are contract workers and their
wage rates are well below the official rates agreed to by the employers and the
trade unions.
   Fishermen very often do not own their boats and nets and therefore have to
pay heavy charges for hire of the equipment. In general, Malay farmers, estate
workers and fishermen earn between $50 and $100 per month.[98]

Apart from landlordism, it was also obvious that the farmers were greatly exploited by money-lenders and middlemen of not only Chinese and Indian but also Malay origin. The plight of the helpless farmer was graphically described in the following:

It very often happens that the merchants who buy the farmers' produce are in a strong economic position. They arrange their business so that farmers are practically compelled to sell to them or not to sell at all. In other words they create a buyers' monopoly. They encourage the farmer to borrow money from them and once he is indebted to them he is in no position to bargain with them.

The farmer must use lorries. The lorries usually belong to the merchant. So the farmer is not able to take his pineapples or coconuts straight to the market where he could get a good price. He has to sell to a merchant who pays him a low price and who takes it in his lorry to the market and sells it at a good profit. There is evidence that some merchants do not weigh or measure the farmer's produce properly. Because of his low income and because of his indebtedness, the farmer may find that finally he has to sell his land to the merchant. Then the merchant becomes a landlord in addition to being a merchant.[99]

In order to remedy the poverty and plight of Malayan farmers it was suggested that the Federation Government should improve its planning system which had thus far been urban-biased by embarking on more realistic and meaningful rural development which would amount to a 'planned process which uses any form of action or communication designed to effect the environment, techniques, institutions and minds of the rural peoples in such a manner as to raise their level of living and improve their way of life'.[100]

It was in recognition of the lack of economic development and equitable benefit among the mainly rural Malays that as early as 1950 the Rural Industrial Development Authority (RIDA) was set up with the express purpose of encouraging Malay participation in commerce and industry by extending loans, forming bus and other transportation services, setting up processing factories, and offering technical, management and marketing assistance to small Malay enterprises.[101] In 1956 the Federal Land Development Authority, at first known as FLDA but later as FELDA was also set up to settle or resettle and provide employment for farmers who were landless or, due to fragmentation, had insufficient land to meet their needs and were consequently underemployed. As with RIDA, the schemes initiated by FELDA were expected to make a contribution to the economic growth of Malaya in the long run.[102]

Yet, despite the steps taken to improve the farmers' lot, rural progress remained rare. Even when Malaysia was about to be inaugurated in 1963, the extent of the problem was implied officially in these words: 'If we can open up new land fast enough to absorb the growing rural population, we should be making a strong start at removing rural poverty, for there will not be growing numbers pressing on a fixed amount of land. We seek also to provide additional land for present farmers whose farms are too small'.[103] More pregnant and disturbing in terms of the development of national unity in Malaya, a second IBRD Report in 1963 pointed out:

Ethnic identification is still fairly strong, not only socially and culturally but also in economic activity. Malays predominate in rice farming and most other non-export agriculture. They are also numerous in the civil service. The Chinese, as well as Indians, are largely concentrated in commerce, finance and industry, in the working force of the estates and mines, and in service activities.[104]

Thus, even as the 1960s unfolded, Malaya's economic problems had by no means been solved.

Notwithstanding the political achievement of independence and the growth engendered by the three economic Plans, the economic disparities among Malaya's multiracial population, particularly that between the Malays and the non-Malays (who in geographical location were mainly rural and urban respectively) had remained acute. In short, by the beginning of the 1960s, a fair fulfilment of the political and economic 'bargain' between the Malays and the non-Malays was still a long way off. The authors of the second IBRD Report conceded that Malaya appeared to be politically stable but, doubtless having in mind the matter of 'ethnic identification', they proceeded to add, 'Stiffer tests of this inter-community stability may be ahead as Malaya enters more uncertain economic and political waters'.[105]

The Socio-economic and Political Bargain and Communal Harmony

Consistent with the provisions made earlier, the Alliance Government proceeded, immediately after independence, to Malayanize the public services. The Alliance had promised to replace expatriate (mostly British) officers with Malayans speedily, at the same time maintaining a high standard of efficiency in the services. While not forgetting the other grades and divisions, the Alliance pledged, 'We consider that a scheme of recruitment and training should be devised so that within 10 years at least 80% of the posts in Division I should be filled by Malayans'.[106] By the beginning of the 1960s, however, almost all the responsible, high public service positions had already been filled by Malayans.[107] Malayanization assisted markedly in the maintenance and promotion of political stability as the nation embarked on its new independent course. At the same time, a sound system of public services was established.

It was part of the constitutional arrangements that the Federal Legislative Council elected in 1955 would continue to function until 1959 when the people would again go to the polls to elect their MPs to the new Dewan Ra'ayat (House of Representatives) of the bicameral Parliament. Whereas the campaigns for the 1955 general elections highlighted the politics of achieving independence, the August 1959 parliamentary poll showed how the political leaders conceived and sought to implement their ideological beliefs for a country which had become their very own. Perhaps the outstanding feature of the 1959 elections was the further development of the democratic political machinery. The 52 constituencies of 1955 were doubled to 104 parliamentary seats in 1959. Electioneering became more sophisticated.

A crop of political parties came forward to offer their manifestos to the electors; the electorate was now not only larger but also more communally representative: as against the 1,280,000 of 1955, the electorate of 1959 totalled 2,177,000; the racial composition of the 1955 electorate had been estimated as 84 per cent Malays, 11 per cent Chinese, and 5 per cent Indian, while that of 1959 was 'estimated to contain over 750,000 Chinese as compared with under 150,000 in 1955 . . . approximately 57 per cent of the increased electorate [was] Malay, 36 per cent Chinese and 7 per cent Indian'.[108] The parties, with the numbers of seats won in brackets, were the Alliance (74), the PMIP (13), the Socialist Front which comprised the Labour Party and Partai Rakyat (8), the People's Progressive Party or PPP (4), the Party Negara (1), and the Malayan Party (1). These parties ranged across the political spectrum but communalism and religion still featured prominently with some of them, especially in the platforms of Party Negara (Malay), the PMIP (Malay), and the PPP (Chinese and Indians). The PMIP's long-term objective was the establishment of a theocratic state in Malaya, based on the tenets of Islam.[109]

Intra-party squabbles and factionalism, not uncommon in more established systems of party politics, surfaced before and during the campaign period;[110] and in general the functional dynamics of politics came into extensive play for the first time.

As we have seen, the political development of Malaya had been a process of evolution rather than revolution; it is also obvious that political maturity was being attained through the adoption and increasingly extensive practice of party politics. The 1955 and 1959 general elections provided wide opportunities to institutionalize that system of party politics:

Prior to the introduction of elections, most political activity in Malaya was limited to that of making representations to the government or organizing public demonstrations in protest over various issues. Practically any person who espoused a political cause could claim to be a political leader, since leadership in some cases required little more than the ability to attract the attention of the public or, perhaps more correctly, to attract the attention of the press. As soon as elections became the primary vehicle to political success and power, political leadership was put to the new task of organizing popular support from diverse and often competing narrow interest groups.... The creation of dependable majorities becomes the overriding consideration of all politics once it becomes established that elections are to be the sole avenue to political power.[111]

*   *   *

The achievement of political independence in Malaya was accomplished side by side with the retention of special Malay rights. The position of the Rulers was not only safeguarded but also enhanced by the creation of the office of Yang di-Pertuan Agong to which they could aspire. Importantly, the Yang di-Pertuan Agong became the custodian of Malay rights. Article 153 (2) of the 1957 Federation of Malaya Constitution stated unequivocally:

Notwithstanding anything in this constitution, but subject to the provisions of Article 40 and of this Article, the Yang di-Pertuan Agong shall exercise his functions under this Constitution and federal law in such manner as may be necessary to safeguard the special position of the Malays and to ensure the reservation for Malays of such proportion as he may deem reasonable to positions in the public service (other than the public service of a State) and of scholarships, exhibitions and other similar educational or training privileges or special facilities given or accorded by the Federal Government and, when any permit or licence for the operation of any trade or business is required by federal law, then, subject to the provisions of that law and this Article, of such permits and licences.[112]

(Article 40 stipulated that the Yang di-Pertuan Agong must act on Ministerial advice.)

In addition, Land Reservations were retained for the Malays in independent Malaya. Another agreement which gave the Malays precedence over the non-Malays was that 'Islam is the religion of the Federation; but other religions may be practised in peace and harmony in any part of the Federation'.[113] It was further agreed in Article 11(4) of the Constitution that 'State law may control or restrict the propagation of any religious doctrine or belief among persons professing the Muslim religion'. The Federation of Malaya was thus peculiar in that it took a step seldom officially promoted by the constitutions of modern nations, namely the adoption of a state or national religion.

The retention and constitutional sanctioning of special Malay rights ensured that political power in Malaya would be increasingly Malay-based. In addition to the enactment of 'the special position of the Malays'

in the 1957 Federation Constitution, it should also be borne in mind that
in the first federal elections in 1955, 84 per cent of the registered electorate
were Malays compared to only 11 per cent Chinese and less than 5 per
cent Indians. As one contemporary writer noted, 'The fact is, the Alliance
walk-over was a Malay rather than a Malayan victory'.[114] In the 1959
elections, as we have seen, only about 57 per cent of the increased
electorate were Malay, while 36 per cent were Chinese and 7 per cent
Indian. Furthermore,

It was the UMNO leadership who realized communal compromises were necessary to achieve independence, and the party workers who have explained the
position, with varying honesty, to the *kampong* (village) Malays. UMNO now
commands the support of the vast majority of the Malays, and its political
dominance assures for the Alliance its leading position in the Federal and state
governments.[115]

The political dominance of UMNO continued well into the future
despite the electoral victory of the PMIP in Kelantan and Trengganu in
1959. In the mid-1960s Milne affirmed, 'Of the three Alliance communal
parties–the United Malays' National Organization (UMNO), the
Malayan Chinese Association (MCA), and the Malayan Indian Congress
(MIC)–UMNO is the strongest and the MIC clearly the weakest'.[116]
     It can be argued that the political ascendancy accorded the Malays in
the public service, in the elections of 1955 and 1959, and in the 1957
Constitution was only part of the political and economic 'bargain' made
in the process of achieving Malayan nationhood. To make this clearer: the
other part of that 'bargain' was that while the Malays were accorded a
special position of advantage in order to enable them to improve and
attain economic and social parity with the non-Malays, the latter were
progressively granted significant concessions in the forms of easier access
to Malayan citizenship, and hence political life, as already recounted;
easier access to the federal public service, in spite of the four-to-one ratio
between recruitment of Malays and non-Malays; the freedom to profess
and practise religions other than Islam; and the opportunity to preserve
various cultural values, including the freedom to set up and maintain
educational institutions other than those in which the medium of instruction was the national language (Malay).[117] Above all, in the course
of fulfilling the essence of that 'bargain', that is to say the uplifting of the
economic and social condition of the Malays, 'The Chinese were to
continue to play their dominant role in business, free from the hindrances
or persecution to which they had been subjected in some other Southeast
Asian countries'.[118]
     The political and economic 'bargain' between the Malays and the non-

Malays involved not simply communal demands but, equally important, the need to foster inter-communal peace and understanding as the people undertook the overriding mission of establishing a Malayan nation. Thus, despite the communal priorities which have invariably and at times unduly occupied the attention of scholars writing on post-war Malaya, it should be emphasized that the years from 1948 to 1957 witnessed a period of cooperation among the multiracial leaders of Malaya in their common endeavour to build a Malayan nation for themselves and their posterity. Behind the 1959 general elections and the social and economic policies implemented after independence was the wish to elect a government as representative as possible of the various ethnic groups and to fulfil an important part of the inter-communal 'bargain', namely to assist the Malays in attaining parity with the non-Malays.

Throughout the period there were clear instances of give-and-take among the leaders. In spite of the writing of 'the special position of the Malays' into the 1957 Federation Constitution, Tunku Abdul Rahman who led the independence campaign could say, 'the Malays are prepared within reason to share their rights with others who owe loyalty to this country'. He went on to remind the Malays, 'No country in the world has won independence without sacrifices by the people. I have no doubt that you are prepared to make sacrifices and to live up to your reputation of tolerance, hospitality and courtesy'.[119]

It was the abiding wish on the part of the multiracial Malayan leaders of the period to arrive at amicable compromise solutions, over and above sectionalist or racialist demands, which ensured the absence of tragic communal riots, the pacific nature of the demands for self-rule, and the rather smooth transition from British rule to Malayan independence. Intrinsically, the same basic desire to preserve and promote inter-communal national cohesion dictated the need for the political and economic 'bargain' between the Malays and the non-Malays.

Yet it was also obvious that the satisfactory fulfilment of that 'bargain' was a long way ahead. After independence, the signing of a treaty of External Defence and Mutual Assistance between Malaya and Britain in October 1957 had helped to ensure the security of the new nation;[120] and Malaya as an independent country had indeed instituted its own policy and priorities in foreign affairs.[121] But the delicate tasks of maintaining inter-communal harmony and further promoting a sense of common Malayan identity among the diverse people of the Peninsula continued to present formidable problems.

Nearly two years after independence, the Prime Minister of the Federation, depicted his hopes and his awareness of what the country could do when he said:

It is my firm conviction that if we in Malaya continue to go forward steadily on these lines then our country and our people will have every reason to be confident of the future of our young nation. Given a good and stable Government, and a Government which stands for the real progress and happiness of the people, the Federation can expect a period of continued progress and prosperity.[122]

After the careful, difficult compromises, after the achievement of independence and amid the plans for economic development, Malayan leaders were still profoundly concerned with the need to mould their people into a more integrated nation. It was in this context that the proposal to form Malaysia emerged in 1961.

1. Awang Had bin Salleh, 'Malay Teacher Training in British Malaya (1878–1941): A General Survey' (B.Ed. Thesis (Post-Graduate), University of Malaya, Kuala Lumpur, 1967), pp. 29–30.

2. Ibid., p. 194.

3. Federation of Malaya, *Report of the Committee to Consider the Problem of Malay Education* (hereinafter referred to as the *Barnes Report*), Kuala Lumpur, 1951, ch. 1, para. 14. See also Malayan Union Government, *Annual Report on Education in the Malayan Union for 1947*, Kuala Lumpur, 1948, pp. 21–6.

4. Malaysia, *Education in Malaysia*, Kuala Lumpur, 1968, p. 6. From the middle of the nineteenth century, Catholic, Methodist and Church of England schools, mostly using English as the medium of instruction, were established in the main towns of Malaya.

5. Malayan Union Government, *Council Paper, No. 53 of 1946*, Kuala Lumpur, 1946, paras. 1–3.

6. Federation of Malaya, *The Federation of Malay Agreement 1948*, Kuala Lumpur, 1948, Second Schedule, Item 79, col. 1.

7. Federation of Malaya, *Annual Report on Education for 1949*, Kuala Lumpur, 1950, p. 29.

8. *Barnes Report*, ch. 1, para. 5.

9. Ibid., ch. 2, para. 4.

10. Ibid., chs. 4 and 12, paras. 2–4.

11. Ibid., ch. 12, para. 5.

12. Ibid.

13. V. Purcell, 'The Crisis in Malayan Education', *Pacific Affairs*, 26, No. 1, 1953, p. 71.

14. The former was widely involved in institutions of higher learning in Taiwan, while the latter was a United Nations official.

15. Federation of Malaya, *Chinese Schools and the Education of Chinese Malayans. The Report of a Mission Invited by the Federation Government to Study the Problem of Education of Chinese in Malaya* (hereinafter referred to as the *Fenn-Wu Report*), Kuala Lumpur, 1951, ch. 1, para. 6.

16. Ibid., ch. 2, para. 6. In its enquiries, the Fenn-Wu Mission encountered pressures 'from Chinese in the non-communist and communist camps'. The former were apprehensive that Chinese language and culture might be threatened with extinction, while the latter, representing the MCP, were interested in seeing that the people of Malaya were not united in a non-communist political system. Interview with Wu Teh-yau, who was Professor of Political Science, University of Singapore, at the time, Singapore, October 1973.

17. V. Purcell, 'The Crisis in Malayan Education', p. 73.

18. Chan Heng Chee, 'The Malayan Chinese Association' (M.A. Thesis, University of Singapore, 1965), p. 59.

19. Means, *Malaysian Politics*, London, 1970, p. 135.

20. 'Alliance Manifesto for Federal Elections', 1955 (?). TCLP.

21. Federation of Malaya, *Report of the Education Committee 1956* (hereinafter referred to as *Razak Education Report*), Kuala Lumpur, 1956, para. 1.

22. F. Wong Hoy Kee and Ee Tiang Hong, *Education in Malaysia*, Singapore, 1971, p. 58, wrote of the *Razak Education Report*, 'The idea of "national schools" as advocated by the Barnes Commission [*sic*] was abandoned, and children would continue to receive their primary education in separate vernacular schools'.

23. *Razak Education Report*, para. 119.

24. Ibid., para. 183(i).

25. *Straits Times*, 1 September 1956.

26. Means, op. cit., p. 201.

27. See *Straits Times*, 24 November 1957.

28. Federation of Malaya, *Report of the Education Review Committee 1960* (hereinafter referred to as *Rahman Talib Education Report*), Kuala Lumpur, 1960. See also C. H. Enloe, *Multi-Ethnic Politics: The Case of Malaysia*, Berkeley, 1970, chs. 2 and 3.

29. *Rahman Talib Education Report*, para. 13.

30. Ibid., para. 371(c).

31. Ibid., para. 371(f).

32. Ibid., para. 42(a) and (b).

33. M. F. Clark, 'The Malayan Alliance and its Accommodation of Communal Pressures, 1952–1962' (M.A. Thesis, University of Malaya, 1964), p. 47.

34. Means, op. cit., p. 201.

35. Ibid.

36. Ratnam, op. cit., p. 164.

37. Federation of Malaya, *Report of the Federation of Malaya Constitutional Commission* (hereafter referred to as *Constitutional Commission Report*), Kuala Lumpur, 1957, para. 36.

38. Ibid.

39. Federation of Malaya, *Federation of Malaya Constitutional Proposals 1957* (hereafter referred to as *Constitutional Proposals*), Kuala Lumpur, 1957, para. 15.

40. *Constitutional Commission Report*, para. 38.

41. In 1962, a modification was enacted which required that at least one parent must be ordinarily resident in the Federation at the time of the child's birth. Federation of Malaya, *Constitution (Amendment) Act 1962*, Kuala Lumpur, 1962. It was further stipulated that the child of a foreign diplomat or of an enemy alien did not qualify.

42. *Constitutional Proposals*, para. 6.

43. *Constitutional Commission Report*, paras. 41 and 42.

44. *Constitutional Proposals*, para. 10.

45. Ibid., para. 14.

46. See H. Miller, *Prince and Premier*, London, 1959, pp. 169–71, 216–17.

47. See Tan Siew Sin, *The National Language*, Department of Information, Kuala Lumpur (1967?), p. 13. See also MCA, *Memorandum on Chinese Education in the Federation of Malaya*, Kuala Lumpur, 1954. On the MIC, see S. Arasaratnam, 'Political Attitudes and Organization among Malayan Indians 1945–1955', *Jernal Sejarah*, 10, 1971/72, pp. 1–6.

48. H. Miller, *A Short History of Malaysia*, New York, 1966, p. 191.

49. 'The Road to Independence' (1955). Mimeographed. TCLP.

50. Ibid.

51. L. W. Pye, *Guerrilla Communism in Malaya*, Princeton, N. J., 1956.

52. See Soh Eng Lim 'Tan Cheng Lock: His Leadership of the Malayan Chinese', *JSEAH*, 1, No. 1, March 1960, pp. 44–7.

53. Dato Onn who founded and led the IMP and Party Negara, apart from holding the post of Member for Home Affairs, has been thought to have 'had ambitions to become the Malay Deputy to the High Commissioner and resented the Rulers' rejection of his plans'. R. Allen, *Malaysia: Prospect and Retrospect*, London, 1968, p. 104.

54. 'The Road to Independence', *TCLP*.

55. Ibid.

56. *Report of the Federation of Malaya Constitutional Conference Held in London in January and February, 1956* (hereinafter referred to as *Constitutional Conference Report*), Kuala Lumpur, 1956.

57. Interview with the present writer, Kuala Lumpur, April 1973. Tun Sambanthan was president of the MIC from 1955 to 1973. He died in 1979.

58. It was because Britain amply succeeded in providing for the future of her economic and strategic interests in Malaya that where the granting of full independence was concerned, 'the Tunku and other ministers went to London in January 1956 expecting some hard bargaining on the issue. To their surprise and gratification their demand was immediately met'. J. M. Gullick, *Malaya*, London, 1964, p. 120.

59. *Constitutional Conference Report*, para. 75.

60. Ibid., paras. 70–2.

61. Ibid., Appendix E, Revised Clause 23(2)(a).

62. 'The Road to Independence', *TCLP*.

63. The 'Round Table' meetings were conducted between the UMNO and MCA leaders with the basic aim of arriving at Sino-Malay agreement on social, economic and political issues while working for full self-government and independence. Minutes of the meetings on 17 and 28 January, and 9 February 1954. *TCLP*.

64. 'The Road to Independence', *TCLP*. Tun Sambanthan confirmed these reasons for appointing the non-Malayan Constitutional Commission in an interview with the present writer, Genting Highlands, March 1974.

65. When the Constitutional Commission was finally approved by Her Majesty the Queen and the Conference of Rulers in March 1956, it comprised Lord Reid (a Lord of Appeal in Ordinary, and chairman of the Commission) and Sir Ivor Jennings (a noted constitutional lawyer) of Britain; Sir William McKell (a former Governor-General) of Australia; Mr B. Malik (a former Chief Justice of the Allahabad High Court) of India; and Mr Justice Abdul Hamid of Pakistan. A member was nominated by the Canadian Government but he had to withdraw at the last moment on medical grounds. *Constitutional Commission Report*, para. 2.

66. 'The Road to Independence', *TCLP*.

67. Tunku Abdul Rahman, 'The Position of the Rulers and Constitutional Reforms', 17 March 1955. Mimeographed. *TCLP*.

68. *Constitutional Commission Report*, para. 179.

69. Ibid., p. 59.

70. It was initially recommended that the Supreme Head of the Federation be called the 'Yang di-Pertuan Besar' but, to avoid confusion with the Head of State of Negri Sembilan who bore the same title, he was subsequently designated 'Yang di-Pertuan Agong'. See *Constitutional Proposals*, para. 15.

71. *Constitutional Commission Report*, para. 58; and *Constitutional Proposals*, para. 19. For the functions of the constitutional monarch in Britain, see Sir Ivor Jennings, *Cabinet Government*, London, 1959.

72. Tunku Abdul Rahman, 'Form of Government', 21 March 1955. Mimeographed. *TCLP.*

73. *Constitutional Commission Report*, ch. IV; and *Constitutional Proposals*, paras. 15–23.

74. *Constitutional Proposals*, para. 22.

75. Menteri Penerangan Republik Indonesia, 'Proklamasi Kemerdekaan Melahirkan Disiplin Bernegara', Panitia Pusat, *Menjambut Malaya Merdeka* [n.p.], Djakarta, 1957, p. 7. 'The independence of Malaya like that of other nations is certain to lay new tasks and burdens on the people's shoulders. The independence of Malaya brings about new consequences which will, in no small way, require sweat and the rolling-up of sleeves in the future. "Independence" is not a supernatural word which can immediately bring earthly bliss to Malaya Merdeka; rather it calls for more sacrifice. The word "independence" cannot function like Alladin's lamp.' All translations from Indonesian into English are by the present writer.

76. For good treatments of the Indonesian nationalist struggle, see G. M. Kahin, *Nationalism and Revolution in Indonesia*, Ithaca, N.Y., 1952; Sartono Kartodirdjo, 'Kolonialisme dan Nasionalisme di Indonesia Abad XIX–XX', *Lembaran Sedjarah*, No. 1, Jogjakarta, December 1967; and Suwondo, 'Sedjarah Pergerakan Nasional', Himpunan Mahasiswa Mesin, Universitas Trisakti, Djakarta [n.d.]. Mimeographed.

77. Ibrahim Manan, 'Chairman's Address at the Closing of the Merdeka Convention', *Merdeka Convention: Papers and Documents* (hereinafter referred to as *Merdeka Convention Papers*), London, 1957. Mimeographed.

78. Ibid.

79. Garieb A. Raouf, 'Menjongsong Kemerdekaan Malaya', *Menjambut Malaya Merdeka*, p. 26. 'Malaya struggled for independence, along an evolutionary line, through a number of stages, giving a demonstration of selfless bravery, sincerity, diplomatic acumen, and extraordinary patience'.

80. E. Z. Muttaqien, 'Mensjukuri Kemerdekaan Malaya', ibid., p. 16, 'facing new citizens of Chinese origin with leftist leanings, who number nearly half the total population'.

81. Rupert Emerson in his Foreword to F. H. H. King, *The New Malayan Nation: A Study of Communalism and Nationalism*, New York, 1957, p. v. See also R. Emerson, *Malaysia: A Study in Direct and Indirect Rule*, Kuala Lumpur, 1964.

82. See his *From Empire to Nation*, Cambridge, Mass., 1967, in which the case is repeatedly and admirably illustrated that nations have usually been first and foremost proclaimed as independent at the formal level—quite often at the stroke of midnight—and only subsequent to the proclamations do they resolutely endeavour to fill the lasting needs of their societies or people for stability and general well-being.

83. Emerson in King, op. cit., p. ix.

84. Great Britain, *Malayan Union and Singapore: Summary of Proposed Constitutional Arrangements*, London, 1946, para. 12(a) and (d). Only 'the personal residences or estates of any Sultan,' or . . . any buildings or lands which are used for the purposes of Muhammadan religion or properties pertaining to the endowment of Muhammadan religious institutions' were exempted from the transfer of Malaya's assets to British control.

85. Anwar Abdullah, *Dato Onn: Riwayat Hidup*, Petaling Jaya, 1971, p. 139. ' . . . all the properties of every Malay state, except the personal possessions of the Rulers, were surrendered to the central government'.

86. Ibid., 'Special Malay rights had been abrogated'.

87. T. H. Silcock, *The Economy of Malaya*, Singapore, 1963, pp. 1–2, classified Malaya's economy into (i) subsistence, (ii) mercantile, and (iii) plantation and mining sectors. See also Lim Chong-Yah, *Economic Development of Modern Malaya*, Kuala Lumpur, 1967, pt. I.

88. Government of Singapore, *The Economic Development of Malaya: Report of a Mission organized by the International Bank for Reconstruction and Development at the request of the Governments of the Federation of Malaya, the Crown Colony of Singapore and the United Kingdom* (hereinafter referred to as *IBRD Mission Report*), Singapore, 1955, p. 9. Malaya overtook Indonesia to become the largest producer of natural rubber in 1959.

89. *IBRD Mission Report*, p. 10.

90. Ibid., p. 16. Unless otherwise stated, all values quoted are in Malayan dollars.

91. Ungku A. Aziz, 'The Causes of Poverty in Malayan Agriculture' in Lim Tay Boh (ed.), *Problems of the Malayan Economy*, Singapore, 1960, p. 22. See also *IBRD Mission Report*, p. 8, for the predominance of the Chinese and Indians in economic sectors other than rice or padi cultivation.

92. Federation of Malaya, *Draft Development Plan of the Federation of Malaya*, Kuala Lumpur, 1950, p. 1.

93. Ibid., p. ii. See also Federation of Malaya, *Progress Report on the Development Plan of the Federation of Malaya 1950–1952*, Kuala Lumpur, 1953; p. 121, which concluded that economic planning should not only be viewed as a continuing process but that it should also be undertaken 'with particular emphasis on what is aimed at by the end of a specific period'.

94. Federation of Malaya, *A Plan of Development for Malaya, 1956–60*, Kuala Lumpur, 1956; *Report on Economic Planning in the Federation of Malaya in 1956 and on the Outcome of the Financial Talks held in London from December the 21st, 1956 to January the 10th, 1957*, Kuala Lumpur, 1957; *The Second Five-Year Plan 1961–1965*, Kuala Lumpur, 1961; and *Malaysia Interim Review of Development in Malaya under the Second Five-Year Plan* (hereinafter referred to as *Development Interim Review 1963*), Kuala Lumpur, 1963.

95. *Development Interim Review 1963*, para. 2.

96. Ibid., paras. 5–13. See also G. D. Ness, *Bureaucracy and Rural Development in Malaysia*, Berkeley, 1967, especially chs. 6 and 7.

97. This pledge was elaborated in 'Finance and Economic Matters' in 'The Road to Independence', *TCLP*.

98. Ungku A. Aziz, 'Facts and Fallacies on Malay Economy', *Merdeka Convention Papers*.

99. Ungku A. Aziz, 'The Causes of Poverty in Malayan Agriculture' in Lim Tay Boh (ed.), op. cit., pp. 23–4.

100. Ibid., p. 28. Economic distress was not restricted to farmers and fishermen. There were a 'decline in the level of living of labour', deterioration of health services, and losses of social, religious, recreational and educational amenities as consequences of the subdivision of rubber estates. See Ungku A. Aziz, *Subdivision of Estates in Malaya*, Vol. 1, Kuala Lumpur, 1963.

101. See Federation of Malaya, *Federal Legislative Council Debates: Official Reports*, Fourteenth Meeting of the Fourth Session of the Second Legislative Council, Kuala Lumpur, 24 June 1959, cols. 6852–3, for a comprehensive written answer by the Minister of Commerce and Industry on RIDA and 'the trades and industries that are now operated by Malays as a result of the implementation of the Government's policy to encourage Malays in the field of commerce and industry'.

102. Interview with Musa Hitam, who was at the time the chairman of FELDA, Kuala Lumpur, January 1972.

103. *Development Interim Review 1963*, para. 60.

104. IBRD, *The Economic Position and Prospects of the Federation of Malaya* (hereinafter referred to as *IBRD Report, 1963*) [n.p.], 1963, para. 3.

105. *IBRD Report, 1963*, para. 5.

106. 'Memorandum by the Hon'ble Dato Abdul Razak bin Hussein for Alliance Round Table', 12 November 1954. Mimeographed. *TCLP*.

107. Interview with Tan Sri Abdul Kadir Shamsuddin, who was secretary to the Malayan delegation to the Constitutional Conference in London from January to February 1956, and was Chief Secretary to the Federal Government and Cabinet at the time of interview. Genting Highlands, March 1974. See also R. O. Tilman, 'The Nationalization of the Colonial Services in Malaya', *South Atlantic Quarterly*, 61, No. 2 (Spring 1962), pp. 183–96.

108. T. E. Smith, 'The Malayan Elections of 1959', *Pacific Affairs*, 33, No. 1, March 1960, p. 40.

109. For the ideological leanings of the main parties which contested the elections, see R. S. Milne and K. J. Ratnam, *The Malayan Parliamentary Election of 1964*, Kuala Lumpur, 1967, chs. 2 and 3.

110. There was, for instance, a dispute within the Alliance regarding the distribution of candidates for the parliamentary election. UMNO wanted 75 of its own ranks, 27 from MCA and 2 from the MIC; but a number of the MCA leaders wanted at least 35 for their party. When the final compromise allocation of 69 UMNO, 31 MCA and 4 MIC candidates was made, some of the MCA members resigned and a number stood for election as Independent candidates. See Means, op. cit., pp. 212–14.

111. Means, op. cit., p. 132.

112. L. A. Sheridan, *Federation of Malaya Constitution*, Singapore, 1961, p. 141.

113. Federation of Malaya, *Federation of Malaya Constitution 1957*, Kuala Lumpur, 1957, Article 3(1). See also *Constitutional Proposals*, para. 57; and Sheridan, op. cit., p. 4.

114. See F. G. Carnell, 'The Malayan Elections', *Pacific Affairs*, 28, No. 4, December 1955, p. 316.

115. King, op. cit., p. 51.

116. R. S. Milne, *Government and Politics in Malaysia*, Boston, 1967, p. 88.

117. Tilman, op. cit., *Constitutional Proposals*, para. 57; and *Federation of Malaya Constitution 1957*, Article 12.

118. Milne, op. cit., p. 39.

119. Miller, *A Short History of Malaysia*, p. 199.

120. Federation of Malaya, *The Text of the Agreement between the Government of the United Kingdom of Great Britain and Northern Ireland and the Government of the Federation of Malaya on External Defence and Mutual Assistance*, Kuala Lumpur, 1957.

121. On this subject see, N. K. Hazra, 'Malaya's Foreign Relations, 1957–1963' (M.A. Thesis, University of Malaya, 1965); J. B. Dalton, 'The Development of Malayan External Policy, 1957–1963' (D.Phil. Thesis, Oxford University, 1967); and Raktakamal Barman, 'The Foreign Policy of Malaya, 31 August 1957 to 16 September 1963' (Ph.D. Thesis, Indian School of International Studies, Delhi, 1967).

122. Dato Abdul Razak bin Hussein, Federation of Malaya, *Legislative Council Debates; Official Reports*, Fourteenth Meeting of the Fourth Session of the Second Legislative Council, Kuala Lumpur, 24 June 1959, col. 6932. Tunku Abdul Rahman had resigned as Prime Minister in April 1959 'for the purpose of touring the whole country to ensure the success of the Alliance Party in the Federal elections'. F. Sullivan, 'A Study in Biography' in S. Durai Raja Singam (ed. & pub.), *Tribute to Tunku Abdul Rahman*, Kuala Lumpur, 1963, p. 115.

5
From Malaya to Malaysia

BEFORE dealing with the developments which led directly to the formation of Malaysia, it is pertinent to take a look at the political and constitutional state of Sarawak and Sabah between the end of the war and the birth of Malaysia.

Political–Constitutional Developments in Sarawak and Sabah, 1946–1961

By contrast with Malaya, which in the immediate post-war years experienced keenly-felt and widely-debated constitutional and political developments, Sarawak and Sabah remained almost apolitical dependencies for long years after 1946. In a significant manner, the 'low level' political response in post-war Sarawak and Sabah was the logical consequence of pre-war policies in the two territories. The paternalism of the Brooke Rajahs and the commercial considerations of the British North Borneo Chartered Company had left the two areas effectively insulated from the spread of nationalist ideas in South-East Asia. It was principally due to this apolitical historical background that Sarawak and Sabah were acquired relatively easily and turned into Crown Colonies by Britain in July 1946.

Britain's motives for acquiring Sarawak and Sabah after the Second World War were not very dissimilar from those which prompted her to regain her pre-war hegemony over Malaya and Singapore. Britain had indirectly but effectively established her imperial influence in northern Borneo during the Brooke rule and Chartered Company administration, which lasted until the Japanese invasion in 1941. As in Malaya, Britain worked for the establishment of a post-war position of dominance in Sarawak and Sabah. For economic and strategic reasons, Britain was prepared to add new acquisitions to her remaining dependencies.[1]

Sabah (known as 'North Borneo' until the inauguration of Malaysia in 1963) received its status of Crown Colony with hardly any dissenting voice. Relative isolation from the outside world and lack of educational facilities during the pre-war period accounted for the inability of most people in Sabah to comprehend the change in their status from that of inhabitants of a mere British Protectorate to that of a directly-governed Crown Colony in 1946.[2] It was on 10 July 1946 that Britain passed the North Borneo Cession Order-in-Council which provided that an agreement had been made between the Secretary of State for the Colonies, on behalf of His Majesty, and the British North Borneo Company, whereby the Company had transferred and ceded all its rights, powers, and interest in the territory with effect from 15 July 1946, and that it was therefore ordered that the State of North Borneo be annexed to and form part of His Majesty's Dominions, and should be called, together with the Settlement of Labuan, the Colony of North Borneo.[3] Malcolm MacDonald, the Governor-General of the Malayan Union and Singapore, was present on 15 July 1946 when the new Colony of North Borneo was proclaimed in Jesselton, as Kota Kinabalu was then called.[4]

As Sabah passed on into the 1950s, the tenor of life was characterized by a preoccupation with 'the peace, order and good government of the Colony'.[5] By 1956 the administration took pride in the fact that 'the Colony maintained its enviable record of freedom from political strife and violence'.[6] Yet, ironically, such 'freedom' ensured that Sabah was far away from freedom from Colonial rule. The transfer to the Colonial Office in 1946 had helped to stem post-war social, economic and administrative dislocations caused by the Japanese occupation in Sabah; beyond that, the territory had little political character, inasmuch as the meticulous application of 'peace, order and good government of the Colony' rendered the growth of political awareness excruciatingly slow among the people of Sabah.

The cession of Sarawak to the British Crown was more eventful, being accompanied and followed by overt protests from many Malays and a number of Iban leaders and their followers. The anti-cession movement, which lasted intermittently until the early 1950s, was the consequence of a series of events which ended in the proclamation of Sarawak as a British Crown Colony on 1 July 1946.

As early as June 1944, the Colonial Office made an initial approach to Rajah Vyner Brooke, who was in exile in Australia and later in Britain during the War. In a secret and personal letter, the Secretary of State for the Colonies, Oliver Stanley, wrote intimating that Britain felt 'responsible for the policies followed in the future development of the State, and its political, social and economic progress'.[7] Sarawak had been a British Protectorate since 1888 and in 1941 a Supplementary Agreement had assigned to the territory a status similar to that of the Malay states *vis-à-vis*

Britain in the pre-war period. Britain's plan by June 1944 was to be able to control Sarawak after the War in the same way as she intended to rule Malaya with the implementation of the Malayan Union scheme.

Rajah Vyner Brooke at this time, however, still took a benignant interest in the people of Sarawak whom he had ruled since 1917 but not seen since 1941. In his reply from London, he declared:

I and my family are Trustees for the State and people of Sarawak, who are well aware that it is not in the position of a 'Colonial Dependency', so their consent to any step which would tend to approach such a relationship would naturally have to be obtained. It can scarcely be obtained at the present time when, owing to the unavoidable inability of the Protecting Power to preserve them from invasion, they are under alien rule.

I have given this matter much thought, and I am convinced that if I were now to enter into a fresh agreement my right to do so would almost certainly be challenged in the future with embarrassing results to myself and possibly to His Majesty's Government.[8]

In preparation for the re-establishment of Brooke rule the Rajah recalled his nephew, Anthony Brooke, from active service in India in December 1944. The latter's title of Rajah Muda, which had been conferred on him in 1939 and withdrawn in 1941, was restored and he proceeded to head a Provisional Government of Sarawak in London. Anthony Brooke re-iterated in February 1945 what his uncle, the Rajah, had contended. In his response to the Colonial Office, which continued to evince its interest in gaining direct control of Sarawak, Anthony Brooke wrote:

Whilst I and my advisers will at all times be very glad, as representing the people of Sarawak, to discuss with you any matter of common interest to our two Governments, we are of the opinion that it would be morally indefensible for the Provisional Government of Sarawak to prejudice the post-war relations of the Government of Sarawak with His Majesty's Government by entering at this time into discussions inconsistent with the existing treaty relationship between the two Governments. This relationship, as defined by the Treaty of Protection of 1888, since amended by the Agreement of 1941, should, in the view of the Provisional Government of Sarawak, form the basis of relationship for such discussions as may take place before the people of Sarawak have been liberated and the *status quo* has been duly restored.[9]

Thus far, it was clear that both Rajah Vyner Brooke and his Rajah Muda, Anthony Brooke, felt that the future of Sarawak should not only be determined through proper constitutional means but that it should be decided in accordance with the wishes of the people of Sarawak. Neither the Rajah nor his nephew appeared to be thinking in terms of relinquishing their sovereignty over Sarawak; both were evidently still imbued with the first of the nine 'Cardinal Principles of the Rule of the

English Rajahs' which enjoined: 'That Sarawak is the heritage of Our Subjects and is held in trust by Ourselves for them'.[10]

The decisive factor, however, was the obvious wish of the British Government to acquire Sarawak as a dependency under the Colonial Office when the war was over. This wish was encouraged by the 72-year-old Rajah's words: 'I should be willing to return to Sarawak *for a short period* on its reoccupation, if thought desirable, but I feel that *the future must lie with those who have the physical vigour* not only to make a fresh start, but to continue firmly *along such lines as will ensure internal peace within the state.*'[11] That candid explanation was enough for the planners in the Colonial Office to make a decisive move. Between the Rajah Muda's reiteration of Brooke policy in February 1945 and October 1945, the Colonial Office succeeded in convincing the Rajah that his nephew and the Provisional Government of Sarawak representatives had 'shown themselves personally unresponsive to the proposals of His Majesty's Government'.[12] On 4 October the Rajah dismissed his Rajah Muda and 'assumed personal control of Sarawak affairs in place of the Provisional Government (which he abolished)'.[13]

The Rajah had decided, with the help of the Colonial Office planners, to cede Sarawak to the British Crown. But his memory of his subjects remained strong, so he dispatched his controversial private secretary, Gerard MacBryan, together with an official from the Colonial Office to Sarawak, 'to consult leading representatives of the people on the question of ceding the territory to His Majesty'. The outcome of this mission was reported as follows:

His emissary has now returned, and the Rajah has informed His Majesty's Government that, in consequence of the very favourable reaction of those representatives, which is, I understand, recorded in letters addressed to him by the leaders of the Malay and Chinese communities in Sarawak, he now feels able to proceed with the cession of the territory. Accordingly the necessary document is being drawn up and will be presented to the representatives of the people for their agreement upon the Rajah's return to the territory, which will probably take place towards the end of March.[14]

The Secretary of State for the Colonies, George Hall, in a heated debate on 6 February 1946 on the proposed Sarawak cession assured Members of the House of Commons that 'so far as we are concerned, if cession takes place, it must take place after full consultation with a properly constituted Supreme State Council in Sarawak'.[15] Rajah Vyner Brooke did arrive in Sarawak and the proposed cession of the territory to the British Crown was the subject of meetings of the Council Negri in Kuching which was opened by the Rajah on 14 May. Reece has summarized the cession proceedings: 'The motion on the second reading was then put and was finally carried by 18 votes to 16, there being a native majority against cession of 13 votes to 12. It was the votes of six European officials which carried the day, although the Residents of the First and Fourth Divisions (Ditmas and Gilbert) and Howes voted against the motion and Barcroft abstained.'[16] On the third reading, the bill was passed by 19 votes to 16. This time Barcroft and Datu Hakim who had earlier abstained voted for cession while Adams who had supported the bill was absent: ill.[17] Thus, with the majority of the non-European (in other words, Sarawakian) members voting against cession, the British Government decided 'that the Rajah's proposal for the cession of the territory to his Majesty is broadly acceptable to the native communities'.[18] The Supreme Council of Sarawak authorized Rajah Vyner Brooke to execute the instrument of cession on 20 May, with British representatives signing it on behalf of His Majesty's Government. A week later the Privy Council in London ordered the annexation of Sarawak to the British Crown. The Brooke kingdom disappeared and Sarawak saw the dawn of a new era with its proclamation as a British Crown Colony on 1 July 1946.

The cession of Sarawak to the British Crown was far from 'broadly acceptable to the native communities' who comprised the majority of the population of the territory. Indeed, the cession evoked strong emotions and reactions from certain sections of the Sarawak population. This was especially true of the Malays and many Ibans in Kuching, Sibu, and the other bigger towns although the indigenous reactions to the cession emerged gradually and rather haltingly.

Two organizations worked to emphasize that Sarawak was an independent state and that Britain was committing an act of injustice in deciding to annex the territory to the British Crown. One of these was the Malay National Union of Sarawak (MNUS) which had existed since 1936 but had not been a distinctly politicized organization before the cession controversy; this forced it to face a situation in which it comprehended the difference between the regime of the Brooke Rajahs (who had always maintained that 'Sarawak belongs to the Malays, Sea Dyaks, Land Dyaks, Kayans, Kenyahs, Milanos, Muruts, Kadayans, Bisayahs, and other tribes, and not to us'[19]) and direct colonial rule which would make Sarawakians the subject people of an alien power. The other organization, the Dayak Association of Sarawak (DAS), was formed after the War and led by Ibans who were mainly in the Brooke service or had served in it previously.[20] Like the MNUS, it was largely a social and welfare body but the cession issue prompted it to encourage Dayak–Malay cooperation in opposing the bequest of Sarawak to the Colonial Office.

The anti-cession movement grew so serious that the new Sarawak

Colonial Government issued an order in December 1946 prohibiting Anthony Brooke from entering Sarawak on the grounds that 'his presence and conduct in Sarawak would inflame feeling', and 'to ensure that the present peaceful state of the country is not unnecessarily disturbed and to protect the people against the danger of disorders which might perhaps be of a grave character'.[21]

Another measure of the seriousness with which the indigenous leaders pursued their endeavour to maintain the 'independence of Sarawak' can be seen in the outcome of a Circular which the new Colonial Government issued on 20 December 1946 to all offices of the Sarawak civil service which stated that the Government

... expects and requires absolute loyalty from all its servants, and since there is no question of a change in the present regime, the Government will not tolerate any association by its servants with activities designed to keep alive the question of cession ... each Government Servant must make up his mind whether to serve the Government loyally or not, and any one who wishes not to continue service under these conditions must inform their Heads of Departments before December 31, 1946.[22]

On 18 January about a thousand Malays, including both sexes, staged an anti-cession demonstration at the Kuching Mosque demanding, among other things, that 'Native wishes must be respected'. Demonstrations of a similar nature continued to be organized in subsequent years, usually on 'cession day', that is to say 1 July each year. The anti-cession movement reached its climax in early December 1949 when the second Governor of Sarawak, Duncan Stewart, was fatally stabbed in Sibu by a Malay Youth, Rosly bin Dhoby. The assassination shocked all parties and with the government taking strong punitive action, the anti-cession movement was practically destroyed by 1950.[23]

The anti-cession movement in Sarawak did not place the British in a predicament as disabling as the Malay reactions to the Malayan Union scheme in the Peninsula. As far as Britain was concerned, the deed was done and Sarawak had been acquired. In answer to Bertram Brooke, who was fighting a losing battle, the Secretary of State for the Colonies stated, as early as July 1946:

I am ... unable to accept the suggestion that there should be some further consultation of the wishes of the people on the cession issue. Now that the territory has been ceded I cannot but feel that anyone who encouraged in any way the small group in Sarawak who persist in voicing their opposition to cession is stirring up dissension and is not servicing the true interest of the territory and its inhabitants.[24]

The last sentence of the passage was a parting shot which was reinforced with the banning of Anthony Brooke from entry into Sarawak as long as the anti-cession movement presented itself as a possible threat.

It is pertinent to add that the Chinese community offered no support to the anti-cession movement. Indeed they felt that British government was likely to confer greater benefits on the Chinese. A Sarawak Chinese wrote recently:

> The Chinese attitude over the cession issue was not difficult to surmise. The Brooke regime had opened Sarawak to Chinese settlement and trade, it is true, and its stable government had encouraged Chinese population growth and the expansion of its economy. Of these benefits they were appreciative; but they also realized that they were not recognized, even the new generations born and bred on Sarawak soil, as true sons of the soil or natives which was (and still is) a privileged position without carrying the pejorative connotation so common elsewhere in Asia and Africa under colonial rule. Until 1931, a Chinese could legally be classified as a native, but the classification denoted nationality rather than ethnic status. After 1931 Chinese and non-Islamic Indians were excluded from native status. This was underlined in the Land Rules of 1933.[25]

Two of the Chinese members in the Council Negri, Tan Bak Kim and Kho Peng Loong, supported the cession bill while two others, Ong Hap Leong and Tse Shuen Sung, were absent.

But, in general, those who were in favour of British colonial administration belonged to the elite of the Chinese community, namely, wealthy merchants and others officially recognized as the leaders of the community. The younger generation from the lower strata of society, especially the Chinese-educated, were inclined towards leftist ideology. In fact, during the Second World War there had existed a communist organization known as the Sarawak Anti-Fascist League which is believed to have been succeeded by the Sarawak Overseas Chinese Democratic Youth League, formed in October 1951. The latter concentrated its efforts on indoctrination of Chinese students, and had contact with the Anti-British League in Singapore, but was dissolved when a state of emergency was declared in the First Division of Sarawak in 1952. Several communist groups existed in Sarawak from then on which the authorities referred to collectively as the Clandestine Communist Organization or CCO. However, it was the Sarawak Liberation League which apparently was able to organize activities in all the five Divisions of the territory. This League appears to have been renamed the Sarawak Advanced Youths' Association (SAYA) in late 1954. It was SAYA which became the most active body for many years and was, principally, the one which the Government called the CCO or the Sarawak Communist Organisation (SCO).

Unlike the MCP, the CCO fell short of executing an all-out war against the British in Sarawak. Armed encounters, human as well as material losses of the magnitude which occurred during the Emergency in Malaya did not take place in Sarawak. Nevertheless, there were basic similarities between the MCP and the CCO. The members of both organizations were primarily Chinese. More cogently, both utilized 'front organizations' to gain support for their identical revolutionary Marxist–Leninist–Maoist ideology. In the case of the CCO, the 'united front' was to include the students, the trade unions, and the peasants of rural Sarawak. In addition, it exploited resentment and fears that government policy would destroy Chinese culture. Both the MCP and CCO were dedicated to the use of 'the most revolutionary means to overthrow British Imperialism'. Both sought to establish an authoritarian communist political system in place of colonial rule. The CCO plan was: 'First of all we should strive for the establishment of a new democratic society, then a socialist society and finally a communist society.'[26]

From the time of the formation of SAYA the CCO stepped up its efforts to recruit support from the Chinese schools and to penetrate the predominantly Chinese trade unions, which had been formed in the main towns, as well as to organize the peasantry. By the late 1950s the CCO was seriously considering the formation of a political party so that there would be an organization with a unified command. That need was expressed in early 1959; by June that year the Sarawak United People's Party (SUPP) was registered. The British authorities thereupon glibly came to the conclusion that the CCO at least actively supported the formation of the SUPP. It is, however, debatable whether the SUPP was the party of the CCO pure and simple. Many of the SUPP leaders were conservative and hailed from propertied families. Although the party included a number of communist and pro-communist elements at the grassroots level, and offered a 'socialist' alternative, SUPP itself reflects elements of traditionalism. Most of the statewide leaders today are medium or small businessmen, not trade unionists or farmers.

At all events, the CCO never managed to establish a commanding position in Sarawak politics. Although it succeeded in forming cells, branches and committees in parts of the first three Divisions of the territory, throughout the British colonial period, and indeed after the formation of Malaysia in the 1960s, the CCO failed to convince more than a tiny minority of the Sarawak population that its revolutionary aim to set up a communist state in the area was a better alternative to the slow but peaceful British-guided constitutional development which had taken place in the post-war period. At the peak of its activities, the CCO had no more than between one and two thousand operational fighting members.

The Malays and indigenous communities largely steered clear of the activities of the CCO.

In general, among the Chinese in Sarawak there was a small group that was passionately China-orientated. On the other hand, there was another small group that was strongly Sarawak-orientated. In between these two groups was the largest segment, namely, the economically depressed, illiterate, and neither greatly China-orientated nor primarily Sarawak-inclined. They were often frustrated, and uneasily placed between the Chinese world and their Bornean habitat. Many of these frustrated and rootless Chinese sometimes embraced a belief that offered an apparently simple solution to the problems of the individual and the state. But they were not Marxist or Maoist ideologues; only the victims of adverse socio-economic circumstances in colonial Sarawak. Therefore, like the anti-cession movement, the Communist movement failed to secure mass support. It is important to note that because of the plural nature of the Sarawak Society, the Chinese-dominated CCO made no attempt to support the anti-British stance of the anti-cessionists.

British colonial rule lasted for seventeen years, from July 1946 to September 1963 in both Sarawak and Sabah. It was an era of benevolent administration. Largely because of the lack of political consciousness in both territories before the Second World War, progress along nationalist lines after 1946 was slow. The Colonial Governments of Sarawak and Sabah wished, above all else, to rehabilitate and reconstruct the economies of the two territories, which were ravaged by the War. It was clearly recognized that social and welfare services were inseparable concomitants of any stable and expanding economy; accordingly, such services were given emphasis at the same time as the principal industries of Sarawak and Sabah such as rubber, oil, pepper, copra, timber, sago and tobacco, were speedily rehabilitated. Sarawak and Sabah under colonial rule experienced British policies very like those carried out in pre-war Malaya.

As in pre-war Malaya, the peoples of Sarawak and Sabah lived in plural societies for many years after 1946. It was not the intention of Whitehall to foster political awareness or nationalistic ideas among them during the 1950s, even though Britain was aware that she would have to relinquish her sovereignty over the territories in the foreseeable future because nationalist movements and successful demands for political independence elsewhere in South-East Asia made it plain that, at best, Britain could only hope to delay the rise of nationalist sentiment among the peoples of Sarawak and Sabah. However, Britain must have reasoned, as she did with respect to Malaya and Singapore, that if the parting of the ways must come with the Borneo territories it was in her best interest that such a break should occur amicably.

In Sarawak, the 1941 Constitution was re-enacted in 1946. This Constitution gave legislative and financial jurisdiction to the Council Negri, a body of 25 members of whom 14 were official members appointed from the Sarawak Civil Service and 11 unofficial, representative of the several peoples of the country and their interests. The Council Negri was the equivalent of a legislative council in other colonies and, typical of colonial legislatures, it 'had the power to make laws for the peace, order and good government of the country, and no public money could be expended or any charge made upon the revenues of the country without the Council's consent'.[27]

Under the resumed 1941 Constitution there was provision for a Supreme Council (the equivalent of an executive council in other colonies) of not less than five members, the majority of whom were members of the Sarawak civil service and the Council Negri. The Governor, in the exercise of his duties, was to consult the Supreme Council; but important exceptions to this rule were made which, in effect, gave him a free hand to direct the affairs of the Colony in the way that the British Government would desire. 'In the exercise of his powers and duties the Governor consulted with the Supreme Council, except in making appointments to the Supreme Council and in cases (a) of such nature that, in the Governor's judgement, Her Majesty would sustain material prejudice by consulting the Supreme Council thereon; or (b) of matters in his judgement too unimportant to require their advice; or (c) of matters in his judgement too urgent to admit of their advice being given by the time action might be necessary'.[28] The people had no franchise and the Governor together with his officials controlled the destiny of the territory.

Gradually, however, local councils were introduced in Sarawak. Because it was obvious that few Sarawakians had the requisite educational qualifications or experience to fill higher posts, it was decided to develop local government institutions as the training ground for future Sarawak leaders. The first five local authorities, as the local councils were termed, were formed at the end of 1947; in November 1948 the Governor informed the Council Negri that by the end of the following year 'in Sarawak no less than one-third of the population of the Colony will be living within the jurisdiction of such Authorities, and nearly one-half of the population will be within the jurisdiction of some kind of Local Government'.[29] From the beginning of 1957 the whole of Sarawak, with the exception of a small area on the coast between Miri and the Brunei border, was under the jurisdiction of some kind of local authority.[30]

Most of the earlier local authorities were established on a racial basis, but as this proved to be detrimental to a common political evolution it was subsequently decided to organize authorities on a mixed or inter-racial pattern 'with jurisdiction over people of all races in the area'.[31] The main functions of each authority were responsibility for primary education and full financial control over expenditure within its area. The local authorities also collected revenue, mainly from a poll-tax, rates, licence-fees, miscellaneous local taxes, and central government grants from Kuching. No less significant was the fact that the local authorities, as the repositories of grassroots democracy, constituted the sub-electoral colleges for the election of representatives to the five Divisional Advisory Councils of Sarawak, which in turn elected members to the Council Negri, according to the provisions of the new Sarawak Constitution promulgated in 1956.

This Constitution, which came into force on 1 April 1957, provided for a new Council Negri consisting of 45 members of whom 24 were elected unofficials, 14 were ex-officio members, four were nominated to represent interests which the Governor considered inadequately re-presented, and the remaining three were 'standing members', two of whose seats were vacant and would not be filled.[32] The new Constitution also provided for a Supreme Council consisting of three ex-officio members, namely the Chief Secretary, the Financial Secretary and the Attorney-General, two nominated members and five elected members who were elected, nominated or standing members of the Council Negri. The introduction of local authorities, which were subsequently renamed 'district councils', had served one of its main purposes, inasmuch as the 1956 Constitution 'embodied the principle, which lasted even beyond the creation of Malaysia in 1963, that a proportion of the members in the higher organs of government would be elected by the members in a lower tier of government'.[33] Thus, while the elective principle was gradually introduced in the elections of members of the district councils, the last also now became sub-electoral colleges for the election of representatives to the five Divisional Advisory Councils mentioned above. These five Councils, the Kuching Municipal Council, and the Urban District Councils of Sibu and Miri, elected from among their members the 24 elected unofficials in the Council Negri.[34] The above system of indirect election was practised until the formation of Malaysia in the early 1960s and did help in a modest way to arouse political awareness among the people of Sarawak.

In the case of Sabah, after being administered by the Governor with the aid of an Advisory Council for four years, a new Legislative Council was established in October 1950. The new legislative body was, however, dominated by official members: 'The Legislative Council consists of the

Governor as President, three ex-officio Members, namely the Chief Secretary, the Attorney-General and the Financial Secretary, nine Official Members and ten Nominated Members'.[35] At the same time, an Executive Council was established which consisted of the same three ex-officio members, two other official members and four nominated members. The latter Council was 'consulted by the Governor on all questions of importance'.[36]

The constitutional arrangements in Sabah throughout the 1950s were more colonial than those in Sarawak. For a full decade until 1960 the British officials dominated the Legislative and Executive Councils. The Sabah colonial legislature advised and assisted the Governor who made 'laws for the peace, order and good Government of the Colony'.[37] Local councils were introduced in Sabah only from 1952 onwards, with functions similar to those in Sarawak but with the exception that the Sabah local councils did not undertake responsibility for education. (The Department of Education in Sabah fully controlled education in the territory.) As in Sarawak, the local councils in Sabah were subsequently renamed 'local authorities' and 'district councils'. By 1956 it was explained: 'Wide powers are conferred upon these Authorities, which have control over their own finances and may levy rates and cesses and make by-laws for such purposes as the improvement of agriculture and animal husbandry, the control of buildings, the provision and maintenance of markets and the safeguarding and promotion of public health.'[38] There was thus an attempt to familiarize the people with ideas of self-government at grassroots level as in Sarawak. Yet it is well to note that the local councils in Sabah never became sub-electoral colleges for a territorial legislature as in Sarawak. Throughout the 1950s, the members of the district councils as well as the unofficials in the Legislative and Executive Councils of Sabah were all nominated by the British Governor with the aid of his officials. In simple language, colonial rule was effective in theory and in practice in the Sabah of the 1950s.

It was only in 1960, just prior to the announcement of the Malaysian proposal, that constitutional changes were introduced which provided for a small unofficial majority in the Legislative Council of Sabah. There were then the Governor as President, 4 ex-officio members, 3 official members and 12 nominated members. However, the Executive Council remained largely in the control of official members who numbered six as against five nominated members.[39] While district and Divisional council elections were held in Sarawak on a territory-wide scale in 1959,[40] the electoral process was never introduced in Sabah before December 1962[41] when Sabah's participation in the formation of Malaysia was already a foregone conclusion.

No discussion of political-constitutional developments in Sarawak and Sabah between 1946 and 1963 would be complete without a reference to the British attempt to establish a Bornean federation.

Bornean Federation

It was largely due to the lack of organized movements among the local population that the first attempts at political unification in northern Borneo came from the colonial leaders themselves. Their idea generally was not to prepare Sarawak, Brunei and Sabah for separate independence but rather to link them in some form of Bornean federation. The first attempt came in the form of a conference in Kuching in April 1953, presided over by Malcolm MacDonald[42] and attended by Sir Anthony Abell, the Governor of Sarawak (and British High Commissioner for Brunei), Sultan Omar Ali Saifuddin of Brunei, and Sir Ralph Hone, Governor of North Borneo. Also in attendance were three representatives from each of the three territories. The main point for discussion was the wish to develop a greater measure of coordination of policy and administration in matters of common interest.[43] It was decided to institute a system of periodic joint meetings between department heads and others in Sarawak, Brunei and Sabah, and to maintain harmony of policy among the three territories.[44] However, very little could be done over the next four years because Brunei refused to entertain the idea of a Bornean federation.[45]

It is interesting to note that since the Second World War there had been several suggestions about linking up all the British territories of Malaya, Singapore and Borneo in some form of confederation. A contemporary academic who took an active interest in the problems of nationhood in the area argued the possibilities and wrote, towards the end of 1946:

A Federation reaching from Perlis to North Borneo is possible, a Federation to which people of many different races gave their loyalty, trying to keep it prosperous and to fit it for independence. There is abundant evidence in the speeches of the Governor-General, and the overall design of local plans, that this is the avowed aim of the present British Government. But no one can spend three months in post-war Malaya without noticing that this plan is being continuously and deliberately thwarted.[46]

Indeed, 'parochialism' reigned even among the senior British officials and in July 1957 Sir Anthony Abell reaffirmed his preference for a Bornean federation. He considered that it was more practical for Sarawak, Brunei and Sabah to chart a common destiny than to look to Malaya and Singapore for unity and progress.[47] This appeared to make sense, one reason being that 'jealousies between the Malayan Union and Singapore are magnified with every appearance of conscious and increasing spite'.[48] Malcolm MacDonald himself affirmed many years later:

I suggested when I was British Commissioner-General for South-East Asia that the three Borneo territories—Sarawak, Brunei and North Borneo—came together in a federation. They had many things in common, for example, administration and economic pattern.... I thought that if the Borneo territories were federated they would be in a stronger position as a larger political entity. They would also be in a stronger bargaining position with any other neighbouring country.[49]

But Brunei, which basically felt unable to bear the probable eventuality that it would end up sharing its oil wealth with poorer Sarawak and Sabah in any Bornean federation, remained uninterested.[50] Sir Anthony Abell renewed his clarion call without much success in February 1958;[51] and in September that year the Council Negri

...approved a resolution that a committee of unofficial members should be appointed to examine the implications of closer association between the three territories of British Borneo and to report back to the Council on the more detailed information which should be presented about this proposal to the people of the territories. A motion in somewhat similar terms was to be passed by the North Borneo Legislative Council and it is expected that the committees of unofficials of both territories will undertake conducted tours of North Borneo and Sarawak in the course of 1959 in order to study the circumstances of each and so be better qualified to make their reports.[52]

Not to be outdone, Sir Roland Turnbull, Hone's successor, had also suggested in April 1958 that the Brunei and Sarawak governments be approached to try to get their agreement to a closer constitutional link between the three territories. An inter-territorial group of people should be formed to study the proposal and make recommendations for the three governments to consider.[53]

Despite the conferences and the efforts of the promoters, the formation of a Bornean federation remained an idea. Apart from Brunei's reluctance, the Sabah authorities also felt that the idea was premature. Sir Roland Turnbull summed up the reasons for the failure thus far to establish a political union in northern Borneo and his hopes for the future in the following passage:

One of the purposes we have conspicuously failed to bring about is the political association of this country with Brunei and Sarawak. Since such purposes cannot be achieved without the ready consent of a substantial majority of the people in each of the countries involved, there is virtually nothing we can do about it at the present time other than to express our continuing goodwill and our desire for such an association.... For the present, let us concern ourselves with the betterment of our own affairs, in the by no means unjustified hope that the years will make us a partner who is not only welcomed but sought.[54]

It can be argued that the Bornean federation proposals mooted from 1953 onwards failed partly because the peoples of the three territories had no significant voice in them. Furthermore, the general idea of forming such a federation was promoted by the representatives of the metropolitan power themselves which gave it the tinge of colonial expediency and so tended to discourage the participation of local leaders such as Sultan Omar Ali Saifuddin, Datu Mustapha bin Datu Harun[55] and Donald A. Stephens.[56] Sir Anthony Abell, for instance, envisaged a very colonial arrangement whereby a Governor-General would act as Her Majesty's representative in Sarawak and Sabah while at the same time being British High Commissioner to Brunei. He would preside over proposed legislatures in Sarawak and Sabah. There would be a Lieutenant-Governor in each of the two territories.[57] The proposals, in some important respects, were reminiscent of the Malayan Union scheme and did not appear to foster the idea of independent nationhood in the three undeveloped territories of northern Borneo.

The Rationale for Malaysia

The wish to associate Malaya, Singapore, and the northern Borneo territories in some form of union had been expressed variously before 1961. Lord Brassey, a North Borneo Chartered Company Director, put forth such a suggestion in 1887, albeit without much effect.[58] During the Second World War, British planners in London 'made a general assessment of the future of all the British areas in the Far East, collectively'.[59] But their deliberations were guided by the wish of the Colonial Office to safeguard British economic and strategic interests in the region rather than by any desire to promote a self-governing con-federation of states there. After the war, Thio Chan Bee, a member of the Legislative Council and Progressive Party of Singapore, which 'opposed merger with Malaya but proposed a confederation of Singapore, Malaya and the Borneo territories',[60] more than once pointed out that this would ensure that the Malayan–Borneo region would fall in with the existing world trend towards larger political groupings such as the Western European Union.[61] Malcolm MacDonald himself, in espousing the prior establishment of a Bornean federation, had in mind, as he later said, that 'After the federation of the Borneo territories, a confederation with Malaya and Singapore could have been attempted.'[62]

Like the Bornean federation proposals, however, the idea of a

Malayan–Singapore–northern Borneo confederation did not progress towards reality until Tunku Abdul Rahman, then Prime Minister of the Federation of Malaya, made an apparently casual statement in the course of a luncheon speech to the Foreign Correspondents' Association of South-East Asia in Singapore on 27 May 1961. The Tunku stated that Malaya could not stand alone in isolation and suggested that sooner or later his country 'should have an understanding with Britain and the peoples of the territories of Singapore, North Borneo (Sabah), Brunei and Sarawak'.[63] He went on to say, 'It is premature for me to say now how this closer undertaking can be brought about but it is inevitable that we should look ahead to this objective and think of a plan whereby these territories can be brought closer together in political and economic co-operation.'[64] To comprehend why the Federation Prime Minister made the statement at that time and what accounted for the subsequent interest in the proposal, we must examine the rationale for Malaysia. Although Malaya had achieved independence, there were old as well as new problems which required solution if the new nation was to continue to progress. Some of these problems concerned the relationship between the Peninsula and Singapore.

Singapore wished to be merged with the Peninsula, mainly for economic and political reasons, as discussed further below. The Malayan leaders, however, were not enamoured of the idea for two main reasons of a different kind. The first was the fact that the racial composition of the population of Malaya differed very markedly from that of Singapore. This posed a serious obstacle to merger. Secondly, it was thought by the leaders in Kuala Lumpur that Singapore's security was being increasingly threatened by a communist take-over. Malaya felt that the inclusion of an increasingly-leftist Singapore would aggravate the problems posed by the Malayan Communist Party (MCP), which had already caused the twelve-year Emergency from 1948 to 1960.

The following Table demonstrates the problem posed by racial composition. The figures shown clearly meant that in a direct Malaya–Singapore merger the numerical superiority of the Malays in the Peninsula would be lost to the Chinese. Furthermore, there was no certainty that the Indians and Others would not tend to side more with the Chinese than with the Malays. The Malays in the Peninsula, where historical processes beyond their control had already created a plural society,[65] had always greatly feared such an eventuality and therefore naturally dreaded the political inclusion of Singapore in their country. In retrospect, it was just as well for the Malays that Britain excluded Singapore from the Malayan Union in 1946 and the Federation of Malaya in 1948.

Yet, the other reason for reluctance in having Singapore as part of a

TABLE 1
Racial Composition of Malaya and Singapore

	Malays and Other Indigenous Groups	Chinese	Indians	Others	Total
Malaya[1]	3,125,474	2,333,756	696,186	123,342	6,278,758
(1957 census)	(49.8%)	(37.1%)	(11.1%)	(2.0%)	
Singapore[2]	197,060	1,090,595	124,084	34,190	1,445,929
(1957 census)	(13.6%)	(75.1%)	(8.6%)	(2.7%)	
Total	3,322,534	3,424,351	820,270	157,532	7,724,687
	(43.0%)	(44.3%)	(10.6%)	(2.1%)	(100%)

[1]Federation of Malaya, *Official Year Book 1961*, Kuala Lumpur, 1961, p. 36; and G. P. Means, 'Malaysia–A New Federation in Southeast Asia', *Pacific Affairs*, 36, No. 2, Summer 1963, p. 140.
[2]Colony of Singapore, *Annual Report 1958*, Singapore, 1959, pp. 27–8.

single Malayan nation, namely the communist threat, increasingly and paradoxically turned into a reason in favour of accepting the Island as a merger partner. It is in this regard that Tunku Abdul Rahman's May 1961 statement on the Malaysia proposal becomes especially significant. It was reasoned that the inclusion of Singapore in such a proposal would enable the Malayan leaders, with the aid of the British, to contain the communists and their tenacious exploitation of anti-colonial feelings, and not only in Singapore. The inveterate anti-communist Tunku explained:

We had successfully overcome the internal threat of Communism in Malaya, but we were only too well aware of its insidious growth in neighbouring areas. I noticed particularly, with growing and grave concern, the increasing influence of Communism in the British territories of Singapore, Sabah, Brunei and Sarawak. The same pattern of Communist exploitation of anti-colonial feelings that we had experienced in Malaya was taking place in those areas. I felt that time was running out, and that the Communist menace had to be swiftly met, otherwise free Malaya would once again be in danger. Therefore, in May 1961 I first announced my hope that the formation of Malaysia would enable the peoples of these states to achieve the independence they desired and at the same time put an end to colonialism in their part of the world.[66]

Thus it was envisaged that the establishment of the enlarged federation would not only speed up but actually consummate the attainment of political independence for Singapore and the three dependent territories in northern Borneo. Nowithstanding internal problems which might occur or remain after the establishment of the enlarged federation, it was intended from the outset that Malaysia was to have the constitutional status of an independent and sovereign nation which its people, including those in Singapore, Sarawak, Brunei (if it became a part) and Sabah, should be equally proud of.

But, there was another reason for Malaysia. This related to the problem of numbers faced by the Malays in the Peninsula in the case of a direct Malaya–Singapore merger. With the inclusion of Sarawak, Brunei and Sabah, each of which contained a majority of indigenous people who were akin in varying degree to the Malays, the proposed Malaysia would maintain the numerical superiority of the Malays and other indigenous peoples together over the Chinese. The following Table makes the point:

TABLE 2

Racial Composition of Malaya, Singapore and the
Borneo Territories (Sarawak, Brunei and Sabah)

	Malays and Other Indigenous Groups	Chinese	All Others	Total
Malaya and Singapore[1]	3,322,534	3,424,351	977,802	7,724,687
The Borneo Territories[2]	872,853	355,491	54,383	1,282,827
Total (i.e. Malaysia)	4,195,387 (46.6%)	3,779,842 (41.9%)	1,032,185 (11.5%)	9,007,514 (100%)

[1]See Table 1 of this chapter.
[2]L. W. Jones, *The Population of Borneo*, London, 1966, Appendix A, p. 203. The figures were for 1960.

Although the numerical factor was not highlighted during the formation of Malaysia, and despite the possibility that the 'only merit of this racial argument seems to lie in the assumption that in extreme racial issues the indigenous population of Borneo might choose to align themselves with the Malays, to whom they were racially akin, rather than to the Chinese',[67] it was none the less 'one reason why the Borneo states are so important as a counterbalance to Singapore's left-leaning Chinese majorities'.[68]

Malaya–Singapore Merger

Although Malayan leaders, notably those who were Malays, had shown an unwillingness to accept the political merger of Singapore with the Peninsula, leaders in Singapore had often argued that their Island was a natural complement of the Peninsula. Philip Hoalim Senior, a long-time resident, a lawyer, and a participant in the early post-war political activities in Singapore, argued in December 1947:

The MDU along with the other members of the Putera-AMCJA, believes that there are three indispensable requisites to the framing of a healthy and progressive constitution for Malaya.

We have consistently fought for these three principles and will continue to do so until we succeed. Firstly, we believe that the whole of Malaya, including Singapore, should come under a central government, democratically elected to power by the citizens of the country. Secondly, that only those who regard Malaya as their real home and the object of their loyalty may become citizens. And thirdly, that democratic political rights should be extended to all citizens.

How all this is connected with our boycott of the Singapore elections may be well understood if we realise, *in the first place, that the welfare of Singapore cannot be considered in isolation from that of the rest of Malaya.* Not the least among the Government's extravagances is the maintenance of a separate governing apparatus for Singapore with all the preposterous duplications this involves.

Singapore, therefore, should be treated as an integral part of Malaya, instead of which the Government proposed to isolate it as a separate British Colony. Then again, *Singapore should be governed by a central authority along democratic lines, and embracing the whole of Malaya.* This will save us from the caprices of a foreign tyranny which by its very nature is incapable of attending to our needs and promoting our welfare.[69]

The fact that these views were expressed immediately after the war exemplifies the earlier development of political attitudes in Singapore as compared to many parts of Malaya and the Borneo territories. The passage quoted also reflects ideals which many Singapore leaders held dear from 1946 right up to the formation of Malaysia: the wish for and belief in a merger with mainland Malaya were uppermost, hence the concept of a common central government for the Peninsula and the Island.

This concept and also the egalitarian, somewhat socialist ideas of the MDU and the AMCJA continued to pervade the atmosphere of Singapore politics in later years. The rather casual Singaporean awareness of a need to make some concessions to the Malays found expression in the grand coalition with PUTERA. These features lend credibility to the assertion that the MDU and its affiliates were in many ways the fore-runners of the People's Action Party (PAP) which emphasized, above all else, that Singapore's political future and independence could only be realized through merger with Malaya.[70] Philip Hoalim's remarks also pointed to one more cogent reason for the wish to merge with Malaya, namely that together the Peninsula and Singapore would have a better chance of political survival.

Throughout the 1950s, the idea of merger never lacked adherents, particularly in Singapore. While the Island was a British Crown Colony from 1946 until it was granted internal self-government in 1959,[71] it was noted that:

In discussion since 1946 political merger has been pronounced as an objective of the majority of parties in Singapore. As an issue, however, it has only come into real prominence with the diminution of British governmental control in Singapore and in conjunction with the swing from restricted political activity, and a restricted franchise, to the participation of the mass of the population in politics and the emergence of parties relying on mass support.[72]

The real 'diminution of British governmental control in Singapore' only began in 1954. In that year it was decided to introduce constitutional reforms which would gradually lead Singapore to independence.[73] The Report of a Commission chaired by Sir George Rendel recommended a partly-elected and partly-nominated legislature:

The Assembly comprised 25 elected members, the 3 official members in the Cabinet, and 4 members nominated by the Governor to represent commercial and minority interests. Although there was an elected majority in the Legislative Council, the Governor had tremendous reserve powers in all matters of defence, foreign affairs and internal security, and the right to suspend the constitution.[74]

The Rendel constitutional reforms provided for a Cabinet consisting of the Governor and nine others, comprising the Chief Secretary, the Financial Secretary and the Attorney-General, an elected Chief Minister and five other elected Ministers.[75] The developments were comparable to the introduction of the Member System in Malaya in 1951 and its extension by 1954. As in Malaya, although the scope was more limited, elections were held in Singapore in 1955 for the 25 Legislative Assembly seats. Sir George Rendel explained many years later that the constitutional reforms proposed by the Commission were intended 'to establish a parliamentary system of government for Singapore in a gradual way, bearing in mind the limited stage of political evolution in the Island. It was felt that a two-party system would be appropriate for Singapore, as this would reduce factionalism and the weakness generally found in coalition governments.'[76]

At all events, the modest constitutional reforms adopted as a result of the Rendel Commission Report did widen the outlook and scope of political activities in Singapore. David Marshall[77] had thought otherwise:

The Rendel Constitution was mainly tailored for the Progressive Party whom everybody, and certainly the British, expected to form the Government and to act as the gold-plated shock absorbers for imperialist rule. To the British the Rendel

Constitution was a suave political ploy–a change of facade to quieten screaming U.N. and world opinion. It was not intended to make any basic change in the realities of government geared for British commercial exploitation.[78]

It is undoubtedly true that the British were far from willing to relinquish their political and economic dominance over Singapore at the time. Yet it was the modest political reforms under the Rendel Constitution which not only promoted party politics in Singapore but also enabled Marshall and his Labour Front to win the most seats in the 1955 elections and become the *primus inter pares* in a coalition government.[79] Marshall himself became Singapore's first Chief Minister in a cabinet government which lasted until his resignation in June 1956. He was succeeded by Lim Yew Hock[80] who remained Chief Minister until the PAP came to power in the elections of 31 May 1959. It should also be noted that Marshall, Lim Yew Hock and the Government lead by the Labour Front from 1955 to 1959 'demanded an early Singapore–Federation merger'.[81] In March 1957 an all-party mission led by Lim Yew Hock went to London and reached agreement on proposals which *inter alia* granted self-government to Singapore. The proposals provided for an Internal Security Council consisting of three British representatives (with the High Commissioner as chairman), three Singapore Ministers and a representative of the Federation of Malaya. A new Legislative Assembly was set up consisting of 51 members elected by universal suffrage on a non-communal roll as in Malaya. In addition to the continuance of cabinet government, the proposals also provided for a Head of State styled the Yang Dipertuan Negara of Singapore.[82]

The PAP, which won 43 of the 51 seats in the 1959 elections,[83] had been founded in late 1954 by Lee Kuan Yew[84] and a number of others:

From the outset, however, it was clear to political observers that the PAP was made up of two groups–the moderates and the communists. Three out of the twelve members of the Party's first Central Executive Committee (CEC) were known to be communist sympathizers, if not yet full-fledged communists. The more prominent non-communists were Lee Kuan Yew, Toh Chin Chye and Goh Keng Swee who had met while studying in London and had discussed many Malayan problems as members of the Malayan Forum.[85]

Under the leadership of the PAP Singapore became an internally self-governing state on 3 June 1959, joined Malaysia in September 1963, and became a sovereign Republic after the Island's separation from Malaysia in 1965. It is significant, however, that the PAP, as the most successful political party in the history of politics in Singapore, had always strongly advocated the independence of the Island through merger with Malaya. The Malayan Forum, which was an important antecedent of the PAP, was a discussion club formed by Malayan and Singapore students in

Britain in 1949 with the aim of arousing interest in and debating the problems of achieving independence for Malaya and Singapore as a single nation.[86] After various people and organizations reflected on the matter over the post-war years, the major reasons for Singapore's wish to merge with Malaya were reviewed by Lee Kuan Yew in 1961:

Merger is going to take place not just because it is the desire of the P.A.P. or merely because it is the wish of the Federation Alliance government. It is as inevitable as the rising and the setting of the sun. The two territories are so intertwined and interwoven in their economic, political and military complex that no man can keep up the artificial barrier at the Causeway for long....

Everyone knows the reasons why the Federation is important to Singapore. It is the hinterland which produces the rubber and tin that keep our shop-window economy going. It is the base that made Singapore the capital city. Without this economic base Singapore would not survive.

Without merger, without a reunification of our two economies, our economic position will slowly and steadily get worse. ... Instead of there being one unified economic development for Malaya, there will be two. The Federation instead of co-operating with Singapore will compete against Singapore for industrial capital and industrial expansion. In this competition both will suffer.

But Singapore will suffer more, because we have less resources to fall back on. We have no rubber and tin, no large land mass. For 140 years we have grown, developed and prospered because we bought and sold for the Federation. Through Singapore they imported what they wanted from the outside world. Through Singapore they sold their rubber and tin.

Merger means that there will be one integrated economic development, and that the wasteful duplication of facilities in the two territories will come to an end.[87]

Undoubtedly, the economic relationship between Singapore and the Peninsula dominated the thinking of the leaders of the former. However, the majority of leading Singaporeans (as well as many of the ordinary citizens of the Island) also had family ties with mainland Malaya, i.e. had relatives who were permanently resident in or citizens of the Federation. This was especially so among the Chinese, but in varying degrees was also true of the Malay and Indian communities.[88] The numerous cultural and familial ties which extended beyond the ends of the Johor Causeway were therefore also seen as compelling reasons for a merger between Singapore and Malaya.

As has been said earlier, political considerations also loomed large in the efforts to arrive at a merger. Apart from the fact that the Peninsula and Singapore had both been governed by Britain since the nineteenth century, and consequently had similarities in systems of administration, communications, judicature, currency, etc., it was noted that 'No iron, rubber or coconut curtain is possible between us. What happens in

Singapore must affect the Federation. From Singapore the Federation can be undermined. Singapore is vital to the security and survival of the Federation.'[89]

Furthermore, since coming to power in 1959 the PAP had encountered an increasing threat from communists in Singapore and pro-communists within its own ranks. To a certain extent this was a bogey fabricated by Lee Kuan Yew and his close associates in the effort to achieve merger with Malaya. But there was a real internal tussle within the PAP. At the Hong Lim by-election in April 1961 a former party member, Ong Eng Guan, who was a strong rival of Lee Kuan Yew, beat the PAP candidate; and again at the Anson by-election the following July, histrionic David Marshall roundly defeated the PAP candidate.[90] For major economic, social and political reasons, therefore, the PAP leaders felt that nationhood should come to Singapore through merger between the Peninsula and the Island.

Tunku Abdul Rahman and his Malayan colleagues took time deciding to admit Singapore as a merger partner in a Malaysia which would include the Borneo territories, from the first serious discussions of the proposal reported to have taken place in July 1960, through another meeting between Duncan Sandys, Lee Kuan Yew and the Tunku in December 1960, until the Federation Prime Minister's speech to correspondents in May 1961,[91] but in Singapore itself the proposal was welcomed at once. A week after the Tunku's luncheon speech, Lee Kuan Yew recapitulated and reaffirmed the entirely pro-merger policy of his Government:

By ties of sentiment as well as of business, we in Singapore have always been closest to the Federation of Malaya. If merger and independence could come sooner and easier through the Borneo sister territories coming in together with us into political integration with the Federation of Malaya, then we support it for it would also mean that we would have a larger and more powerful economic base for our new nation.

... we welcome and support the declaration of the Prime Minister of the Federation of Malaya that it is inevitable that we should look ahead to this objective of closer political and economic association between the Federation, Singapore, Brunei, Sarawak and North Borneo. This declaration should accelerate the speed of political progress towards complete independence for us.[92]

From then on the PAP Government never relented in its single-minded determination to unify Singapore with Malaya through the formation of Malaysia. Notwithstanding the defeats in the Hong Lim and Anson by-elections, Lee Kuan Yew and his loyal colleagues worked adroitly to isolate the pro-communist leaders who were against the PAP bringing Singapore into political union with Malaya under the Alliance Government. When the Singapore leftists broke away and formed the Barisan Sosialis in July 1961, about 70 per cent of the PAP rank and file membership crossed over to join the new party.[93] But the PAP Government remained in office (still having 25 Assemblymen out of 51 in the legislature by August 1962) and proceeded assiduously towards its merger goal.

After Britain and the Federation of Malaya jointly announced on 1 August 1962 that 'subject to the necessary legislation, the proposed Federation of Malaysia should be brought into being by 31st August 1963,'[94] the PAP Government held a 'referendum' on 1 September 1962. The people were asked to choose the type of merger they favoured not whether they were for or against merger and 71 per cent of the electorate voted for constitutional merger arrangements, contained in a white paper, 'giving Singapore autonomy in education and labour'.[95] From then on, Singapore's wish to merge with Malaya was as good as fulfilled. While S. Rajaratnam had earlier said that the partners were 'trying to build a Malayan nation not by force, but by consent',[96] Tunku Abdul Rahman remarked shortly after the Singapore referendum that it was 'impossible to grant independence to Singapore [on its own] because of the danger of it going communist, and if it goes communist it would with the help of the communist powers try to overrun the whole of Malaya'.[97] The Tunku affirmed that 'the only course open to us would be to accept Singapore as a member of the Federation of Malaysia'.[98]

Singapore was so accepted when Malaysia was inaugurated on 16 September 1963. Apart from being granted autonomy in education and labour, Singapore was allocated 15 seats in the 159-member Dewan Rakyat of the new nation;[99] although broadcasting and television were federal matters, the Singapore Government was to be responsible for administration and day-to-day programmes within Singapore, while all licence and advertising fees from broadcasting and television in Singapore were to be State revenue;[100] and in general Singapore was granted a substantial part of its state revenue to support its education, housing, and other social services.[101] Importantly, the economic aspect of merger received attention when the Malaysia Agreement provided:

The Federal Government, in order to facilitate the maximum practicable degree of economic integration of the territories of Malaysia, while taking account of the interests of the entrepot trade of Singapore, Penang and Labuan and those of existing industries in Malaysia, and the need to ensure a balanced development of these territories, shall progressively establish a common market in Malaysia for all goods or products produced, manufactured or assembled in significant quantities in Malaysia, with the exception of goods and products of which the principal terminal markets lie outside Malaysia.[102]

By and large Singapore was afforded much leeway in economic matters. For the first five years after Malaysia Day the appointment of the chairman of a Tariff Advisory Board, which was to be set up to advise the Federal Government generally on the establishment of the common market, required the concurrence of the Singapore Government; over the same period 'the Singapore Government shall have the right to require a delay not exceeding twelve months in the imposition in Singapore of any protective duty on the grounds that the duty would significantly prejudice the entrepot trade'; with certain exceptions, all revenues collected in Singapore were to be divided between the Federal and Singapore Governments 'and paid to them at least once in every year, in the proportion of 60 per cent to the Singapore Government and 40 per cent to the Federal Government'; and '60 per cent of income tax collected in the States of Malaya but attributable to income derived from Singapore shall be paid to the Singapore Government'.[103] The Malaysia Agreement, however, also provided that the Singapore Government should make available to the Federal Government two 15-year loans totalling $150 million 'to assist development in the Borneo territories'.[104]

Northern Borneo and Malaysia

Tunku Abdul Rahman's Malaysia proposal in May 1961 was initially opposed by leaders in Sarawak, Brunei and Sabah. One main reason was that the three territories had long been conditioned into thinking that their common colonial rulers, the British, would eventually lead them to sovereignty and independence. The failure of the Bornean federation proposals of the 1950s was itself evidence that Sarawak, Brunei and Sabah were each inclined to hope and work for their own separate independence, even if the ideal of nationhood might take until the year 2000 or longer to achieve. Because of this frame of mind, the announcement of the Malaysia proposal not only took the leaders of the three territories by surprise but also elicited strong reactions against the proposal from some of them. A number of them formed a United Front; and the main personalities involved, A. M. Azahari of Brunei, Ong Kee Hui of Sarawak, and Donald A. Stephens of Sabah, declared on 9 July 1961 that 'any plan in accordance with the pronouncements made by Tengku Abdul Rahman ... would be totally unacceptable to the people of the three territories'.[105]

Soon after his speech in May 1961, Tunku Abdul Rahman had paid a familiarization visit to Brunei and Sarawak in the course of which he endeavoured to explain the Malaysia proposal. It was not an easy task, however, to project such a federation proposal to peoples who, as we have seen, were still relatively unschooled in the art of party politics and lacking in nationalist fervour.

As we have also seen, the local leaders of the Borneo territories were in such a handicapped position that the first overt moves *vis-à-vis* the Malaysia proposal were taken by the colonial authorities themselves. In June 1961 the British leaders of northern Borneo—Governor Sir Alexander Waddell of Sarawak, High Commissioner to Brunei D. C. White, and Governor Sir William Goode of Sabah—were summoned by Britain's Commissioner-General for Southeast Asia, Lord Selkirk; and after two days of talks in Singapore they suggested 'that the Borneo territories should bind themselves closer together before joining the Malaysia confederation'.[106] The British Prime Minister, Harold Macmillan, had stated a week earlier that he had observed with interest the Tunku's Malaysia proposal. He added, 'Tunku Abdul Rahman's statement is already stimulating discussion in these countries, and the Government will wish to take their reactions into account in their consideration of the suggestion'.[107]

The British Government might indeed have been involved in suggesting the Malaysia proposal as a more amenable alternative to direct Malaya–Singapore merger. Implying that he had discussed the proposal with the Malayan Prime Minister, Malcolm MacDonald once said, 'Tunku Abdul Rahman called me, months before his 27 May 1961 speech in Singapore'.[108] The usually well-regarded if conservative London *Times* put Britain's stakes in the Malaysia region in proper perspective when it concluded, 'British strategic interest in the area is shared by Australia and New Zealand and some common policy will have to be evolved. If strategic needs can be satisfied there should be no further political objection from Britain'.[109] A contemporary writer affirmed, 'Because of the obvious advantages accruing to Great Britain from the Malaysian Federation, the opponents of Malaysia charge that the idea originated with the British'.[110] Indeed, as the formation of Malaysia proceeded, left-wing opponents of the proposal in the region charged that Malaysia represented 'a sinister conspiracy on the part of the British and Malayan Governments which will enable Britain to protect her military and economic interests and Malaya to crush socialism in the area and make second-class citizens of the Chinese'.[111]

A series of developments ensured the continuance of attention to the Malaysia plan in northern Borneo. The leaders in the area took their political cues largely from their British rulers, at least initially but, for the reasons stated above, their British rulers appeared to be increasingly favourable to the formation of Malaysia. British officials gave the impression that although the prior establishment of a Bornean federation comprising the three territories was not to be completely ruled out, the Malaysia proposal was a constructive one and that the crucial factor was proper timing in forming the larger federation. 'The quicker you try to do it, the more difficult it would be for the Borneo territories because they feel they lag behind Singapore and the Federation politically.'[112] The United Front leaders themselves were aware of and perturbed by the political handicaps of their territories. It was for this reason that they implored:

We believe that it is vitally important that the constitutional advance in the three territories should be speeded up and with this in view elections should be held in the territories, where an undertaking has been given by the Governments concerned so that the legitimate aspirations of the people for political advancement can be satisfied.[113]

Britain for her part had become resigned to the realities of the situation: Malaya had achieved independence, Singapore had been increasingly resolute in its demand for self-rule, and the northern Borneo territories would be following the same path to political emancipation either of their own volition or with the aid and moral support of friendly neighbours. The British also seem to have decided that the parting with the Borneo territories should be on good terms so as to avoid 'endangering their stand on self-determination in Africa and elsewhere in the world'.[114] It appeared that colonial rule was inevitably coming to an end in northern Borneo, at any rate in Sarawak and Sabah.

In July 1961 the British authorities arranged for local Sarawak and Sabah leaders to be present at the Commonwealth Parliamentary Association (CPA) conference in Singapore. Both Malaya and Singapore were represented and both very much wanted to realize Malaysia; but it was Lee Kuan Yew, who appeared to be at the apex of his political agility in the early 1960s, who really worked hard to establish rapport with the mostly suspicious Borneo leaders: 'I would suggest that at the conference you speak your minds frankly. Let us know what are the things that you feel have to be safeguarded. Let us know how they can be done and when'.[115] The Borneo leaders did begin to speak their minds on the Malaysia proposal, while Malaya and Singapore lent their willing ears. The CPA conference decided to set up a Malaysia Solidarity Consultative Committee (MSCC), which comprised delegations from Malaya, Singapore and the three Borneo territories, to continue discussions on the Malaysia proposal as well as to identify the matters regarding which the Borneans wanted safeguards. (Brunei was not represented at the first meeting, and sent only observers to the remaining three meetings of the MSCC.)

In view of what subsequently developed, the MSCC can be considered as a path-finding body in the formation of Malaysia. It was not a mere coincidence that Donald Stephens, the most vocal Borneo leader at the time, was chosen to be chairman of the MSCC. By entrusting him with that important job, the Malayans and Singaporeans ensured that the representatives from the Borneo territories would feel that they were playing major roles in discussing the Malaysia plan from the beginning. The MSCC held four fruitful meetings, the first in Jesselton, the second in Kuching, the third in Kuala Lumpur and the fourth in Singapore, between August 1961 and February 1962.

While the Borneans were gaining in political understanding as the Malaysia proposal increasingly became a topic of conversation among the people in town and kampong, their leaders were gaining expertise in negotiations as they sat in conference with their Malayan and Singapore counterparts. It is evident that during the four meetings of the MSCC the pervading theme was that of nationhood; and it became increasingly clear that what the Borneo leaders wanted was no longer separate independence before joining Malaysia but rather acceptable conditions and safeguards regarding important aspects of social, economic and political life.

At the first MSCC meeting in Jesselton, the Malayan delegates told their Borneo counterparts, 'The facts of geography and economics further reinforce our growing intimacy in our joint effort in many practical fields such as administration, education, technical assistance, the law and exchange of experts and training programmes in various fields'.[116] At the second MSCC meeting in Kuching the Malayan delegation reinforced the case for nationhood by reiterating that the Malaysia region shared a common cultural heritage, links forged in history, common economic factors, common threats to security and consequently the need for similar defence thinking, administrative and judicial services produced out of the same mould and for decades a common currency.[117]

The persuasive approach of the Malayans and Singaporeans soon convinced an increasing number of Borneo leaders that the Malaysia proposal was constructive and advantageous to the future of their territories. Recalling the beginning of favourable Borneo response to Malaysia, Datuk Ong Kee Hui stated many years later:

At the Commonwealth Parliamentary Association conference in Singapore in July 1961, the Borneo leaders (no Britishers were present) met Lee Kuan Yew who was the greatest supporter of the Malaysia idea. Lee Kuan Yew used all his power of persuasion to try to convince the Borneo leaders to support the Tengku's proposal. He said that the British were made up in their minds to give up Singapore and the Borneo territories. If the Borneans did not unite with

Malaya and Singapore, then it would be 'everyone for himself' and the chances of political survival would be almost nil.[118]

Donald Stephens had initially warned, 'If we join Malaya, the people who will come and take most of the top jobs will be from Malaya'.[119] But soon after the United Front declaration, Tunku Abdul Rahman sent invitations to Borneo leaders to go to Kuala Lumpur to exchange views. 'Donald Stephens did not even bother to communicate with his United Front colleagues and flew to Kuala Lumpur'.[120] However, as late as August 1961 Stephens could say, 'My people feel that if North Borneo joins Malaya now as a state, it would in fact mean that North Borneo would become not a state but a colony of the Federation of Malaya'.[121] Yet by the time the fourth meeting of the MSCC took place in Singapore in February 1962, the delegations from the five areas had 'reached common ground on the broad constitutional and political issues, like a strong effective Central Government in charge of defence, external affairs and internal security, and on details such as control of migration, religion, education, national language, and other safeguards for local interests'.[122] In fine, the Malaysia proposal had come to embody the major institutional aspects of nation-building.

That Britain supported the formation of Malaysia became very evident when the Sarawak and Sabah Governments each published a white paper in January 1962 urging the peoples of the two territories to support the Malaysia proposal.[123] To adhere to well-known British practice in granting self-rule to dependencies, it was decided to set up a commission of enquiry on Malaysia 'to ascertain the views of the peoples of North Borneo and Sarawak on this question; and, in the light of their assessment of these views, to make recommendations'. The Commission comprised Lord Cobbold (chairman), Sir Anthony Abell and Sir David Watherston, who were nominated by the British Government; and Dato Wong Pow Nee and Muhammad Ghazali Shafie, who were nominated by the Federation of Malaya.[124] The Commission undertook its tasks from 19 February to 17 April 1962. It held 50 hearings at 35 different centres (20 in Sarawak and 15 in Sabah). Over 4,000 persons appeared before the Commission in some 690 groups which varied in size from one to fifty. The Commission received nearly 600 letters and memoranda in Sabah and over 1,600 in Sarawak.[125] In giving its assessment the Commission concluded:

About one-third of the population in each territory strongly favours early realisation of Malaysia without too much concern about terms and conditions. Another third, many of them favourable to the Malaysia project, ask, with varying degrees of emphasis, for conditions and safeguards varying in nature and extent. . . The remaining third is divided between those who insist on independence before Malaysia is considered and those who would strongly prefer to see British rule continue for some years to come.[126]

The Cobbold Commission made recommendations on matters similar to those already discussed and agreed upon by the MSCC. These included issues such as representation in the federal parliament, the special position of the indigenous communities, development, the judiciary, the head of state, the public services, the federal constitution, finance, tariffs and trade, education, and regionalization of federal services.[127] The Commission urged that these be dealt with in detail by a Working Party. The chairman of the Commission made one very pertinent observation:

It is a necessary condition that, from the outset, Malaysia should be regarded by all concerned as an association of partners, combining in the common interest to create a new nation but retaining their own individualities. If any idea were to take root that Malaysia would involve a 'take-over' of the Borneo territories by the Federation of Malaya and the submersion of the individualities of North Borneo and Sarawak, Malaysia would not, in my judgment, be generally acceptable or successful.[128]

This observation served to allay the fears of the Borneo leaders that Malaysia might 'come about by a process of large units like the Federation of Malaya taking in smaller units', or that it might mean the Borneo territories 'being bulldozed' into the proposed federation.[129]

The recommendation to have a Working Party was taken up when an Inter-Governmental Committee (IGC) was formed consisting of members from Britain, Malaya, Sarawak and Sabah. The IGC divided into constitutional, fiscal, legal and judicial, public service and departmental organization sub-committees which met variously between August and December 1962.[130] The IGC Report contained the framework of Malaysia as a nation. In so far as Sarawak and Sabah had indicated their wish to be parts of Malaysia, the IGC Report embodied the conditions and safeguards which the two territories wanted before they gave their final consent. Many of the constitutional aspects of statehood that were worked out by the IGC were based on the 1957 Federation of Malaya Constitution and Malayan experience in nation-building.

Briefly, in Malaysia Islam was to be the religion of the Federation. There were to be constitutional guarantees for religious freedom. Immigration would remain a federal subject but, with certain exceptions, entry into the Borneo states would require the approval of the state concerned. This legislation could not be amended or repealed in its application to a Borneo state without the agreement of the state concerned. Education was a federal subject, but the existing policy and system of educational administration in Sarawak and Sabah remained under the control of each state government until it otherwise agreed.[131]

Any citizen of the United Kingdom and her Colonies who was born, naturalized or registered in Sarawak or Sabah and ordinarily resident there when Malaysia came into existence, became a citizen by operation of law. Any other person over the age of seventeen years and ordinarily resident in the Borneo territories was entitled to apply for Malaysian citizenship by registration within eight years of Malaysia Day, subject to certain qualifications including residence for seven out of the previous ten years. An applicant for citizenship by registration had to pass a Malay language test, and was required to take the citizenship oath as prescribed in the existing Federal Constitution.[132]

Two members of the Dewan Negara (Senate) of the Parliament of Malaysia would be elected by each Borneo legislature, while six other Senators would be appointed by the Yang di-Pertuan Agong from the two Borneo states of Sarawak and Sabah. The existing Dewan Rakyat (House of Representatives) was enlarged from 104 to 159. Of the new MPs, 16 were to be elected from Sabah, and 24 from Sarawak. The remaining 15 were to come from Singapore. In Sarawak the Head of State was styled Governor; in Sabah he was Yang di-Pertuan Negara. The Sarawak executive council was named Supreme Council and the legislative assembly Council Negri as both bodies had been during the pre-Malaysia period. The lists of federal and state powers, with some modifications, were based on the distribution of legislative powers under the Federation of Malaya Constitution.[133]

With certain exceptions, taxation remained a federal matter. Taxes in Sarawak and Sabah would be gradually raised to federal levels. Some revenues additional to those already assigned to the states in the existing Federation of Malaya, such as certain duties on petroleum products timber and minerals, revenue from state sales taxes and port dues, were assigned to the Borneo states. In Sabah, for as long as the state retained responsibility for medicine and health, 30 per cent of all other customs revenue was assigned to it. The Federation Government would use its best endeavours to enable Sarawak to secure and disburse M$300 million during the first five years after Malaysia Day for capital expenditure on development. The Federation Government also noted an estimate of desirable development expenditure in Sabah of M$200 million for the same period after Malaysia Day, and recognized that funds from outside the territory would be required. Britain promised a grant of £1.5 million per year for five years for the development of the Borneo states.[134]

Members of the Parliament of Malaysia from Sarawak and Sabah were initially elected by the state legislative assemblies. Direct elections to

Parliament and the Borneo state legislatures would be held with the first general elections after the fifth anniversary of Malaysia Day or earlier if the state government agreed. Elections would be the responsibility of the Federal Election Commission which would be enlarged with an additional member from the Borneo states.[135]

In addition to the Supreme Court of Malaysia, which was to be known as the Federal Court, there were to be three High Courts for the states of the existing Federation, for Singapore, and for the Borneo states. The Federal Court determined disputes between the states or a state and the Federation and certain constitutional questions, as well as appeals from the three High Courts, while the latter determined appeals from inferior courts in the states. Native law and custom and native courts remained a state matter.[136]

Separate Public Service Commissions were to be established in each Borneo state. The Federal Public Service Commission would establish, for at least five years, branches in Sarawak and Sabah, and members of the State Public Service Commissions were to serve on the Federal Public Service Commission's state branches. Malay was the national language, but for a period of ten years after Malaysia Day and thereafter until the state legislatures of Sarawak and Sabah otherwise provided, English would remain an official language. Significantly, the provisions in the Federation of Malaya Constitution relating to Malays were made applicable to the indigenous peoples of the Borneo states as if they were Malays.[137]

The IGC Report satisfied Borneo demands for conditions and safeguards to a large extent. It met most of the 'Twenty Points' which Sabah leaders and their Sarawak counterparts wanted from the Federation Government if the two territories were to become parts of Malaysia.[138] The provisions for social and economic aid to the Borneo states were very substantial. It may also be supposed that the Borneo leaders came to favour Malaysia because, upon reflection, it could be seen that the plan did not in any serious manner threaten their ambitions to become or remain pre-eminent in their states if they joined Malaysia. After all, Sarawak and Sabah were each provided with a state cabinet complete with a Chief Minister and a complement of other state Ministers.[139] Leaders of Sarawak and Sabah could, and did, enthusiastically aspire to these high, influential and often lucrative positions after Malaysia Day.

Before the Malaysia proposal was made in May 1961 there were three political parties in Sarawak, the Sarawak United People's Party (SUPP), the Party Negara Sarawak (PANAS), and the Sarawak National Party (SNAP); Azahari's Partai Rakyat existed in Brunei; and there was none in Sabah. Asked why he did not form a political party, Donald Stephens replied only months before the Malaysia plan was propounded, 'I want to learn from the mistakes of SUPP and PANAS first'.[140] At that time the two Sarawak parties were engaged in furious conflict with each other and political mud-slinging.

The Malaysia proposal, besides triggering decolonization, greatly accelerated the development of party politics in northern Borneo. By the first half of 1962 five political parties had been formed in previously apolitical Sabah. The United National Kadazan Organization (UNKO), led by Donald Stephens, was formed in August 1961. As the name implies, its majority support came from the Kadazans of the West Coast and Interior Residencies. Soon after its formation the UNKO decided to support the Malaysia proposal. The United Sabah National Organization (USNO) appeared next in December 1961 and was led by Datu Mustapha bin Datu Harun. It commanded support largely from the Muslim groups, and like the UNKO it soon decided to support the Malaysia plan with some reservations. In 1962 several parties emerged. Among these was the United National Pasok Momogun Organization (Pasok Momogun) which wanted self-government before Sabah joined Malaysia and gained support from the interior indigenous people. (It merged with the UNKO in June 1964 to form the United Pasok Momogun Kadazan Organization (UPKO).) The Chinese of Sabah formed the Democratic Party and the United Party (which, after merging and undergoing two changes of name, finally became the Sabah Chinese Association (SCA) in May 1965[141]). The Chinese parties at first opposed Malaysia but, like all the political parties of Sabah of the period, they soon decided to support the proposal on condition that certain safeguards were agreed upon.

In addition to the mainly Chinese-supported SUPP which was inaugurated in June 1959, the largely Malay PANAS which was brought into being in April 1960, and SNAP which began as a predominantly Dayak-based party in April 1961, new parties emerged in Sarawak in the wake of the Malaysia Plan. The Barisan Raayat Jati Sarawak (BARJASA) was formed in December 1961 with Malay and Muslim Melanau support. The conservative well-to-do Chinese led the formation of the Sarawak Chinese Association (SCA) in July 1962; and in August 1962 the Party Pesaka Anak Sarawak (Pesaka) came into being with the principal support of Ibans and other Dayaks in the Third Division. With the exception of the SUPP, which argued for Sarawak independence first, all these parties in time decided to support the Malaysia proposal. It may be mentioned, however, that while all the parties in Sabah formed a pro-Malaysia grand coalition, the Sabah Alliance, in August 1962, the parties in Sarawak only succeeded in establishing a similar coalition, the

Sarawak Alliance, in January 1963. The SUPP remained on the opposition side until 1970.[142]

Thus the Malaysia proposal engendered the development of political thinking in northern Borneo. The formation of the parties allowed the articulation of political preferences and enabled the leaders of the Borneo territories and their counterparts from Malaya and Singapore to identify and give adequate consideration to the major problems which had to be solved or taken into account in the course of establishing the new nation. Concurrently with the spread of political awareness, the Malaysia proposal fostered the development of nationalist consciousness in northern Borneo. The idea of belonging to an independent nation, a central and essential feature of the Malaysia proposal, gradually gained currency and accounted for the willingness of increasing numbers of people in Sarawak and Sabah to look favourably at and in the end to accept that proposal.

The formation of Malaysia took twenty-eight months, from May 1961 to September 1963, and it was basically an enlargement of the Federation of Malaya despite the reservations expressed earlier on this point. Although substantial state autonomy was accorded Singapore, and conditions and safeguards were agreed upon to satisfy Bornean demands, the three new areas became additional states of fundamentally the same Federation, renamed Malaysia. The Malaysia Agreement provided for a series of adaptations of and additional provisions in the existing 1957 Federation of Malaya Constitution rather than the framing of an entirely new document. Thus the content of the Federal Constitution of Malaysia was to a great extent the same as that of the 1957 Federation of Malaya Constitution.[143]

When Malaysia was inaugurated on 16 September 1963, Tunku Abdul Rahman's earlier wish seemed almost fulfilled: 'If the three Borneo territories are included in the Federation, it will become 14 states'.[144] With the inclusion of Singapore, there were indeed fourteen states, but one of the Borneo territories was missing, for Brunei had decided in the end to stay out of Malaysia.

Brunei and Malaysia

In July 1961 Tunku Abdul Rahman and the Yang di-Pertuan Agong had attempted to persuade the Bruneians that the Sultanate and the Peninsula had much in common and that this warranted the closer union of the two areas. The Agong eloquently said:

We came to Brunei on a mission of friendship and goodwill, and we have found them waiting for us in abundance—the same nationality, the same culture and the same customs. . . . It is my earnest hope that the ties of friendship and goodwill in our hearts, ties which link our lands and peoples today as they have throughout recorded time, will endure as long as the sea which washes both our shores.[145]

But even at this early stage there were signs that Brunei was disinclined to accept the Malaysia proposal. A number of Malayan officers who were trained at Brunei Government expense and were serving in the Sultanate could not get along with their local colleagues. While Tunku Abdul Rahman attempted to resolve the 'officers affair', Azahari claimed 'the people are angry with Malayan seconded officers who do not want to fit themselves into their environment'.[146] The issue hardly augured well for the future of Brunei–Malayan relations.

While Brunei sent observers to the Kuching, Kuala Lumpur and Singapore meetings of the MSCC, the Sultan of Brunei himself appointed a Commission early in 1962 to consider the Malaysia proposal; this consisted of the Menteri Besar as chairman, two Malays, one Chinese and one Iban. No report of the Commission was published, but those who gave evidence, 'among whom there would, no doubt, have been a large majority of members of the Partai Rakyat',[147] preferred the unification of the Borneo territories to joining Malaysia. There were among the Bruneians those who harped on the past greatness of the Sultanate and wished to reunify Sarawak and Sabah, which were once parts of Brunei.[148] Indeed it was partly for this reason that, while Brunei sent observers to the crucial meetings of the IGC, on 8 December 1962 Azahari and his cohorts in the Partai Rakyat staged a revolt; they managed to hold parts of Brunei Town and controlled Seria and Kuala Belait for a short while. From his comfortable hotel suite in Manila, Azahari declared, 'We want history to say it was our sweat and struggle and not Malaysia which gave Brunei independence'.[149] With the assistance of British troops, however, the revolt was over within a week. The Partai Rakyat was also dissatisfied with the snail's pace of constitutional development in Brunei itself. The British Government, which controlled the Sultanate's relations and also had profound influence in its domestic affairs, had repeatedly advised the Sultan not to convene the State Legislative Council for fear that the Partai Rakyat might overcome the protected Brunei Government.[150]

After the 1962 revolt the Sultan evidently tried harder to assess the possibility of joining Malaysia. In February 1963 Dato Neil Lawson, the Sultan's legal adviser, said that any alternative to Bruneians joining the proposed federation was not only illusory but 'indeed fraught with danger to their political, social and economic development'.[151] The Sultan proceeded to lead a delegation to Kuala Lumpur for talks with the

Federation Government the following month, and intimated that except for a few minor issues Brunei was ready to be part of Malaysia. The Sultan also led a delegation to London where he joined others from Sabah, Sarawak, Singapore and Malaya for concluding discussions on the proposed federation. But when the Malaysia Agreement was being signed by all the other heads of delegations on 9 July 1963 the Sultan decided that Brunei should remain outside Malaysia.

Several reasons accounted for Brunei's decision. First, neither the public nor the personal relations between Brunei and Kuala Lumpur leaders improved or grew cordial after the visit of the Yang di-Pertuan Agong and Tunku Abdul Rahman in July 1961. In fact many of the Malayan officers serving in Brunei asked to return to Malaya soon after that visit.[152] It was unfortunate that as negotiations between the Sultan and his officers and the Malayan leaders went on, problems of protocol tended to obstruct the growth of cordial relations. When it appeared that Brunei was within an ace of becoming a part of Malaysia in April 1963, an unintentional but to some extent culpable slip soured relations between the two sides. This concerned a letter which the Malayan Cabinet was to have written confirming the agreed terms of Brunei's entry into Malaysia. Tunku Abdul Rahman stated at a press conference that the letter had been sent. The Brunei delegates waited for two days at their *Istana* (palace) in Kuala Lumpur, but the letter did not come. The Brunei delegation thereupon called a press conference and stated that no letter had been received. The Malayan side ruefully complained, 'Why are they doing this to us?' The Tunku and others subsequently went to see the Sultan of Brunei and his delegation off at the Kuala Lumpur Airport, but the Malayan Prime Minister did not get the opportunity of handing a letter he had with him to the Sultan.[153]

Another major reason for Brunei's decision to stay out of Malaysia was the settlement of the Sultanate's rich oil revenue. The negotiations on the matter narrowed down to the question of control of the revenue in Malaysia. The Malayan leaders, who were destined to become the federal leaders of Malaysia, wanted Brunei to have control over the oil only for the first ten years after Malaysia Day; thereafter the Federal Government would take over jurisdiction. But Brunei stipulated that it must have control of its oil wealth in perpetuity within Malaysia.[154] The Sultan's legal adviser subsequently explained:

On the economic side, it was not only a question of who would have jurisdiction over the petroleum but also of who would exercise power over land where new oil fields might well be found in the future. Although land had been a state matter in the existing Federation of Malaya, Sarawak and Sabah, a constitutional amendment had enabled the Federation Government to take over control of tin mining and production. There was a suspicion that the same might eventually happen to the oil industry of Brunei in Malaysia.[155]

Thus the same major factor which rendered the Bornean federation proposals of the 1950s unworkable had appeared again in bold relief. So long as the Brunei oil fields remained productive and the revenue derived from them proved adequate to sustain the protected state, there appeared to be little prospect of the Sultanate wanting to achieve nationhood through merger or union with any of its neighbours.

The other consequential reason why Brunei opted out of Malaysia had to do with the system of rotating monarchy and the Conference of Rulers which were retained in the Malaysian Constitution.[156] Unlike the Governor of Sarawak and the Yang di-Pertua Negara of Sabah, the Sultan of Brunei was made eligible for election as the Yang di-Pertuan Agong of Malaysia. This raised the question of his position in relation to the nine Malay Rulers of the Peninsula. Among them, precedence and seniority were determined by the lengths of their reigns on their respective state thrones. This criterion accordingly affected the order in which they expected to succeed to the office of Yang di-Pertuan Agong. Now Brunei was one of the few surviving Sultanates of the Malay world that had existed for centuries and was much older than most of the states of the Malay Rulers of the Peninsula. The Sultan of Brunei never said anything in public about his position but it may be supposed that, proud of the long history and traditions of his state, he expected to become the next Agong when the incumbent—who visited Brunei in July 1961—had completed his term of five years in September 1965. Unfortunately, it was reported that he was offered the position of the most junior candidate to the office of Agong and the Brunei Ruler found this unacceptable.[157]

Despite this, it has been said that 'The Sultan was not really interested in becoming the Yang di-Pertuan Agong. The main reason why Brunei stayed outside Malaysia was financial. In ten years' time Brunei would have lost its oil riches to the Federal Government.'[158] Thus Brunei chose to remain a protected state under Britain.

Malaya, Singapore, Sabah and Sarawak, on the other hand, had announced, by December 1962, their agreement to form Malaysia on 31 August 1963. But opposition from Indonesia and the Philippines to the proposed federation forced Malaya to accept, in early August, the proposal of the other two countries that the Secretary-General of the United Nations or his representative be asked to head an international commission to ascertain whether the elections which had recently been held in Sarawak and North Borneo accurately indicated the wishes of the majority of the population in those two territories to enter Malaysia.

The nine-member neutral nation UN Commission conducted its

survey in Sabah and Sarawak from 16 August to 5 September. U Thant's report, based on the findings of the mission, was released on 14 September. It confirmed that a sizeable majority of the people of both the territories wished to join in the Federation of Malaysia which, accordingly, was proclaimed on 16 September 1963, 'an independent and sovereign democratic State founded upon liberty and justice, ever seeking to defend and uphold peace and harmony among its peoples and to perpetuate peace among nations'.[159] But, because Malaysia's inauguration was initially set for 31 August 1963, it is '31 August' which is officially recognized as the anniversary of the birth of Malaysia.

1. See C. N. Parkinson, *Britain in the Far East: The Singapore Naval Base*, Singapore, 1955; S. Rose, *Britain and South-East Asia*, London, 1962.

2. See M. H. Baker, *Sabah: The First Ten Years as a Colony, 1946–1956*, Singapore, 1965, p. iv.

3. Colony of North Borneo, *The Laws of North Borneo in Force on the 30th June 1953*, London, 1954, Vol. 6, pp. 49–52; and *Annual Report on North Borneo for the Year 1947*, London, 1948, p. 48.

4. Jesselton (which was renamed Kota Kinabalu on 22 December 1967) became the post-war capital of Sabah. The first capital was Kudat (1881–4) and the second was Sandakan (1884–1941).

5. Colony of North Borneo, *Annual Report 1954*, Jesselton, 1955, p. 142.

6. Colony of North Borneo, *Annual Report 1956*, London, 1957, p. 1.

7. Colonial Office to Rajah Vyner Brooke, 19 June 1944. Reproduced in [Anthony Brooke], *The Facts About Sarawak* (hereinafter referred to as *FAS*), London, 1946, pp. 65–6.

8. Rajah Vyner Brooke to Stanley, 3 August 1944, *FAS*, p. 67.

9. Rajah Muda Anthony Brooke to Stanley, 28 February 1945, *FAS*, p. 68.

10. Government of Sarawak, *The Sarawak Government Gazette*, Government Press, Kuching, 24 September 1941, p. 616.

11. Rajah Vyner Brooke to Stanley, 3 August 1944, *FAS*, p. 67. Emphasis added.

12. Stanley to Rajah Vyner Brooke, 17 July 1945, *FAS*, p. 70.

13. *FAS*, p. 7.

14. Great Britain, *Hansard* (*House of Commons*), 6 February 1946. Reproduced in *FAS*, p. 45.

15. *FAS*, p. 49.

16. R. H. W. Reece, *The Name of Brooke: The End of White Rajah Rule in Sarawak*, Kuala Lumpur, 1982, p. 236. See also *Sarawak Gazette*, 2 September 1946. Datuk Sockalingam, a former Speaker of the Council Negri, stated that 'those Native Council Negri members who voted for the cession were offered money'. Interview by the present writer, Kuching, November 1971.

17. Reece, op. cit., p. 236.

18. Secretary of State for the Colonies George Hall in a reply in Parliament. Great Britain, *Hansard* (*House of Commons*), 27 March 1946. Also in *FAS*, p. 51.

19. R. Payne, *The White Rajahs of Sarawak*, London, 1960, p. 182.

20. Interview with Datuk Benedict Sandin, an Iban specialist on local history, an active member of the DAS and also Government Ethonologist and Curator of the well-known

Sarawak Museum and Archives until his retirement in October 1973; Kuching, November 1971.

21. *Sarawak Tribune*, 20 December 1946.

22. *Sarawak Tribune*, 15 January 1947.

23. *Sarawak Tribune*, 20 January 1946. See also Reece, op. cit., p. 276.

24. Hall to Bertram Brooke, 26 July 1946, *FAS*, p. 107.

25. See John M. Chin, *The Sarawak Chinese*, Oxford University Press, 1981, pp. 102–3. See also Reece, op. cit., p. 237.

26. Government of Sarawak, *The Danger Within: A History of the Clandestine Communist Organisation in Sarawak*, Kuching, 1963, p. 4. The account of the CCO given here is based mainly on this source. See also M. B. Leigh, *The Chinese Community of Sarawak: A Study of Communal Relations*, Singapore, 1964, p. 42 and Chin, op. cit., pp. 111, 119, 122, 126 and 127.

27. See *Annual Report on North Borneo for the Year 1948*, London, 1949; and Colony of Sarawak, *Annual Report on Sarawak for the Year 1948*, Kuching, 1949, for progress reports on economic, social and welfare development in the two territories. See also Colony of Sarawak, *Sarawak Annual Report, 1956*, Kuching, 1957, p. 163.

28. Colony of Sarawak, *Sarawak Annual Report, 1953*, Kuching, 1954, p. 177.

29. I. Morrison, 'Local Self-Government in Sarawak', *Pacific Affairs*, 22, No. 2, June 1949, p. 181.

30. Colony of Sarawak, *Sarawak Annual Report, 1958*, Kuching, 1959, p. 163.

31. Ibid.

32. Colony of Sarawak, *Sarawak Annual Report, 1960*, Kuching, 1961, p. 216.

33. R. S. Milne, *Government and Politics in Malaysia*, Boston, 1967, p. 58.

34. *Sarawak Annual Report, 1960*, p. 217.

35. Colony of North Borneo, *Annual Report on North Borneo for the Year 1950*, Jesselton, 1951, p. 64.

36. Ibid., pp. 63–4.

37. Colony of North Borneo, *North Borneo Annual Report, 1955*, Jesselton, 1956, p. 144.

38. Colony of North Borneo, *Annual Report, 1956*, p. 163.

39. Colony of North Borneo, *North Borneo Annual Report, 1961*, Jesselton, 1962, p. 200.

40. See R. O. Tilman, 'Elections in Sarawak', *Asian Survey*, 3, No. 10, October 1963.

41. See K. J. Ratnam and R. S. Milne, *The Malayan Parliamentary Election of 1964*, Singapore, 1967, pp. 295–311.

42. For the background of Malcolm MacDonald, see note 23 of Chapter 3, above.

43. See *Sarawak Tribune*, 23 April 1953.

44. *Straits Times*, 23 April 1953.

45. Brunei's subsequent decision not to join Malaysia is discussed below.

46. T. H. Silcock, *Towards a Malayan Nation*, Singapore, 1961, p. 18.

47. *Sarawak Tribune*, 24 July 1957.

48. Silcock, loc. cit.

49. Interview with the present writer, Kuching, November 1971.

50. Oil was discovered at Seria, Brunei, in 1929. The workable oil-field along the coastal belt 'gave added importance to the State and its revenue increased and Brunei became prosperous'. State of Brunei, *Annual Report, 1958*, Kuching, 1959, p. 200.

51. *Sarawak Tribune*, 18 February 1958.

52. *Sarawak Annual Report, 1958*, p. 1.

53. *North Borneo News and Sabah Times*, Jesselton, 12 and 13 April 1958.

54. Colony of North Borneo, *North Borneo Annual Report, 1959*, Jesselton, 1960, p. 4.

55. Datu Mustapha bin Datu Harun, a well-known post-war Sabah leader, had little

176   NATION-BUILDING IN MALAYSIA

formal education; he was a house-boy to Chartered Company officers in the pre-war days and a member of the Filipino guerrilla movement against the Japanese during the Second World War. Nominated a member of the Sabah Legislative Council in 1954 and became a member of the Executive Council in 1956. Founder president of the United Sabah National Organization (USNO) formed in 1961, took an active part in the formation of Malaysia, became federal Minister of Sabah Affairs and Civil Defence after relinquishing the post of Yang Di Pertuan Negara in September 1965. He was Chief Minister of Sabah from April 1967 until October 1975. He has not fully retired from politics but has achieved no success in his attempt to regain his previous position of pre-eminence.

56. Donald Aloysius Stephens was a veteran journalist who organized the first Sabah English daily, *The North Borneo News and Sabah Times*, in 1953. Became unofficial member of the North Borneo Legislative and Executive Councils, initially opposed Malaysia but later agreed that it was in the best interests of Sabah. Organized and became founder president of the United National Kadazan Organizaton (UNKO) in 1961 and the United Pasok Momogun Kadazan Organizaton (UPKO) in 1964. A Eurasian of partly Kadazan descent who espoused the political aspirations of the Kadazans, Stephens became Chief Minister of Sabah upon its entry into Malaysia in September 1963 and held the post until he was appointed federal Minister of Sabah Affairs and Civil Defence in January 1965, a post he held until September 1965 when, having resigned, he was replaced by Datu Mustapha. With his party colleagues, he worked hard for the success of UPKO in the Sabah state election of April 1967 but in December the same year, disenchanted with political developments in Sabah, the leadership of UPKO decided to dissolve the party. Stephens returned to active politics as the president of Berjaya, a party formed in 1975 by some of the former members of USNO. Meanwhile he had been appointed Malaysia's High Commissioner to Australia in 1968. In January 1971, he embraced Islam and became Mohammed Fuad Stephens. Appointed Yang Di Pertua Negara of Sabah in August 1973, the same year he was conferred the title of 'Tan Sri'. In 1976 he was made a 'Tun' but he died in an air crash in June that year.

57. See B. Simandjuntak, *Malayan Federalism, 1945–1963*, Kuala Lumpur, 1969, p. 123.

58. S. Runciman, op. cit., p. 195.

59. Lord Ogmore (formerly D. R. Rees-Williams) in an interview with the present writer, London, April 1972.

60. D. Marshall, *Singapore's Struggle for Nationhood, 1945–1959*, Singapore, 1971, p. 5.

61. Yeo Kim Wah, *Political Development in Singapore 1945–1955*, Singapore, 1973, p. 48.

62. Interview with the present writer, Kuching, November 1971.

63. Federation of Malaya, *Malaysia in Brief*, Kuala Lumpur, 1963, pp. 108–9; and *Malaysia*, Kuala Lumpur, No. 2, April 1962, p. 6.

64. Dato Ong Yoke Lin, *Malaysia at the United Nations*, Kuala Lumpur, 1963, p. 10.

65. See I. Morrison, 'Aspects of the Racial Problem in Malaya', *Pacific Affairs*, 22, No. 3, September 1949, pp. 239–53; and F. G. Carnell, 'Communalism and Communism in Malaya', *Pacific Affairs*, 26, No. 2, June 1953, pp. 99–117.

66. Tunku Abdul Rahman 'Malaysia: Key Area in Southeast Asia', *Foreign Affairs*, 43, No. 4, July 1965, p. 661.

67. Simandjuntak, op. cit., p. 134. See also Mohammad Hatta, 'One Indonesian View of the Malaysia Issue', *Asian Survey*, 5, No. 3, March 1965, pp. 139–43.

68. Means, op. cit., p. 140.

69. P. Hoalim Senior, *The Malayan Democratic Union: Singapore's First Democratic Political Party*, Singapore, 1973, pp. 12–13. Emphasis added. The boycott referred to elections to the Legislative Council of Singapore in 1948. There were six elected seats. Active participation in politics then was confined to British subjects. Only 22,395 voters registered out of a potential electorate of nearly 300,000 and 6 per cent cast their votes. Marshall, op. cit., p. 3.

70. See Yeo Kim Wah, 'The Anti-Federation Movement in Malaya, 1946–48', *JSEAS*, 4, No. 1, March 1973, pp. 31–51; and Cheah Boon Kheng, 'The Malayan Democratic Union, 1945–1948' (M.A. Dissertation, University of Malaya, Kuala Lumpur, 1974).

71. T. E. Smith & J. Bastin, *Malaysia*, London, 1967, pp. 70–3; and V. Purcell, *Malaysia*, London, 1965, p. 11.

72. M. E. Osborne, *Singapore and Malaysia*, Ithaca, N.Y., 1964, p. 2.

73. See Colony of Singapore, *Report of the Rendel Constitutional Commission* (hereinafter referred to as *Rendel Commission Report*), Singapore, 1954.

74. Marshall, op. cit., p. 6.

75. Ibid., see also Yeo Kim Wah, *Political Development in Singapore, 1945–1955*, pp. 58–62; and F. G. Carnell, 'Constitutional Reform and Elections in Malaya', *Pacific Affairs*, 27, No. 3, September 1954, pp. 216–20.

76. Interview with the present writer, London, June 1972.

77. David Marshall was born in 1908 in Singapore. Educated in Singapore schools, gained LL B (London, external), and Barrister-at-Law, Middle Temple. Advocate and solicitor in Singapore. Enlisted in 1938 and fought in Singapore Volunteer Corps, and was taken POW by the Japanese in 1942. A founder of the Labour Front, formed in 1954. Elected to the Singapore Legislative Assembly in 1955 and became Chief Minister. Led all-party missions to London in late 1955 and April–May 1956 for talks with Britain on the constitutional future of Singapore. Resigned as Chief Minister in June 1956 because of failure of talks. Formed the Workers' Party of which he was president until 1962. President of the Singapore Jewish Welfare Board, and has continued to practise law in Singapore. From being a lawyer and politician, he has become, in recent years, a diplomat.

78. Marshall, op. cit., p. 7. For the backgrounds and role of the main political parties in Singapore, see Yeo Kim Wah, *Political Development in Singapore, 1945–1955*, ch. 3.

79. Sir George Rendel's hope for a two-party system for Singapore remained unfulfilled even until this writing. The 2 April 1955 elections saw the 25 seats won in the following manner: Labour Front–10; Progressive Party–4; People's Action Party–3; Alliance–3; Democractic Party–2; Independents–3. A coalition government was then formed incorporating the Labour Front and the Alliance (which was the Singapore extension of the Malayan tripartite Alliance).

80. Lim Yew Hock was a professional trade unionist who was nominated to the Singapore Legislative Council in 1948. Played an active part in the Labour Party which was formed in the same year; and teamed up with David Marshall to form the Labour Front in 1954. Took over from Marshall when he resigned the post of Chief Minister in June 1956. Lim Yew Hock was Chief Minister until Lee Kuan Yew and the PAP came to power in June 1959. Thereafter he moved to Malaysia. He died in 1984.

81. Yeo Kim Wah, *Political Development in Singapore, 1945–1955*, p. 115.

82. See Great Britain, *Report of the Singapore Constitutional Conference held in London in March and April 1957*, London, 1957.

83. The remaining seats were won by the following: Singapore People's Alliance (under Lim Yew Hock)–4; Alliance (UMNO–MCA)–3; and Independent–1.

84. Lee Kuan Yew was born in Singapore in 1923. Attended Raffles Institution, Singapore, graduated in Law (placed first in honours list) from Cambridge in 1950 when he returned to Singapore and became increasingly involved in politics. Actively involved in advising and defending trade unionists in disputes and litigation. Founding member and secretary-general of the PAP since its inception in November 1954. Led the PAP to victory in 1959 when he formed his first government and became Prime Minister of an internally self-governing Singapore. Convincingly argued for Singapore's merger with Malaya, and brought the Island into Malaysia in September 1963. Became Prime Minister of the independent Republic of Singapore after the separation of the Island from Malaysia in

August 1965. Married Kwa Geok Choo, his Raffles College mate just before the Second World War and who studied with him at Cambridge until their return to Singapore where they married in September 1950. They have three children: Lee Hsien Loong, Lee Wei Ling and Lee Hsien Yang.

85. Pang Cheng Lian, *Singapore's People's Action Party: Its History, Organization and Leadership*, Kuala Lumpur, 1971, p. 1.

86. Ibid., and Yeo Kim Wah, *Political Development in Singapore, 1945–1955*, pp. 117–18.

87. Lee Kuan Yew, *The Battle for Merger*, Singapore, 1961, pp. 3–4. The Johor Causeway linking Singapore to Malaya was first opened to traffic in 1923.

88. Discussion with the late Wong Lin Ken, Professor of History, University of Singapore, Singapore, June 1974.

89. Lee Kuan Yew, op. cit., p. 5.

90. See Pang Cheng Lian, op. cit., pp. 11–13.

91. Means, op. cit., p. 141n; and *Malayan Times*, 21 June 1962. Duncan Sandys was Britain's Minister of State for Commonwealth Relations.

92. *Singapore Free Press*, 3 June 1961.

93. T. J. Bellows, *The People's Action Party of Singapore: Emergence of a Dominant Party System*, New Haven, 1970, pp. 41–7; and Pang Cheng Lian, op. cit., pp. 14–15.

94. Federation of Malaya, *Joint Public Statement Issued by the British and Malayan Governments on 1 August 1962*, Kuala Lumpur, 1962, para. 3.

95. Osborne, *Singapore and Malaysia*, pp. 23–8. In addition, 25 per cent of the 624,000 registered electors cast blank votes which were counted as votes for the Government that is, for merger on the terms of the White paper. There were two other types of merger arrangements, each of which, however, commanded less than 2 per cent votes from the electorate: (a) a complete and unconditional merger as a state on an equal basis with the other eleven states in accordance with the constitutional documents of the Federation of Malaya; and (b) entry into Malaysia on terms no less favourable than the terms for the Borneo territories. See also Pang Cheng Lian, op. cit., p. 16.

96. *Singapore Free Press*, 31 May 1961. S. Rajaratnam was born in Ceylon in 1915. Early education in Seremban and Victoria Institution, Kuala Lumpur. Went into journalism, was editor of *Singapore Standard* from 1950 to 1954 and was on the editorial staff of *Straits Times* until he resigned in 1959 to give his full time to PAP politics. He was a founder member of the party. An MP in the Malaysian Parliament until Singapore's separation in 1965. Over the years, he has held the portfolios of Minister for Culture, Labour, and Foreign Affairs in Singapore.

97. *Malayan Times*, 25 September 1962.

98. Ibid.

99. Great Britain, *Malaysia: Agreement concluded between the United Kingdom of Great Britain and Northern Ireland, the Federation of Malaya, North Borneo, Sarawak and Singapore* (hereinafter referred to as *Malaysia Agreement*), London, 1963, Annex A, Article 9.

100. Ibid., Annex K.

101. Simandjuntak, op. cit., p. 139; and Government of Singapore, *Memorandum Setting out Heads of Agreement for a Merger between the Federation of Malaya and Singapore*, Singapore, 1961.

102. *Malaysia Agreement*, Annex J, para. 1(1). Like Penang and Singapore, Labuan, off the south-west coast of Sabah, had been an entrepôt for the greater part of its history since Britain acquired it from the Sultan of Brunei and made it a Crown Colony in 1846. See N. Tarling, 'The Entrepot at Labuan and the Chinese' in J. Ch'en and N. Tarling (eds.), *Studies in the Social History of China and Southeast Asia*, London, 1970, pp. 355–73; and K. G. Tregonning, *North Borneo*, London, 1960, ch. 13.

103. *Malaysia Agreement*, Annex J, para. 2(1) and (2); and 6(1) and (2). The Tariff Advisory Board was established only in July 1964.

104. *Malaysia Agreement*, Annex J, para. 9(a).

105. *Straits Times*, 10 July 1961. A. M. Azahari was a Brunei political leader who had spent time in Indonesia, taking an active part in opposing Dutch rule together with the Indonesian revolutionaries after 1945. President of Partai Rakyat Brunei which opposed the participation of the Sultanate in Malaysia. Centrally involved in the December 1962 Brunei revolt, after which he avoided public appearance, at any rate in Malaysia and Brunei; but is believed to be in Indonesia now (notably Kalimantan). Ong Kee Hui was a veteran Sarawak politician who was a founding member and president of the Sarawak United People's Party (SUPP). He initially opposed the Malaysia plan; and his party remained in the opposition until it formed a coalition with the Sarawak Alliance in July 1970. Soon after, Ong Kee Hui was awarded the title of 'Datuk' and became a member of the Federal Cabinet as Minister of Technology, Research and Local Government. He became Minister of Local Government and Environment after being returned in the 1974 Malaysian general elections. He has lately retired from politics.

106. *Singapore Free Press*, 28 June 1961.

107. *The Times*, London, 21 June 1961.

108. Interview with the present writer, Kuching, November 1971.

109. *The Times*, 28 July 1961.

110. Means, op. cit., p. 141.

111. T. E. Smith, *The Background to Malaysia*, London, 1963, p. 27.

112. Sir William Goode in *Straits Times*, 29 June 1961.

113. *Straits Times*, 10 July 1961. Brunei had been promised elections by September 1961. These were eventually held the following year. Azahari's Partai Rakyat 'won all 55 constituencies in the 1962 local elections, and consequently occupied the 16 unofficial seats in the 33-member State Legislative Council through the operation of the electoral college system'. Simandjuntak, op. cit., p. 151.

114. *The Bulletin*, Sydney, 25 November 1961. See also R. Emerson, *From Empire to Nation*, Cambridge, Mass., 1962, Pt. 4.

115. *Straits Times*, 22 July 1961.

116. *Straits Times*, 25 August 1961.

117. *Straits Times*, 19 December 1961.

118. Interview with the present writer, Kuala Lumpur, November 1973.

119. *Straits Times*, 19 July 1961.

120. Interview with Datuk Ong Kee Hui, Kuala Lumpur, November 1973. In the course of 1961 and 1962 the Federation Government and Singapore invited numerous leaders from Sarawak and Sabah to undertake study tours of the Peninsula and Singapore. Many of these visitors were doubtful about Malaysia, but subsequently became ardent supporters of the proposal. See J. P. Ongkili, *The Borneo Response to Malaysia, 1961–1963*, Singapore, 1967, ch. 4.

121. R. McKie, *Malaysia in Focus*, Sydney, 1963, p. 199.

122. *Straits Times*, 2 February 1962. See also 'Malaysia–An Economic Challenge', *United Asia*, Bombay, March 1962, pp. 175–6.

123. See Colony of Sarawak, *Malaysia and Sarawak*, Kuching, 1962; and Colony of North Borneo, *North Borneo and Malaysia*, Jesselton, 1962.

124. Colony of Sarawak, *Report of the Commission of Enquiry, North Borneo and Sarawak, 1962* (hereinafter referred to as *Cobbold Commission Report*), Kuching, 1962, p. vi.

125. Ibid., paras. 5–8.

126. Ibid., para. 144.

127. Ibid., para. 236.

128. Ibid., para. 237.

129. *Straits Times*, 25 and 26 August 1961.

130. Colony of North Borneo, *Malaysia: Report of the Inter-Governmental Committee* (hereinafter referred to as *IGC Report*), Jesselton, 1963, paras. 4–8.

131. Ibid., paras. 15–17.

132. Ibid., para. 18.

133. Ibid., paras. 19–21. See also Ahmad Ibrahim, 'Malaysia as a Federation', *Jernal Undang-Undang, Journal of Malaysian and Comparative Law*, 1, Pt. 1, May 1974, pp. 1–27.

134. *IGC Report*, para. 24.

135. Ibid., para. 25.

136. Ibid., para. 26.

137. Ibid., paras. 27–9.

138. For the text of the 'Twenty Points', see J. P. Ongkili, *Modernization in East Malaysia, 1960–1970*, Kuala Lumpur, 1972, Appendix I. Sarawak leaders agreed that their demands for conditions and safeguards in joining Malaysia in general coincided with those contained in the 'Twenty Points'. Information obtained from interviews with Sarawak leaders.

139. See *Malaysia Agreement*, Annex B, ch. 2; and Annex C, ch. 2.

140. Discussion with the present writer, Jesselton, October 1960.

141. SCA Secretary-general to the present writer, 27 July 1966.

142. For a more comprehensive treatment of the political parties of Sarawak and Sabah, see Ongkili, *Modernization in East Malaysia, 1960–1970*, ch. 4.

143. *Malaysia Agreement*, Annex A. See also Malaysia, *Malaysia Federal Constitution*, Kuala Lumpur, 1964; and H. E. Groves, *The Constitution of Malaysia*, Singapore, 1964.

144. *Straits Times*, 5 July 1961.

145. Ibid.

146. *Straits Times*, 7 July 1961.

147. Smith, op. cit., p. 22.

148. See J. P. Ongkili, 'Pre-Western Brunei, Sarawak and Sabah', *Sarawak Museum Journal*, 20, Nos. 40–41 (New Series), January–December 1972, pp. 1–20.

149. *The Sunday Mail*, Brisbane, 9 December 1962; and J. A. C. Mackie, 'Azahari's Young Men', *Nation*, Sydney, 12 January 1963, p. 7.

150. See R. S. Milne, 'Malaysia: A New Federation in the Making', *Asian Survey*, No. 2, February 1963, p. 80.

151. *Straits Times*, 8 February 1963.

152. *Straits Times*, 7 July 1961.

153. Interview with a Brunei leader who asked to remain anonymous.

154. *Straits Times*, 8 June 1963.

155. Interview with Justice Neil Lawson, Q.C., Lewes, England, June 1972.

156. *Malaysia Agreement*, Annex A, Clause 6.

157. *Malayan Times*, 17 June 1963. The Agong who visited Brunei in July 1961 was the Raja of Perlis, Tuanku Syed Putra ibni Al-Marhum Syed Hassan Jamalullail, who was succeeded as Agong by the Sultan of Terengganu, Tuanku Ismail Nasiruddin Shah ibni Al-Marhum Sultan Zainal Abidin on 21 September 1965. See also Ongkili, 'Pre-Western Brunei, Sarawak and Sabah'.

158. Interview with Pehin Pengiran Abdul Momen, State Secretary of Brunei, Bandar Seri Begawan (Brunei Town), November 1971.

159. Malaysia, *Proclamation of Malaysia*, Kuala Lumpur, 1963. See also Means, op. cit., pp. 315–17.

6

The Challenges to the Malaysian Concept

THE desire to form a bigger and, it was hoped, more viable nation led to the establishment of Malaysia in 1963. But crises arose almost immediately and in the following years which imposed a severe strain on the Malaysian political leadership and the nation as a whole. There were external threats in the form of the Indonesian *Konfrontasi* (Confrontation) and the Philippines' claim to Sabah[1] but these two developments will not be dealt with here at any great length since the present study is primarily concerned with the internal process and problems of nation-building. These external threats were, nevertheless, significant in amplifying the strains within the society and *Konfrontasi*, in particular, brought to the surface the inherent communal tensions.[2] There were two internal crises which emerged within less than ten years after the birth of Malaysia, namely, the 'Singapore Separation' and the 1969 racial riots. They were not unrelated events for both were continuations of the long-drawn conflict between Malays and Chinese. The Indians were not entirely uninvolved but because their number in Malaysia is relatively small, they tended to be overshadowed by the larger Chinese community.

'Malaysian Malaysia' and the Singapore Separation

It can be argued that the political ambition of Singapore leaders, particularly Lee Kuan Yew, which unavoidably led to racial polarization, was mainly responsible for the separation of the island-state in 1965. Although Singapore was allotted 15 Dewan Ra'ayat seats in the Malaysian Parliament, no Singapore leader was appointed to the Federal Cabinet throughout the 23 months during which the Island was a part of Malaysia. (In the same period there were several Bornean members of the

Cabinet.[3]) It was clearly this exclusion from the highest echelon of national government which increasingly frustrated Lee Kuan Yew and his PAP colleagues and prompted them to assert themselves in an increasingly strident manner after Malaysia Day. The fact that Singapore, with a population of 1,750,000 people was allocated only 15 Dewan Ra'ayat seats as against, for instance, Sarawak's 24 seats for no more than 800,000 people[4] served to insulate the rest of Malaysia from Singapore political influence.[5] From the beginning of Singapore's participation as a state in Malaysia, the PAP leaders resented these restrictions on their political roles.

The fact that the PAP Government virtually made a unilateral declaration of independence on 31 August 1963 instead of complying with the decision of the Malayan Parliament to proclaim Malaysia on 16 September 1963 presaged the subsequent deterioration of relations between the Singapore and the federal leaders.[6] On 31 August Lee Kuan Yew declared, 'Federal powers over defence and external affairs from today till September 16 [shall] be reposed in our Yang Di-pertuan Negara. We look upon ourselves as trustees for the Central Government of Malaysia in these fifteen days'.[7] Singapore held a snap general election in September 1963, five days after Malaysia Day, and the PAP, which just two years before had lost 70 per cent of its members to the Barisan Sosialis, won 37 of the 51 Legislative Assembly seats. The Singapore Alliance Party which was openly supported by the mainland Malayan Alliance captured none and relations between Singapore and Kuala Lumpur headed for disaster.[8] The Alliance was humiliated; the Tunku was 'shocked'.[9]

The Malayan Alliance leaders received more shocks when the PAP decided to extend its branches and field eleven candidates in the Malayan parliamentary elections of April 1964. There was, according to Malayan Alliance leaders, an understanding when Malaysia was formed that Singapore politicians would confine their party activities to Singapore. Tunku Abdul Rahman stated that it had been written in the Malaysia Agreement that Singapore 'should have representation in our Parliament and fit into the pattern by having her own administration machinery, and her own elections. The first sign of Singapore's attempt to have a hand in the affairs of Malaysia was in the last elections when the PAP contested some of the constituencies. That was quite contrary to what we agreed.'[10] Replying to this contention later, when Singapore–Kuala Lumpur relations had further deteriorated, Dr Toh Chin Chye, the chairman of the PAP, maintained: 'Charges have been made that the PAP has ambitions to capture power at the centre. Surely any political party, big or small, which is worth its salt and receives the support of the people, must have such an objective if it is to put into practice its political ideals.'[11] It should be noted that earlier, on 9 September 1963, Lee Kuan Yew himself had said that the PAP would not contest the 1964 Malayan elections. He declared, 'we want to show the MCA that even if the PAP keeps out of the elections on the mainland, the MCA will still lose.'[12]

It was clear that the political marriage between Malaya and Singapore did not rest on a firm foundation, and even in the first few uncertain months the partners were increasingly not seeing eye to eye. Of the eleven PAP candidates nominated in the 1964 Malayan parliamentary elections, two did not campaign actively for their Johor constituencies because it turned out that the Alliance candidates there came from UMNO instead of the MCA which the PAP particularly wanted to see defeated in the elections; three others lost their deposits and only one, C. V. Devan Nair, won—largely by the votes of the Indians in the Bungsar constituency of Kuala Lumpur.[13] The PAP made no bones about its wish to replace the MCA in the ruling Malayan Alliance. Lee Kuan Yew thought that the effective leadership which could sustain Malaysia was 'that of the Tengku and Tun Razak in UMNO' but the PAP secretary-general added, 'the Chinese leadership in the Alliance as represented by the Malayan Chinese Association is replaceable'.[14] However it has been correctly pointed out, 'Though the PAP was anxious to co-operate with UMNO, the latter preferred to stand by its ally, the MCA.'[15] At all events, although the PAP had not wanted to become an opposition to the Federal Government, as it considered that that 'would be to court disaster for the country', it was the case that from the moment of its startling defeat in the 1964 Malayan elections 'the PAP seemed to turn its efforts more and more clearly towards opposition to the Alliance and the Central Government, and to have given up the idea of joining and cooperating with the Tunku and his political entourage'. The ensuing battle clearly did 'court disaster for the country'.[16]

Tan Siew Sin, the MCA president, alleged that Lee Kuan Yew had suggested to the Tunku that the PAP replace the MCA in the Singapore Alliance Party. Lee Kuan Yew replied that Malayan Alliance leaders themselves had suggested that the PAP establish a united front with the Singapore Alliance Party.[17] The PAP grew increasingly contemptuous of MCA leaders. 'Lee reserved his harshest phrases for MCA leaders. In his most notorious attack, he described them as political eunuchs. He called them greedy and inept and said they were expendable. No wonder those Malaysians who personally hated Lee most were to be found in the top echelons of MCA leadership.'[18] But the direct attack on the MCA boomeranged on the PAP. In the first place, it dismayed the UMNO leaders, who wished to ensure the continued unity of the Malayan

Alliance, and prompted them to rally behind the MCA against the PAP. Secondly, and more profoundly in terms of the realities of Malaysian politics, the confrontation between the MCA and the PAP from the 1964 elections until the separation of Singapore in 1965 belied the presumption that the Chinese in Malaysia would always act in concert against the Malays or other non-Chinese in the region.

In July 1964 racial riots took place in Singapore. The incidents were repeated in September. Lee Kuan Yew went on the radio to explain that there had been organization and planning behind the riots. He thereby implied the involvement of what he called the 'ultra Malays'. Among these was the UMNO Secretary-General Syed Jaafar Albar who, nine days prior to the July riots, 'arrived in Singapore to mount a campaign to secure for the Singapore Malays the special privileges which he felt they deserved'.[19] Tunku Abdul Rahman subsequently explained that the Singapore Malays 'expected the Government to improve their lot but the State Government of Singapore made no provision for special treatment of one particular race or community. They, therefore, felt aggrieved.'[20] Sober moments for reflection became increasingly scarce as both sides continued making charges and counter-charges. Eight months before separation took place, the Tunku, as if premonitorily, said 'If the politicians of various colours and tinges and flashes in Singapore disagree with me, *the only solution is a break-away*, but what a calamity that would be for Singapore and Malaysia'.[21]

In point of fact, it was increasingly obvious that the PAP wished to achieve control of the Federal Government. The most concrete manifestation of this wish was the promotion of the concept of 'Malaysian Malaysia', a political campaign for equality for all in Malaysia, irrespective of class, colour or creed. Spearheaded by the PAP, the movement gained momentum when five opposition parties in Malaysia met in Singapore on 9 May 1965 and formed the Malaysian Solidarity Convention (MSC). The five parties were almost entirely non-Malay and principally Chinese-supported: the PAP; the SUPP and MACHINDA, a tiny multiracial group from Sarawak; and the United Democratic Party (UDP) and People's Progressive Party (PPP) from the states of Malaya. The MSC Declaration proclaimed:

Support for the ideal of a Malaysian Malaysia means, in theory as well as in practice, educating and encouraging the various races in Malaysia to seek political affiliation not on the basis of race and religion but on the basis of common political ideologies and common social and economic aspirations, which is the real basis of ensuring the emergence of a truly free prosperous and equitable national community.[22]

The wish to gain control of the Federal Government became plain a fortnight after the formation of the MSC when Lee Kuan Yew stated that if it was 'necessary to have a Malaysian Malaysia through such a group of parties making an effort to win the majority of seats in Malaysia to form the Government, well so be it'. In fact he added, 'It has to be done'.[23]

'Malaysian Malaysia' and the MSC in effect challenged one of the most fundamental provisions of the Malaysia Agreement, namely that the special position of the Malays and the indigenous communities of northern Borneo would be upheld.[24] While Singapore had agreed to these provisions, by March 1965 Lee Kuan Yew could state during a well-publicized international tour, 'My charge is not that there are these special rights but that these special rights will not solve the problem. How does giving bus licences or licences to run bus companies to one or two hundred Malay families solve the problem of Malay poverty?'[25] The MSC Declaration argued: 'The people of Malaysia did not vote for a non-democratic Malaysia. They did not vote for a Malaysia assuring hegemony to one community. Still less would they be prepared to fight for the preservation of so meaningless a Malaysia'.[26]

Increasingly, the Malays were perturbed by the growing challenge emanating from the non-Malays, notably from the platform of the MSC. The influential Utusan Melayu declared in April 1965, 'The Malays must not think that non-Malays could help them. If the Malays join other parties, especially those that are led by non-Malays, the consequences will be very grave'.[27] Many Malays began to demand the arrest of Lee Kuan Yew. On 12 May 1965 a group of UMNO youths assembled outside the Kampung Datuk Keramat Community Hall in Kuala Lumpur to burn the effigy of the Singapore Prime Minister. Four days later Utusan Zaman reported that the Malays had picketed the Dewan Bahasa dan Pustaka building in the federal capital with posters which inter alia read 'Suspend Singapore's Constitution' and 'Detain Lee Kuan Yew'.[28] The Dewan Bahasa dan Pustaka (Language and Literature Agency) had been the visible symbol and means of widening research on and usage of the national language, Malay.

A truce agreed upon by the Alliance and the PAP in September 1964 whereby all sides were to 'avoid sensitive issues' for two years had all but broken down.[29] By July 1965 Utusan Melayu was reporting the repeated 'accusation that the People's Action Party was opposing the sovereignty of the Malay Rulers, Special Malay Rights, Islam and the National Language'.[30] Verily the Malayan leaders and their PAP counterparts were headed for an impasse. 'Ultimately, both sides came to view the contest as a question of whether Singapore's or Malaya's approach to communal issues would become the pattern for all states in

Malaysia. Or, to put it more bluntly, who was the genuine non-communal leader—Tunku Abdul Rahman or Lee Kuan Yew'.[31]

But Tunku Abdul Rahman had already made his decision. While convalescing in a London clinic in June 1965 he felt that if the PAP leaders persisted in challenging the federal leadership, communal feelings would be exacerbated to the point of causing the disintegration of Malaysia. Returning to Malaysia, rather reticent but solemn, he passed through Singapore and proceeded to Kuala Lumpur on 5 August 1965. The next day Lee Kuan Yew, who was on his 'annual breather' with his family in the cool Cameron Highlands, received a trunk call from Dr Goh Keng Swee in Kuala Lumpur. Lee Kuan Yew rushed to the federal capital. The following day, 7 August, he met the Tunku and signed the separation agreement.[32] Lee Kuan Yew asked for a brief note from the Tunku for Dr Toh Chin Chye, the chairman of the PAP who, Lee said, would otherwise be unwilling to sign the separation agreement. The Tunku wrote:

I am writing to tell you that I have given the matter of our break with Singapore my utmost consideration and I find that in the interest of our friendship and the security and peace of Malaysia as a whole there is absolutely no other way out.

If I were strong enough and able to exercise complete control of the situation I might perhaps have delayed action, but I am not, and so while I am able to counsel tolerance and patience I think the amicable settlement of our differences in this way is the only possible way out.[33]

The Malaysian Parliament was hurriedly convened, and in his speech on Singapore's separation on 9 August 1965 the Tunku traced the origins of the conflict which led to the unfortunate break. He said that repressive measures could have been taken against the Singapore Government, but concluded:

I believe the second course of action which we are taking, that is the breakaway, is the best and the right one, sad as it may be. We are pledged to form Malaysia with Singapore but having given it a trial we found that if we persist in going on with it, in the long run there will be more trouble to Malaysia than what Singapore is worth to us. The separation will be made on the understanding that we shall cooperate closely on matters of defence, trade and commerce.[34]

On the same day, with all the Singapore leaders having withdrawn to their Island, Lee Kuan Yew proclaimed that 'Singapore shall be forever a sovereign democratic and independent nation, founded upon the principles of liberty and justice and ever seeking the welfare and happiness of her people in a more just and equal society'.[35] Singapore was out of Malaysia, twenty-three months after the inauguration of the new nation.

Bornean Reactions to the Separation

Reactions to Singapore's separation from Malaysia occurred in both Sarawak and Sabah. In Sarawak, the SUPP and MACHINDA called for a referendum to decide if the people of the state still wished to remain in Malaysia following the expulsion of an important sister state. Ong Kee Hui perhaps represented the feelings of many who were genuinely perturbed by the separation when he stated:

The Government seems to have little respect for the Constitution. There was no time to assess reaction and public opinion. The Government has made nonsense of parliamentary democracy. The SUPP has tried to make Malaysia work. Now that Singapore is out, what justification is there for it to continue? . . . What will be the position of the Borneo states if there should emerge governments there not so pliable to Alliance ways? The London treaty on the formation of Malaysia has been abrogated. Had the Borneo people no right to be consulted? A referendum should be held to establish the people's wishes.[36]

The federal leaders, however, did not take kindly to their actions being queried in this manner. The Tunku visited Kuching following the separation and warned about government opponents whom he described as communist sympathizers: 'I look upon all enemies of the State who try to overthrow the Government by force as Communists'.[37] It was a rather oversimplified view, but the message was clear: because the SUPP was often charged with being infiltrated by communists in Sarawak, its criticism of the separation of Singapore could be taken as a pretext for accusing the Sarawak party of being an enemy of the state. The SUPP demand for a referendum fizzled out for lack of support.

In Sabah some poignant reactions were witnessed. The Sabah Alliance was in a commotion for a while as the UPKO leaders felt vehemently dissatisfied with 'the Federal Government's failure to consult Sabah and Sarawak over Singapore's expulsion from Malaysia and [there were] fears of Central Government rule at the expense of the greater local autonomy sought by Dato Stephens and his colleagues'.[38] In view of the fact that Dato Donald Stephens was bound by collective responsibility as Minister of Sabah Affairs and Civil Defence in the Federal Cabinet, he offered to resign his presidency of UPKO. His party colleagues refused his proposal, explaining that the Dato was not to blame for the separation of Singapore. The outspoken UPKO leaders called for 'a re-examination of arrangements made in respect of Sabah's entry into Malaysia in view of Singapore's separation from the federation'.[39] The Sabah Alliance went so far as to appoint a ten-man committee to take up the UPKO demand for re-examination. However, the attempt to question the Federal Government on its alteration of the agreed basis of Malaysia rapidly lost appeal, as in Sarawak, when the Tunku also visited Sabah and soon afterwards Dato Stephens resigned his portfolio in the Federal Cabinet. As in Sarawak, reactions against the Singapore separation failed to command widespread support in Sabah.

The lack of support for the re-examination of the terms on which Sarawak and Sabah entered Malaysia consequent upon the separation of Singapore was largely due to the experiences of the Borneans since 1963. In the first place, many of the ruling Alliance leaders in Sarawak and Sabah had achieved their cherished ambitions to be at the helm of politics and government in their own states. Secondly, there was no opposition party to speak of in Sabah, UPKO being itself a member of the ruling Sabah Alliance;[40] while in Sarawak the SUPP had come under suspicion, since it took part in the MSC, of supporting the strident and uncompromising challenge to the basic foundations of Malaysia by the PAP. But no less important in determining Bornean attitudes were the threats to Malaysia which had come from beyond its borders.

While the Philippines under President Diosdado Macapagal had been pursuing its claim to a part of Sabah and refusing to recognize Malaysia until the issue was settled, Indonesia under President Soekarno and his foreign minister Dr Subandrio had stepped up their undeclared war–'Konfrontasi'–against Malaysia. From April 1963 Indonesia began sending 'volunteers' and 'irregular forces' to the border areas between northern Borneo and Kalimantan. During the first half of 1964, as armed encounters became prevalent in these areas, diplomatic moves were initiated with Thailand acting as the mediator between Malaysia and Indonesia.

Little progress was made on the diplomatic front; confrontation continued and indeed reached a critical juncture when the Indonesians made sea and air landings at Pontian and Labis in Johor state in August and September 1964. Although these landings involved only about 140 Indonesians and although they failed, the two incidents bore some significance. It appears that the Indonesian Government organized the landings in the hope of creating communal discord in the states of Malaya. In the case of Pontian, which is less than forty miles from Singapore, the intention seemed to be to cause the Malays in the district to rally to the support of their 'oppressed Malay brothers' in predominantly Chinese Singapore. In Labis, which had been from the beginning a mainly Chinese area, it was hoped that the remnants of the communists who made it one of their strongholds during the Emergency would collaborate with the parachuted infiltrators among whom were ten Malaysian Chinese defectors, two of them girls: 'Apparently, the Indonesian aim was to set up a jungle camp deep in the forest reserve near the mountains and to use local Chinese defectors to recruit other dissidents who would help to stir up the embers of the earlier Communist insurrection'.[41]

That was, however, the beginning of the end of confrontation for the unfruitful landings led to the gradual abatement of Indonesian intransigence towards Malaysia. Following the *coup d'état* of 30 September 1965 the threat from Soekarno rapidly diminished. Yet, despite its failure for Indonesia, confrontation had nationalist significance for Malaysia. As a real threat to the viability of the new nation, confrontation demonstrated that even the 'fence-sitters' in Malaysia proved by and large unwilling to exchange their political rights for whatever was offered by the Soekarno regime. Most non-Malay Malaysians remained tacitly loyal to their new nation.

In so far as the Philippine claim was concerned, from the beginning of assertive local political attitudes in the early 1960s when the claim was also first vociferously put forward by President Macapagal, the leaders of Sabah not only rejected it but also sought the support of their Malayan and Singapore partners in Malaysia to demonstrate that the Philippines had no case. The problem of secessionist Muslims in the southern Philippines had not yet arisen to complicate matters; but even later in the 1960s Datu Mustapha and the other Sabah leaders made it amply clear that they preferred nationhood within Malaysia to membership of a Filipino community directed from and controlled by Manila.[42]

Both the Philippine claim and Indonesian confrontation were overt foreign acts of unfriendliness towards the people of Malaysia. Their overall impact was to solidify nationalist sentiments within the young federation. The leaders of Sabah consistently rejected the Philippine claim while the 1964 Malayan elections demonstrated strong support for the Federal Government in the face of Soekarno's confrontation. While British Commonwealth troops assisted in defending Malaysia against Indonesian onslaughts, the Malaysians themselves showed their awareness of nationhood in a patriotic, even xenophobic, manner. An example was the following statement made by Dato Donald Stephens: 'What the Sukarno Government wants to do is to drag us down to their level. They will only win if we, the people of Malaysia, are divided and if racism is allowed to rear its ugly head in Malaysia. As long as we are united, we need have no fear of confrontation or even an all out war.'[43] In Sarawak, nationalist awareness was not wanting. The Chief Minister, Dato Stephen Kalong Ningkan, explained, 'There is no point in Sabah and Sarawak leaving Malaysia. We benefit from Malaysia. We could not stand alone'.[44] The Council Negri of Sarawak overwhelmingly passed a resolution to the effect: 'That the Council unreservedly support the Federation of Malaysia Government regarding its policy of resisting Indonesian aggression against Sarawak and of taking strong, positive action against the Clandestine Communist Organization and other subversive organisations in Sarawak which support Indonesians in their aggressive acts.'[45] Indeed, Malaysia survived as a nation after the separation of Singapore to a considerable degree because the peoples of Sarawak and Sabah had begun to grow accustomed to being a part of the federation. They had helped to prevent the undoing of the nation by hostile foreign forces; and the totality of Malaysia had come to mean the political anchorage of their nationalist fervour, hopes and aspirations. Singapore was gone; but it was not pre-ordained that Sarawak and Sabah must tread the same path to political loneliness as the island city-state was fated to follow.

The Anatomy of Separation

The separation of Singapore took place because of a number of points of conflict between the Malayan and Singapore leaders. Both groups of leaders believed that there must be inter-communal cooperation in order to form a workable government which would ensure the political survival of the nation. With their socialist orientation and declared platform, the PAP leaders believed that the political survival of Singapore rested on multiracialism. It was basically this belief in inter-communal effort which impelled the party to spearhead the 'Malaysian Malaysia' movement. The MSC declared, 'A Malaysian Malaysia is the antithesis of a Malay Malaysia, a Chinese Malaysia, a Dyak Malaysia, an Indian Malaysia or Kadazan Malaysia and so on'.[46] But for the MSC to achieve its non-communal objectives, surely there had to be inter-communal cooperation and harmony.

At the same time, the Malayan Alliance also believed in the need to maintain inter-communal leadership in order to foster nationhood. As late as March 1965 Tunku Abdul Rahman maintained that in the country 'everyone was trying to create a Malaysian nation'.[47] The Tunku, however, emphasized one of the conflicting factors which led to separation when he charged that Lee Kuan Yew and the PAP wanted a 'Malaysian Malaysia' impatiently—'here and now'—instead of allowing the passage of time to blunt gradually the edges of communal animosities and lingering suspicions among the newly-united but multiracial Malaysian people. When the 'Malaysian Malaysia' movement was being promoted by the PAP leaders the Malaysian Prime Minister described them as young men who wanted to rush things: 'Instead of doing what they want in a quiet and practical way, they tread on everybody's toes, knock everybody's head and bring about chaos, suspicion, misunderstanding, hatred and trouble'.[48]

Aside from the difference in timing for the realization of a 'Malaysian Malaysia', there were also differences in outlook between the Alliance and PAP leaderships which aggravated the problem of achieving consensus:

The Tunku was as deeply wedded to mutli-racialism as Lee, and personally as racially unconscious. But the two men were otherwise poles apart. The Tunku was simplicity personified, Lee was highly complex. The Tunku cherished mass popularity, Lee spurned it. The Tunku was sincere to the point of being embarrassing; Lee was all cleverness. The Tunku's responses sprang from the heart and from his identification with the people, Lee's from the mind and his studied aloofness from the crowd. The Tunku was utterly human, Lee a machine.[49]

The differences in outlook remained incidental during the earlier months when Lee Kuan Yew was prepared to try to win the support of the Tunku and UMNO while at the same time striving to replace the MCA with the PAP in the national Alliance. But when the PAP and its MSC platform sought openly to challenge the Malayan Alliance, it became obvious not only 'that Malaysia was born in atmosphere of conflict and bitterness', but also that 'The PAP in attempting to impose the Singapore style of politics on Malaya was destined to be unsuccessful'.[50]

Conflict and bitterness between Kuala Lumpur and Singapore were exacerbated by the fact that both sides found it difficult to implement even the written agreements relating to economic matters after merger. The PAP leaders considered the establishment of a common market within Malaysia as a fundamental consideration in the merger settlement. 'Merger with Malaya would brighten the prospect of trade by forming a common market between Singapore and the Peninsula.... The federal leaders dragged their feet on the agreed common market proposal.'[51] The administrative machinery designed to facilitate the establishment of the common market, the Tariff Advisory Board, was only set up a year after merger, largely because 'Kuala Lumpur did not want the common market to be established before a national industrialization policy had been worked out, for fear that it would lead to an even greater industrial imbalance between Singapore and the other states of the federation'.[52]

The Federal Government was meant to ask the consent of the Singapore Government before imposing new import duties for the first five years after Malaysia Day; but the 1965 federal budget imposed a number of new taxes which Singapore objected to on the grounds that the state government had not been consulted beforehand and that the new taxes, which the Federal Government explained were necessary because of added defence expenditure in the face of Indonesian confrontation, had not been foreseen in the original merger agreements.[53] More indicative of future inability to reach agreement on financial matters was the fact that differences on the allocations of revenues derived from Singapore led the two Governments to submit their cases to the World Bank for arbitration.[54]

Singapore for its part failed to fulfil important aspects of the merger agreements. The PAP Government paid nothing towards development in the Borneo states, although it had been agreed that Singapore should make available to the Federal Government two 15-year loans totalling $150 million 'to assist development in the Borneo territories'.[55] In refusing to honour the agreement the Singapore leaders maintained that the Borneo loans were a quid pro quo for implementing the common market arrangement. Since the Federal Government appeared to procrastinate over the common market issue, the PAP leaders decided that the Borneo loans were not due for delivery.

Thus the Singapore separation involved the political, socio-cultural and economic aspects of nation-building. Many of the factors which the PAP leaders believed made merger imperative, paradoxically became the very causes of separation. At any rate, the non-fulfilment of some of the PAP's main aims rendered separation all the more likely. A writer who had personal acquaintance with many of the PAP leaders believed that Lee Kuan Yew fought for Malaysia 'because this was the only way that Singapore could free itself entirely from the remnant shackles of colonialism'.[56] It is hardly necessary to argue that Singapore wished to achieve independence from the British. Malaya had successfully achieved independence and it was evident that the British, through the granting of the Rendel Constitution, the demands of the Marshall and Lim Yew Hock all-party constitutional missions to London, and internal self-government in 1959, were aware that they would have to give independence to Singapore in the foreseeable future. Yet Lee Kuan Yew and his PAP colleagues preferred to campaign for independence through merger with Malaya.

It is one of the enigmas of the period that Lee Kuan Yew and his colleagues, having skilfully championed the merger of Singapore with Malaya, Sarawak and Sabah, with a manifest understanding of the political, socio-cultural and economic factors involved, then proceeded to challenge, and challenge in a hurry, the very federal leadership which they had originally acknowledged as their trustee in keeping the new nation viable and united. A former Singapore Minister of the Interior and Defence, Professor Wong Lin Ken, who first met Lee Kuan Yew in London in 1956, explained:

The PAP went into Malaysia with a promise that it would protect and promote the interests and welfare of the people of Singapore. It could not let down the people by ignoring that undertaking made to them when they were asked to support the PAP's merger stand. . . . The PAP leaders believed in what they stated and did on the merger issue. That was why Lee Kuan Yew was very emotionally affected by separation.[57]

That the Kuala Lumpur–Singapore conflict was unfortunate and indeed largely unintended may be seen from Lee Kuan Yew's words upon separation:

You see, this is a moment of. . . . You know, every time we look back on this moment when we signed this Agreement which severed Singapore from Malaysia, it will be a moment of anguish. I mean, for me it is a moment of anguish because all my life. . . . You see, the whole of my adult life I had believed in merger and the unity of these two territories. You know, as a people connected by geography, economics and ties of kinship. . . . Will you mind if we stop for a while?[58]

Lee Kuan Yew was indeed 'very emotionally affected'. He did not complete the sentence before he asked for a pause in that televised press conference on 9 August 1965. One of his arch political adversaries during the twenty-three months Singapore was in Malaysia, Tun Tan Siew Sin,[59] retired from active politics in April 1974. Like Lee Kuan Yew, he said the separation of Singapore affected him deeply: 'It was a tragedy for both countries. It was the failure of a dream.'[60]

After all that has been said, it is only too clear that the most significant underlying factor which resulted in the need for separation was the mounting tension in the Sino–Malay relationship. Lee Kuan Yew's call for a 'Malaysian Malaysia' reminded the Malays of the British attempt to create a Malayan Union where Malays and non-Malays were to enjoy equal political rights and this, in Malay eyes, was an attempt to wrest from them all that they considered their birthright. In endeavouring to justify his cause, Lee Kuan Yew opened up issues most hurtful to Malay feelings; he questioned what the British themselves always accepted until 1946—that Malaya belonged to the Malays. The effect of Singapore's withdrawal from Malaysia was to postpone racial clashes for about four years.

Political Trends, 1965–1969

When Singapore became a sovereign and independent nation, Malaysia was not destroyed, but the departure of the recalcitrant and oppositionist member-state did not bring halcyon days to the reduced federation either. In explaining the need to detach Singapore from Malaysia, Tunku Abdul Rahman had said, 'It appeared that as soon as one issue was resolved, another cropped up. Where a patch was made here, a tear appeared elsewhere, and where one hole was plugged, other leaks appeared.'[61] The separation was followed by feelings of disappointment and much heaping of blame for the failure of an experiment in nation-building by each of the two parties concerned upon the other: strained relations continued for sometime between Singapore and Malaysia.

However the earlier external threats began, fortuitously, to ebb away. While the Philippines all but dropped its contentious claim to Sabah after President Ferdinand Marcos took office in early 1966,[62] the gradual but almost inevitable downfall of President Sukarno following the *coup d'état* of 30 September 1965 led to the demise of Confrontation.[63] In July 1966 an exchange of Notes in Manila normalized relations between Malaysia and the Philippines, while the signing of the Djakarta Agreement of August 1966 marked the resumption of diplomatic relations between Malaysia and Indonesia. Thereafter, Malaysia was relatively at peace with its neighbours,[64] and could devote greater energy and time to the domestic problems which continued to emerge.

In general, the departure of Singapore from Malaysia caused fore-boding among the non-Malays that with the subtraction of one and a half million Chinese from the federation the Alliance Government under the political dominance of the United Malays National Organization (UMNO) might implement increasingly pro-Malay policies. Hence the Chinese, through the Malaysian Chinese Association (MCA), once more agitated for a 'more liberal use' of the Chinese language for official communications and purposes.[65] The Selangor, Perak and Penang branches of the MCA urged their national party headquarters to champion the issue to the extent that the latter endorsed the demand for a liberal use of the Chinese language in government notices, forms, signboards and announcements. A twenty-man Alliance Committee was established to resolve disputes within the Alliance and 'to solve the language problem'.[66]

It will be recalled that as early as the 1950s, language had featured prominently as one of the major issues in the political development of Malaya. In the prolonged effort to establish a national system of edu-cation, the matter of language was a prime consideration. The indepen-dence negotiations dwelt on it, and Article 152 of the 1957 Federation Constitution embodied the agreement among the multiracial leaders that 'the national language shall be the Malay language'. But for a period of ten years from Merdeka Day, that is to say until 1967, English could be used for all official purposes.[67] For the states of Malaya, these provisions were retained in the Constitution of Malaysia. So was the provision that 'no person shall be prohibited or prevented from using (otherwise than for official purposes) or from teaching or learning any other language'.[68]

It was indicative of the continuing importance of language as an aspect of nation-building in Malaysia that sections of the Malay population began early to exert pressure on the Federal Government so that no concession would be made to the non-Malays on the proposal to make Malay the sole official language by 1967. Led by Syed Nasir bin Ismail, the Director of the Dewan Bahasa dan Pustaka, the Malays set up in early 1965 a *Barisan Bertindak Bahasa Kebangsaan*, or National Language Action Front, 'to assist the government in the implementation of Malay as the official language by 1967'.[69] This was actually a manifestation of Malay feelings aroused in response to Lee Kuan Yew's attack on the Malays. As a result, the Chinese in the Peninsula (as we have seen) but also the Indians to some extent, began to demand a 'more liberal use' of their languages for official purposes.

In spite of the basic agreement that Malay would be the sole official language by 1967, it was a measure of the problem of choosing a common language for a multiracial society that when the national language bill was passed in March 1967 it in fact contained indirect provisions for the continued official use of languages other than Malay. The Act gave 'the right to the Federal Government or any State Government to use any translation of official documents or communications in the language of any other community in the Federation for such purposes as may be deemed necessary in the public interest'.[70] In addition, the Act empowered the Yang di-Pertuan Agong to allow the use of English for such official purposes as might be deemed fit; and provisions were made for the continued use of English in the Parliament, state Assemblies, the texts of laws passed by the various legislatures and in the law courts of the country.[71] Although these indirect concessions to the non-Malays *vis-à-vis* the official use of their languages might have been necessary at that stage of nation-building, they also delayed the wider use of the national language and its implementation as the unifying factor among the communities which it was meant to be, until well into the 1970s.

Political trends continued along communal lines for the remainder of the 1960s in West and in East Malaysia.[72] The Alliance remained safely in power, despite internal haggling among the three component parties: 'Much of the democratic struggle goes on within the Alliance, so that by the time the level of Alliance policy is reached, many of the potential conflicts are already compromised'.[73] That had been the nature and pattern of Alliance politics since the formation of the UMNO–MCA alliance in 1952 and continued to be so until the 1969 general elections. Nonetheless, consensus did not prevail across the political spectrum of Malaysia as was evidenced by the formation of parties which opposed the

Alliance between the 1959 and the 1969 elections. The United Democratic Party (UDP) formally came into being in April 1962. It was founded by the key figures who had resigned from the MCA after a crisis in 1959.[74] The UDP, led by Dr Lim Chong Eu, Too Joon Hing and others, attempted to project a multiracial image but its leaders found it difficult to carry through an inter-communal platform inasmuch as they knew their main supporters were Chinese. The UDP was a party on the horns of a dilemma; for while it criticized the Federal Government's policy towards Chinese education, it also supported the reservation of special privileges for the Malays for a specific period and approved of Malay as the sole official language.[75]

The parties which contested the 1964 general elections in Malaya were (with the numbers of parliamentary seats they won in brackets): the Alliance (89); the Pan-Malayan Islamic Party or PMIP (9); the Socialist Front (2); the People's Progressive Party or PPP (2); UDP (1); and PAP (1). These parties were mostly the same as in the 1959 elections. Apart from the UDP, the other new party to enter the later poll was the People's Action Party (PAP) of Singapore which fielded only eleven candidates although there were, as in 1959, a total of 104 parliamentary constituencies. The PAP entered the 1964 elections primarily to test its appeal among the Malayan electorate and to begin realizing its wish to replace the MCA in the ruling Malayan Alliance, with the disastrous results we have seen earlier. K. J. Ratnam and R. S. Milne, who made an exhaustive study of the 1964 elections, accounted for the better performance of the Alliance compared to its victory in the 1959 elections in the following manner:

The main feature of the election was perhaps the pre-eminence of a single issue. This was the Indonesian 'confrontation' of Malaysia and the threat it posed to the country's security.... The Alliance argued that it was the only party which could safeguard national integrity and that the difference between voting for it and voting for the other parties was in essence the difference between being loyal and being sympathetic to Indonesian aggression.[76]

The 1964 elections thus tended to be more of a referendum on Indonesian confrontation than a normal periodical opportunity for parties and the electorate to voice their feelings on national and local issues. However, that is not to say that these issues, particularly language and the education system, special rights of the Malays, Islam (between UMNO and the PMIP), need for communal harmony, economic and rural development, foreign capital, foreign policy and internal security, were ignored.[77] On the contrary, they were extensively and often vigorously debated; but the issue of Indonesian confrontation hovered over the whole election campaign. The non-Malays, in particular, gladly supported the Alliance Party because it was prepared to resist Indonesian aggression; there was widespread fear that should Malaysia become a part of Indonesia, the non-Malays would be completely overwhelmed.

Two other political parties subsequently emerged to challenge the dominance of the Alliance in West Malaysia. The first, the Democratic Action Party (DAP), was registered in March 1966 and was in many ways a successor to the PAP, which was de-registered concurrently with the separation of Singapore from Malaysia on 9 August 1965. For some time the new party in fact continued to be led by C. V. Devan Nair, the only PAP candidate to have won a seat in the 1964 parliamentary elections. In opposing the Alliance the DAP continued to espouse many of the 'Malaysian Malaysia' objectives of the PAP. For example, the DAP argued in favour of racial equality and rejected the division of the citizens of Malaysia into *bumiputra* and non-*bumiputra*. (The term *bumiputra* literally means 'son of the soil' or 'native' and is used to designate the Malays and other indigenous peoples of Malaysia, such as the Dayaks of Sarawak, and Kadazans and Bajaus of Sabah.) It disagreed that the 'propagation and permanence of the national language can only be finally secured on the basis of the eventual deculturation of two major communities in Malaysia—the Chinese and the Indians'.[78] As the 1969 general elections drew nearer, the DAP appeared to be increasingly strident in its criticism of Malay rights and the lack of use of Chinese and Tamil as languages for official purposes. Indeed, when the 1969 poll took place the DAP in its pursuit of 'political democracy, social and economic democracy, and cultural democracy' declared: 'All Malaysians must have an equal place under the Malaysian sun. Hence our plea for "A Malaysian Malaysia"'.[79]

The Gerakan Rakyat Malaysia (Gerakan) was inaugurated in March 1968 by former leaders of the Labour Party of Malaya, Dr Tan Chee Khoon and V. Veerappan; Dr Lim Chong Eu of the UDP, which had failed to make a good showing and appeared ready to wind up its affairs; Professor Syed Hussein Alatas of the University of Singapore; and Professor Wang Gungwu of the University of Malaya.[80] It also worked to gain the support of the trade unions and eventually Yeoh Teck Chye, the president of the Malaysian Trade Union Congress, as well as V. David, another unionist of long standing, were elected vice-chairman and deputy secretary-general respectively. The Gerakan was a moderate party which sought genuinely to pursue a non-communal platform. While many of its leaders were non-Malays, it sought to attract Malays to its membership and leadership. Eventually a perceptible number did join and Professor Syed Hussein Alatas became the first party chairman.

The Gerakan's moderate, somewhat intellectual and non-communal approach to politics was evident in the following statement, made in April 1968:

We strive for a Malaysian nationhood evolved out of the existing communities in Malaysia. The process of formation should be left to historical growth. The state participates in its formation by eliminating obstacles to harmony and inter-community acculturation. It should not impose cultural elements or indulge in artificial experiments such as introducing a common dress, dance, ritual and ceremony without regard to the receptivity of the communities in Malaysia. We emphasise common experience and the sense of a common destiny as the decisive essentials of nationhood rather than cultural, religious or ethnic uniformity.[81]

As the 1969 elections approached the Gerakan strove harder to project a non-communal image before the electorate. It especially wished to reduce the Alliance majority in Parliament in order to deny it the two-thirds majority which a ruling party needed before it could seek to amend the Federal Constitution. The Gerakan reaffirmed its abiding wish 'to establish an *integrated society* of Malaysians sharing a common outlook and a common destiny'.[82]

After becoming member-states of Malaysia on 16 September 1963, Sarawak and Sabah proceeded to institutionalize the forms and framework of nationhood which they had settled for in the negotiations to establish the enlarged federation. Politically both tended to follow trends in the Peninsula and the Alliance pattern of inter-communal party grouping was adopted in both. In each Borneo state, the Alliance group captured power during the formation of Malaysia and continued in office through the 1960s, and indeed until 1974. The component parties of the Alliance groups in Sarawak and Sabah represented ethnic communities but the ethnic spectrum differed, of course, from that in the Alliance in the Peninsula.

Between 1963 and 1969, there was only one state election, that in Sabah in April 1967, which saw an electorate in Borneo vote directly for their representatives in the state legislature; understandably, the election issues pertained largely to state matters. During this period federal–state relations featured prominently not in any election but rather in the course of differences between federal and state leaders such as the conflict between Dato Stephen Kalong Ningkan and Kuala Lumpur in 1966.[83] Nevertheless it may be said that the politicization of the people of Sarawak and Sabah advanced considerably in the 1960s; and the sense of being states in a new nation, of belonging to one Malaysian national community, was gaining ground as the 1969 general elections approached.[84]

The 1969 Elections and 13 May

The political parties which contested the 1969 elections in West Malaysia were the Alliance, the DAP, the Gerakan, the PPP and the PMIP. Two other parties, the Labour Party and the Partai Rakyat, boycotted the poll while a 'United Malaysian Chinese Organization' (UMCO) played a negligible role.[85] On the face of it, the 1969 general elections did not differ fundamentally from the two previous polls held in the Peninsula since independence. With the exception of the DAP (which was a successor of the PAP) and the Gerakan, the parties were the same ones which contested the 1959 and 1964 elections and the election issues were substantially those which had preoccupied the parties in the previous polls. The fact that the parties and issues were mainly the same as twice before tended to give the 1969 general elections a pedestrian and routine outlook while the existence of electoral arrangements not to field candidates against each other among the DAP, the Gerakan and the PPP ought to have decided the major issues in a more clear-cut and tidier manner between them and their common adversary, the Alliance. Yet the 1969 elections had consequences far beyond the expectations of most Malaysians. They brought about electoral losses for the Alliance, corresponding gains for the opposition parties, tragic racial riots in Kuala Lumpur on 13 May and for days after, suspension of elections in East Malaysia, and the imposition of a state of emergency through the nation.

The Alliance went to the voters with a feeling of confidence. Television and radio, which were under its control, were fully utilized to project the image of the Government as the architect and well-spring of the phenomenal progress and socio-economic development which the country had experienced in the years since the achievement of Merdeka. Television newsreels recording the activities of the Alliance Government over the years were incessant during the weeks before polling day on 10 May 1969. The Alliance Manifesto confidently declared:

Today we have made available to the overwhelming majority of our rural people the amenities hitherto known only to our urban dwellers. Electricity, water, roads, bridges, schools, clinics and community centres have all been laid on.

While enjoying these amentities we have also endeavoured to ensure that the means to enjoy them are also made equally available. Through land development schemes, the encouragement of oil palm growing, double cropping of padi, the planting of high yielding rubber, and the provision of financial and other forms of assistance to the farmer and the fisherman, we have steadily raised the income levels of our rural people.

With rural development, there has been a concurrent concentration on industrialisation. Our efforts have resulted in a per capita level of income of about

$1,000/- which is one of the highest in Asia. This compares very favourably with $700/- at the time when we took office.[86]

The PMIP's platform remained largely the same as in previous elections. Against the PMIP the Alliance, particularly UMNO, charged that the Kelantan-based party had links with the Malayan Communist Party (MCP) in South Thailand. UMNO leaders alleged that MCP members crossed to the Malaysian border areas to call on people to vote for the PMIP. The Alliance denigrated the PMIP for having kept Kelantan backward since it won control of the state in 1959. Indeed, the Alliance put forward an election manifesto specially for Kelantan which outlined an extensive programme of development with a planned expenditure of $550 million for the only opposition-held state of the country provided the Alliance came to power there in the election.

The DAP campaigned largely for non-Malay votes. In order to help erase the identification of the party with the PAP, its early leader, C. V. Devan Nair retreated to Singapore permanently in 1968. While it did not overtly advocate a socialist system of government, the DAP significantly argued 'that the have-nots in Malaysia are of all races. They are found in rural areas as well as in urban slums'. The party's manifesto unequivocally added:

We give full support to all genuine moves to eradicate poverty and backwardness among our rural population. It must be the paramount concern of all Malaysians to eradicate the economic, social and educational imbalance between our rural and urban sectors. Malaysian prosperity and progress are indivisible. The elimination of Malay peasant poverty and the raising of rural income and of the standards of living of Malay peasantry must therefore be given a major priority.[87]

But it was clear to all and sundry that the DAP was essentially a Chinese party. The PPP, which effected a close electoral link with the DAP, maintained its policy of rejecting the special position of the Malays and other *bumiputra* peoples and reaffirmed that 'a Malaysian Malaysia is the antithesis of a Malay Malaysia. They cannot co-exist'. The PPP manifesto explained clearly why the party was opposed to special privileges:

Special rights and privileges have brought no material or other benefits to the Malay Ra'ayat who after 10 years of independence find themselves in the same social and economic plight they were in before Merdeka.

What has happened is that the Alliance has abused its powers and under the guise of enforcing the special rights, has created a Malay capitalist class which is now exploiting the Malay masses.

The result of this policy is that without bringing any benefits to the Malay Ra'ayat it has served as a constant irritant to non-Malays, disrupting the unity of the people and perpetuating racial prejudices.[88]

Like the DAP, the PPP argued in favour of greater use of the Chinese, Tamil and English languages as media of instruction and examination in the country's education system. All students after completion of their studies should be treated equally in the matter of selection for jobs, irrespective of which school or college they were educated in. The PPP was more strident in its attack on *bumiputra* privileges than the DAP which tended to criticize them only obliquely. Like the DAP, the PPP, although led by the Ceylonese brothers, S. D. and D. R. Seenivasagam, was basically a Chinese party.

The Gerakan, in its efforts to be a non-communal party, understandably trod a moderate course. Its preoccupation with preventing the Alliance from scoring a two-thirds majority in the Dewan Ra'ayat was the overt manifestation of the Gerakan's belief in representative government and its wish 'to safeguard the *rights* and *liberties* of our people from corrosive and abusive legislation and ministerial decrees which undermine the Constitution'.[89] The Gerakan, while not opposed to them, nevertheless wanted 'to prevent Malay privileges from being abused by unscrupulous leaders'. The party also promised 'to eliminate the causes that create *poverty, suffering and ill-health* and *inertia* especially in the rural areas'.[90]

Thus all the main parties contesting the 1969 elections took definite stands on major issues affecting the country. Their manifestos were almost all presented in a sober and serious manner. But the communal feelings generated rapidly increased in intensity. The verbal battles, the insults and innuendos directed at one group or another and the strong support for or opposition to the 'Malaysian Malaysia' concept ought to have alerted the government to the dire consequences that could ensue. The by and large incident-free campaign period, however, generated complacency all round. After all it was almost twenty-five years ago that the country had experienced a serious communal outbreak. A probable conflict had been nipped in the bud in 1965. Voting day again gave no indication of what was to follow.

The results were unexpected. Table 3 which follows shows the position of the parties in the 1964 and 1969 parliamentary elections. The Table clearly shows that the Alliance had suffered large losses. All the opposition parties which actively contested the 1969 elections did better than in the 1964 poll. This general trend was repeated in the state elections, as illustrated in Table 4.

A number of Alliance leaders lost their seats. Senu bin Abdul Rahman, the Minister of Information and Broadcasting, lost to a PMIP candidate in his home state of Kedah; Dr Mahathir bin Mohamad, another UMNO leader of considerable standing from Kedah, also conceded defeat to a

TABLE 3
Parliamentary Election Results

Parties	Seats Won 1964	Seats Won 1969	Votes Polled 1964	Per Cent of Total 1969
Alliance	89	66	58.37	48.41
PMIP	9	12	14.45	23.75
DAP	1*	13	2.06	13.73
PPP	2	4	3.59	3.87
Gerakan	–	8	–	8.57
Partai Rakyat	–	–	–	1.24
Independents	–	–	0.66	0.34

Source: Adapted from R. Vasil, *The Malaysian General Election of 1969*, Appendix II, Table 2(a).
*This was the sole seat (Bungsar) won by PAP.

TABLE 4
State Election Results

Parties	Seats Won 1964	Seats Won 1969	Votes Polled 1964	Per Cent of Total 1969
Alliance	241	162	57.62	47.95
PMIP	25	40	15.25	22.80
DAP (DAP in 1964)	–	31	0.90	11.76
PPP	5	12	4.51	4.79
Gerakan	–	26	–	8.78
Partai Rakyat	*	3	*	1.53
Independents	–	3	1.09	2.29

Source: Adapted from R. Vasil, *The Malaysian General Election of 1969*, Appendix II, Table 1(a).
*In the 1964 poll the Partai Rakyat was a member of the Socialist Front which won seven state seats in those elections.

PMIP candidate; Dr Lim Swee Aun, the Minister of Commerce and Industry, was defeated by a Gerakan candidate; and Dr Ng Kam Poh, the Minister of Social Welfare, lost to an unknown bus driver (a DAP candidate) in the town of Teluk Anson (re-named Teluk Intan in 1982).

Because the Alliance won only 66 of the 104 seats in West Malaysia and was expected to win little more than half of the 40 parliamentary seats in East Malaysia (24 from Sarawak and 16 from Sabah), it seemed likely that the ruling Alliance might not get the coveted two-thirds majority in Parliament. (The elections in East Malaysia were suspended consequent upon the imposition of a national state of emergency in May 1969. When the polls in Sarawak and Sabah were eventually held in June and July 1970, the Alliance won only 23 out of the total of 40 parliamentary seats.)[91]

Although the Alliance remained in power, it had sustained losses in a number of its traditional strongholds and crucial areas. The following passage described its weakened position *vis-à-vis* and other parties:

A new pattern was emerging in the four Northern states. On the east coast the Alliance just about held its own in terms of votes, its gains in Kelantan almost balancing its losses in Trengganu, but it lost heavily to the PMIP in Kedah and to the PMIP and Partai Rakyat in Perlis. . . . In the remaining states the opposition successes were achieved largely by parties appealing to non-Malay electors: The Democratic Action Party (DAP), the Gerakan Ra'ayat Malaysia (Gerakan) and the People's Progressive Party (PPP). The DAP provided the main opposition in Perak, Negri Sembilan, and Malacca, the Gerakan in Penang, while both were strong in Selangor. The Gerakan actually won a majority of the state seats in Penang and took over the state government from the Alliance. The Alliance held on to control of the state government in Selangor and Perak but without having won a majority of the seats in either state assembly.[92]

The Gerakan capture of Penang meant that the Alliance had lost control of two state governments, Kelantan having been retained by the opposition PMIP.

Adding to the surprise that the Alliance had been dealt a severe electoral blow was the fact that the MCA did poorly in the states where Chinese and other non-Malays predominated, namely Selangor, Perak and Penang. In Selangor, the Alliance won only 14 out of the total of 28 state seats; in Perak it secured only 19 out of the total of 40; and in Penang only 4 out of the total of 24 seats went to the Alliance. To aggravate the humiliation of the Alliance, virtually all the federal ministers who retained their seats were returned with reduced majorities.

The main opposition parties were joyful and ebullient over their successes and in their jubilation many of their members and supporters cast caution and decency to the winds. Their irresponsible behaviour contributed directly to the outbreak of communal riots in and around Kuala Lumpur on 13 May 1969. The DAP and Gerakan held 'victory' processions in and around Kuala Lumpur on 11 and 12 May 1969 and it is generally agreed among residents of Kuala Lumpur, who experienced the consequences of the disastrous riots, that the processions were not only noisy but also provocative, arrogant and abusive.[93]

It was officially reported five months after the May riots that some of the highly irresponsible and insulting utterances during the processions were 'Apa polis boleh buat—kita raja!' (What can the police do—we are king!); 'Buang semua polis Melayu!' (Chuck out all Malay policemen!); and 'Mati Melayu, sakai pergi masok hutan!' (Death to the Malays, aborigines go back to the jungle!). Supporters in the Gerakan processions were reported to have shouted: 'Melayu balek kampong' (Malays go back to your kampong); 'Melayu sekarang ta'ada kuasa lagi' (Malays have lost power), 'sekarang kita kontrol' (we are now in control); 'Butoh Melayu' (Balls to the Malays), 'Pergi matilah' (Better go and die); 'Ini negeri bukan Melayu punya, kita mahu halau semua Melayu' (This country does not belong to the Malays, we will chase out all Malays); 'MARA butoh, MARA tundun' (an obscene jeer at MARA). A combined DAP–Gerakan procession was reported to have shouted 'Apa ini Melayu kita negeri dia sudah perintah? Ini negeri bukan Melayu punya'. (Why should the Malays rule our country? This country does not belong to the Malays); 'Mata-mata lanchau' (Balls to the police).[94]

The remarks were not only cruel, arrogant and insulting; they were specially directed at the Malays. The jeer at MARA had the same intention since this organization, the Majlis Amanah Ra'ayat or Council of Trust for the People, is a government-endowed corporation, established in 1966 to assist the *bumiputra* in achieving advancement in the social, economic, technical and—indirectly—political fields. The *NOC Report* stated, 'The common features in all these [processions] were the complete and deliberate defiance of traffic regulations, vulgar and obscene language and gestures, and deliberately provocative slogan attacking the Malays'.[95]

The DAP and Gerakan had reason to be joyful on 11 and 12 May 1969, by virtue of their electoral successes. But when their jubilation was carried to the extent of purposely offending and humiliating a whole community, it can be said simply that the procession organizers and their followers were asking for trouble. The Government at any rate, interpreted the mood of the Malays in these words:

Despite these extreme provocations, the Malay communities in the areas most affected by these insults showed patience and restraint. However, they brooded on the fact that even with the winning of only a few additional seats the non-Malays, particularly the Chinese, had shown arrogance beyond belief. To the Malays as a whole, the events from the 9th to 12th May gave cause for fear over their future. On 12th May for instance, the restraint of the Police, and the freedom with which the Chinese flouted the law, caused the Malays to harbour doubts as to the willingness or ability of the Government to deal firmly with such lawless elements. A feeling of dismay and uncertainty, coupled with their memories of the 1945 kangaroo courts, swept the Malay community in the Federal Capital.[96]

If it had been the Malays who had treated the Chinese in the abrasive way in which the latter behaved towards the former during the Kuala Lumpur processions, it is reasonable to assume that the Chinese would not have sat still and felt forgiving and happy about it. At any rate, the Malays were not happy, nor were they willing to take things lying down; there was little or no sensible reason for the insults hurled at them, other than exuberance following the opposition's election successes and these were actually quite small compared to the total of 66 parliamentary and 162 state seats won by the Alliance. The Malays around Kuala Lumpur decided to organize a procession on 13 May 1969 to show the opposition parties that UMNO also had a good reason to celebrate since it had won the largest number of seats for the Alliance, and far more parliamentary and state seats than the DAP and Gerakan put together. UMNO had won 51 parliamentary seats compared to 13 by the DAP and 8 by the Gerakan; and at the state level UMNO won 133 seats compared to 31 by the DAP and 26 by Gerakan.[97] On those figures, the UMNO members certainly had better reasons to celebrate if they wished to do so.

The organizers decided that the UMNO procession would begin at the residence of the Menteri Besar of Selangor, Datuk Harun bin Haji Idris, at Kampung Bahru, the largest Malay area in Kuala Lumpur, at 7.30 p.m. on 13 May. The Menteri Besar, who was also chairman of Selangor UMNO, in a later statement to the police said he agreed to the procession after the organizers had assured him that it would be held in a peaceful and orderly manner and that a police permit would be obtained for it. Datuk Harun added, 'In order to lend respectability to it and to ensure that the participants behaved themselves, I agreed to take part and lead the procession. As I felt that I should advise the crowd before the procession commenced, I told them that the participants should assemble in my compound'.[98]

Since the morning of 11 May there had been rumours that the DAP and Gerakan might come together and attempt to form the new Selangor Government. The Alliance had won 14 of the 28 State seats in Selangor, the DAP 9 and the Gerakan 4; there was one Independent. It is difficult to see how a DAP–Gerakan coalition could have operated, even if it had had the support of the Independent member. The fact remains that such a scheme was discussed and caused much agitation. By the afternoon of 13 May, however, the Gerakan had announced that it would remain neutral in the Selangor State Assembly and this enabled the Alliance, as the party with the largest number of seats, to form the next Selangor Government. The Selangor UMNO, which had organized the procession and invited all branches in the state to send participants, 'decided that it would proceed with the proposed victory procession to celebrate the formation of the new Government'.[99]

   Being the federal capital, Kuala Lumpur was buzzing with hearsay and
rumour from the time most of the election results for West Malaysia
became known on 11 May. There were uncertainties as to how the new
Federal Cabinet would be formed, in the light of the electoral set-back
sustained by the Alliance. At 2.00 p.m. on 13 May the MCA president,
Tun Tan Siew Sin, who was Minister of Finance in the previous Federal
Cabinet and had for many years proved amenable to UMNO leaders,
announced that because of its poor performance in the elections the MCA
would not participate in the new Federal Government, although it would
remain in the Alliance.[100] Thus, while there was anxiety regarding the
formation of the new Selangor Government until dusk on 13 May, the
MCA decision at 2.00 p.m. not to take part in the Federal Cabinet actually
helped to charge the atmosphere in Kuala Lumpur with increasing
suspense. Any long-time resident of Kuala Lumpur who was interested in
public affairs could feel the atmosphere of foreboding on that fateful
afternoon and evening of 13 May 1969.[101]

   The UMNO procession was to have assembled at Datuk Harun's
residence in Jalan Raja Muda by 7.00 p.m. and to have proceeded at 7.30
p.m. via Jalan Raja Muda and Jalan Tuanku Abdul Rahman to Sulaiman
Court where a mass rally was to be held. No clear report has been made,
but it appears that by 6.00 p.m. on 13 May the atmosphere of anxiety and
anger among the crowd in front of the Menteri Besar's residence was
bordering on the point of explosion. A Malaysian academic wrote over a
year after 13 May, 'The timing and location of the first fatal incidents
were not co-incidental. The mass violence broke out within the vicinity
of the Selangor Menteri Besar's house at about 6.00 p.m. on 13 May,
approximately sixty hours after the last [election] result in the state of
Selangor was declared'.[102] The *NOC Report*, however, recounted that a
commander leading his troop from the Federal Reserve Unit (FRU) to
Jalan Tuanku Abdul Rahman

... passed in front of the Menteri Besar's residence at about 6.30 p.m. There was
no trouble there at that time and he proceeded without stopping but he passed on
an observation to the Selangor Police Control Centre by wireless that 'a crowd of
four or five thousand' was swamping the roadside in front of the Menteri Besar's
residence and spilling over into the compounds of the Residency and neighbouring houses. Some of the Malays carried sticks and banners and 'a few were
seen to be armed with parangs and kris'.[103]

The commander, Assistant Superintendent of Police Tham Kong Weng,
assessed that there would be real trouble if the scheduled procession was
attacked. It was noted that 'the Malay would-be participants were highly
emotional on the evening of May 13 as a result of the previous two days of

insults and provocations'.[104] There had been rumours in Kuala Lumpur that the UMNO procession would be attacked by non-Malay elements that evening and that the Malays were determined to retaliate if attacked.[105] Those who heard the rumours were to that extent forewarned.

When and where exactly the first fatal incident occurred on 13 May is still unclear. The *NOC Report* indicated that violence first took place at Setapak, some 3 to 4 miles from Kampung Bahru, at about 6.00 p.m. or approximately forty minutes before the procession participants at the Menteri Besar's residence got out of hand at about 6.40 p.m. It also stated that at about 6.30 p.m., just before pandemonium broke along Jalan Raja Muda, '. . . a Malay youth, riding a scooter, heading towards the Menteri Besar's residence shouted "Setapak sudah kena langgar" (Setapak has been attacked)'; and added: 'The news that Malay would-be participants in the procession had been attacked in Setapak by Chinese groups whilst en route to Kampong Bharu from Gombak, had lashed through the Malays gathered on the roadside opposite the houses of the Menteri Besar and his Political Secretary, Haji Ahmad Razali. There was a spontaneous and violent anti-Chinese reaction but who its first victim was had not been positively established.'[106]

The bloody and tragic communal incidents which followed are depicted in the following passage which appears to be fairly representative of what happened in Kuala Lumpur on 13 May 1969:

A clear picture of Kuala Lumpur's macabre nightmare of May 13 may never be produced. The mosaic that emerges from eyewitness accounts is gruesome, conflicting, and incomplete. At about 6.45 p.m. belligerent Malay mobs were seen surging from the Menteri Besar's residence and Kampung Bahru, armed with rocks, bricks, sharpened poles, knives, homemade fire bombs, shovels and pieces of pipe, charging in menacing phalanxes down Jalan Raja Muda and Jalan Hale toward nearby Chinese neighbourhoods. At the traffic circle junction of Jalan Raja Muda and Jalan Tuanku Abdul Rahman (Batu Road) Malay bands confronted similarly armed Chinese mobs from Chow Kit area. The Malays, some wearing white or red battle headbands, raged through the area randomly smashing, hacking and burning; any Chinese person or belonging became a target of opportunity. Enraged Chinese and Indian rioters (some with pistols and shotguns as well as homemade weapons) launched a similar mayhem of mutilation and destruction upon persons and things Malay. There were chopped limbs and savage decapitations. Scores of cars and scooters were smashed, overturned, and burned. Cinemas were raided and unsuspecting film watchers were killed in their seats. Homes and shops were looted and burned. Mob madness had seized the city.[107]

A curfew was declared on Kuala Lumpur at 8.00 p.m.[108] But apart from the severely affected Kampung Bahru, Chow Kit and Setapak–Gombak areas the communal riots spread like wildfire to Jalan Tuanku Abdul Rahman, Jalan Campbell, Jalan Bangsar, and the suburban areas of Kampung Datuk Keramat, Kampung Pandan, Kampung Kerinchi, Pudu, Cheras, and a number of others where smaller clashes occurred. With the federal capital in confusion, the ideals of nationhood in Malaysia appeared to have gone to pieces.

As the situation worsened and was getting out of hand, the Deputy Prime Minister, Tun Abdul Razak, gave permission for the military to be called in to assist; army deployment in Kampung Bahru and Chow Kit commenced at about 10.00 p.m. on 13 May. Police and military reinforcements were rushed to Kuala Lumpur throughout the night but much confusion and lack of coordination prevailed during the first critical hours after the outbreak of violence and the authorities did not gain full control of the situation before the morning of 14 May.[109] Violence, arson and pillaging erupted intermittently but at times on a considerable scale for the next four days. The government, initially, did appear nonplussed. Repeated appeals to the people in the national capital seemed to fall on deaf ears. There were rumours that people from outside Kuala Lumpur were coming into the capital to join in the fray. In many other towns too, the situation was tense. As one scholar remarked, '...most of the earliest responses to the crises were a result not of deliberate policy but of demoralization...'.[110] The government, however, regained its balance towards the end of the turbulent week.

Malaysia indeed has had a continual heritage of racial conflict since 1945–6. Feelings, for example, ran high for several years after the declaration of Emergency in the middle of 1948. Although there was no actual racial disturbance arising directly from the Emergency, the Malay-dominated local armed forces fought bitterly against the Chinese-dominated MCP. Between 1957 and 1967, isolated Sino-Malay conflicts did occur several times. Sino-Malay fighting occurred in Pangkor, Perak, in 1957 and again in Bukit Mertajam, Penang, in 1964. In late 1967, the Labour Party (with a majority of Chinese members) protested against the devaluation of the Malaysian dollar; it led to Sino-Malay clashes in Butterworth, Penang. Less serious racial skirmishes were also reported in Kuala Lumpur and Johor.[111]

None of the conflicts since 1945–6, however, was comparable in intensity to the riots of 1969. Although fighting did not spread to other parts of the country, the Kuala Lumpur riots gave rise to widespread despondency in the Peninsula. Not a few Malaysians believed that it would be impossible to rebuild from the ashes of 13 May. Accusations and counter-accusations were cast about and conversations at private gatherings often became heated, though they remained furtive, out of nervousness. Compared, therefore, to the Malaysia–Singapore separation which saddened many hearts and, for a brief moment, threatened to split asunder the young Malaysian nation, the conflict of 1969 was a far more critical development. Still the nation survived.

1. Both these subjects have been discussed at some length in J. P. Ongkili, *Modernization in East Malaysia, 1960–1970*, Kuala Lumpur, 1972, ch. 2. See also J. A. C. Mackie, *Konfrontasi: The Indonesia–Malaysia Dispute, 1963–1966*, Kuala Lumpur, 1974; M. O. Ariff, *The Philippines' Claims to Sabah*, Kuala Lumpur, 1970; D. Hyde, *Confrontation in the East*, Singapore, 1965; M. Leifer, *The Philippine Claim to Sabah*, Hull, 1968; H. James and D. Sheil-Small, *The Undeclared War*, London, 1971.

2. See Mohamed Noordin Sopiee, *From Malayan Union to Singapore Separation*, Kuala Lumpur, 1974, pp. 194–5.

3. From 16 September 1963 there was a Minister of Sarawak Affairs, and a Minister for Sabah Affairs in the Federal Cabinet. The incumbents, Temenggong Jugah anak Barieng and Peter Lo, each came from the state concerned. In addition, Abdul Rahman Yakub of Sarawak was appointed federal Assistant Minister of Rural Development in November 1963, Assistant Minister of Justice from May 1964 and Minister of Lands and Mines from February 1965 while Datuk Donald Stephens of Sabah was Minister of Sabah Affairs and Civil Defence from January to September 1965.

4. Malaysia, *Official Year Book, 1963*, Kuala lumpur, 1964, p. 42.

5. See R. S. Milne, 'Singapore's Exit from Malaysia: The Consequences of Ambiguity', *Asian Survey*, 6, No. 3, March 1966, pp. 177–9.

6. On 29 August the Yang di-Pertuan Agong signed the proclamation fixing 16 September 1963 as the new Malaysia Day.

7. *Straits Times*, 1 September 1963. The Yang di-Pertuan Negara was the constitutional Head of State of Singapore.

8. Of the remaining 14 seats, 13 went to the Barisan Sosialis and 1 to the United People's Party. See Pang Cheng Lian, *Singapore's People's Action Party: Its History, Organization, and Leadership*, Kuala Lumpur, 1971, Appendix D. The Malayan Alliance was composed of the United Malays National Organization (UMNO), the Malayan Chinese Association (MCA) and the Malayan Indian Congress (MIC).

9. *Straits Budget*, 2 October 1963.

10. *Straits Times*, 21 September 1964. It was stated in *Malaysia Agreement*, Annex A, Clause 31 (1) that 'a Singapore citizen is not qualified to be an elected member of either House of Parliament except as a member for or from Singapore; and a citizen who is not a Singapore citizen is not qualified to be a member of either House *from Singapore*'. This provision, however, did not prevent Singapore political parties from extending their activities to other states of Malaysia by establishing branches, enrolling members and choosing leaders from among them. Such members were not 'Singapore citizens' but Malaysians resident in those states themselves.

11. *Straits Times*, 20 April 1965.

12. *Straits Times*, 10 September 1963.

13. See K. J. Ratnam and R. S. Milne, *The Malayan Parliamentary Election of 1964*, Kuala Lumpur, 1967, pp. 385–9.

14. *Straits Budget*, 25 March 1964. Abdul Razak bin Dato Hussein was born in 1922 at Pekan, Pahang. Educated at Malay College, Kuala Kangsar and Raffles College, Singapore. A member of Force 136, a largely Malay resistance movement against the Japanese. Went to

England in 1947 to study law and was called to the Bar in May 1950. State Secretary of Pahang, 1952. Made Acting Menteri Besar of Pahang in February 1955, but resigned in June to enter politics. A member of the Merdeka Mission to London in January 1956. Conferred title of 'Tun' in 1959. As Deputy Prime Minister of Malaya he took a leading part in discussions on the formation of Malaysia. Deputy Chairman of IGC. Remained Deputy Prime Minister of Malaysia until Tunku Abdul Rahman retired in September 1970 when Tun Razak became Prime Minister. Died in February 1976.

15. Pang Cheng Lian, op. cit., p. 19n.

16. N. M. Fletcher, *The Separation of Singapore From Malaysia*, Ithaca, N.Y., 1969, p. 39.

17. Ibid., p. 36n.

18. T. J. S. George, *Lee Kuan Yew's Singapore*, London, 1973, p. 76.

19. Fletcher, op. cit., p. 41 and *Straits Times*, 22 July 1964. 'The Secretary-General of UMNO in particular developed an animosity towards the PAP and especially against Lee Kuan Yew. The climax of the conflict between the two men came in April 1965 when Lee Kuan Yew sued the former for libel.' Pang Cheng Lian, op. cit., p. 19n.

20. *Straits Times*, 7 September 1964. See also M. Leifer, 'Communal Violence in Singapore', *Asian Survey*, 4, No. 10, October 1964, pp. 1115–21.

21. *Straits Times*, 10 December 1964. Emphasis added.

22. Government of Singapore, *Separation: Singapore's Independence on 9th August 1965* (hereinafter referred to as *Separation*), Singapore [n.d.], p. 17.

23. *Straits Times*, 25 May 1965.

24. See *Malaysia Agreement*, Annex A, Clause 62.

25. Government of Singapore, *Malaysia–Age of Revolution*, Singapore [n.d.], p. 54.

26. *Separation*, p. 17.

27. Ibid., p. 12.

28. Ibid., pp. 13–15.

29. *Straits Budget*, 4 November 1964.

30. *Separation*, p. 25.

31. G. P. Means, *Malaysian Politics*, London, 1970, pp. 343–4.

32. George, op. cit., p. 86.

33. See Mohamed Noordin Sopiee, op. cit., p. 317.

34. Malaysia, *Parliamentary Debates (Dewan Ra'ayat)*, Vol. 2, 9 August 1965, col. 1466.

35. Government of Singapore, *Proclamation of Singapore*, Singapore, 1965.

36. *Borneo Bulletin*, 14 August 1965.

37. *Straits Budget*, 25 August 1965.

38. *Borneo Bulletin*, 28 August 1965

39. *Straits Budget*, 25 August 1965.

40. See M. Roff, 'The Rise and Demise of Kadazan Nationalism', *JSEAH*, 10, No. 2, September 1969, pp. 326–43.

41. Mackie, op. cit., p. 260.

42. For another extended discussion of the Philippine claim, see J. P. Ongkili, *The Borneo Response to Malaysia, 1961–1963*, Singapore, 1967, pp. 87–94. See also note 62 below.

43. *Sabah Times*, 13 January 1964.

44. *Straits Budget*, 1 April 1964. Stephen Kalong Ningkan was born in 1920 in Betong, Sarawak. Educated at St. Augustine School, Betong, and was a hospital assistant with the Shell company, Brunei, before entering politics by forming SNAP and becoming its secretary-general in 1961. Secretary-general of the Sarawak Alliance; Chief Minister of Sarawak from August 1963 to September 1966. He remained chairman of SNAP from January 1964 until 1976.

45. *Straits Budget*, 22 April 1964.

46. *Separation*, p. 17.

47. Mohamed Noordin Sopiee, op. cit., p. 200. Three months later Tun Dr Ismail bin Dato Abdul Rahman, the Minister of Internal Security and Home Affairs, remarked, 'There are two ways of establishing a Malaysian Malaysia. First is the platform of the PAP–non-communalism straightaway. The other–the method adopted by the Alliance–requires two steps. First, inter-racial harmony; second, and ultimate state of non-communalism'. *Straits Times*, 1 June 1965.

48. *Straits Times*, 8 March 1965.

49. George, op. cit., p. 77.

50. Chan Heng Chee, *Singapore: The Politics of Survival, 1965–1967*, Kuala Lumpur, 1971, pp. 6–7 and 10.

51. Interview with a PAP leader and Member of Parliament, Singapore, who asked to remain anonymous, Singapore, August 1974.

52. Fletcher, op. cit., p. 14.

53. See *Malaysia Agreement*, Annex J, para. 3(3); and *Straits Budget*, 11 August 1965.

54. Fletcher, op. cit., p. 18.

55. *Malaysia Agreement*, Annex J, para. 9.

56. A. Josey, *Lee Kuan Yew: The Struggle for Singapore*, Sydney, 1974, p. 10.

57. Discussion with the present writer, Singapore, August 1974.

58. From a tape-recording in the possession of the present writer.

59. Tan Siew Sin, the only son of Tan Cheng Lock (Note 70, Chapter 2), was born in Malacca in 1916. Educated in Raffles College, Singapore. Member of the Federal Legislative Council 1948. Chairman of Malacca branch of the MCA from 1957. Became president of the MCA in 1961, a post he held until his retirement in April 1974. Treasurer of the Alliance from 1958 until his retirement. Appointed Minister of Commerce and Industry in 1957; and Minister of Finance in 1959, a portfolio which he held until 1969. The same year he was conferred the title of 'Tun'. Appointed Minister with Special Functions after the May 1969 general elections. Continued to be active in MCA and Alliance politics until his retirement. He was appointed Special Economic Adviser to the Prime Minister, after his retirement. Much of his time is now devoted to Sime Darby Berhad of which he is Chairman.

60. *Straits Times*, Kuala Lumpur, 10 April 1974.

61. Malaysia, *Parliamentary Debates (Dewan Ra'ayat)*, Vol. 2, 9 August 1965, col. 1460; see also *Straits Times*, 10 August 1965.

62. For the present writer's analyses of this issue, see *The Borneo Response to Malaysia, 1961–1963*; 'The Philippine Claim', *Opinion*, 1, No. 4, Kuala Lumpur, June 1969; *Modernization in East Malaysia, 1960–1970*, ch. 2; 'The Sabah Claim', *Sunday Mail*, Kuala Lumpur, 8 July 1973; and 'Analysis... The Sabah Claim', *Sunday Mail*, 15 July 1973. See also M. Meadows, 'The Philippine Claim to North Borneo', *Political Science Quarterly*, 77, No. 3, September 1962, pp. 321–35.

63. The steps towards Indonesian–Malaysian peace which eventuated after the 'September 30th Movement' are succinctly presented in G. P. Means, op. cit., ch. 19.

64. For sometime after separation, Singapore and Malaysia engaged in verbal recriminations. It was the continuation of pre-separation rivalry when 'statesmanship and compromise were abandoned for political oneupmanship', Chan Heng Chee, op. cit., p. 8. However, even Singapore progressively adopted a more sober attitude towards Malaysia. When the new Indonesian Government under General Suharto proposed peace negotiations with Singapore in April 1966, 'sensitive of Malaysian fears and opinion, Lee Kuan-yew indicated that no agreement would be possible which might prejudice the interests or security of Malaysia'. Means, op. cit., p. 362.

65. *Malay Mail*, 4 October 1966.

66. *Straits Times*, 2 September 1965; and 21 October 1966. See also M. Roff, 'The Politics of Language in Malaya', *Asian Survey*, 7, No. 5, May 1967, pp. 316–28.

67. Federation of Malaya, *Federation of Malaya Constitution 1957*, Kuala Lumpur, 1957, Article 152(1) and (2); and *Malayan Constitutional Documents*, Kuala Lumpur, 1959, p. 101.

68. See H. E. Groves, *The Constitution of Malaysia*, Singapore, 1964, p. 150; and Malaysia, *Malaysia Federal Constitution*, Kuala Lumpur, 1970, Article 152(1)(a).

69. *Straits Times*, 6 April 1965.

70. Malaysia, *Speech by the Prime Minister, Malaysia: The National Language*, Kuala Lumpur, 1967, p. 4.

71. Ibid., pp. 5–7.

72. When Malaysia was inaugurated in September 1963, Malaya was first referred to as 'the states of Malaya' in Malaysia while Sarawak and Sabah retained their names. From 6 August 1966 'the states of Malaya' were officially named West Malaysia and at the same time Sarawak and Sabah became East Malaysia by virtue of the same gazette notification. Significantly, soon after the traumatic partition of West and East Pakistan into Pakistan and Bangladesh in late 1971, the Malaysian Federal Government casually introduced, in its radio, television and public statements, a change from West and East Malaysia into Peninsular Malaysia for the former West Malaysia and simply Sarawak and Sabah for the former East Malaysia. Accordingly, in this study, Malaya, Sarawak and Sabah are used for the period until August 1966; East and West Malaysia from then until the end of 1971; and Peninsular Malaysia and Sarawak and Sabah for the period thereafter.

73. G. S. Maryanov, 'Political Parties in Mainland Malaya', *JSEAH*, 8, No. 1, March 1967, p. 109.

74. K. J. Ratnam and R. S. Milne, *The Malayan Parliamentary Election of 1964*, Singapore, 1967, p. 52.

75. Ibid., pp. 52–3.

76. Ibid., pp. 110–11. See also R. K. Vasil, 'The 1964 General Elections in Malaya', *International Studies*, 7, No. 1, July 1965, pp. 20–65.

77. See Ratnam and Milne, op. cit., ch. 4; Means, op. cit., pp. 335–41; and Malaysia, *Report on the Parliamentary (Dewan Ra'ayat) and State Legislative Assembly General Elections 1964 of the States of Malaya*, Kuala Lumpur, 1965, pp. 14–15.

78. Democratic Action Party, 'The Setapak Declaration', *Who Lives if Malaysia Dies?*, Kuala Lumpur, 1969, p. 20. The 'Setapak Declaration' was made on 29 July 1967.

79. Democratic Action Party, 'Towards a Malaysian Malaysia?' [1969 DAP Election Manifesto]. Mimeograph copy, Pt. 1.

80. Professor Wang Gungwu subsequently explained that he did not formally become a member of the Gerakan and had merely helped in the formation of the party 'as a gesture to Dr. Tan Chee Khoon'. Discussion with the present writer, Kuala Lumpur, December 1971.

81. R. K. Vasil, *The Malaysian General Election of 1969*, Kuala Lumpur, 1972, p. 20.

82. Gerakan Rakyat Malaysia, *Election Manifesto: 3rd General Elections 1969*, Kuala Lumpur, 1969, paras. 1 and 17. Emphasis in the original.

83. Political developments and trends in Sarawak and Sabah have been discussed at length by the present writer in his *Modernization in East Malaysia, 1960–1970*, chs. 4, 5 and 7.

84. See R. S. Milne and K. J. Ratnam, *Malaysia: New States in a New Nation*, London, 1974; and M. C. Roff, *The Politics of Belonging: Political Change in Sabah and Sarawak*, Kuala Lumpur, 1974.

85. See K. J. Ratnam and R. S. Milne, 'The 1969 Parliamentary Election in West Malaysia', *Pacific Affairs*, 43, No. 2, Summer 1970, p. 204. In the 1959 elections the parties were the Alliance, PMIP, Socialist Front, PPP, Party Negara and Malayan Party. For the

electoral strengths of the parties in the two elections, see Ratnam and Milne, *The Malayan Parliamentary Election of 1964*, p. 361.

86. Alliance, 'The Alliance Manifesto (1969 Elections)', Kuala Lumpur, 1969, paras. 12–14.

87. Democratic Action Party, 'Towards a Malaysian Malaysia', p. 2.

88. People's Progressive Party, 'People's Progressive Party of Malaya Manifesto 1969', Ipoh, 1969, paras. 5 and 10–12. Mimeographed.

89. Gerakan Rakyat Malaysia, *Election Manifesto: 3rd General Elections, 1969*, Kuala Lumpur, 1969, para. 8. Emphasis in the original.

90. Ibid., paras. 21–22. Emphasis in the original.

91. See Ongkili, *Modernization in East Malaysia, 1960–1970*, ch. 5, 'Elections and Politicization'.

92. Ratnam and Milne, 'The 1969 Parliamentary Election in West Malaysia', pp. 204–5.

93. From interviews and discussions over the following five years after 13 May with residents of Kuala Lumpur (which in this study is taken to include the suburb of Petaling Jaya). The present writer was resident in Kuala Lumpur during the May 1969 riots.

94. All the procession utterances are reproduced from National Operations Council, *The May 13 Tragedy* (hereinafter referred to as *NOC Report*), Kuala Lumpur, 1969, pp. 29–33. The NOC was set up on 17 May 1969 to take control of government during the emergency situation following the outbreak of violence. See also Chapter 7.

95. *NOC Report*, p. 36.

96. Ibid., pp. 36–7. The '1945 kangaroo courts' were instruments of the MPAJA's vendetta against alleged collaborators with the Japanese. See chapter 1, above.

97. Ratnam and Milne, 'The 1969 Parliamentary Election in West Malaysia', p. 204.

98. *NOC Report*, pp. 40–1. Datuk Harun bin Haji Idris was born in 1925 at Petaling. Educated at Victoria Institution, Kuala Lumpur and Middle Temple, London. Assistant District Officer Gemas and Tampin; joined Attorney-General's Chambers as Deputy Public Prosecutor; later was Registrar of Societies and Official Assignee of the Federation of Malaya, then State Legal Adviser, Selangor. Contested the 1964 elections and became Menteri Besar, Selangor; re-elected in the 1969 elections and was Menteri Besar again till 1976 when he was convicted of corruption. Pardoned in 1981.

99. *NOC Report*, p. 43.

100. Tunku Abdul Rahman, *May 13–Before and After*, Kuala Lumpur, 1969, p. 86.

101. From personal experience at the time, and discussions with many Kuala Lumpur residents since then.

102. Goh Cheng Teik, *The May Thirteenth Incident and Democracy in Malaysia*, Kuala Lumpur, 1971, p. 18. The author subsequently successfully contested the Nibong Tebal parliamentary seat in the August 1974 elections, and has been Deputy Minister in several portfolios of the Federal Government.

103. *NOC Report*, p. 50. The parang is a common heavy household single-edged sheath-knife 12–18 inches long and 2–4 inches wide; while a kris is a traditional Malay Dagger with double-edged wavy blades tapering to a sharp point, usually 8–12 inches long.

104. NOC Report, p. 44.

105. Ibid.

106. Ibid., pp. 45–51.

107. F. V. Gagliano, *Communal Violence in Malaysia 1969: The Political Aftermath*, Athens, Ohio, 1970, pp. 16–17. For typically freelancing and tendentious descriptions of the incidents of 13 May, see G. Alexander, *Silent Invasion: The Chinese in Southeast Asia*, London, 1973, pp. 96–110; and J. Slimming, *Malaysia: Death of a Democracy*, London, 1969.

108. The curfew 'was imposed on all areas except Kampong Bharu, the reason being that

the area was swamped with several thousands from out-of-town who had come to participate in the proposed procession and those who sought shelter from surrounding areas. The
majority of them could not be physically accommodated in Kampong Bharu houses and
mosque. The only possible solution was to cordon off Kampong Bharu and to treat it as one
large curfew area.' *NOC Report*, p. 64.

109. A. Reid, 'The Kuala Lumpur Riots and the Malaysian Political System', *Australian
Outlook*, No. 23/3, December 1969, pp. 269–70.

110. Ibid., pp. 270–2.

111. There has been no in-depth study of the racial clashes between 1957 and 1967. The
tendency has been to look at the Kuala Lumpur riots as a phenomenon which happened
from out of the blue when they should be more appropriately seen as the culmination of a
period of suspicion, distrust and animosity between Malays and non-Malays.

7
The 'Bargain' and the New Economic Policy

DESPITE the severity of the 1969 conflict, Malaysia's political leadership managed to act quickly and without undue panic. By 17 May there had been established a 'National Operations Council' (NOC) following the declaration of a national state of emergency by the Yang di-Pertuan Agong on 15 May. In effect, parliamentary democracy was suspended and the NOC, under Tun Abdul Razak as chairman and Director of Operations, co-ordinated executive action, in particular the work of the military and police in restoring law and order in Kuala Lumpur and confidence throughout the nation. Patterned after the Operations Council which existed during the 1948–60 Emergency, the NOC, comprising nine members, was not originally intended to supersede the Federal Cabinet. But the wide powers given to the Director of Operations enabled the NOC to emerge rapidly as the centre of decision-making in the months following 13 May. The top military and police officers were brought into the NOC in order to ensure the execution of swift and decisive action.[1]

In the event, the NOC did concentrate much of its effort on restoring the situation in the affected areas to pre-13 May conditions. However, other aspects of government were also given attention and by mid-July 1969 the NOC had issued decrees which *inter alia* initiated the setting up of a National Goodwill Committee headed by Tunku Abdul Rahman. There were similar committees at state and district levels, all with the prime objective of re-establishing tolerance among the different communities of West Malaysia. Leaders of opposition parties were invited to participate in the activities of these committees. At the end of July Tunku Abdul Rahman was beginning—in opposition-held Penang—a state-to-state goodwill tour of the nation in an endeavour to repair the damage done to the process of nation-building in Malaysia.[2] By the beginning of August 1969 the situation had eased and there were clear signs of a return to normal.

Notwithstanding the formation of a new Federal Cabinet on 20 May 1969, the NOC continued to issue directives and decrees. The Tunku admitted, 'During the Emergency period the Cabinet is playing a secondary role to the National Operations Council.' However, he remained Prime Minister and three MCA leaders, Tun Tan Siew Sin, Khaw Kai Boh and Lee Siok Yew, participated in the Cabinet as Ministers with Special Functions.[3]

While Parliament remained suspended until March 1971, a National Consultative Council (NCC) was formed comprising representatives of various political, economic, professional, religious and other groups. Tun Razak, in announcing its formation in October 1969, said that in the NCC 'issues affecting our national unity will be discussed fully and frankly. In this way it is hoped to reach an understanding and agreement on these national issues that would ensure the future peace, security and unity of our country and that the May 13 tragedy would not recur'.[4] While the representatives in the NCC, meeting in Parliament House, proceeded to discuss problems affecting the nation, a Department of National Unity was also established to study in depth the problems of race relations which were plainly crucial to the future of the Malaysian nation. As 1970 dawned, it seemed that Malaysian leaders were turning over a new leaf with the approach of a new decade. The racial incidents of May 1969 had had a chastening effect and there were obvious and genuine attempts at establishing consensus and seeking new and more realistic solutions to the problems of national unity.

The 'Bargain' in Retrospect

One of the fundamental steps taken by the NOC, the NCC and the Federal Government between May 1969 and the general elections in 1974 was to make a more profound assessment of the causes of the communal antagonisms which had reached a cathartic point on 13 May. On the basis of that assessment, a more decisive approach was adopted towards identifying and ordering the priorities of the country and meeting the challenges of nation-building. It was felt that, basically, the political and economic 'bargain' between the Malays and the non-Malays in the course of working for self-rule and achieving independence in the 1950s had not been fulfilled.

It will be remembered that in the course of working out the constitutional and national foundations of an independent Malaya, 'The Communities Liaison Committee had come to the conclusion that the Malays would sacrifice their privileged position only if they could be aided in securing a greater share of their country's wealth'.[5] There is no doubt that the leaders of Malaya were aware of and believed in the necessity of implementing the 'bargain'. The words of an 'elder statesman' of Peninsular Malaysia, E. E. C. Thuraisingham, were quoted in an earlier chapter: 'It is true. I and others believed that the backward Malays should be ... assisted to attain parity with non-Malays to forge a united Malayan Nation of equals'.[6] This inter-communal understanding became a cardinal formula in the life of the ruling Alliance from 1955 onwards: 'In time, a guiding theme and informal *quid pro quo* emerged in this elite bargaining forum: exchange of Chinese co-operation in improving the Malay economic position, in return for Malay co-operation in improving the Chinese political position'.[7]

However, despite the achievement of political independence in 1957, social and economic progress among the Malays had been manifestly slow. Although the Malayan Government began implementing socio-economic development programmes for the Peninsula as early as 1950, the two Plans between then and 1960 had failed to bring about more than marginal improvement in the lives of the Malays. Of particular significance, rural poverty had continued to be widespread even as Malaysia was being formed in the early 1960s.[8] Developments throughout the 1960s continued to demonstrate that the Malays were economi-

TABLE 5[1]
Expenditure on Rural Development,
Second Malayan Five Year Plan, 1961–1965
($ thousand)

Rural Health Centres	39,390
Rural Roads	163,773
Rubber Replantmg Scheme	104,768
Rural Electrification	15,000
Land Development Authority	191,707
Rural Industries	7,600
Minor Rural Development Schemes	12,177
Group Development Schemes	29,293
Agriculture	28,506
Co-operative Development	66,839
Drainage and Irrigation	120,615
Fisheries	7,273
Forestry	4,805
Veterinary	10,333
Total	712,079

[1]*Interim Review of Second Malayan Plan*, p. 7.

cally behind the non-Malays, notwithstanding the truism that there were also non-Malay poor members of society, mainly in urban areas.

National development outlays increased from $5,050 million in the Second Malayan Five Year Plan (1961–5) to $10,500 million in the First Malaysia Plan (1966–70).[9] Under the former Plan, $712 million was allocated for rural development; the latter Plan earmarked $1,087 million for similar purposes, $900 million of which was for expenditure in the states of Malaya. These development Plans of the 1960s gave priority to matters such as rural roads, land development, drainage and irrigation, agriculture, rubber replanting, rural health, group settlement schemes, and crop subsidies. Tables 5 and 6 illustrate the scope and emphases of rural development programmes undertaken by the Malayan (and subsequently Malaysian) Government during the 1960s.

The estimates for most of the items on rural and agricultural development under the Second Malayan Five Year Plan and the First Malaysia Plan were used up and, indeed, in many cases were augmented by supplementary votes in Parliament.[10]

The First Malaysia Plan stated clearly the objectives of public devel-

TABLE 6[1]

Expenditure on Agricultural Development
First Malaysia Plan, 1966–1970
($ million)

	Malaya	Sabah	Sarawak	Malaysia
Agriculture	166.5	11.7	89.3	267.5
Research	17.0	4.5	1.7	23.2
Education	10.0	0.8	4.9	15.7
Extension	10.6	0.4	1.5	12.5
Rubber Replanting Grants	93.9	5.3	61.0	160.2
Other crops subsidies	35.0	0.7	20.2	55.9
Animal Husbandry	28.0	2.1	3.7	33.8
Fisheries	17.0	1.3	4.0	22.3
Forestry	10.0	1.1	1.3	12.4
Drainage and Irrigation	319.2	7.0	6.5	332.7
Land Development	335.0	27.8	13.1	375.9
Rural Credit & Marketing	19.5	4.0	13.5	37.0
Emergency Contract Personnel Services	5.0	–	–	5.0
Total	900.2	55.0	131.4	1,086.6

[1]First Malaysia Plan, 1966–1970, p. 121.

opment expenditure in so far as it pertained to the rural sector of the economy and nation in the 1960s:

The substantial increases in expenditure on drainage and irrigation, land development, rural industry and certain social services, such as schools and rural health centres, will have direct effects in raising the productivity of resources in the rural economy. In addition, much of the investment in roads and bridges, utilities and community facilities will provide benefits for the rural population. The purpose of the emphasis on rural development in the public investment programme has been to provide a more balanced distribution of economic benefits and opportunities between the rural and urban sectors of the economy.[11]

One of the First Malaysia Plan's declared aims was 'to increase the well-being of Malaysia's rural inhabitants and other low-income groups, primarily by raising their productivity and thus their income-earning capacity'.[12] In moving the adoption of the First Malaysia Plan in Parliament, the Deputy Prime Minister and Minister of National and Rural Development, Tun Abdul Razak, said, 'No one can dispute that a radical change for the better has been effected in the face of the rural countryside'.[13]

The Alliance, which had been a prime mover in the process of nation-building and particularly in the constitutional and political negotiations leading to the attainment of Merdeka in 1957 and the formation of Malaysia in 1963, had undoubtedly been aware of the need to fulfil that part of the 'bargain' which undertook to improve the social and economic position of the Malays and, after the formation of Malaysia, other *bumiputras*. In its 1964 election manifesto the ruling party had reiterated that it would 'continue to be a cardinal objective of the Alliance economic policy to undertake rural development on an increasing scale in order to correct the imbalance between the urban and rural areas of our country'. It added:

It will be Alliance policy to ensure that rural development will result in increased output and increased rural incomes. In order to ensure that increased rural income would result from increased output, the Alliance Government will take measures to achieve more effective control over land rents, improved marketing of rural produce and the provision to our farmers of short, medium and long term credit on reasonable terms.[14]

In the same election campaign, the Alliance declared, 'We were given a mandate to make our Country a better place to live in. Millions of projects, the pillars of our prosperity, are proof of our determination and dynamic drive in Development. We were given a Mandate for progress. Our rural people are no longer insecure!'[15] In moving the adoption of the First Malaysia Plan in 1965, the Deputy Prime Minister told the Dewan

Rakyat, 'The development effort of the Government has also resulted in improving the long-run productivity of our natural and human resources, particularly in the rural areas.'[16] As has been discussed, the Alliance campaigned in the 1969 elections largely by emphasizing to the voters how much progress that ruling party had achieved for the people since independence.

However, despite all the visible signs of progress, despite the continued exhortations on development, despite even the impressive figures and projections contained in the development Plans, there were major defects in these programmes as a careful examination of Tables 5 and 6 above clearly shows. The areas in which the rural farmers really needed assistance in order to improve their social and economic conditions were sorely neglected: rural industries, fisheries, cooperative development, agricultural education and extension, rural credit and marketing. (See Tables 5 and 6 above.) In terms of financial allocations under the development Plans, these items received almost farcical amounts compared to those which in the long run benefited big business, non-Malay contractors and middlemen: the rubber replanting scheme, land development and group development schemes; even the large expenditure on drainage and irrigation boosted the incomes of landlords rather than the earnings of tenant farmers. It cannot be denied that the national and rural development programmes were extensive. But their implementation was spasmodic and some of the priorities lacked realism.

Even as the 1960s were coming to a close, rural poverty and economic handicaps remained conspicuous. The unemployment rate was 6.8 per cent during 1967-8 (as against 6.3 per cent in 1965 and 6 per cent in 1962). It was more serious if attention were focused on the young (15-19 age group); the rate was up to 26 per cent with the overall figure for urban areas being 11.2 per cent. Agriculture, unable to absorb the increase in the rural labour force, failed to prevent migration to the cities.[17] Writing just over a year before 13 May, a Malaysian who had had extensive involvement in Malaysia's development programmes pointed out:

Even within West Malaysia there is a distinction between what is known as the West Coast and the East Coast States, because the former have between seventy and eighty percent of the wealth and urban centers. Surveys of household budget spending and income tax returns indicate that people in the urban centers have a much higher level of individual and family income than those in rural areas, both on the West Coast, and the East Coast, and in the Borneo states. Moreover, most of the urban dwellers are Chinese, whereas two-thirds of our population, in fact, live in rural areas, and most of them are Malays.[18]

Those disparities between the urban and rural areas, which coincided with the geographical location of the non-*bumiputra* and *bumiputra* communities, had prevailed throughout the 1960s, in spite of the development activities of government. What is equally significant is the fact that during that decade the Malays learned that they held 'only around one per cent of investment in registered business; Malay unemployment in 1965 was running at 11.2 per cent, compared with 5.6 per cent for Chinese and 9.6 per cent for Indians; the Government's much vaunted rural development scheme had failed to lift living standards in rural areas'.[19] There lay the crux of the problem of nation-building.

It is indisputable that the Malays and other *bumiputras* had continued to lag behind the non-*bumiputra* communities until the end of the 1960s. It was often alleged that the Malays were given privileges in government jobs to the *exclusion* of non-Malays, and that the Malays controlled the administration and the uniformed services, particularly in the top echelon ('Division One') of the government services. The 13 May incident

TABLE 7

Figures Relating to Division One Government Officers
by Racial Groups, as on 1 November 1968[1]

Total 3,392 (Excluding Armed Forces and the Police)		
Malays 1,142		36.26%
Non-Malays 2,250		63.74%
Administrative Services		
Total	1,221	
Malays	706	57.8%
Non-Malays	515	42.2%
Professional Services (Excluding Education)		
Total	1,998	
Malays	385	19.2%
Non-Malays	1,613	80.8%
Education Officers		
Total	173	
Malays	51	29.9%
Non-Malays	122	70.1%
Police (absolute figures withheld for security reasons)		
Malays		38.76%
Non-Malays		61.24%
Armed Forces (absolute figures withheld for security reasons)		
Malays		64.5%
Non-Malays		35.5%

[1]These figures are reproduced from *NOC Report*, pp. 22–3.

prompted the NOC to present figures which showed the true position. These are reproduced in Table 7. It can be seen that the Malays had a fairly narrow majority in Division One of the Administrative Services and a rather larger majority in Division One of the Armed Forces. Elsewhere in the Government Service they were clearly outnumbered.

It was noted that in other (lower) Divisions of government services and statutory authorities the ratio of Malay to non-Malay officers was even less favourable to the Malays. The notable exceptions, which probably encouraged the allegations of Malay preponderance, were in the lower ranks of the Armed Forces and the Police, that is to say areas of employment long avoided by non-Malays. The NOC crisply concluded:

Allegations that the non-Malays are excluded are regarded by the Malays as deliberate distortion. *The Malays who already felt excluded in the country's economic life, now began to feel a threat to their place in the public services. No mention was ever made by non-Malay politicians of the almost closed-door attitude to the Malays by non-Malays in large sections of the private sector in this country.*[20]

The findings of a Malaysian scholar are very relevant in showing the inferior economic position of the Malays. At the end of the 1960s, when traditional rural income was compared to modern urban income, 'There was a differential of close to 1 : 4. This meant that 58 per cent of the total Malay labour force were working in areas where incomes were only one-quarter the size of incomes in areas dominated by 25 per cent of the total non-Malay labour force'.[21] Another Malaysian of Chinese origin, Alex Lee, who was one of the 'young Turks' in the MCA following 13 May, and who was critical of the *bumiputra* policy of the government, aptly summed up the situation:

The twelve years following Merdeka did not, in fact, bring forth the wealth and power which the Malays had expected. They found themselves still to be the rural people with control of the towns very much in the hands of the non-Malays. Even in the rural areas their position was being encroached upon by the Chinese New Villages, the prosperous Chinese tin miners and the large European dredges and large foreign plantations. Their control of the civil service was also being eroded by the influx of many non-Malays into the government services and their supremacy in the police force was reduced by the recruitment of non-Malay officers during the Emergency. Their only area of control, therefore, was in the political arena, especially in Parliament where they controlled two-thirds of the seats. However, the 1969 election results gave the impression that even this political control was being threatened, and in some States the balance of power seemed to shift to political parties which appealed to Chinese chauvinism.[22]

In regard to the shift in political power, it bears recalling that at the time of independence in 1957 non-Malays had been granted a very significant political concession in the form of *jus soli* citizenship. The continued official use of English, Chinese and Tamil after the stipulated ten-year period expired in 1967 was seen as a further concession to the non-Malays. But the Malays had not made equivalent economic gains. The economic dominance of the Chinese had prevailed without any consequential restrictions or control by the Government, as implicitly required by the 'bargain'.

Clearly, the social and economic disparities which the fathers of nation-building in Malaysia had understood and agreed to rectify still remained by 13 May 1969.

The NEP and Nation-building

It was in recognition of the continuing serious imbalance between the position of the Malays and other *bumiputras* and that of the non-*bumiputras* that the Malaysian Government embarked on political and economic reforms soon after the 13 May incident. The NOC itself initiated the move when it sought, first of all, to entrench certain 'sensitive' provisions of the Federal Constitution by placing them beyond the possibility of public discussion. These provisions were the whole of Part III, and Articles 71, 152, 153 and 159. These pertained to citizenship; the federal guarantee of the constitution of each state and the rights and prerogatives of the Malay Rulers; the Malay language as the national language and ultimately the sole official language of the nation; the responsibility of the Yang di-Pertuan Agong to safeguard the special position of the Malays and legitimate interests of other communities; and the proviso 'that any amendment of the provisions relating to the Malay Rulers (Articles 38, 70 and 71) and the special position of the Malays (Article 152) shall not be passed without the consent of the Conference of Rulers'.[23] A White Paper was published to explain the need for entrenching those provisions:

It is now clear that unless certain restraints are placed on public discussions on issues which are likely to generate anxiety and fear among the races and unless measures are taken to assure the people that their rights and legitimate interests under the Constitution will not be threatened, this nation runs the risk of another, possibly worse, racial conflict.[24]

What the Government had set out to do can be likened to creating a 'mechanism designed to de-radicalize democratic politics' through the establishment of 'a constitutional contract which sets out the terms of inter-communal relations'.[25]

At the same time the Department of National Unity spent nearly a year until early 1971 to draft meticulously the *Rukunegara* (National Ideology) which thereafter went through frank and careful deliberation in the NCC. Again in anticipation of the formulation and implementation of economic reforms, the *Rukunegara*, which subsequently became included in the study of civics in schools and was referred to in gatherings or associations of a goodwill nature, enunciated the wish to establish a Malaysia 'dedicated to achieving a greater unity of all her peoples; to maintaning a democratic way of life; to creating a just society in which the wealth of the nation shall be equitably shared; to ensuring a liberal approach to her rich and diverse traditions; to building a progressive society which shall be oriented to modern science and technology'.[26] After Tunku Abdul Rahman voluntarily stepped down from the post of Prime Minister and Tun Abdul Razak took over from him on 22 September 1970, it became increasingly obvious that the new Federal Cabinet under Tun Razak was directing its energy to the need to redress the unfulfilled part of the 'bargain', that the Malays and other *bumiputras* be uplifted to achieve economic parity and balance with the non-indigenous communities in Malaysia. The principal means adopted was the New Economic Policy (NEP).

The decision to embark on the NEP was a measure of realization on the part of the Malaysian Government of the simple fact that 'Poverty arises because of the inequality in the distribution of income and inequality in the distribution of wealth'.[27] But it was also a recognition of the fact that 'the Malay intellectuals saw that the *status quo* benefited the non-Malays more than the Malays'.[28] The NEP was spelled out in and became the underlying objective of the *Second Malaysia Plan, 1971–1975*:

The Plan incorporates a two-pronged New Economic Policy for development. The first prong is to reduce and eventually eradicate poverty, by raising income levels and increasing employment opportunities for all Malaysians, irrespective of race. The second prong aims at accelerating the process of restructuring Malaysian society to correct economic imbalance, so as to reduce and eventually eliminate the identification of race with economic function. The process involves the modernization of rural life, a rapid and balanced growth of urban activities and the creation of a Malay commercial and industrial community in all categories and at all levels of operation, so that Malays and other indigenous people will become full partners in all aspects of the economic life of the nation.[29]

The Second Malaysia Plan also devoted attention to the need to foster and maintain national unity:

Our people of all races and all social groups should therefore regard the Second Malaysia Plan as a great opportunity to participate in the whole process of social change and nation-building. It is now, more than ever before, necessary for each member of our society, whether a politician, civil servant, farmer, employer, worker, trade unionist or journalist, to join in the common endeavour to ensure the progress and well-being of the community and the nation as a whole. ... To achieve our overall objective of national unity, Malaysia needs more than merely a high rate of economic growth. While devoting our efforts to the task of achieving rapid economic development, we need to ensure at the same time that there is social justice, equitable sharing of income growth and increasing opportunities for employment.[30]

At last there appeared to be a clearer perception of the fact that 'the key to the eradication of Malay poverty was to be found in the eradication of exploitation and in the consequent introduction of modern technology into rural economic activity',[31] and a willingness to act on this fact.

The Second Malaysia Plan provided for institutional development designed to foster 'rural development programmes that deal adequately with the three main causes of poverty: low productivity, exploitation and neglect'.[32] Apart from FELDA (the Federal Land Development Authority) and MARA, other institutions had already been set up to enhance and speed up development in the rural and agricultural sector generally. The Federal Agricultural Marketing Authority (FAMA) was established in 1965 to improve the efficiency of the agricultural marketing system; the Malaysian Agricultural Research and Development Institute (MARDI) was set up in 1968 to undertake production research on all crops except rubber, livestock, poultry and freshwater fisheries; and the expressively-named Federal Land Consolidation and Rehabilitation Authority (FELCRA), was established in 1966.

Under the Second Malaysia Plan the activities of these institutions were broadened. Bank Pertanian (the Agricultural Bank) made funds available 'for lending to producers through rural co-operatives and Farmers Associations and to FAMA for programme use'; and a National Padi and Rice Authority (Lembaga Padi dan Beras Negara or LPN) was set up 'to co-ordinate the various aspects of production, processing and marketing of padi and rice'.[33] The total allocation for agricultural development under the Second Malaysia Plan amounted to $1,956 million, or about 80 per cent higher than the allocation to that sector in the First Malaysia Plan. The largest allocation of $909 million or nearly 47 per cent was for land development.[34] A well-known authority on the rural economy of Malaysia, Professor Ungku A. Aziz conceded that the 'programmes in the Second Malaysia Plan are obviously a great step forward for Malaysian economic development, in theory and in practice'.[35]

In practice, some of the positive results of the reforms could be seen by the beginning of 1974. One of the significant developments following 13 May was the decision to use the national language, renamed Bahasa Malaysia, as the medium of instruction in Standard One of all English-medium primary schools beginning wth the 1970 school-year. Thereafter there would be a progressive conversion to Bahasa Malaysia until 1982 when all the primary and secondary schools in Peninsular Malaysia, with the exception of the Chinese and Tamil schools, would be using the national language fully. Sabah began the process of converting all English-medium primary schools to the Bahasa Malaysia medium in 1971; Sarawak began doing so in 1977. However, in all three cases (Peninsular Malaysia, Sabah and Sarawak) language subjects, such as English, Tamil and Chinese, would continue to be taught in those languages.

The position of Malays in tertiary education was improved abruptly with the establishment of Universiti Kebangsaan Malaysia (the National University of Malaysia) in 1970. In the 1960s Malay enrolment had progressed at a snail's pace in the existing University of Malaya and was particularly poor in the technical faculties, i.e., Science, Engineering, Medicine and Agriculture.[36] However, by 1974 Ungku Aziz—who had become Vice-Chancellor of the University of Malaya in 1968—was able to say:

Since 1969, access to higher education and to many areas of vocational and technical education have been substantially expanded for the Malays. Some effort is being made to ensure access for Malay workers into manufacturing industry. A class of Malays (or bumiputra) millionaires has been fostered. However, it remains to be seen whether their charitable instincts will match those of the non-Malays mentioned by Za'ba half a century ago and who continue to benefit educational institutions today.[37]

The Mid-Term Review of the Second Malaysia Plan takes the assessment of progress under the Plan to the end of 1973.[38] In reviewing the two-pronged strategy of the NEP, the Mid-Term Review of the Second Malaysia Plan demonstrated that a number of cogent results had been achieved by the close of 1973 in the endeavour to 'eradicate poverty ... irrespective of race' and in 'restructuring Malaysian society to correct economic imbalance so as to reduce and eventually eliminate the identification of race with economic function'.

In an effort to get rid of money-lenders and middle-men and to promote the commercialization of agriculture, government agencies continued to extend credits: from 1971 to 1973 loans given to small-scale agro-based industries by MARA, the Malaysian Industrial Development Finance Berhad (MIDF), and Bank Bumiputra amounted to about $300 million. In the same period FELDA developed 224,000 acres of land, representing 81 per cent of the original Second Malaysia Plan target, to accelerate the movement of rural farmers from traditional to modern agriculture; and FELCRA dealt with 46,000 acres or 47 per cent of its target.

State Economic Development Corporations (SEDCs) had been set up in all states and were engaged in various commercial and industrial projects while the Urban Development Authority (UDA) was set up in November 1971 to implement a variety of short-term and long-term projects for commercial and property development. Significantly, among its short-term projects had been the 'the leasing, purchase and construction of commercial premises for Malays and other indigenous people for printing, tailoring, offices, restaurants, shops, a mini-market, travel agency and wholesale trade'.[39] Also within the scope of eradication of poverty, and in 'assisting the movement of Malays from traditional agriculture to the modern industrial and commercial sectors, MARA, SEDCs and UDA played an indirect role by providing technical, financial and capital assistance for Malays and other indigenous people to enter such sectors'.[40]

The eradication of poverty in the most depressed and exploited rural areas was to be stepped up during the remaining two years of the Second Malaysia Plan as summed up in the following:

The recently established Farmers' Organization Authority (FOA) will co-ordinate farming activities and ensure better credit and marketing facilities. FAMA will participate in the processing and marketing of fruits, maize, pepper, cocoa, groundnuts and other cash crops, while Bank Pertanian will expand its operations in the rural areas, particularly in padi areas. Research and extension services will be stepped up by MARDI, RISDA [Rubber Industry Smallholders' Development Authority] and FOA. Other agencies such as the Fisheries Development Authority (MAJUIKAN) and the National Livestock Corporation (MAJUTERNAK) will undertake several projects to increase productivity and income in these sections.[41]

Although the Mid-Term Review did not show quantitatively how far modernization of the rural sector had taken place, the activities carried out during the 1971–3 period did indicate that a genuine and more steadfast attempt was being undertaken to eradicate poverty and uplift the social and ecnomic conditions of the long-neglected rural dwellers throughout the nation.

By the beginning of 1974 employment and ownership imbalance among the different races remained serious, but some progress had been achieved. In pioneer industries, which constituted the fastest-growing sector in the manufacturing field, participation by Malays accounted for about 45 per cent of total employment. However, about 55 per cent of the Malays employed were still unskilled labour, while the Chinese accounted for 77 per cent of the professional and managerial group and 73 per cent of the technical and supervisory group.[42] To ensure increased representation of professionals in the private sector, the Government was encouraging Malay scholarship holders to enter that sector on completion of their studies.

The overriding aim of the NEP in the private sector was the creation of a Malay commercial and industrial community in which 'within a period of 20 years, Malays and other indigenous people ... [would] own and manage at least 30% of the total commercial and industrial activities of the economy in all categories and scales of operations'.[43] Pertubuhan Nasional (The National Corporation or PERNAS) was incorporated as a public company in 1969, and by 1973 had formed seven wholly-owned subsidiaries covering insurance, construction, trading, properties, engineering and securities while its joint-venture activities were in mining, containerization, consultancy, hotels and trading. In all these activities the prime objective was to prepare the ground for ownership by *bumiputras* as soon as they had the wherewithal. The initial allocation in the Plan of $100 million for PERNAS had been disbursed and an additional $50 million was made available for 1974-5 to help it expand and accelerate its programmes in industry and commerce.[44] The following sums up the methods of the NEP in so far as the restructuring of society in gradual fulfilment of the socio-economic 'bargain' was concerned:

The agencies which spearhead the Government's efforts in the creation of a Malay commercial and industrial community include MARA, FIMA [Federal Industrial Marketing Authority], PERNAS, UDA and the SEDCs. Their activities are wide-ranging and comprise, *inter alia*, the development of modern commercial and industrial activities in the rural areas, new growth centres and in existing urban centres. They have an important role in expanding opportunities for participation by Malays and other indigenous people in these sectors through financial, technical and other assistance to help them start and sustain their own commercial ventures. They also have the role of acquiring share capital in existing and new enterprises to be held in trust for the Malays and other indigenous groups until such time as they are in a position to acquire these shares on their own.[45]

Thus the endeavour to fulfil the ideals of independence and nation-building through the achievement of greater equity in society was being undertaken more determinedly and realistically by the beginning of 1974.

1. The membership of the NOC was as follows: Director of Operations—Tun Abdul Razak bin Hussein. Ordinary members: Tun (Dr) Ismail bin Datuk Abdul Rahman; Hamzah bin Datuk Abu Samah; Tun Tan Siew Sin; Tun V. T. Sambanthan; Tan Sri Abdul Kadir Shamsuddin; Tan Sri Muhammad Ghazali Shafie; General Tunku Osman Jewa; Tan Sri Mohammad Salleh. See Goh Cheng Teik, *The May Thirteenth Incident and Democracy in Malaysia*, Kuala Lumpur, 1971, p. 27n.

2. *Straits Times*, 30 July 1969.

3. *Straits Times*, 26 July 1969.

4. *NOC Report*, p. vi.

5. G. P. Means, *Malaysian Politics*, London, p. 130n.

6. Dato E. E. C. Thuraisingham to the present writer, 20 November 1973. Cf. Chapter 3, p. 138.

7. F. V. Gagliano, *Communal Violence in Malaysia 1969: The Political Aftermath*, Athens, Ohio, 1970, p. 5.

8. The development Plans were discussed in Chapter 4 above; see also M. Rudner, 'The Draft Development Plan of the Federation of Malaya, 1950–55', *JSEAS*, 3, No. 2, March 1972, pp. 63–96.

9. Malaysia, *Interim Review of Development in Malaya Under the Second Five-Year Plan* (hereinafter referred to as *Interim Review of Second Malayan Plan*), Kuala Lumpur, 1963, p. 1; and Malaysia, *First Malaysia Plan, 1966–1970*, Kuala Lumpur, 1965, p. v.

10. Malaysia, *First Malaysia Plan, 1966–1970*, pp. 28–9; and Malaysia, *Second Malaysia Plan, 1971–1975*, Kuala Lumpur, 1971, p. 28.

11. *First Malaysia Plan, 1966–1970*, p. 27.

12. Ibid., p. 2.

13. Tun Abdul Razak bin Hussein, *First Malaysia Plan: Full Text of Speech . . . at the House of Representatives on 15th December 1965*, Kuala Lumpur, p. 10.

14. Alliance, *To A Happier and Greater Malaysia*, Kuala Lumpur, 1964, p. 5.

15. Alliance, *We the Alliance: Results in Rural Development*, Kuala Lumpur, 1964, pp. 2–3.

16. Tun Abdul Razak bin Hussein, op. cit., p. 9.

17. Gagliano, op. cit., p. 30n.

18. Siew Nim Chee, *Development Challenge in Malaysia*, Athens, Ohio, 1968, p. 3.

19. J. H. Funston, 'Writings on May 13', paper presented to Seminar Aliran Kini Dalam Sains Kemasyarakatan dan Kemanusiaan, Universiti Kebangsaan Malaysia, 23–25 October 1974, p. 7. Mimeographed.

20. Ibid., pp. 23–4. Emphasis in the original.

21. Lim Lin Lean, *Some Aspects of Income Differentials in West Malaysia*, Faculty of Economics and Administration, University of Malaya, Kuala Lumpur, 1971, p. 69.

22. A. Lee 'The Chinese and Malay Dilemmas in Malaysia', *Pacific Community*, 3, No. 3, April 1972, pp. 562–3.

23. *NOC Report*, pp. 82–3. See also these provisions in Malaysia, *Malaysia Federal Constitution*, Kuala Lumpur, 1970.

24. Malaysia, *Towards National Harmony*, Kuala Lumpur, 1971, paras. 6 and 8.

25. K. von Vorys, *Democracy without Consensus*, Princeton, 1975, p. 434.

26. Malaysia, *Rukunegara*, Kuala Lumpur, 1970. See also the wide coverage given in *Straits Times*, 1 September 1970.

27. Ungku A. Aziz, 'Poverty and Rural Development in Malaysia', *Kajian Ekonomi Malaysia*, 1, No. 1, June 1964, p. 75.

28. Wang Gungwu, 'Malaysia: Contending Elites', *Current Affairs Bulletin*, University of Sydney, 47, No. 3, 28 December 1970, p. 46.

29. Malaysia, *Second Malaysia Plan, 1971–1975* (hereinafter referred to as *Second Malaysia Plan*), Kuala Lumpur, 1971, para. 2.

30. *Second Malaysia Plan*, Foreword by the Prime Minister, Tun Abdul Razak bin Dato Hussein, p. vi.

31. Ungku A. Aziz, 'Footprints on the Sands of Time—The Malay Poverty Concept over 50 Years from Za'ba to Aziz and the Second Malaysia Five Year Plan'. Paper presented at the Malaysian Economic Association Meeting on Malaysian Economic Development and Policies, Kuala Lumpur, March 1974, p. 20.

32. Ibid., p. 18.

33. *Second Malaysia Plan*, Chapter 9.

34. Ibid., p. 144.

35. Aziz, 'Footprints on the Sands of Time', p. 23.

36. See Malaysia, *Towards National Harmony*, Appendix, for figures which amply substantiate this point.

37. Aziz, 'Footprints on the Sands of Time', p. 12. Za'ba wrote about the social and economic helplessness of the Malays in the 1920s.

38. Malaysia, *Mid-Term Review of the Second Malaysia Plan, 1971–1975*, Kuala Lumpur, 1973.

39. Ibid., pp. 6 and 14–15.

40. Ibid., pp. 6–7.

41. Ibid., p. 8.

42. Ibid., p. 13.

43. Ibid., pp. 13 and 81.

44. Ibid., p. 14.

45. Ibid.

Epilogue

THE existence of a nation does not necessarily follow the formal declaration of its independence. The words of an Indonesian neighbour proved prophetic: '*Perkataan kemerdekaan bukan lah perkataan keramat jang langsung dapat melahirkan sjurga dunia keatas bumi Malaya Merdeka; malah dia meminta pengorbanan jang lebih banjak lagi.*'[1] Indicative of the problem of political legitimacy faced by a newly-independent nation, the greatest challenges to Malaysia came from two quarters. One was Lee Kuan Yew's conception of and demand for a more liberal and less centralist 'Malaysian Malaysia'; the other was the communal riots in Kuala Lumpur in May 1969 which led to a basic reassessment of the underlying causes of such challenges.

Both these events were not unrelated. It would be accurate to say that the 'Singapore Separation' in 1965 was to forestall a possible outbreak of communal violence. Although the immediate objective was achieved, the underlying problems remained unsolved. Tension abated momentarily only to increase in intensity in the political campaign prior to the 1969 elections leading to the outbreak of 13 May.

As indicated earlier,[2] there had been sporadic communal conflicts since 1945. While it is not unfair to conclude that such conflicts reveal only too plainly that the efforts to build an integrated nation have encountered formidable obstacles, it is nonetheless true that the national leadership has, apart from the 'Singapore Separation', successfully held together the disjunctive parts. However, it has taken the lessons of 1965 and 1969 seriously. The belief is that preoccupation with the constitutional aspects of nation-building during the earlier phase of independence had led to an unconscious neglect of the importance of achieving socio-economic balance and parity among the different racial groups in Malaysia. The five-year development plans, started as early as 1950, and the First Malaysia Plan (1966–70), brought far greater benefit to the urban area hence perpetuating the imbalance between the Malays and non-Malays.

What has made the socio-economic imbalance so pertinent and

poignant is the tacit belief among the Malays that at the time the country achieved independence in 1957, there was a political and economic 'bargain' between Malay and non-Malay leaders. In return for the former's acceptance of the principle of *jus soli*, the latter should expect that the government would direct special efforts towards the socio-economic upliftment of the Malays.

The New Economic Policy (NEP) was meant to achieve that immediate objective. Admittedly, it has been araugued that the NEP has opened up a new dimension of dissension between Malays and non-Malays, but it is equally pertinent to argue that without special steps taken to reduce the economic imbalance, it would be impossible to remove Malay grievances. The effects of the NEP, politically, economically and socially, belong to another study. Suffice it to say that, having been launched, it has to be allowed, at least, to run its course; and there is little doubt that if its immediate objective is not achieved by 1990, its continuance will be a matter of foregone conclusion.

Despite the obvious importance of the NEP and the wide discussion and debate that it has generated, it should not be forgotten that another major step had been taken, after the 1969 riots, to try to circumvent the problem of communal conflict—namely the formation of the Barisan Nasional. It was, in a sense, an admission of the inadequacy of the 'Alliance' approach confined as it was to only three political parties. There never was, however, any illusion that the Barisan Nasional concept would completely eradicate communal conflict; its principal aim was to reduce political competition and strife along racial lines. Again, analogous to the 'Singapore Separation', a major component of the coalition—Parti Islam—subsequently withdrew; but the Barisan Nasional has proved itself to be extremely viable and flexible. It has periodically admitted new parties and expelled one. Soon after its formation, yet another party—the Parti Bangsa Dayak Sarawak (PBDS) was added to the coalition.

Repeatedly it has been pointed out that dissension within the Barisan Nasional has been all too frequent—between MCA and Gerakan, BERJAYA and USNO, and lately a serious dispute within the SNAP gave birth to the PBDS. But, this pertinent question has never been seriously considered: in the absence of the Barisan Nasional would such differences not have led to more serious consequences? As it is, although friction, either within a component party or between component parties of the Barisan Nasional, remains a fact of life, the degree of its intensity is contained largely by not allowing it to extend beyond the confines of the coalition.

Whether the Barisan Nasional will successfully, in future, prevent excessive politicking from threatening the integrity of the nation is open to speculation but its continued existence despite periodic internal dissension demonstrates all too clearly that the leaders of Barisan Nasional have placed utmost priority on the need to maintain the viability of the coalition without which political strife may repeatedly intensify communal divisiveness given the nature of Malaysia's plural society. The methods adopted by Malaysia's leaders since 1955 until now have no doubt shown inherent shortcomings but this is because there is, despite the stricture of critics, no obvious answer to Malaysia's problem of communalism. Suffice it to say that methods have been periodically reviewed and, if the past is any indication, will continue to be reviewed as and when circumstances demand. It is highly probable that communalism will for long remain a perennial problem but conflict within a nation is not necessarily an aberration from the norm of perfect harmony and integration. No society is completely cohesive and Malaysia is no exception.

1. See Chapter 4, footnote 75.
2. See Chapter 6, *passim*.

Bibliography

1. Select List of Persons Interviewed or with whom Discussions were Held

(The places and dates of interviews and discussions are given at the end of each entry.)

Abdul Kadir Shamsuddin, Tan Sri. Chief Secretary to the Federal Government; secretary of the Malayan delegation to the Constitutional Conference in London, January–February 1956. Genting Highlands, March 1974. (Deceased –1978)

Abdul Momen, Pehin Pengiran. State Secretary of Brunei. Bandar Seri Begawan (Brunei Town), November 1971.

Abdul Samad Ahmad. Malay linguist and writer who took part in the political activity of the early post-war years and the 1950s. Kuala Lumpur, January 1975.

Abdul Samad Ismail. Active member of the Malay leftist movement beginning from 1945, a veteran journalist who was Editor-in-Chief of *Berita Harian* at the times of discussions. Kuala Lumpur, August and October 1972; and May 1973.

Aishah binti Haji Abdul Ghani. Senator and later federal Minister of Welfare Services. On a rail journey from Johor Bahru to Kuala Lumpur, December 1972.

Ansibin, Assistant Superintendent of Police, Sabah, who was active during the Japanese Occupation. Kuala Lumpur, June 1971.

Corry, W. C. S. Formerly of the Malayan Civil Service, and secretary of the British Association of Malaysia and Singapore. London, April 1972. (Deceased)

Cruz, Gerald de. A co-founder of the Malayan Democratic Union, and an acknowledged ex-member of the Malayan Communist Party. Singapore, December 1972.

Dzulkifli bin Abdul Hamid, Senator Datuk. Federal Deputy Minister of Defence, and formerly Assistant Minister to the Chief Minister, Sabah. Kuala Lumpur, October 1974.

Foster, Sir John, K.B.E., Q.C., M.P. (Britain). One of the legal advisers to the Malay Rulers during the Malayan Union period. Letter to the present writer, 11 December 1973.

Gilong, Datuk Ganie (later Abdul Ghani). Federal Minister of Justice, and subsequently of Works and Power. Kuala Lumpur, March 1970.

Harun bin Haji Idris, Datuk, Menteri Besar of Selangor. Kuala Lumpur, September 1973.

Jugah anak Barieng, Tan Sri Datuk Amar Temenggong. Paramount leader of the Dayaks, especially in the Third Division of Sarawak. Federal Minister of Sarawak Affairs from September 1963 to his retirement in August 1974. Kuala Lumpur, March 1971; and Kuching, February 1974. (Deceased—1981)

Jugah, Leonard Linggi. Son of Tan Sri Datuk Amar Temenggong Jugah. Was Minister with Special Functions, and later of Local Government, Sarawak, until August 1974. Now back at his practice as advocate and solicitor. Kuching, November 1971, and February 1974.

Lawson (Dato) Justice Neil, Q.C. Adviser to the Sultan of Brunei during the crucial period of the Malaysia negotiations in 1962 and 1963. Lewes, England, June 1972.

Luping, Datuk Herman James. Former United Pasok Momogun Kadazan Organization leader. Assistant Minister of Co-ordination, and later appointed Assistant Minister to the Chief Minister, Sabah. Kota Kinabalu, November 1969, and February 1974.

MacDonald, Malcom. Governor-General of the Malayan Union and Singapore, May–July 1946; Governor-General of Malaya, Singapore and British Borneo, 1946–8; and Commissioner-General for the United Kingdom in Southeast Asia, 1948–55. Kuching, November 1971.

Melan Abdullah. Veteran journalist who was active in Malay political movements, initially with the leftist groups, after the Japanese Occupation. Parliament House, Kuala Lumpur, July 1970.

Mohd. Asri bin Haji Muda, Datuk Haji. A member of API in his youth; he took over the Presidency of the PMIP in 1964. He left the party in 1982 and in 1983 formed a new party called Hizbul Muslimin (Hamim). Kuala Lumpur, March 1979.

Mohamed bin Rahmat, Datuk. An active student leader during his years of study in Jakarta. Federal Deputy Minister of Co-ordination of Public Corporations. Kuala Lumpur, September 1971; and Cairo, January 1972.

Mohamed Yassin Anik, Assistant Superintendent of Police, Sabah. An active participant in the resistance movement during the Japanese occupation. Kuala Lumpur, June 1971.

Mojuntin, Datuk Peter Joinod. Former secretary-general of the United Pasok Momogun Kadazan Organization. Attempted to form the Union of Sabah People party in 1971; and became Assistant Minister of Industrial Development, Sabah, in October 1971. Kuala Lumpur, February 1971; and Penampang, Sabah, February 1974. (Deceased—1976)

Muhammad Ghazali bin Shafie, Tan Sri. Permanent secretary of the Ministry of Foreign Affairs before becoming a Senator, and Minister with Special Functions. Federal Minister of Home Affairs since August 1973. Kuala Lumpur, March 1971.

Musa Hitam, Datuk. An active youth leader at national and international levels who later took up politics. Following his criticism of Tunku Abdul Rahman's handling of the 13 May 1969 incident, he was dismissed from his post of Deputy Minister in the Prime Minister's Department. Returned to power politics after the Tunku's retirement in September 1970; was appointed a Deputy Minister of Trade and Industry, before he became Minister of Primary Industries in August 1974, and later Minister of Education and Deputy Prime Minister. Bangkok, October 1970; and Kuala Lumpur, January 1972.

Muthucumaru, M. President of the Negri Sembilan Indian Association. Seremban, August 1972.

Ningkan, Datuk Stephen Kalong. President of the Sarawak National Party, and Chief Minister of Sarawak from September 1963 to September 1966. Kuala Lumpur, July 1970; and Kuching, November 1971.

Ong Kee Hui, Datuk. President of the Sarawak United People's Party from its inauguration in 1959. Keen observer of the Malaysian political scene from the opposition side until his party formed a coalition with the Sarawak Alliance in July 1970. Became federal Minister of Technology, Research and Local Government in February 1971, and was later Minister of Local Government and the Environment from August 1974. Now retired from politics.

Ratnam, K. J. Professor of Political Science, University of Singapore, before he joined the University of Penang (later University of Science, Malaysia) and became dean of the School of Comparative Social Sciences from September 1970 to January 1974. He was later director of the Centre for Policy Research, Penang, from February 1974. Penang, August 1973.

Rees-Williams, D. R. (Lord Ogmore). A lawyer in Penang from 1930 to 1934. Member of a two-MP British mission to observe the cession of Sarawak to the British Crown in 1946. He was also confidentially asked by the Secretary of State for the Colonies to cross over to Malaya to watch and report on the 1946 Malayan Union scheme, particularly the reactions of the Malays against it. London, April 1972.

Rendel, Sir George. A retired career diplomat who was appointed by Her Majesty's Government to head a Commission to decide on the constitutional future of Singapore in 1953. London, June 1972.

Sambanthan, Tun V. T. Leader and President of the Malayan Indian Congress from 1955 to 1973. Held portfolios in the Federal Government, including those of Minister of Posts and Telecommunications and Minister of National Unity before he partly retired from active politics in 1974. Kuala Lumpur, April 1973; and Genting Highlands, March 1974. (Deceased–1978)

Sandhu, Kernial Singh. Associate Professor of Georgraphy, University of British Columbia, Vancouver, when he took up the post of Director of the Institute of Southeast Asian Studies, Singapore in July 1972. Singapore, April 1974.

Sandin, Datuk Benedict. A Sarawak career civil servant who took special interest in Iban folklore and traditions and was curator and ethnologist at the Sarawak Museum and Archives from 1967 to his retirement in 1973. Kuching, October 1969, and November 1971.

Smith, A. G. Former Director of Education, Sarawak. Hull, England, March 1972.

Stephens, Donald Aloysius (later Tan Sri Mohammed Fuad). A veteran journalist who organized the first Sabah English daily, *The North Borneo News and Sabah Times*, in 1953. Became Unofficial Member of the North Borneo Legislative and Executive Councils. Organized and became founder president of the United National Kadazan Organization (UNKO) in 1961 and the United Pasok Momogun Kadazan Organization (UPKO) in 1964. Became Chief Minister of Sabah upon its entry into Malaysia in September 1963 and held the post until he was appointed federal Minister of Sabah Affairs and Civil Defence in January 1965. Stephens returned to active politics as the president of Berjaya. Meanwhile he had been appointed Malaysia's High Commissioner to Australia in 1968. In January 1971, he embraced Islam and became Mohammed Fuad Stephens. Appointed Yang Di Pertua Negara of Sabah in August 1973, the same year he was conferred the title of 'Tan Sri'. In 1976 he was made a 'Tun' but he died in an air crash in June that year.

Tajem, Daniel. An independent-minded Iban graduate from New Zealand who was advocate and solicitor while keenly observing the Sarawak political scene. Became president of the Sarawak Dayak National Union; and successfully contested in the 1974 Sarawak state elections. Simanggang, Sarawak, October 1969; and Bandar Seri Begawan, Brunei, November 1971.

Templer, General Sir Gerald. Well-known British High Commissioner and Director of Operations, Malaya, from January 1952 to June 1954. London, June 1972. (Deceased–1978)

Thuraisingham, Datuk Sir E. E. Clough. Ceylonese leader of the 1950s in Malaya. Believed that the people should be 'equal and united' in Malaya. Letter to the present writer, 20 November 1973. (Deceased–1978)

Wang Gungwu. Professor of History, University of Malaya, before taking up the Chair of Far Eastern History at the Australian National University, Canberra, in August 1968. Kuala Lumpur, December 1971; and London, March 1972.

Wong, Datuk James. Vice-President of the Sarawak National Party, and was Deputy Chief Minister in the Ningkan cabinet from September 1963 to September 1966. Detained under the Preservation of Public Security Regulations (Sarawak) and the Internal Security Act on 30 October 1974. Kuala Lumpur, February 1971; and Kuching, February 1974.

Wu Teh-yao. Remembered for his part in the Fenn-Wu report on Chinese education in Malaya, 1951. Professor of Political Science, University of Singapore. Singapore, October 1973.

2. *Official Sources*

(a) **Malayan Union Government**

Advisory Council Proceedings, 1st April 1946, Kuala Lumpur, 1946.
Annual Report on Education in the Malayan Union for 1947, Kuala Lumpur, 1948.
Annual Report on the Malayan Union, 1946, Kuala Lumpur, 1946.
Annual Report on the Malayan Union, 1947, Kuala Lumpur, 1947.
Constitutional Proposals for Malaya: Report of the Consultative Committee Together with Proceedings of Six Public Meetings, a Summary of Representations Made and

Letters and Memoranda Considered by the Committee, Kuala Lumpur, 1947.

Constitutional Proposals for Malaya: Report of the Working Committee Appointed by a Conference of His Excellency the Governor of the Malayan Union, Their Highnesses the Rulers of the Malay States and the Representatives of the United Malays National Organization, Kuala Lumpur, 1946.

Council Paper, No. 53 of 1946, Kuala Lumpur, 1946.

Report on a Mission to Malaya by Sir Harold MacMichael, G.C.M.G., D.S.O., Kuala Lumpur, 1946.

(b) Federation of Malaya

A Plan of Development for Malaya, 1956–60, Economic Secretariat, Kuala Lumpur, 1956.

Annual Report, 1951, Kuala Lumpur, 1952.

Annual Report, 1952, Kuala Lumpur, 1953.

Annual Report, 1953, Kuala Lumpur, 1954.

Annual Report on Education for 1949, Kuala Lumpur, 1950.

Annual Report on the Federation of Malaya, 1948, Kuala Lumpur, 1949.

Chinese Schools and the Education of Chinese Malayans. The Report of a Mission Invited by the Federation Government to Study the Problem of Education of Chinese in Malaya (Fenn-Wu Report), Kuala Lumpur, 1951.

Communist Banditry in Malaya: The Emergency, Kuala Lumpur (n.d.).

Constitution (Amendment) Act 1962, Kuala Lumpur, 1962.

Draft Development Plan of the Federation of Malaya, Kuala Lumpur, 1950.

Federal Legislative Council Debates: Official Reports, 14th Meeting of the 4th Session of 2nd Legislative Council, 24 June 1959.

Federation of Malaya (Amendment) Ordinance, 1952, Kuala Lumpur, 1952.

Federation of Malaya Constitution 1957, Kuala Lumpur, 1957.

Federation of Malaya Constitutional Proposals 1957, Kuala Lumpur, 1957.

Joint Public Statement Issued by the British and Malayan Governments on 1 August 1962, Kuala Lumpur, 1962.

Malayan Constitutional Documents, Kuala Lumpur, 1959.

Malaysia in Brief, Kuala Lumpur, 1963.

Official Year Book, 1961, Kuala Lumpur, 1961.

Proceedings of the Federal Legislative Council of the Federation of Malaya, 4th Session, February 1951–February 1952.

Progress Report on the Development Plan of the Federation of Malaya 1950–1952, Kuala Lumpur, 1953.

Report by the Chief Minister of the Federation of Malaya on the Baling Talks, Kuala Lumpur, 1956.

Report of a Commission to Enquire into Matters Affecting the Integrity of the Public Services, Kuala Lumpur, 1955.

Report of the Commission on University Education in Malaya (Carr-Saunders Report), Kuala Lumpur, 1948.

Report of the Committee Appointed to Examine the Question of Elections to the Federal Legislative Council, Kuala Lumpur, 1954.

Report of the Committee on the Malayanization of the Government Service, Kuala Lumpur, 1954.

Report of the Committee to Consider the Problem of Malay Education (L. J. Barnes, Chairman), Kuala Lumpur, 1951.

Report of the Constituency Delineation Commission, Kuala Lumpur, 1954.

Report of the Education Committee 1956 (Dato Abdul Razak bin Dato Hussein, Chairman), Kuala Lumpur, 1956.

Report of the Education Review Committee 1960 (Abdul Rahman bin Haji Talib, Chairman), Kuala Lumpur, 1960.

Report of the Federation of Malaya Constitutional Commission (Lord Reid, Chairman), Kuala Lumpur, 1957.

Report of the Federation of Malaya Constitutional Conference Held in London in January and February, 1956, Kuala Lumpur, 1956.

Report of the First Election of Members to the Legislative Council of the Federation of Malaya (by T. E. Smith), Kuala Lumpur, 1955.

Report of the Land Administration Commission, Kuala Lumpur, 1958.

Report of the Special Committee Appointed on the 20th day of September 1951 to Recommend Legislation to Cover All Aspects of Educational Policy for the Federation of Malaya, Kuala Lumpur, 1952.

Report on the Barnes Report on Malay Education and the Fenn-Wu Report on Chinese Education, Kuala Lumpur, 1951.

Report on Economic Planning in the Federation of Malaya in 1956 and on the Outcome of the Financial Talks held in London from December the 21st, 1956 to January the 10th, 1957, Kuala Lumpur, 1957.

Report on the Introduction of Elections in the Municipality of George Town, Penang, 1951, Kuala Lumpur, 1953.

Report on the Parliamentary and State Elections, 1959, Kuala Lumpur, 1960.

Resettlement and the Development of New Villages in the Federation of Malaya, Kuala Lumpur, 1952

State Nationality Enactments, 1952, Kuala Lumpur, 1952.

The Emergency Regulations Ordinance 1948 (amended up to 31 March 1953), Kuala Lumpur, 1953.

The Federation of Malaya Agreement 1948, Kuala Lumpur, 1948.

The Second Five-Year Plan 1961–65, Kuala Lumpur, 1961.

The Text of the Agreement between the Government of the United Kingdom of Great Britain and Northern Ireland and the Government of the Federation of Malaya on External Defence and Mutual Assistance, Kuala Lumpur, 1957.

(c) Malaysia

A Plot Exposed, Kuala Lumpur, 1965.

Background to Indonesia's Policy Towards Malaysia, Kuala Lumpur, 1963.

Communist Threat to Sarawak, Kuala Lumpur, 1966.

Education in Malaysia, Dewan Bahasa dan Pustaka, Kuala Lumpur, 1968.

First Malaysia Plan, 1966–1970, Kuala Lumpur, 1965.

Indonesian Involvement in Eastern Malaysia, Kuala Lumpur, 1964.

Interim Review of Development in Malaya Under the Second Five-Year Plan, Kuala
    Lumpur, 1963.
Malaysia Federal Constitution, Kuala Lumpur, 1970.
Mid-Term Review of the First Malaysia Plan, 1966–1970, Kuala Lumpur, 1969.
Mid-Term Review of the Second Malaysia Plan, 1971–1975, Kuala Lumpur, 1973.
National Operations Council, *The May 13 Tragedy*, Kuala Lumpur, 1969.
Official Year Book, 1963, Kuala Lumpur, 1964.
Parliamentary Debates (Dewan Ra'ayat); Official Reports, Vol. 2, 9 August 1965.
Proclamation of Malaysia, Kuala Lumpur, 1963.
*Report on the Parliamentary (Dewan Ra'ayat) and State Legislative Assembly General
    Elections 1964 of the States of Malaya*, Kuala Lumpur, 1965.
Report on the Sabah State Legislative Assembly General Election 1967, Kuala Lumpur,
    1967.
Rukunegara, Kuala Lumpur, 1970.
Second Malaysia Plan, 1971–1975, Kuala Lumpur, 1971.
Speech by the Prime Minister, Malaysia: The National Language, Kuala Lumpur,
    1967.
The Militant Communist Threat to West Malaysia, Kuala Lumpur, 1966.
Towards National Harmony, Kuala Lumpur, 1971.
United Nations Malaysia Mission Report, Kuala Lumpur, 1963.

(d) Government of Sarawak

Annual Report on Sarawak for the Year 1948, Kuching, 1949.
Malaysia and Sarawak, Kuching, 1962.
Report of the Commission of Enquiry, North Borneo and Sarawak, 1962 (Lord
    Cobbold, Chairman), Kuching, 1962.
Report of the Land Committee, 1962, Kuching, 1963.
Sarawak And Its Government, Kuching, 1954.
Sarawak Annual Report, 1953, Kuching, 1954.
Sarawak Annual Report, 1955, Kuching 1956.
Sarawak Annual Report, 1956, Kuching, 1957.
Sarawak Annual Report, 1958, Kuching, 1959.
Sarawak Annual Report, 1959, HMSO, London, 1961.
Sarawak Annual Report, 1960, Kuching, 1961.
*The Danger Within: A History of the Clandestine Communist Organisation in
    Sarawak*, Kuching, 1963.
The Sarawak Government Gazette, 24 September 1941.

(e) Government of Sabah (formerly North Borneo)

Annual Report, 1954, Jesselton (now Kota Kinabalu), 1955.
Annual Report, 1956, HMSO, London, 1957.
Annual Report on North Borneo for the Year 1947, HMSO, London, 1948.
Annual Report on North Borneo for the Year 1948, HMSO, London, 1949.
Annual Report on North Borneo for the Year 1950, Jesselton, 1951.

British North Borneo Chartered Company, *Handbook of British North Borneo, 1886*, William Clowers and Sons, London, 1886.

British North Borneo (Chartered) Company, *Handbook of the State of North Borneo*, London, 1934.

Malaysia: Report of the Inter-Governmental Committee, Jesselton, 1963.

North Borneo and Malaysia, Jesselton, 1962.

North Borneo Annual Report, 1955, Jesselton, 1956.

North Borneo Annual Report, 1959, Jesselton, 1960.

North Borneo Annual Report, 1961, Jesselton, 1962.

Standing Orders of the Legislative Assembly of State of Sabah (by G. E. N. Oehlers, Speaker), Jesselton (n.d.).

The Laws of North Borneo in Force on the 30th June 1953, Vol. 6, HMSO, London, 1954.

(f) Government of Singapore

Annual Report, 1958, Singapore, 1959.

Malaysia—Age of Revolution, Singapore (n.d.).

Memorandum Setting out Heads of Agreement for a Merger between the Federation of Malaya and Singapore, Singapore, 1961.

Proclamation of Singapore, Singapore, 1965.

Report of the Rendel Constitutional Commission, Singapore, 1954.

Separation: Singapore's Independence on 9th August 1965, Singapore, (1965?).

The Economic Development of Malaya: Report of a Mission organized by the International Bank for Reconstruction and Development at the Request of the Government of the Federation of Malaya, the Crown Colony of Singapore and the United Kingdom, Singapore, 1955.

(g) Great Britain

British Dependencies in the Far East, 1945–1949, HMSO, London, 1949.

Colonial Office Records, C.O. 273/535, *Malayan Bulletin of Political Intelligence*, October 1926.

Federation of Malaya: Summary of Revised Constitutional Proposals, Cmd. 7171 of 1947, HMSO, London, 1947.

Hansard (House of Commons), Vol. 414, 1945/1946; and Vol. 420, 1946/1947.

Malaya: The Making of a Nation, HMSO, London, 1957.

Malayan Union and Singapore: Statement of Policy on Future Constitution, Cmd. 6724, HMSO, London, 1946.

Malayan Union and Singapore: Summary of Proposed Constitutional Arrangement, Cmd. 6749 of 1946, HMSO, London, 1946.

Malaysia: Agreement concluded between the United Kingdom of Great Britain and Northern Ireland, the Federation of Malaya, North Borneo, Sarawak and Singapore, Cmd. 2094 of 1963, HMSO, London, 1963.

Report of the Federation of Malaya Constitutional Conference, London 1956, London, 1956.

Report of the Singapore Constitutional Conference Held in London in March and April 1957, Cmd. 147 of 1957, HMSO, London, 1957.

The Colonial Empire (1939–1947), Cmd. 7167 of 1948, HMSO, London, 1948.

The Colonial Empire (1947–1948), Cmd. 7433 of 1948, HMSO, London, 1948.

(h) Republic of Indonesia

Panitia Pusat, *Menjambut Malaya Merdeka* (n.p.), Djakarta, 1957.

  1. Menteri Penerangan Republik Indonesia, 'Proklamasi Kemerdekaan Melahirkan Disiplin Bernegara'.

  2. Garieb A. Raouf, 'Menjongsung Kemerdekaan Malaya'.

  3. E. Z. Muttaqien, 'Mensjukur Kemerdekaan Malaya'.

(i) Government of Brunei

State of Brunei, *Annual Report, 1958*, Kuching, 1959.

3. Books

Abdul Rahman Omar, *Aliran Gerakan Nasionalisme di Asia Tenggara*, Pustaka Aman, Kota Bharu, 1969.

Adams, R. M., *The Malayan Union: A Study in British Empire Federation*, Boulder, Colorado, 1948.

Agastja, I. K. (Ibrahim Yaacob), *Sedjarah dan Perjuangan di Malaya*, Jogjakarta, 1951.

Ahmad Boestamam, *Dr. Burhanuddin: Putera Setia Melayu Raya*, Penerbitan Pustaka Kejora, Kuala Lumpur, 1972.

———, *Merintis Jalan Ke Puncak*, Penerbitan Pustaka Kejora, Kuala Lumpur, 1972.

Alatas, S. H., *The Myth of the Lazy Native*, Frank Cass, London, 1977.

Alexander, G., *Silent Invasion: The Chinese in Southeast Asia*, MacDonald and Company, London, 1973.

Ali Al-Haji Riau, *Tuhfat al-Nafis*, Malaysia Publications, Singapore, 1965.

Allen, G. C. and Donnithorne, A. G., *Western Enterprise in Indonesia and Malaya*, Macmillan Company, New York, 1957.

Allen, J. V., *Malayan Union*, Yale University, New Haven, 1967.

Allen, R., *Malaysia: Prospect and Retrospect*, Oxford University Press, London, 1968.

Anwar Abdullah, *Dato Onn: Riwayat Hidup*, Pustaka Nusantara, Petaling Jaya, 1971.

Arasaratnam, S., *Indians in Malaysia and Singapore*, Oxford University Press, Kuala Lumpur, 1970.

Ardizzone, M., *A Nation is Born: Being a Defence of Malayan Union*, The Falcon Press, London, 1946.

Ariff, M. O., *The Philippines' Claim to Sabah*, Oxford University Press, Kuala Lumpur, 1970.

Awberry, S. S. and Dalley, G. W., *Labour and Trade Union Organisation in the Federation of Malaya and Singapore*, Government Press, Kuala Lumpur, 1948.

Baker, M. H., *Sabah: The First Ten Years as a Colony, 1946–1956*, Malaysia Publishing House, new edn., Singapore, 1965.

Bali, K., *Sayang Sarawak*, Pustaka Aman, Kota Bharu, 1966.

Barber, N., *The War of the Running Dogs: How Malaya Defeated the Communist Guerrillas*, Fontana Books, London, 1972.

Baring-Gould, S. and Bampfylde, C. A., *A History of Sarawak Under its Two White Rajahs, 1839–1908*, Henry Sotheran and Company, London, 1909.

Barlow, Colin, *The Natural Rubber Industry: Its Development, Technology, and Economy in Malaysia*, Oxford University Press, Kuala Lumpur, 1978.

Barth, F., *Ethnic Groups and Boundaries*, George Allen and Unwin, London, 1969.

Bastin, J. and Smith, T. E., *Malaysia*, Oxford University Press, London, 1967.

Bedlington, Stanley S., *Malaysia and Singapore: The Building of New States*, Ithaca, N.Y., 1978.

Bellows, T. J., *The People's Action Party of Singapore: Emergence of a Dominant Party System*, Yale University Press, New Haven, 1970.

Benham, F. C., *The National Income of Malaya, 1947–49*, Government Press, Singapore, 1951.

Bird, I. L., *The Golden Chersonese and the Way Thither*, Oxford University Press, Kuala Lumpur, 1967 (reprint of 1883 edition).

Blythe, W., *The Impact of Chinese Secret Societies in Malaya (A Historical Study)*, Oxford University Press, Kuala Lumpur, 1969.

Bonney, R., *Kedah, 1771–1821: The Search for Security and Independence*, Oxford University Press, Kuala Lumpur, 1971.

Bowle, J., *The Nationalist Idea*, Ampersand, London, 1955.

Boyce, P., *Malaysia and Singapore in International Diplomacy: Documents and Commentaries*, Sydney University Press, Sydney, 1968.

Brimmell, J. H., *A Short History of the Malayan Communist Party*, Donald Moore Press, Singapore, 1956.

———, *Communism in Southeast Asia*, Oxford University Press, London, 1959.

Brooke, A., *The Facts about Sarawak*, William Crocker, London, 1946.

Brown, C. C., *Sejarah Melayu or Malay Annals*, Oxford University Press, Kuala Lumpur, 1970.

Brown, D. E., *Brunei: The Structure and History of a Bornean Malay Sultanate*, Brunei Museum, Bandar Seri Begawan, 1970.

Carr, E. H., *Nationalism and After*, Macmillan Company, London, 1945.

Chai Hon-chan, *The Development of British Malaya, 1896–1909*, Oxford University Press, Kuala Lumpur, 1964.

Chan Heng Chee, *Singapore: The Politics of Survival, 1965–1967*, Oxford University Press, Kuala Lumpur, 1971.

Chapman, F. S., *The Jungle is Neutral*, Chatto and Windus, London, 1949.

Chater, W. J., *Sarawak Long Ago*, Borneo Literature Bureau, Kuching, 1969.

Cheah Boon Kheng, *The Masked Comrades: A Study of the Communist United Front in Malaya, 1945–1948*, Times Books International, Singapore, 1979.

Ch'en, Jerome and Nicholas Tarling (eds.), *Studies in the Social History of China and Southeast Asia*, Cambridge University Press, London, 1970.

Chin, John M., *The Sarawak Chinese*, Oxford University Press, Kuala Lumpur, 1981.

Chin Kee Onn, *Malaya Upside Down*, Jits and Company, Singapore, 1946.

Clutterbuck, R., *Riot and Revolution in Singapore and Malaya, 1945–1963*, Faber and Faber, London, 1973.

———, *The Long Long War: The Emergency in Malaya, 1948–1960*, Cassell and Company, 2nd edn., London, 1967.

Comber, L. F., *Chinese Secret Societies in Malaya: A Survey of the Triad Society from 1800 to 1900*, J. J. Augustin Incorporated, New York, 1959.

Cooper, A. M., *Men of Sarawak*, Oxford University Press, Kuala Lumpur, 1968.

Corry, W. C. S., *Malaya Today*, British Commonwealth Affairs, No. 9, London, 1955.

Cowan, C. D., *Nineteenth Century Malaya: The Origins of British Political Control*, Oxford University Press, London, 1961.

Crabb, C. H., *Malaya's Eurasians—An Opinion*, Eastern Universities Press, Singapore, 1960.

Dawson, T. R. P., *Tan Siew Sin: The Man From Malacca*, Donald Moore Press, Singapore, 1969.

Desai, A. R. (ed.), *Essays on Modernization of Underdeveloped Countries*, Vol. 1, Thacker & Co., Bombay, 1971.

Deutsch, K. W., *Nationalism and Social Communication*, M.I.T. Press, 2nd edn., Cambridge, Mass., 1966.

Donnison, F. S. V., *British Military Administration in the Far East 1943–1946*, HMSO, London, 1957.

Dow, M. W., *Nation Building in Southeast Asia*, Pruett Press, Boulder, Colorado, 1965.

Drabble, J. H., *Rubber in Malaya 1876–1922: The Genesis of the Industry*, Oxford University Press, Kuala Lumpur, 1973.

Durai Raja Singam S. (ed. & pub.), *Tribute to Tunku Abdul Rahman*, Kuala Lumpur, 1963.

Elsbree, W. H., *Japan's Role in Southeast Asian Nationalist Movements, 1940 to 1945*, Harvard University Press, Cambridge, Mass., 1953.

Emerson, R., *From Empire to Nation*, Harvard University Press, Cambridge, Mass., 1962.

———, *Malaysia: A Study in Direct and Indirect Rule*, University of Malaya Press, Kuala Lumpur, 1964 (reprint of 1937 edition).

——— (ed.), *Government and Nationalism in Southeast Asia*, Institute of Pacific Relations, New York, 1942.

Enloe, C. H., *Ethnic Conflict and Political Development*, Little Brown & Co., Boston, 1973.

———, *Multi-Ethnic Politics: The Case of Malaysia*, University of California, Berkeley, 1970.

Esman, M. J., *Administration and Development in Malaysia: Institution Building and Reform in a Plural Society*, Cornell University Press, Ithaca, N.Y., 1972.

Evans, I. H. N., *Among Primitive Peoples in Borneo*, Cambridge University Press, London, 1922.

Evans, S. R., *Guide for Sabah Native Courts*, Borneo Literature Bureau, Kuching, 1967.

Fatimi, S. Q., *Islam Comes to Malaysia*, Malaysian Sociological Research Institute, Singapore, 1963.

Fisher, C. A., *Southeast Asia: A Social, Economic and Political Geography*, Methuen and Company, London, 1966.

Fletcher, N. M., *The Separation of Singapore From Malaysia*, Cornell University Press, Ithaca, N.Y., 1969.

Franck, T. M., *Why Federations Fail*, New York University Press, New York, 1968.

Freeman, J. D., *Report on the Iban*, University of London Press, London, 1970.

Fujiwara Iwaichi, Lt.-Gen., F. *Kikan Japanese Army Intelligence Operations in Southeast Asia during World War II*, Heinemann Asia, Hong Kong, 1983. Translated by Akashi Yoji.

Furnivall, J. S., *Colonial Policy and Practice*, New York University Press, New York, 1956.

Gagliano, F. V., *Communal Violence in Malaysia 1969: The Political Aftermath*, Ohio University, Athens, Ohio, 1970.

Gamba, C., *The Origins of Trade Unionism in Malaya*, Eastern Universities Press, Singapore, 1962.

Geddes, W. R., *Land Dayaks of Sarawak*, HMSO, London, 1954.

_____, *Nine Dayak Nights*, Oxford University Press, London, 1957.

George, T. J. S., *Lee Kuan Yew's Singapore*, Andre Deutsch, London, 1973.

Gibson, W. S. and Maxwell, W. G. (eds.), *Treaties and Engagements affecting the Malay States and Borneo*, Truscott and Son, London, 1924.

Ginsburg, N. and Robert, Jr., C. F., *Malaya*, University of Washington Press, Seattle, 1958.

Goh Cheng Teik, *The May Thirteenth Incident and Democracy in Malaysia*, Oxford University Press, Kuala Lumpur, 1971.

Gould, J. W., *The United States and Malaysia*, Harvard University Press, Cambridge, Mass., 1969.

Groves, H. E., *The Constitution of Malaysia*, Malaysia Publications, Singapore, 1964.

Guillemard, L., *Trivial Fond Records*, Methuen and Company, London, 1937.

Gullick. J. M., *Indigenous Political Systems of Western Malaya*, University of London Press, London, 1958.

_____, *Malaya*, Ernest Benn, 2nd edn., London, 1964.

Gwee Hock Aun, *The Emergency in Malaya*, Sinaran Brothers, Penang, 1966.

Hall, J. M., *Kinabalu Guerrillas (An Account of the Double Tenth 1943)*, Sarawak Press, Kuching (1949?).

_____, *Labuan Story*, Chung Nam Printing Company, Jesselton (now Kota Kinabalu), 1958.

Hanna, W. A., *Sequel to Colonialism: The 1957–1960 Foundations for Malaysia*, American University Field Staff, New York, 1965.

――――, *The Formation of Malaysia: New Factor in World Politics*, American University Field Staff, New York, 1962.

――――, *The Separation of Singapore from Malaysia*, American University Field Staff, New York, 1965.

Hanrahan, G. Z., *The Communist Struggle in Malaya*, University of Malaya Press, Kuala Lumpur, 1971 (reprint of 1954 edition).

Hayes, C. J. H., *The Historical Evolution of Modern Nationalism*, Macmillan Company, New York, 1931.

Ho Seng Ong, *Education for Unity in Malaya: An Evaluation of the Educational System of Malaya with Special Reference to the Need for Unity in its Plural Society*, Malayan Teachers' union, Penang, 1952.

Hoalim, Sr., P., *The Malayan Democratic Union: Singapore's First Democratic Political Party*, Institute of Southeast Asian Studies, Singapore, 1973.

Holland, W. L. (ed.), *Asian Nationalism and the West*, Macmillan Company, New York, 1953.

Hyde, D., *Confrontation in the East*, Donald Moore Books, Singapore, 1965.

Ibrahim Yaacob, *Sekitar Malaya Merdeka*, Kesatuan Malaya Merdeka, Djakarta, 1957.

International Bank for Reconstruction and Development, *The Economic Development of Malaya*, Johns Hopkins University Press, Baltimore, 1955.

International Labour Office, *The Trade Union Situation in the Federation of Malaya*, Geneva, 1962.

Irwin, G., *Nineteenth-Century Borneo*, Donald Moore Press, Singapore, 1965.

Ishak bin Haji Muhammad, *Bersatu Sekarang* (Annies Print Works?), Johor Bahru, 1956.

Jackson, R. N., *Immigrant Labour and the Development of Malaya, 1786–1920*, Government Press, Kuala Lumpur, 1961.

James, H. and Sheil-Small, D., *The Undeclared War*, Leo Cooper, London, 1971.

Jang Aisjah Muttalib, *Pemberontakan Pahang 1891–1895*, Penerbitan Kelantan, Kota Bharu, 1972.

Jasni, R. M., *Sejarah Sabah*, Sinaran Brothers, Penang, 1965.

――――, *Tanah Ayer Kita, Negeri Sabah*, Sinaran Brothers, Penang, 1969.

Jennings, Sir Ivor, *Cabinet Government*, London, 1959.

Jones, L. W., *The Population of Borneo*, University of London Press, London, 1966.

Jones, S. W., *Public Administration in Malaya*, Royal Institute of International Affairs, London, 1953.

Josey, A., *Lee Kuan Yew*, Donald Moore Press, Singapore, 1968.

――――, *Lee Kuan Yew: The Struggle for Singapore*, Angus and Robertson, Sydney, 1974.

――――, *Trade Unionism in Malaya*, Donald Moore Press, Singapore, 1954.

Kahin, G. M., *Nationalism and Revolution in Indonesia*, Cornell University Press, Ithaca, N.Y., 1952.

Kamenka, E. (ed.), *Nationalism: The Nature and Evolution of an Idea*, Australian National University Press, Canberra, 1973.

Kedourie, E., *Nationalism*, Hutchinson University Library, 3rd edn., London, 1964.

Kennedy, J., *Asian Nationalism in the Twentieth Century*, Macmillan & Company,

London, 1968.

Khoo Kay Kim, *The Western Malay States, 1850–1873*, Oxford University Press, Kuala Lumpur, 1972.

King, F. H. H., *The New Malayan Nation: A Study of Communalism and Nationalism*, Institute of Pacific Relations, New York, 1957.

Kohn, H., *Nationalism: Its Meaning and History*, D. Van Nostrand Company, Princeton, New Jersey, 1965.

_____, *The Idea of Nationalism*, Collier Books, New York, 1967.

Komer, R. W., *The Malayan Emergency in Retrospect: Organization of a Successful Counterinsurgency Effort*, Rand Corporation, Santa Monica, 1972.

Kroef, J. M. van der, *Communism in Malaysia and Singapore*, Martinus Nijhoff, The Hague, 1967.

Kunstadter, P. (ed.), *Southeast Asian Tribes, Minorities and Nations*, Princeton University Press, Princeton, New Jersey, 1967.

Lafalombara, J. and Weiner, M. (eds.), *Political Parties and Political Development*, Princeton, New Jersey, 1966.

Lee Kuan Yew, *Malaysia—Age of Revolution*, Government Press, Singapore, 1965.

_____, *The Battle for a Malaysian Malaysia*, Government Press, Singapore, 1965.

_____, *The Battle for Merger*, Government Press, Singapore 1961.

Lee Yong Leng, *North Borneo (Sabah): A Study in Settlement Geography*, Eastern Universities Press, Singapore, 1965.

Leifer, M., *The Philippine Claim to Sabah*, University of Hull, Hull, 1968.

_____, (ed.), *Nationalism, Revolution and Evolution in Southeast Asia*, University of Hull, Hull, 1970.

Leigh, M. B., *The Chinese Community of Sarawak: A Study of Communal Relations*, Malaysia Publishing House, Singapore, 1964.

_____, *The Rising Moon: Political Change in Sarawak*, University of Sydney Press, Sydney, 1974.

Liang Kim Bang, 'Sarawak, 1941–1957', *Number Five: Singapore Studies on Borneo and Malaya*, University of Singapore, Singapore, 1964.

Lim Chong-Yah, *Economic Development of Modern Malaya*, Oxford University Press, Kuala Lumpur, 1967.

Lim Lin Lean, *Some Aspects of Income Differentials in West Malaysia*, Faculty of Economics and Administration, University of Malaya, Kuala Lumpur, 1971.

Lim Tay Boh, *The Co-operative Movement in Malaya*, Cambridge University Press, Cambridge, 1950.

_____, (ed.), *Problems of the Malayan Economy*, Eastern Universities Press, 3rd -rev. edn., Singapore 1960.

Loh Fook Seng, P., *The Malay States, 1877–1895*, Oxford University Press, Kuala Lumpur, 1969.

MacIntyre, S. C., *Through Memory Lane*, University Education Press, Singapore, 1973.

Mackenzie, W. J. M., *Political Identity*, Manchester University Press, Manchester, 1978.

Mackie, J. A. C., *Konfrontasi: The Indonesia–Malaysia Dispute 1963–1966*, Oxford University Press, Kuala Lumpur, 1974.

McKie, R., *Malaysia in Focus*, Angus and Robertson, Sydney, 1963.

McVey, R. T., *The Calcutta Conference and the Southeast Asian Uprisings*, Cornell University, Ithaca, N.Y., 1958.

Mahathir bin Mohamad, *The Malay Dilemma*, Federal Publications, Kuala Lumpur, 1970.

Majul, C. A., *Muslims in the Philippines*, University of the Philippines Press, Quezon City, 1973.

Marshall, D., *Singapore's Struggle for Nationhood, 1945–1959*, University Education Press, Singapore, 1971.

Masanobu Tsuji, *Singapore: The Japanese Version*, Mayflower-Dell, London, 1966.

Maxwell, G., *The Civil Defence of Malaya*, Hutchinson and Company, London, 1944.

Maxwell, W. G. and Gibson, W. S. (eds.), *Treaties and Engagements Affecting the Malay States and Borneo*, Truscott and Son, London, 1924.

Means, G. P., *Malaysian Politics*, University of London Press, London, 1970.

Mehden, F. R. van der, *Religion and Nationalism in Southeast Asia*, University of Wisconsin Press, Madison, 1963.

Miller, H., *A Short History of Malaysia*, Frederick A. Praeger, New York, 1966.

———, *Menace in Malaya*, George G. Harrap, London, 1954.

———, *Prince and Premier: A Biography of Tunku Abdul Rahman Putra al-Haj, First Prime Minister of the Federation of Malaya*, George G. Harrap, London, 1959.

Mills, L. A., *British Malaya, 1824–1867*, Oxford University Press, Kuala Lumpur, 1967 (reprint of 1960 edition).

———, *Malaya: A Political and Economic Appraisal*, University of Minnesota Press, Minneapolis, 1958.

——— and Thompson, V., *Government and Nationalism in Southeast Asia*, Institute of Pacific Relations, New York, 1942.

Milne, R. S., *Government and Politics in Malaysia*, Houghton Mifflin Company, Boston, 1967.

——— and Ratnam, K. J., *Malaysia: New States in a New Nation*, Frank Cass, London, 1974.

———, *The Malayan Parliamentary Election of 1964*, University of Malaya Press, Singapore, 1967.

Minogue, K. R., *Nationalism*, B. T. Batsford, London, 1967.

Mohamed Noordin Sopiee, *From Malayan Union to Singapore Separation*, Penerbit Universiti Malaya, Kuala Lumpur, 1974.

Mohamed Suffian bin Hashim, *An Introduction to the Constitution of Malaysia*, Government Press, Kuala Lumpur, 1972.

Morais, V. J. (compiler and publisher), *Who's Who in Malaysia and Singapore*, Kuala Lumpur, 1959–.

Muhammad Ghazali bin Shafie, *Confrontation: A Manifestation of the Indonesian Problem*, Government Press, Kuala Lumpur, 1964.

Muhammad Yunus Hamidi, *Sejarah Pergerakan Politik Melayu Semenanjong*, Kuala Lumpur, Pustaka Antara (1961?).

Nabir bin Haji Abdullah, *Maahad Il Ihya Assyariff Gunung Semanggol, 1934–1959*,

Jabatan Sejarah, Universiti Kebangsaan Malaysia, Kuala Lumpur, 1976.

Ness, G. D., *Bureaucracy and Rural Development in Malaysia*, University of California Press, Berkeley, 1967.

Nyce, R., *Chinese New Village in Malaya: A Community Study*, Malaysian Sociological Research Institute, Singapore, 1973.

O'Balance, E., *Malaya: The Communist Insurgent War, 1948–60*, Faber and Faber, London, 1966.

One of them [Abdul Majid bin Haji Zainuddin], *The Malays in Malaya*, Malaya Publishing House, Singapore, 1928.

Ong Yoke Lin, *Malaysia at the United Nations*, Government Press, Kuala Lumpur, 1963.

Ongkili, J. P., *Modernization in East Malaysia, 1960–1970*, Oxford University Press, Kuala Lumpur, 1972.

———, *Susuzan Totopot do Sabah (History of Sabah)*, Borneo Literature Bureau, Kuching, 1965.

———, *The Borneo Response to Malaysia, 1961–1963*, Donald Moore Press, Singapore, 1967.

Onraet, R., *Singapore—A Police Background*, Dorothy Crisp, London, 1947.

Ooi Jin-bee, *Land, People and Economy in Malaya*, Longmans, Green and Company, London, 1963.

Osborne, M. E., *Singapore and Malaysia*, Cornell University Press, Ithaca, N.Y., 1964.

Owen, F., *The Fall of Singapore*, Michael Joseph, London, 1960.

Palit, D. K., *The Campaign in Malaya*, English Book Store, New Delhi, 1960.

Pang Cheng Lian, *Singapore's People's Action Party: Its History, Organization and Leadership*, Oxford University Press, Kuala Lumpur, 1971.

Panikkar, K. M., *Asia and Western Dominance*, George Allen and Unwin, new edn., London, 1959.

Parkinson, C. N., *Britain in the Far East: The Singapore Naval Base*, Eastern Universities Press, Singapore, 1955.

———, *British Intervention in Malaya 1867–1877*, University of Malaya Press, Singapore, 1960.

Parmer, J. N., *Colonial Labor Policy and Administration: A History of Labor in the Rubber Plantation Industry in Malaya, c.1910–1941*, J. J. Augustin Incorporated, New York, 1960.

Payne, R., *The White Rajahs of Sarawak*, Robert Hale, London, 1960.

Peet, G. L., *Political Questions in Malaya*, Cambridge University Press, London, 1949.

Pringgodigdo, A. K., *Sedjarah Pergerakan Rakjat Indonesia*, Penerbitan Dian Rakyat, tjetakan ketudjuh, Djakarta, 1970.

Pringle, R., *Rajahs and Rebels: The Ibans of Sarawak under Brooke Rule, 1841–1941*, Macmillan Company, London, 1970.

Purcell, V., *Malaya: Communist or Free?*, Victor Gollancz, London, 1954.

———, *The Chinese in Malaya*, Oxford University Press, London, 1948.

———, *The Chinese in Modern Malaya*, Donald Moore Press, Singapore, 1956.

———, *The Revolution in Southeast Asia*, Thames and Hudson, London, 1962.

Puthucheary, J. J., *Ownership and Control in the Malayan Economy*, Donald Moore, Singapore, 1960.

Pye, L. W., *Guerrilla Communism in Malaya (Its Social and Political Meaning)*, Princeton University Press, Princeton, N.J., 1956.

Ratnam, K. J., *Communalism and the Political Process in Malaya*, University of Malaya Press, Kuala Lumpur, 1965.

——— and Milne, R. S., *The Malayan Parliamentary Election of 1964*, University of Malaya Press, Singapore, 1967.

Reece, R. H. W., *The Name of Brooke: The End of White Rajah Rule in Sarawak*, Oxford University Press, Kuala Lumpur, 1982.

Rees-Williams, D. R., *et al.*, *Three Reports on the Malayan Problem*, Institute of Pacific Relations, New York, 1949.

Reid, A. J. S., *The Contest of North Sumatra*, Oxford University Press, Kuala Lumpur, 1969.

Richards, A. (ed.), *The Sea Dayaks and Other Races of Sarawak*, Kuching, 1963 (reprint of 1912 edition).

Robinson, A., *The Malayan Campaign in the light of the Principles of War*, Royal United Service Institution, London, 1964.

Robinson, J. B. P., *Transformation in Malaya*, Secker and Warburg, London, 1956.

Roff, M. C., *The Politics of Belonging: Political Change in Sabah and Sarawak*, Oxford University Press, Kuala Lumpur, 1974.

Roff, W. R., *The Origins of Malay Nationalism*, University of Malaya Press, Singapore, 1967.

Rokkan, S., *Citizens' Election Parties*, Universitetsforlaget, Oslo, 1970.

Romulo, C. P., *Contemporary Nationalism and the World Order*, Asia Publishing House, New York, 1964.

Rose, S., *Britain and South-East Asia*, Chatto and Windus, London, 1962.

———, *Socialist Parties in Southeast Asia*, Oxford University Press, London, 1959.

Royal Institute of International Affairs, *Nationalism*, Oxford University Press, London, 1939.

Runciman, S., *The White Rajahs*, Cambridge University Press, London, 1960.

Ruslan Abdulgani, *Nasionalisme Asia*, Jajasan Pantjaka, Djakarta, 1964.

Rutter, O., *British North Borneo*, Constable and Company, London, 1922.

Sadka, E., *The Protected Malay States 1874–1895*, University of Malaya Press, Singapore, 1968.

Salleh Daud, *UMNO, Image and Reality*, UMNO Headquarters, Kuala Lumpur (1966?).

Sandhu, K. S., *Indians in Malaya: Some Aspects of Their Immigration and Settlement (1786–1957)*, Cambridge University Press, London, 1969.

Sandin, B., *The Sea Dayaks of Borneo*, Macmillan, London, 1967.

Scott, J. C., *Political Ideology in Malaysia*, Yale University Press, New Haven, 1968.

Senu Abdul Rahman (ed.), *Revolusi Mental*, Penerbitan Utusan Melayu, Kuala Lumpur, 1971.

Shellabear, W. G., *Sejarah Melayu*, Oxford University Press, Kuala Lumpur, 1967 (reprint of 1898 edition).

Sheridan, L. A., *Federation of Malaya Constitution*, University of Malaya Law Review, Singapore, 1961.

Short, Anthony, *The Communist Insurrection in Malaya, 1948–1960*, Frederick Muller Limited, London, 1975.

Siew Nim Chee, *Development Challenge in Malaysia*, Ohio University, Athens, Ohio, 1968.

Silcock, T. H., *The Economy of Malaya*, Eastern Universities Press, 4th edn., Singapore, 1963.

_____, *Towards a Malayan Nation*, Donald Moore Press, Singapore, 1961.

_____ and Fisk, E. K. (eds.), *The Political Economy of Independent Malaya*, Australian National University Press, Canberra, 1963.

Simandjuntak, B., *Malayan Federalism, 1945–1963*, Oxford University Press, Kuala Lumpur, 1969.

Simson, I., *Singapore; too little, too late—the failure of Malaya's Defences in 1942*, Asia Pacific Press, Singapore, 1970.

Skinner, C., *The Civil War in Kelantan, 1839*, Malaysian Branch, Royal Asiatic Society, Singapore, 1965.

Slimming, J., *Malaysia: Death of a Democracy*, J. Murray, London, 1969.

Smith, T. E., *Population Growth in Malaya*, Royal Institute of International Affairs, London, 1952.

_____, *Report of the First Election of Members to the Legislative Council of the Federation of Malaya*, Government Press, Kuala Lumpur, 1955.

_____, *The Background to Malaysia*, Oxford University Press, London, 1963.

Snyder, L. L., *The Dynamics of Nationalism*, D. Van Nostrand Company, New York, 1964.

Soekarno, *Nationalism, Islam and Marxism*, Cornell University, Ithaca, N.Y., 1969.

Soetan Sjahrir, *Nationalism and Internationalism*, U Hla Aung, 2nd edn., Rangoon, 1953.

Song Ong Siang, *One Hundred Years' History of the Chinese in Singapore*, University of Malaya Press, Singapore, 1967 (reprint of 1923 edition).

Stenson, M. R., *Industrial Conflict in Malaya*, Oxford University Press, London, 1970.

_____, *Repression and Revolt: The Origins of the 1948 Communist Insurrection in Malaya and Singapore*, Ohio University, Athens, Ohio, 1969.

_____, *The 1948 Communist Revolt in Malaya: A Note on Historical Sources and Interpretation*, Institute of Southeast Asian Studies, Singapore, 1971.

Swettenham, F., *British Malaya*, John Lane the Bodley Head, London, 1907.

Swift, M. G., *Malay Peasant Society in Jelebu*, University of London Press, London, 1965.

Syed Husin Ali, *Malay Peasant Society and Leadership*, Oxford University Press, Kuala Lumpur, 1975.

Tan Cheng Lock, *A Collection of Correspondence* (privately published), Singapore, 1950.

_____, *A Collection of Speeches and Writings*, Tiger Standard Press, (n.p., n.d.).

_____, *Malayan Freedom and Independence* (privately published) (n.p.), 1953.

————, *Malayan Problems from a Chinese Point of View*, Tannsco Publishers, Singapore, 1947.

————, *Miscellaneous Speeches* (privately published), Malacca (n.d.).

————, *National Service Broadcast*, Government Press, Kuala Lumpur, 1952.

Tan Siew Sin, *The National Language*, Department of Information, Kuala Lumpur (1967?).

Tarling, N., *Britain, the Brookes and Brunei*, Oxford University Press, Kuala Lumpur, 1971.

————, *British Policy in the Malay Peninsula and Archipelago, 1824–1871*, Oxford University Press, Kuala Lumpur, 1969.

Thayer, P. W., *Nationalism and Progress in Free Asia*, Johns Hopkins Press, Baltimore, 1956.

Thio, E., *British Policy in the Malay Peninsula 1880–1910*, University of Malaya Press, Singapore, 1969.

Thompson, V., *Postmortem on Malaya*, Macmillan Company, New York, 1943.

————, and Adloff, R., *The Left Wing in Southeast Asia*, William Sloane Associates, New York, 1950.

————and Mills, L. A., *Government and Nationalism in Southeast Asia*, Institute of Pacific Relations, New York, 1942.

T'ien Ju-Kang, *The Chinese of Sarawak*, University of London, London, 1953.

Tilman, R. O., *Bureaucratic Transition in Malaya*, Cambridge University Press, London, 1964.

————(ed.), *Man, State and Society in Contemporary Southeast Asia*, Pall Mall Press, London, 1963.

Tregonning, K. G., *North Borneo*, HMSO, London, 1960.

————, *Under Chartered Company Rule*, University of Malaya Press, Singapore, 1958; 2nd edn., 1965, as *A History of Modern Sabah, 1881–1963*, with an additional chapter covering 1946–63.

Tufo, M. V. del, *Malaya: A Report on the 1957 Census of Population*, Government Press, Singapore, 1948.

Tunku Abdul Rahman, *May 13–Before and After*, Utusan Melayu Press, Kuala Lumpur, 1969.

Turnbull, C. M., *The Straits Settlements, 1826–67*, University of London Press, London, 1972.

Ungku A. Aziz, *Renchana2 Ekonomi dan Kemiskinan*, Pustaka Melayu Singapura, 1959.

————, *Subdivision of Estates in Malaya*, Government Press, Vol. 1, Kuala Lumpur, 1963.

Usha Mahajani, *The Role of Indian Minorities in Burma and Malaya*, Vora and Company Publishers, Bombay, 1960.

Vasil, R. K., *Politics in a Plural Society*, Oxford University Press, Kuala Lumpur, 1971.

————, *The Malaysian General Election of 1969*, Oxford University Press, Kuala Lumpur, 1972.

Vaughan, J. D., *The Manners and Customs of the Chinese of the Straits Settlements*, Oxford University Press, Kuala Lumpur, 1971 (reprint of 1879 edition).

Vorys, Karl von, *Democracy without Consensus; Communalism and Political Stability in Malaysia*, Princeton University Press, Princeton, N.J., 1975.

Wang Gungwu, *A Short History of the Nanyang Chinese*, Donald Moore, Singapore, 1959.

———— (ed.), *Malaysia: A Survey*, Frederick A. Praeger, New York, 1964.

Wheare, K. C., *Federal Government*, Oxford University Press, London, 1967.

Wheatley, P., *The Golden Khersonese*, University of Malaya Press, Kuala Lumpur, 1961.

Wheeler, R. L., *The Modern Malay*, George Allen and Unwin, London, 1928.

Wilber, D. N. (ed.), *The Nations of Asia*, Hart Publishing Company, New York, 1966.

Wilkinson, R. J. (ed.), *Papers on Malay Subjects*, Kuala Lumpur, 1925.

Williams, T. R., *The Dusun: A North Borneo Society*, Holt, Rinehart and Winston, New York, 1965.

Winstedt, R. O., *Britain and Malaya, 1786–1948*, Longmans, Green and Company, revised edn., London, 1949.

————, *Malaya and its History*, Hutchinson University Library, 2nd edn., London, 1951.

Wolters, O. W., *The Fall of Srivijaya in Malay History*, Lund Humphries Publishers, London, 1970.

Wong Choon San, *A Gallery of Chinese Kapitans*, Dewan Bahasa dan Kebudayaan Kebangsaan, Singapore, 1963.

Wong Hoy Kee, F. and Ee Tiang Hong, *Education in Malaysia*, Singapore, 1971.

Wong Lin Ken, *The Malayan Tin Industry to 1914*, University of Arizona Press, Tucson, 1965.

Wright, L. R., *The Origins of British Borneo*, University of Hong Kong Press, Hong Kong, 1970.

Yeo Kim Wah, *Political Development in Singapore, 1945–1955*, Singapore University Press, Singapore, 1973.

Yoji Akashi, *The Nanyang Chinese National Salvation Movement, 1937–1941*, Centre for East Asian Studies, University of Kansas, 1970.

Zainal Abidin bin Abdul Wahid (ed.), *Glimpses of Malaysian History*, Dewan Bahasa dan Pustaka, Kuala Lumpur, 1970.

Zaini bin Mohd. Isa, *Kebudayaan dan Adat Resam Kadazan dan Murut*, Pustaka Aman, Kota Bharu, 1969.

4. Articles

Abdul Rahman bin Karim, 'Northern Borneo Nationalism; the Threat to Malaysia', *Eastern World*, 17, No. 6, London, June 1963, pp. 14–17.

Ahmad Ibrahim, 'Malaysia As A Federation', *Jernal Undang-Undang; Journal of Malaysian and Comparative Law*, 1, Pt. 1, Kuala Lumpur, May 1974, pp. 1–27.

Akashi, Yoji, 'Japanese Military Administration in Malaya–Its Formation and Evolution in Reference to Sultans, the Islamic Religion, and The Moslem-Malays, 1941–1945', *Asian Studies*, 7, No. 1, April 1969, pp. 81–110.

————, 'Education and Indoctrination Policy in Malaya and Singapore under the

Japanese Rule, 1942–1945', *Malaysian Journal of Education*, 13, No. 1/2, December 1976, pp. 1–46.

Allen, R., 'Britain's Colonial Aftermath in Southeast Asia', *Asian Survey*, 3, No. 9, September 1963, pp. 403–14.

Arasaratnam, S., 'History, Nationalism and Nation Building; The Asian Dilemma', an Inaugural Lecture delivered at the University of New England, Armidale, New South Wales, on 29 April 1974.

———, 'Political Attitudes and Organization Among Malayan Indians, 1945–1955', *Jernal Sejarah*, 10, 1971/72, pp. 1–6.

Armstrong, H. F., 'The Troubled Birth of Malaysia', *Foreign Affairs*, 41, No. 4, New York, July 1963, pp. 673–93.

Bass, J., 'Malaysia and Singapore; Moving Apart?', *Asian Survey*, 9, No. 2, February 1969, pp. 122–9.

Bellows, T. J., 'The Singapore Party System', *JSEAH*, 8, No. 1, March 1967, pp. 122–38.

Bradley, C. P., 'Rupture in Malaysia', *Current History*, 50, No. 294, February 1966, pp. 98–105.

———, 'The Formation of Malaysia', *Current History*, 46, No. 271, February 1964, pp. 89–94.

Burridge, K. O. L., 'Racial Relations in Johore', *Australian Journal of Politics and History*, 2, No. 2, May 1957, pp. 151–68.

Butwell, R., 'A Chinese University for Malaya', *Pacific Affairs*, 26, No. 4, December 1953, pp. 344–8.

———, 'Malaysia and its Impact on the International Relations of Southeast Asia', *Asian Survey*, 4, No. 7, July 1964, pp. 940–6.

Carnell, F. G., 'Communalism and Communism in Malaya', *Pacific Affairs*, 26, No. 2, June 1953, pp. 99–117.

———, 'Constitutional Reform and Elections in Malaya', *Pacific Affairs*, 27, No. 3, September 1954, pp. 216–35.

———, 'The Malayan Elections', *Pacific Affairs*, 28, No. 4, December 1955, pp. 315–30.

Chaudhuri, N. C., 'Subhas Chandra Bose–His Legacy and Legend', *Pacific Affairs*, 26, December 1953, pp. 349–57.

Ch'en Su-ching, 'The Chinese in Malaya', *Pacific Affairs*, 26, No. 3, September 1948, pp. 291–5.

Cohen, S. P., 'Subhas Chandra Bose and the Indian National Army', *Pacific Affairs*, 36, No. 4, Winter 1963–64, pp. 411–29.

Corry, W. C. S., 'The Malayan Scene', *Journal of the Royal Central Asian Society*, 48, London, Pt. 1, January 1956, pp. 20–8.

Crisswell, C. N., 'The Origins of the Limbang Claim', *JSEAS*, 2, No. 2, September 1971, pp. 218–29.

Dhu Renick, Jr., R., 'The Emergency Regulations of Malaya; Causes and Effect', *JSEAH*, 6, No. 2, September 1965, pp. 1–39.

Dobby, E. H. G., 'Malayan Prospect', *Pacific Affairs*, 23, No. 4, December 1950, pp. 392–401.

Enloe, C., 'Issues and Intergration in Malaysia', *Pacific Affairs*, 41, No. 3, Fall 1968, pp. 372–85.

Freedman, M., 'The Growth of a Plural Society in Malaya', *Pacific Affairs*, 33, No. 2, June 1960, pp. 158–68.

Funston, J., 'The Origins of Parti Islam Se Malaysia', *JSEAS*, 7, No. 1, March 1976, pp. 58–73.

_____, 'Writings on May 13', paper presented to Seminar Aliran Kini Dalam Sains Kamasyarakatan dan Kemanusiaan, Universiti Kebangsaan Malaysia, 23–25 October 1974. Mimeographed.

Gamba, C., 'Labour and Labour Parties in Malaya', *Pacific Affairs*, 31, No. 2, June 1958, pp. 117–30.

_____, 'Singapore–City and State', *Australian Journal of Politics and History*, 5, No. 2, Brisbane, November 1959, pp. 180–90.

Ghosh, K. K., 'The Indian National Army–Motives, Problems and Significance', *Asian Studies*, 7, No. 1, April 1969, pp. 4–30.

Glick, H. R., 'The Chinese Community in Sabah and the 1963 Elections', *Asian Survey*, 5, No. 3, March 1965, pp. 144–51.

Grossholtz, J., 'An Exploration of Malaysian Meanings', *Asian Survey*, 6, No. 4, April 1966, pp. 227–40.

Hairi Abdullah, 'Kebangkitan dan Gerakan Tentera Selendang Merah dalam Sejarah Daerah Muar dan Batu Pahat', *JEBAT*, 3/4, 1972/75, pp. 6–15.

Hawkins, G., 'First Steps in Malayan Local Government', *Pacific Affairs*, 26, No. 2, June, pp. 155–8.

_____, 'Reactions to the Malayan Union', *Pacific Affairs*, 19, No. 3, September 1946, pp. 279–85.

Hughes-Hallett, H. R., 'A Sketch of the History of Brunei', *JMBRAS*, 17, Pt. 2, August 1940, pp. 23–42.

Ingleson, J. E., 'Britain's Annexation of Labuan 1846; The Role of James Brooke and Local Influences', *University Studies in History*, 5, No. 4, Nedlands, Perth, 1970, pp. 33–71.

Ishak bin Tadin, 'Dato Onn and Malay Nationalism, 1946–1951', *JSEAH*, 1, No. 1, March 1960, pp. 56–88.

Itagaki, Yoichi, 'Some Aspects of the Japanese Policy for Malaya under the Occupation, with Special Reference to Nationalism' in K. G. Tregonning (ed.), *Papers on Malayan History*, University of Malaya Press, Singapore, 1962, pp. 256–67.

John, D. W. and J. C. Jackson, 'The Tobacco Industry of North Borneo: A Distinctive Form of Plantation Agriculture', *JSEAS*, 4, No. 1, March 1973, pp. 88–106.

Kahin, G. M., 'Malaysia and Indonesia', *Pacific Affairs*, Vol. 37, No. 3, 1964, pp. 253–70.

Khoo Kay Kim, 'Komunisma di Tanah Melayu: Peringkat Awal', *Jernal Sejarah*, 10, 1971/72, pp. 89–97.

_____, 'The Origin of British Administration in Malaya', *JMBRAS*, 39, Pt. 1, 1966.

_____, 'Malay Society, 1874–1920's', *JSEAS*, 5, No. 2, September 1974, pp. 179–98.

————, 'Ibrahim Yaacob dan KMM', *Widya*, No. 21, May 1979, pp. 34–41.

Lebra, J., 'Japanese Policy and the Indian National Army', *Asian Studies*, 7, No. 1, April 1969, pp. 31–49.

Lee, A., 'The Chinese and Malay Dilemmas in Malaysia', *Pacific Community*, 3, No. 3, April 1972, pp. 561–71.

Lee, E., 'The Emergence of Towkay Leaders in Party Politics in Sabah', *JSEAH*, 9, No. 2, September 1968, pp. 306–24.

Lee Ting Hui, 'Singapore under the Japanese', *JSSS*, 16, Pt. 1, 1961, pp. 31–69.

Leifer, M., 'Astride the Straits of Johore; The British Presence and Commonwealth Rivalry in Southeast Asia', *Modern Asian Studies*, 1, 1967, pp. 283–312.

————, 'Communal Violence in Singapore', *Asian Survey*, 4, No. 10, October 1964, pp. 1115–21.

————, 'Indonesia and Malaysia; The Diplomacy of Confrontation', *The World Today*, June 1965, pp. 250–60.

————, 'Singapore in Malaysia; The Politics of Federation', *JSEAH*, 6, No. 2, September 1965, pp. 54–70.

Leys, Peter, 'Observations on The Brunei Political System 1883–1885' (with notes by Robert M. Pringle), *JMBRAS*, 41, Pt. 2, December 1968.

Lim San Kok, 'Some Aspects of the Malayan Chinese Association, 1949–69', *JSSS*, 26, No. 2, 1971, pp. 31–48.

Lockard, C. A., 'Leadership and Power within the Chinese Community of Sarawak; A Historical Survey', *JSEAS*, 2, No. 2, September 1971, pp. 195–217.

————, 'Parties, Personalities and Crisis Politics in Sarawak', *JSEAH*, 8, No. 1, March 1967, pp. 111–21.

Loh Fook-Seng, P., 'A Review of the Educational Development in the Federated Malay States to 1939', *JSEAS*, 5, No. 2, September 1974, pp. 225–38.

Low, H., 'Selesilah (Book of Descent) of the Rajas of Brunei', *et al.*, *JSBRAS*, No. 5, June 1880, pp. 1–35.

MacFadyen, E., 'A Political Future for British Malaya', *Pacific Affairs*, 17, No. 1, March 1944, pp. 49–55.

McGee, T. E., 'The Malayan Elections of 1959; A Study in Electoral Geography', *The Journal of Tropical Geography*, 16, October 1962, pp. 70–99.

McIntyre, D., 'Political History 1896–1946' in Wang Gungwu (ed.), *Malaysia—A Survey*, Frederick A. Praeger, New York, 1964, pp. 138–48.

Mackie, J. A. C., 'Azahari's Young Men', *Nation*, Sydney, 12 January 1963, p. 7.

Maryanov, G. S., 'Political Parties in Mainland Malaya', *JSEAH*, 8, No. 1, March 1967, pp. 99–110.

Maxwell, G., 'Problems of Administration in British Malaya', *British Malaya*, February and April–June 1943.

————, 'Britain's Intervention in Malaya: The Origin of Lord Kimberley's Instructions to Sir Andrew Clarke in 1873', *JSEAH*, 2, No. 3, 1966.

Meadows, M., 'The Philippine Claim to North Borneo', *Political Science Quarterly*, 77, No. 3, September 1962, pp. 321–35.

Means, G. P., 'Eastern Malaysia: The Politics of Federation', *Asian Survey*, 8, No. 4, April 1968, pp. 289–308.

_____, 'Malaysia–A New Federation in Southeast Asia', *Pacific Affairs*, 36, No. 2, Summer 1963, pp. 138–59.

_____, 'The Role of Islam in the Political Development of Malaysia', *Comparative Politics*, 1, No. 2, January 1969, pp. 264–84.

Milne, R. S., 'Malaysia: A New Federation in the Making', *Asian Survey*, 3, No. 2, February 1963, pp. 76–82.

_____, 'Malaysia', *Asian Survey*, 4, No. 2, February 1964, pp. 695–701.

_____, 'National Ideology and Nation-Building in Malaysia', *Asian Survey*, 10, No. 7, July 1970.

_____, 'Patrons, Clients and Ethnicity: The Case of Sarawak and Sabah in Malaysia', *Asian Survey*, 13, No. 10, October 1973, pp. 891–907.

_____, 'Political Parties in Sarawak and Sabah', *JSEAH*, 6, No. 2, September 1965, pp. 104–17.

_____, 'Singapore's Exit from Malaysia: The Consequences of Ambiguity', *Asian Survey*, 6, No. 3, March 1966, pp. 175–84.

_____ and Ratnam, K. J., 'Patterns and Peculiarities of Ethnic Voting in Sabah 1967', *Asian Survey*, 9, No. 5, May 1969, pp. 373–81.

_____, 'The 1969 Parliamentary Election in West Malaysia', *Pacific Affairs*, 42, No. 2, Summer 1970, pp. 203–26.

_____, 'The Sarawak Elections of 1970: An Analysis of the Vote', *JSEAS*, 3, No. 1, March 1972, pp. 111–22.

Mohammad Hatta, 'One Indonesian View of the Malaysia Issue', *Asian Survey*, 5, No. 3, March 1965, pp. 139–43.

Morrison, I., 'Aspects of the Racial Problem in Malaya', *Pacific Affairs*, 22, No. 3, September 1949, pp. 239–53.

_____, 'Local Self-Government in Sarawak', *Pacific Affairs*, 22, No. 2, June 1949, pp. 178–85.

Ness, G. D., 'Modernization and Indigenous Control of the Bureaucracy in Malaysia', *Asian Survey*, 5, No. 9, September 1965, pp. 467–73.

Ongkili, J. P., 'A Decade of Growth for People of Sarawak', *Straits Times*, Kuala Lumpur, 12 February 1974.

_____, 'A Look at Sabah's Progress: A Decade of Growth', *Straits Times*, Kuala Lumpur, 7 March 1974.

_____, 'Adult Education for the British Borneans', *North Borneo News and Sabah Times*, 25 October 1962.

_____, 'Analysis ... The Sabah Claim', *Sunday Mail*, Kuala Lumpur, 15 July 1973.

_____, 'Darurat dan British, 1948–1960: Suatu Penghargaan', *Jernal Sejarah*, 12, 1973/74, pp. 58–73.

_____, 'Kelekaan Ekonomi Kompeni Berpiagam Sabah, 1881–1941', *Malaysia in History*, Malaysian Historical Society, 16, No. 1, June 1973, pp. 9–15.

_____, 'Malaysian History: The Challenges', *The Sunday Mail*, Kuala Lumpur, 21 October 1973. (Also as 'Writing Malaysia's National History', *Kinabalu Sabah Times*, 12 January 1974.)

_____, 'National Integration in Malaysia', *Southeast Asian Affairs 1974*, Institute of Southeast Asian Studies, Singapore, pp. 162–72. Also in *The Sarawak*

Tribune, 21 and 22 February 1975.

———, 'Nationalisma Filipina dan Konvenshen Perlembagaan 1971', *Jernal Sejarah*, 10, 1971/72, pp. 112–33.

———, 'Penggunaan Sejarah Socio Budaya dalam Usaha Memupok Keperibadian Kebangsaan (The Use of Socio-Cultural History in the Efforts to Form a National Identity)', *Southeast Asian Archives*, Petaling Jaya, 5, July 1972, pp. 76–83.

———, 'Penulisan Sejarah Malaysia Dari Segi Politik', *Kinabalu Sabah Times*, 13 September 1974.

———, 'Perkembangan Nasionalisma', *JEBAT*, Bil. 1, 1971/72, pp. 24–43.

———, 'Pre-Western Brunei, Sarawak and Sabah', *Nusantara*, Bil. 3, January 1973, pp. 49–68. Also in *Sarawak Museum Journal*, 20, Nos. 40–41 (New Series), January–December 1972, pp. 1–20.

———, 'Sarawak Politics and Future', *Opinion*, 2, No. 6, August 1969.

———, 'Students and Political Change in Southeast Asia', *Kinabalu Sabah Times*, 29 June 1970.

———, 'The Birth of Nationalism in Sarawak; The 1946 Cession and its Historical Significance', *The Sarawak Tribune*, 9 November 1971.

———, 'The British and Malayan Nationalism, 1946–1957', *JSEAS*, 5, No. 2, September 1974, pp. 255–77.

———, 'The Philippine Claim', *Opinion*, 1, No. 4, Kuala Lumpur, June 1969.

———, 'The Sabah Claim', *Sunday Mail*, Kuala Lumpur, 8 July 1973.

———, 'White Rajahs', *Far Eastern Economic Review*, 78, No. 41, 7 October 1972.

Parmer, J. N., 'Malaysia 1965: Challenging the Terms of 1957', *Asian Survey*, 6, No. 2, February 1966, pp. 111–18.

Pluvier, J. M., 'Malayan Nationalism: A Myth', *JHSUM*, 6, 1967/68, pp. 26–40.

P'ng Poh Seng, 'The Kuomintang in Malaya, 1912–1941', *JSEAH*, 2, No. 1, March 1961, pp. 1–41.

Purcell, V., 'A Malayan Union: The Proposed new Constitution', *Pacific Affairs*, 19, No. 1, March 1946, pp. 20–40.

———, 'The Crisis in Malayan Education', *Pacific Affairs*, 26, No. 1, March 1953, pp. 70–6.

Radin Soenarno, 'Malay Nationalism', *JSEAH*, 1, No. 1, March 1960, pp. 1–28.

Ratnam, K. J., 'Constitutional Government and the "Plural Society"', *JSEAH*, 2, No. 3, October 1961, pp. 1–10.

———, 'Political Parties and Pressure Groups', in Wang Gungwu (ed.), *Malaysia—A Survey*, Frederick A. Praeger, New York, 1964, pp. 336–45.

Rees-Williams, D. R., 'The Constitutional Position in Malaya', *Pacific Affairs*, 20, No. 2, June 1947, pp. 174–8.

Reid, A., 'The Kuala Lumpur Riots and the Malaysian Political System', *Australian Outlook*, 23, No. 3, December 1969, pp. 258–78.

Roff, M. C., 'Sabah's Political Parties and the 1967 State Election', *International Studies*, 9, No. 4, Bombay, April 1968, pp. 431–56.

———, 'The Malayan Chinese Association, 1948–65', *JSEAH*, 4, No. 2, September 1965, pp. 40–53.

———, 'The Politics of Language of Malaya', *Asian Survey*, 7, No. 5, May 1967, pp. 316–28.

_____, 'The Rise and Demise of Kadazan Nationalism', *JSEAH*, 10, No. 2, September 1969, pp. 326–43.

Roff, W. R., 'Kaum Muda-Kaum Tua: Innovation and Reaction Amongst the Malays 1900–1941' in K. G. Tregonning (ed.), *Papers on Malayan History*, University of Malaya Press, Singapore, 1962, pp. 162–92.

_____, 'The Persatuan Melayu Selangor: An Early Malay Political Association', *JSEAH*, 9, No. 1, March 1968, pp. 117–46.

Rudner, M., 'The Draft Development Plan of the Federation of Malaya 1950–55', *JSEAS*, 3, No. 2, March 1972, pp. 63–96.

_____, 'The Malaysian General Election of 1969: A Political Analysis', *Modern Asian Studies*, 4, No. 1, 1970, pp. 1–21.

_____, 'The Organization of the British Military Administration in Malaya, 1946–48', *JSEAH*, 9, No. 1, March 1968, pp. 95–106.

Sadka, E., 'Malaysia: The Political Background' in T. H. Silcock and E. K. Fisk (eds.), *The Political Economy of Independent Malaya*, Australian National Univesity Press, Canberra, 1963, pp. 28–58.

_____, 'Singapore and the Federation: Problems of Merger', *Asian Survey*, 1, No. 8, August 1961, pp. 17–25.

Sandhu, Kernial Singh, 'Emergency Resettlement in Malaya', *The Journal of Tropical Geography*, 18, August 1964, pp. 157–83.

_____, 'The Saga of the Malayan Squatter', *JSEAH*, 5, No. 1, March 1964, pp. 143–77.

Sartono Kartodirdjo, 'Kolonialisme dan Nasionalisme di Indonesia Abad XIX–XX', *Lembaran Sedjarah*, No. 1, Jogjakarta, December 1967.

Short, A., 'Communism and the Emergency' in Wang Gungwu (ed.), *Malaysia—A Survey*, Frederick A. Praeger, New York, 1964, pp. 149–60.

_____, 'Nationalism and the Emergency in Malaya' in M. Leifer (ed.), *Nationalism, Revolution and Evolution in Southeast Asia*, University of Hull, Hull, 1970, pp. 43–58.

Sidhu, J. S., 'Decentralisation of the Federated Malay States 1930–34', *Peninjau Sejarah*, 1, No. 1, June 1966, pp. 17–28.

Silcock, T. H. and Ungku A. Aziz, 'Nationalism in Malaya' in W. L. Holland (ed.), *Asian Nationalism and the West*, Macmillan, New York, 1953, pp. 269–345.

Singhal, D. P., 'Nationalism and Communism in South-East Asia', *JSEAH*, 3, No. 1, March 1962.

_____, 'The United States of Malaysia', *Asian Survey*, 1, No. 8, August 1961, pp. 16–22.

Smith, T. E., 'The Malayan Elections of 1959', *Pacific Affairs*, 33, No. 1, March 1960, pp. 38–47.

Soh Eng Lim, 'Tan Cheng Lock: His Leadership of the Malayan Chinese', *JSEAH*, 1, No. 1, March 1960, pp. 29–55.

Starner, F. L., 'Malaysia and the North Borneo Territories', *Asian Survey*, 3, No. 11, November 1963, pp. 519–34.

Stenson, M. R., 'The Malayan Union and the Historians', *JSEAH*, 10, No. 2, September 1969, pp. 344–54.

Straits Times, 'Malay–Chinese Goodwill Move–Nine Leaders Work for Racial Harmony', 11 January 1949.

Subky Latif, 'Pasang Surut Politik Hussein Onn', *Mastika*, No. 10, October 1973, pp. 2–8.

Suryanarayan, V., 'Singapore in Malaysia', *International Studies*, 10, No. 1, July 1969, pp. 1–43.

Suwondo, 'Sedjarah Pergerakan Nasional', *Himpunan Mahasiswa Mesin*, Universitas Trisakti, Djakarta (n.d.). Mimeographed.

Takdir Alisjahbana, S. *et al.* (eds.), *The Cultural Problems of Malaysia in the Context of Southeast Asia*, Public Printers, Kuala Lumpur, 1967.

Tilman, R. O., 'Elections in Sarawak', *Asian Survey*, 3, No. 10, October 1963, pp. 507–18.

_____, 'Malaysia and Singapore: The Failure of a Federation' in R. O. Tilman (ed.), *Man, State and Society in Contemporary Southeast Asia*, Pall Mall Press, London, 1963, pp. 490–505.

_____, 'The Alliance Pattern in Malaysian Politics; Bornean Variations on a Theme', *South Atlantic Quarterly*, 43, No. 1, Winter 1964, pp. 60–74.

_____, 'The Nationalization of the Colonial Services in Malaya', *South Atlantic Quarterly*, 61, No. 2, Spring 1962, pp. 183–96.

_____, 'The Sarawak Political Scene', *Pacific Affairs*, 37, No. 4, Winter 1964–5, pp. 412–25.

Traeger, F. N., 'The Federation of Malaysia' in T. M. Franck (ed.), *Why Federations Fail*, New York University Press, New York, 1968, pp. 125–66.

Tregonning, K. G., 'North Borneo, 1957' *Pacific Affairs*, 31, No. 1, March 1958, pp. 65–73.

_____, 'The Mat Salleh Revolt (1894–1905)', *JMBRAS*, 29, Pt. 1, 1956, pp. 20–36.

_____ (ed.), *Papers on Malayan History*, University of Malaya Press, Singapore, 1962.

Trocki, Carl A., 'The Origin of the Kanchu Systems, 1740–1860', *JMBRAS*, 44, Pt. 2, 1976.

Tunku Abdul Rahman, 'Malaysia: Key Area in Southeast Asia', *Foreign Affairs*, 43, No. 4, July 1965, pp. 659–70.

Turnbull, C. M., 'British Planning For Post-War Malaya', *JSEAS*, 5, No. 2, September 1974, pp. 239–54.

Ungku A. Aziz, 'Co-operation is the Key to Rural Success', *Straits Times*, 17 October 1963.

_____, 'Footprints on the Sands of Time–The Malay Poverty Concept over 50 Years from Za'ba to Aziz and the Second Malaysia Plan'. Paper presented at the Malaysian Economic Association meeting on Malaysian Economic Development and Policies, Kuala Lumpur, March 1974.

_____, 'Poverty and Rural Development in Malaysia', *Kajian Ekonomi Malaysia*, 1, No. 1, June 1964, pp. 71–96.

_____, 'The Causes of Poverty in Malayan Agriculture' in Lim Tay Boh (ed.), *Problems of the Malayan Economy*, Eastern Universities Press, 3rd revised edn., Singapore, 1960, pp. 19–26.

_____, 'The Development and Utilization of Labour Resources in Southeast Asia' in P. W. Thayer, *Nationalism and Progress in Free Asia*, Johns Hopkins University Press, Baltimore, 1956, pp. 193–203.

_____, 'The Remedy for Rural Poverty' in Lim Tay Boh (ed.), *Problems of the Malayan Economy*, Eastern Universities Press, 3rd revised edn., Singapore, 1960, pp. 27–32.

van der Kroef, J. M., 'Communism and Chinese Communalism in Sarawak', *The China Quarterly*, No. 20, October–December 1964, pp. 38–66.

_____, 'Indonesia, Malaya and the North Borneo Crisis', *Asian Survey*, 3, No. 4, April 1963, pp. 173–81.

_____, 'The Sarawak–Indonesian Border Insurgency', *Modern Asian Studies*, 2, No. 3, 1963, pp. 245–65.

Vasil, R. K., 'The 1964 General Elections in Malaya', *International Studies*, 7, No. 1, July 1965, pp. 20–65.

Vlieland, C. A., 'The 1947 Census of Malaya', *Pacific Affairs*, 22, No. 1, March 1949, pp. 59–63.

Wan A. Hamid, 'Religion and Culture of the Modern Malay' in Wang Gungwu (ed.), *Malaysia: A Survey*, Frederick A. Praeger, New York, 1964, pp. 179–89.

Wang Gungwu, 'Communism in Asia', *JHSUM*, 5, 1966/67, pp. 1–12.

_____, 'Malayan Nationalism', *Journal of the Royal Central Asian Society*, 49, Pt. 3, pp. 317–28.

_____, 'Malaysia: Contending Elites', *Current Affairs Bulletin*, University of Sydney, 47, No. 3, 28 December 1970, pp. 35–48.

_____, 'Nation Formation and Regionalism in Southeast Asia', in M. Grant (ed.), *South Asia Pacific Crisis*, Dodd, Head and Company, New York, 1964, pp. 125–35.

_____, 'Political Change in Malaysia', *Pacific Community*, 2, No. 4, July 1970, pp. 687–96.

_____, 'Sun Yat-sen and Singapore', *JSSS*, 15, Pt. 2, December 1959, pp. 55–68.

_____, 'Traditional Leadership in a New Nation; The Chinese in Malaya and Singapore' in S. Takdir Alisjahbana *et al.* (eds.), *The Cultural Problems of Malaysia in the Context of Southeast Asia*, Public Printers, Kuala Lumpur, 1967, pp. 170–87.

Yarwood, A. T., 'The Overseas Indians: A Problem in Indian and Imperial Politics at the end of World War I', *Australian Journal of Politics and History*, 14, No. 2, August 1968, pp. 204–18.

Yeo Kim Wah, 'The Anti-Federation Movement in Malaya, 1946–48, *JSEAS*, 4, No. 1, March 1973, pp. 31–51.

Zikmund II, J., 'National Anthems as Political Symbols', *Australian Journal of Politics and History*, 15, No. 3, December 1969, pp. 73–80.

5. *Party Documents*

Alliance, 'Alliance Manifesto for [the 1955] Federal Elections'. Mimeographed. TCLP.

_____, 'Memorandum by the Hon'ble Dato Abdul Razak bin Hussein for

Alliance Round Table', 12 November 1954. Mimeographed.

———, 'The Alliance Manifesto (1969 Elections)'. Mimeographed.

———, *To a Happier and Greater Malaysia*, Alliance Headquarters, Kuala Lumpur, 1964.

———, *We the Alliance: Results in Rural Development*, Alliance Headquarters, Kuala Lumpur, 1964.

Alliance National Council, 'The Road to Independence (Menuju Kearah Kemerdekaan)', Alliance Headquarters, Kuala Lumpur, 1955. Mimeographed.

Democratic Action Party, 'Towards a Malaysian Malaysia!' [1969 DAP Election Manifesto]. Mimeographed.

———, *Who Lives If Malaysia Dies?*, Kuala Lumpur, 1969.

Gerakan Rakyat Malaysia, *Election Manifesto: 3rd General Elections 1969*, Kuala Lumpur, 1969.

Malay Nationalist Party, 'The Manifesto of the Malay Nationalist Party, Malaya, with Regard to the British "White Paper on Malayan Union"'. Central Committee, Kuala Lumpur, 1946.

Malayan Chinese Association, *Memorandum of Chinese Education in the Federation of Malaya*, Kuala Lumpur, 1954.

———, *Speech by Tan Cheng Lock on the 27th February 1949, at the Inaugural Meeting of the Proposed Malayan Chinese Association at Kuala Lumpur*, privately published (n.p., n.d.).

Malayan Communist Party, 'Party Directive of 1 October 1951'.

———, 'Strategic Problems of the Malayan Revolutionary War', December 1948.

Malaysian Chinese Association, *MCA 20th Anniversary Souvenir*, Kuala Lumpur, 1969.

Penang Chinese Constitutional Consultative Committee, *The Humble Petition of the Chinese Town Hall–Penang, the Chinese Chamber of Commerce–Penang, the Straits Chinese British Association–Penang to the Right Honourable Arthur Creech Jones, P.C., M.P., H.M. Secretary of State for the Colonies*, 9 March 1947.

People's Progressive Party, 'People's Progressive Party of Malaya Manifesto 1969', Ipoh, 1969. Mimeographed.

PUTERA–AMCJA, *The People's Constitutional Proposals for Malaya*, Ta Chong Press, Kuala Lumpur, 1947.

Sarawak Alliance, 'Constitution and Rules of the Sarawak Alliance Party; Adopted by the Sarawak Alliance National Council on 21st January 1963, and amended by the National Council on 30th and 31st March 1964 and on 18th October 1965', Alliance Headquaters, Kuching (n.d.).

Sarawak Chinese Association, 'Sarawak Chinese Association Manifesto, "We Believe in Unity"', Kuching (n.d.).

Sarawak United People's Party, 'Constitution and Rules of the Sarawak United People's Party', Kuching (n.d.).

United Malays National Organization, *Penyata Tahunan UMNO Malaysia 1968–70*, Pejabat Setiausaha Agong UMNO Malaysia, Kuala Lumpur (n.d.).

———, *Ten Years of UMNO*, Daud Press, Penang, 1957.

———, *UMNO Dua Puloh Tahun*, Ibu Pejabat UMNO, Kuala Lumpur (1966).

_____, *Undang2 Tuboh Pertubohan Kebangsaan Melayu Bersatu*, Life Printers, Kuala Lumpur, 1960.

United Party, 'Constitution and Rules of the United Party (Sabah)', Jesselton (n.d.).

United Sabah National Organization, 'Constitution of the United Sabah National Organization', Jesselton (n.d.).

6. Unpublished Theses and Documents

Abdul Latiff bin Sahan, 'Political Attitudes of the Malays, 1945–1955', B.A. Academic Exercise, University of Malaya, 1959.

Abdul Majid, 'The Malayan Union and the Malay Press', B.A. Academic Exercise, University of Malaya, 1963.

Abd. Malek Hj. Md. Hanafiah, 'Sejarah Perjuangan Kesatuan Melayu Muda, 1937–1945', B.A. Hons. Academic Excercise, Department of History, Universiti Kebangsaan Malaysia, 1974.

Abdul Razak bin Hussein, Tun, *First Malaysia Plan: Full Text of Speech ... at the House of Representatives on the 15th December 1965*, Kuala Lumpur. Printed.

Awang Had bin Salleh, 'Malay Teacher Training in British Malaya (1878–1941): A General Survey', B.Ed. Thesis (Post-Graduate), University of Malaya, 1967.

Bamadhaj, Halinah, 'The Impact of the Japanese Occupation of Malaya on Malay Politics and Society', M.A. Thesis, Auckland University, 1975.

Chan Heng Chee, 'The Malayan Chinese Association', M.A. Thesis, University of Singapore, 1965.

Cheah Boon Kheng, 'The Malayan Democratic Union, 1945–1948', M.A. Dissertation, University of Malaya, 1974.

Clark, M. F., 'The Malayan Alliance and its Accommodation of Communal Pressures, 1952–1962', M.A. Thesis, University of Malaya, 1964.

Dalton, J. B., 'The Development of Malayan External Policy, 1957–1963', D.Phil. Thesis, Oxford University, 1967.

Funston, N. J., 'Writings on May 13', paper presented to Seminar Aliran Kini Dalam Sains Kemasyarakatan dan Kemanusiaan, Universiti Kebangsaan Malaysia, 23–25 October 1974.

Ghazali Basri, 'Hilir Perak: Sejarah Hubungan Ras Zaman Pendudukan Jepun sehingga Pemerintahan Tentera Inggeris (BMA), 1942–1946', B.A. Hons. Thesis, Department of History, University of Malaya, 1974/75.

Haas, R. H., 'The Malayan Chinese Association, 1958–1959: An Analysis of Differing Conceptions of the Malayan Chinese Role in Independent Malaya', M.A. Thesis, University of Northern Illinois, 1967.

Hazra, N. K., 'Malaya's Foreign Relations, 1957–1963', M.A. Thesis, University of Malaya, 1965.

Ishak bin Tadin, 'The United Malays National Organization under Dato' Onn, 1946–1951', B.A. Academic Exercise, University of Malaya, 1959.

Institute of Southeast Asian Studies, 'Tan Cheng Lock Papers' ('*TCLP*'), eighteen folios, mostly in mimeographed form, deposited with the Institute in 1971.

Jan, J. P., 'Nationality and Treatment of Overseas Chinese in Southeast Asia', Ph.D. Thesis, New York University, 1960.

Khong Kim Hoong, 'Communalism and the Eviction of Singapore from Malaysia', B.A. Academic Exercise, University of Malaya, 1969.

Khoo Kay Kim, 'The Beginnings of Political Extremism in Malaya, 1915–1935', Ph.D. Thesis, University of Malaya, 1974.

Lau Teik Soon, 'Malaysia–Singapore Foreign Policies in Southeast Asia 1965–1970', Ph.D. Thesis, Australian National University, 1973.

Lee Ah-chai, 'Policies and Politics in Chinese Schools in the Straits Settlements and Federated Malay States, 1786–1941', M.A. Thesis, University of Malaya, 1957.

Lee, E., 'Chinese Towkays in the Political Process of Sabah (North Borneo): From Colony to Malaysian State', M.A. Dissertation, Cornell University, 1970.

Leong, Stephen, 'Sources, Agencies and Manifestations of Overseas Chinese Nationalism in Malaya, 1941–1945', Ph.D. Thesis, University of California, Los Angeles, 1976.

Lim Huck-tee, E., 'The Malayan Civil Service, 1896–1941', B.A. Thesis, University of Malaya, 1960.

MacDougall, J. A., 'Shared Burdens: A Study of Communal Discrimination by Political Parties in Malaysia and Singapore', Ph.D. Dissertation, Harvard University, 1968.

Merdeka Convention, 'Merdeka Convention; Papers and Documents', London, 1957. Mimeographed.

Moore, D. E., 'The United Malays National Organization and the 1959 Elections', Ph.D. Dissertation, University of California, Berkeley, 1960.

Musak Mantrak, 'Sejarah Masyarakat Majemuk di Mukim VII, Batu Pahat, Johor, 1900–1945', B.A. Hons. Thesis, Department of History, University of Malaya, 1974/75.

Nam Tae Yue, 'Malaysia and Singapore: The Failure of a Political Experiment', Ph.D. Thesis, University of Iowa, 1969.

Nik Ahmad bin H. N. Hassan, 'The Malay Vernacular Press', B.A. Thesis, University of Malaya, 1958.

Nisperos, 'Philippine Foreign Policy on the North Borneo Question', Ph.D. Thesis, University of Pittsburgh, 1969.

Peritz, R., 'The Evolving Politics of Singapore', Ph.D. Thesis, University of Pennsylvania, 1964.

Rahmat Saripan, 'Kegiatan2 Politik Orang2 Melayu di Tahun2 1930an', B.A. Academic Exercise, University of Malaya, 1970.

Raktakamal Barman, 'The Foreign Policy of Malaya, 31 August 1957 to 16 September 1963', Ph.D. Thesis, Indian School of International Studies, Delhi, 1967.

Reinhardt, J. M., 'Nationalism and Confrontation in the Southeast Asian Islands; The Sources of Indonesian Foreign Policy', Ph.D. Thesis, Tulane University, 1967.

Renick, Roderick, 'Emergency Regulations of Malaya: Background Organization Administration and Use as a Socialising Technique', M.A. Thesis, Tulane University, 1964.

Richards, R. A., 'Government in North Borneo', University of New England, 27 September 1961.

Samuel, D. S., 'A Comparative Study of the Malayan and Singapore Legislatures, 1945–1959', M.A. Thesis, University of Singapore, 1966.

Stephens, D. A., 'Why UPKO was Dissolved', February 1969. Original Typescript. In possession of author.

Stockwell, Anthony John, 'The Development of Malay Politics During the Course of the Malayan Union Experiment, 1942–1948', Ph.D. Dissertation, University of London, 1973.

Tan Cheng Lock Papers: *see* Institute of Southeast Asian Studies (above).

Tan Hock Seng, 'The Left-Wing in Malaya, 1945–1957', B.A. Academic Exercise, University of Malaya, 1960.

Tan, K. C., 'The Federation of Malaysia; Some Aspects of Political Geography', Ph.D. Thesis, University of London, 1965.

Taylor, S. R., 'The North Borneo Dispute: Its Political and Legal Implications', M.A. Thesis, The American University, 1968.

Tunku Abdul Rahman, 'Form of Government', 21 March 1955. Mimeographed, *TCLP*.

_____, 'The Position of the Rulers and Constitutional Reforms', 17 March 1955. Mimeographed, *TCLP*.

Ungku A. Aziz, 'Facts and Fallacies on Malay Economy', 'Merdeka Convention; Papers and Documents', London, 1957. Mimeographed.

_____, 'Poverty and Rural Development in Malaysia', Inaugural Lecture, University of Malaya, 1963.

Wang Gungwu, 'Chinese Politics in Malaya', Undated Essay, Institute of Southeast Asian Studies, Singapore. Mimeographed.

Yap Hyun-phen, 'The Founding of Labuan, 1846', B.A. Academic Exercise, University of Singapore, 1958.

Yung, Yuet-hing, R. M., 'Contributions of the Chinese to Education in the Straits Settlements and the Federated Malay States, 1900–1941', M.A. Thesis, University of Malaya, 1967.

7. Select List of Newspapers Used

Borneo Bulletin (Kuala Belait)

Majlis (Kuala Lumpur)

Malay Mail (Kuala Lumpur and Singapore)

Malaya Tribune (Singapore)

Malayan Times (Kuala Lumpur and Singapore)

North Borneo News and Sabah Times (subsequently *Sabah Times* and latterly *Kinabalu Sabah Times*, Jesselton/Kota Kinabalu)

Sarawak Tribune (Kuching)

Singapore Free Press (Singapore)

Singapore Standard (Singapore)

Straits Budget (Kuala Lumpur and Singapore)
Straits Echo (Penang)
Straits Times (Kuala Lumpur and Singapore)
Sunday Mail (Kuala Lumpur and Singapore)
Sunday Times (Kuala Lumpur and Singapore)
Sunday Tribune (Kuching)
The Times (London)
Utusan Malaysia (Kuala Lumpur)
Utusan Melayu (Kuala Lumpur)
Utusan Zaman (Kuala Lumpur)
Warta Negara (Penang and Kuala Lumpur)

8. Select List of Periodicals Used

Asian Studies (Quezon City)
Asian Survey (Berkeley)
Australian Journal of Politics and History (Brisbane)
British Malaya (London and Kuala Lumpur)
Far Eastern Economic Review (Hong Kong)
JEBAT (Universiti Kebangsaan Malaysia, Kuala Lumpur)
Jernal Sejarah (formerly *Journal of the Historical Society, University of Malaya*–JHSUM–Kuala Lumpur)
Journal of Southeast Asian History (*JSEAH*; later renamed *Journal of Southeast Asian Studies*–JSEAS–Singapore)
Journal of the Malayan Branch, Royal Asiatic Society (*JMBRAS*; formerly *Journal of the Straits Branch, Royal Asiatic Society*–JSBRAS; later *Malayan* was changed to *Malaysian*–Singapore)
Journal of the Royal Central Asian Society (London)
Mastika (Kuala Lumpur)
Modern Asian Studies (London)
Pacific Affairs (Vancouver)
Pacific Community (Tokyo)

Index